Lecture Notes in Computer Science 5832

Commenced Publication in 1973
Founding and Former Series Editors:
Gerhard Goos, Juris Hartmanis, and Jan van Leeuwen

Pieter Koopman   Rinus Plasmeijer
Doaitse Swierstra (Eds.)

Advanced Functional Programming

6th International School, AFP 2008
Heijen, The Netherlands, May 19-24, 2008
Revised Lectures

 Springer

Volume Editors

Pieter Koopman, Rinus Plasmeijer
Radboud University Nijmegen
Institute for Computing and Information Sciences
Heijendaalseweg 135
6525AJ Nijmegen, The Netherlands
E-mail: {pieter,rinus}@cs.ru.nl

Doaitse Swierstra
Utrecht Universiy
Department of Information and Computing Sciences
Padualaan 14
3584CH Utrecht, The Netherlands
E-mail: doaitse@cs.uu.nl

Library of Congress Control Number: 2009934860

CR Subject Classification (1998): D.2, F.4.1, D.1, D.1.1, D.2.3, D.3.3, F.4

LNCS Sublibrary: SL 1 – Theoretical Computer Science and General Issues

ISSN   0302-9743
ISBN-10   3-642-04651-7 Springer Berlin Heidelberg New York
ISBN-13   978-3-642-04651-3 Springer Berlin Heidelberg New York

springer.com

© Springer-Verlag Berlin Heidelberg 2009
Printed in Germany

Typesetting: Camera-ready by author, data conversion by Scientific Publishing Services, Chennai, India
Printed on acid-free paper   SPIN: 12757787   06/3180   5 4 3 2 1 0

Preface

This volume contains the revised lecture notes corresponding to the lectures given at the 6th International School on Advanced Functional Programming, AFP 2008, held in Heijen, a little village in the woodlands near the city of Nijmegen, The Netherlands, May 19-24, 2008. AFP 2008 was co-located with TFP 2008, the 9th Symposium on Trends in Functional Programming [see P. Achten, P. Koopman, M. Marazán: Trends in Functional Programming volume 9, ISBN 978-1-84150-277-9, Intellect]. The school attracted 62 participants from 19 countries, a record, including the lecturers and organizers. This event was preceded by five earlier instances in Båstad, Sweden (1995, LNCS 925), Olympia, WA, USA (1996, LNCS 1129), Braga, Portugal (1998, LNCS 1608), Oxford, UK (2002, LNCS 2638) and Tartu, Estonia, (2004, LNCS 3622).

The goals of the series of Advanced Functional Programming schools are:

- Bringing computer scientists, in particular young researchers and programmers, up to date with the latest functional programming techniques.
- Showing how to use advanced functional programming techniques in "programming in the real world".
- Bridging the educational gap between results presented at conferences on the one side and material as presented in introductory textbooks on the other side.

The approach we take to achieve these goals in the schools is having in-depth lectures about functional programming techniques which emerged or were established recently. The lectures are taught by experts in the field who actively contribute to the development and application of these new techniques and are accompanied by practical problems to be solved by the students during the school. It is our experience that solving such problems guides the students' learning to a great extent. Finally we stimulate group work, especially because the practical exercises set will typically be too large for a single person to solve in the time given.

The scientific programme of AFP 2008 covered eight subjects, presented by:

Umut Acar Toyota Technological Institute, University of Chicago, USA
Richard Bird University of Oxford, UK
Olivier Danvy University of Aarhus, Denmark
Johan Jeuring Utrecht University, The Netherlands
Mark Jones Portland State University, USA
Ulf Norell Chalmers University, Sweden
Satnam Singh Microsoft Research, UK
Rinus Plasmeijer Radboud University Nijmegen, The Netherlands

Following the school seven lecturers revised the notes they had prepared for the school, based on the experiences in the school and the feedback of the students. Each of these revised notes was carefully checked by at least two experienced readers and then revised once more by the lecturers. We want to especially thank Ralf Hinze and Neil Jones for their very detailed and constructive reviews. We are proud to recommend the final texts to everyone wishing to acquire first-hand knowledge about some of the exciting and trendsetting developments in functional programming.

We are very grateful to our sponsors, Getronics Apeldoorn, The Netherlands Organization for Scientific Research (NWO), and The Netherlands Defence Academy. Thanks to them we were able to give substantial scholarships to the PhD students attending the AFP summer school.

July 2009

Pieter Koopman
Rinus Plasmeijer
Doaitse Swierstra

Organization

Host Institutions

AFP 2008 was organized by the Institute for Computing and Information Sciences, section Model-Based System Development of the Radboud University Nijmegen, The Netherlands and the Software Technology Group of Utrecht University, The Netherlands.

Program Committee	Pieter Koopman	Radboud University Nijmegen
	Rinus Plasmeijer	Radboud University Nijmegen
	Doaitse Swierstra	Universiteit Utrecht
Organizing Committee	Peter Achten	Radboud University Nijmegen
	Pieter Koopman	Radboud University Nijmegen
	Rinus Plasmeijer	Radboud University Nijmegen
Local Arrangements	Simone Meeuwsen	Radboud University Nijmegen
Sponsoring Institutions	Getronics	Apeldoorn
	The Netherlands Organization for Scientific – Research (NWO)	
	The Netherlands Defence Academy	

Table of Contents

Libraries for Generic Programming in Haskell 165

*Johan Jeuring, Sean Leather, José Pedro Magalhães, and
Alexey Rodriguez Yakushev*

A Tutorial on Parallel and Concurrent Programming in Haskell 267

Simon Peyton Jones and Satnam Singh

Self-adjusting Computation with Delta ML

Umut A. Acar[1] and Ruy Ley-Wild[2]

[1] Toyota Technological Institute
Chicago, IL, USA
umut@tti-c.org
[2] Carnegie Mellon University
Pittsburgh, PA, USA
rleywild@cs.cmu.edu

Abstract. In self-adjusting computation, programs respond automatically and efficiently to modifications to their data by tracking the dynamic data dependences of the computation and incrementally updating the output as needed. In this tutorial, we describe the self-adjusting-computation model and present the language ΔML (Delta ML) for writing self-adjusting programs.

1 Introduction

Since the early years of computer science, researchers realized that many uses of computer applications are *incremental* by nature. We start an application with some initial input to obtain some initial output. We then observe the output, make some small modifications to the input and re-compute the output. We often repeat this process of modifying the input incrementally and re-computing the output. In many applications, incremental modifications to the input cause only incremental modifications to the output, raising the question of whether it would be possible to update the output faster than recomputing from scratch.

Examples of this phenomena abound. For example, applications that interact with or model the physical world (e.g., robots, traffic control systems, scheduling systems) observe the world evolve slowly over time and must respond to those changes efficiently. Similarly in applications that interact with the user, application-data changes incrementally over time as a result of user commands. For example, in software development, the compiler is invoked repeatedly after the user makes small changes to the program code. Other example application areas include databases, scientific computing (e.g., physical simulations), graphics, etc.

In many of the aforementioned examples, modifications to the computation data or input are external (e.g., the user modifies some data). In others, incremental modifications are inherent. For example, in motion simulation, objects move continuously over time causing the property being computed to change continuously as well. In particular, if we wish to simulate the flow of a fluid by modeling its constituent particles, then we need to compute certain properties of moving objects, e.g., we may want to triangulate the particles to compute the

P. Koopman and D. Swierstra (Eds.): AFP 2008, LNCS 5832, pp. 1–38, 2009.
© Springer-Verlag Berlin Heidelberg 2009

forces exerted between particles, and update those properties as the points move. Since the combinatorial structure of the computed properties change slowly over time, we can often view continuous motion as an incremental modification; this makes it possible to compute the output more efficiently than re-computing it from-scratch at fixed intervals.

Although incremental applications abound, no effective general-purpose technique or language was known for developing incremental applications until recently (see Section 10 for the discussion of the earlier work on the subject). Many problems required designing specific techniques or data structures for remembering and re-using results to ensure that computed properties may be updated efficiently under incremental modifications to data. Recent advances on self-adjusting computation (Section 10.2) offer an alternative by proposing general-purpose techniques for automatically adapting computations to data modifications by selectively re-executing the parts of the computation that depend on the modifications and re-using unaffected parts. Applications of the technique to problems from a reasonably diverse set of areas show that the approach can be effective both in theory and practice.

We present a tutorial on a language for self-adjusting computation, called ΔML (Delta ML), that extends the Standard ML (SML) language with primitives for self-adjusting computation.

In self-adjusting computation, programs consist of two components: a self-adjusting *core* and a top- or meta-level *mutator*. The self-adjusting core is a purely functional program that performs a single run of the intended application. The mutator drives the self-adjusting core by supplying the initial input and by subsequently modifying data based on the application. The mutator can modify the computation data in a variety of forms depending on the application. For example, in a physical simulation, the mutator can insert a new object into the set of objects being considered. In motion simulation, the mutator changes the outcomes of comparisons performed between objects as the relationship between objects change because of motion. After modifying computation data, the mutator can update the output and the computation by requesting *change propagation* to be performed. Change propagation is at the core of self-adjusting computation: it an automatic mechanism for propagating the data modifications through the computation to update the output.

To support efficient change propagation, we represent a computation with a *trace* that records the data and control dependences in the computation. Change propagation uses the trace to identify and re-execute the parts of the computation that depend on the modified data while re-using the parts unaffected by the changes. The structure and the representation of the trace is critical to the effectiveness of the change propagation. Techniques have been developed for implementing both tracing and change propagation efficiently (Section 10.2).

The ΔML language provides linguistic facilities for writing self-adjusting programs consisting of a core and a mutator. To this end, the language distinguishes between two kinds of function spaces: conventional and self-adjusting. The mutator consists solely of conventional functions. The self-adjusting core consists of self-adjusting functions and all pure (self-adjusting or conventional) functions that they call directly or indirectly (transitively).

ΔML enables the programmer to mark the computation data that is expected to change across runs (or over time) by placing them into *modifiable references* or *modifiables* for short. For implementing a self-adjusting core, ΔML provides facilities for creating and reading modifiables within a self-adjusting function. In this tutorial, we do not include the update operation on modifiables in the core—modifiables are write-once within the self-adjusting core.[1] ΔML also provides facilities for defining self-adjusting functions to be memoized if so desired. For implementing a mutator, ΔML provides meta-level facilities to create, read, and update modifiables, and to perform change propagation. The mutator can use the update operation to modify destructively the contents of modifiables—this is how mutators modify the inputs of the self-adjusting core. After such modifications are performed, the mutator can use change propagation to update the result of the core.

Writing a self-adjusting program is very similar to writing a conventional, purely functional program. Using the techniques described in this tutorial, it is not hard to take an existing purely functional SML program and make it self-adjusting by annotating the code with ΔML primitives. Annotated code is guaranteed to respond to modifications to its data correctly: the result of an updated run is equivalent to a (from-scratch) run. Guaranteeing efficient change propagation, however, may require some additional effort: we sometimes need to modify the algorithm or use a different algorithm to achieve the optimal update times.

When an algorithm does not yield to efficient change propagation, it is sometimes possible to change it slightly to regain efficiency, often by eliminating unnecessary dependences between computation data and control. For example, the effectiveness of a self-adjusting mergesort algorithm can be improved by employing a divide-and-conquer strategy that divides the input into two sublists randomly instead of deterministically dividing in the middle. Using randomization eliminates the dependence between the length of the list and the computation, making the computation less sensitive to modiciations to the input (e.g. when a new element is inserted the input length changes, causing the divide-and-conquer algorithm to create different splits than before the insertion, ultimately preventing re-use). Sometimes, such small changes to the algorithm do not suffice to improve its efficiency and we need to consider an entirely different algorithm. For example, the quicksort algorithm is inherently more sensitive to input modifications than the mergesort algorithm, because it is sensitive to values of the pivots, whereas the mergesort algorithm is not. Similarly, an algorithm that sums a list of numbers by performing a traversal of the list and maintaining an accumulator will not yield to efficient change propagation, because inserting an element can change the value of the accumulator at every recursive call. No

---

[1] The actual ΔML language places no such restrictions on how many time modifiables can be written in the core.

small modification will improve this algorithm as we would like. Considering a different, random sampling algorithm addresses the problem (Section 8).

The structure of the rest of the tutorial is as follows. In Section 2 we describe how incremental modifications arise and why they can lead to improved efficiency and why having general-purpose techniques and languages can help take advantage of this potential. In Section 3 we describe the self-adjusting computation model and the core and the meta primitives for writing self-adjusting programs. In Section 4 we describe an example self-adjusting application, called CIRCLES, and how the user can interact with such a program. In the rest of the tutorial, we use this example to illustrate how the ΔML language may be used to implement self-adjusting programs.

2   Motivation

We consider the two kinds of modifications, discrete and continuous, that arise in incremental applications via simple examples and describe how we may take advantage of them to improve efficiency. We then describe how and why language-based techniques are critical for scalability.

2.1   Discrete and Continuous Modifications

Close inspection of incremental applications reveal that two kinds of modification arise naturally: discrete/dynamic and continuous/kinetic.

Discrete/Dynamic: A discrete or dynamic modification is a *combinatorial* modification to the input of the program that modifies the set of objects in the input.

Continuous/Kinetic: A continuous or kinetic modification affects the relationship between the input objects but does not affect the set of objects itself. By a relationship we broadly mean any function mapping objects into a discrete set. For example, comparisons between objects are relationships because the co-domain contains true and false.

As an example, consider sorting a list of numbers and how discrete and continuous modifications may arise in this application.

Suppose that we sort a list of numbers, e.g., [30,10,20,0], and then we insert a new number to the list, e.g. [7,30,10,20,0]. Since the set of objects itself is modified this is a discrete modification. Note that inserting/deleting an element from the input only causes an in incremental modification to the output, that of inserting/deleting the new element into/from the output (at the right position). Thus we can expect to be able to update the output significantly faster than recomputing from scratch. In fact, we can update the output for a sorting application in optimal logarithmic time, instead of the $O(n \log n)$ time a re-computation would require.

As an example of continuous modifications, consider a set of numbers that change as a function of time $a(t) = 40.0 - 0.3t$, $b(t) = 20.0 - 0.3t$, $c(t) = 10$, and

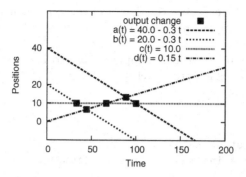

Fig. 1. Numbers varying with time

$d = 0.15t$. Suppose that we want to keep the numbers sorted as they change over time. More specifically, we want to start at time zero ($t = 0$), and then update the output whenever the ordering changes. Since time changes continuously, the values of the functions also change continuously. But the sorting changes discretely—only when the outcomes of comparisons between the moving numbers change.

For example, at time 0, sorted output is $[d(t), c(t), b(t), a(t)]$, which remains the same until the time becomes 33.$\dot{3}$, when $b(t)$ falls below $c(t)$ changing the output to $[d(t), b(t), c(t), a(t)]$. The output then remains the same until 44.$\dot{4}$, when $b(t)$ falls below $d(t)$, and the output becomes $[b(t), d(t), c(t), a(t)]$. The output then changes at 66.$\dot{6}$ to $[b(t), c(t), d(t), a(t)]$, and at 88.$\dot{8}$ to $[b(t), c(t), a(t), d(t)]$. The final change takes place at time 100.0, when the output becomes $[b(t), a(t), c(t), d(t)]$. Although the output changes continuously, we only need to update the computation at these times, i.e., when the output changes combinatorially.

Note that when the outcome of the comparison changes, the change in the output is small—it is simply a swap of two adjacent numbers. This property enables treating motion as a form of incremental modification. In fact, in this example, we can model continuous modifications as discrete modifications that affect the outcomes of comparisons. In general, if the computed property only depends on relationships between data whose values range over a discrete domain, then we can perform motion simulation by changing the values of these relationships as they take different values discretely.

2.2   Taking Advantage of Incrementality

When an incremental modification to computation data causes an incremental modification to the output, we can expect to update the output faster than by re-computing from scratch. In this tutorial, we propose language-based general purpose techniques for taking advantage of incremental modifications to update outputs faster. An alternative approach would be to design and implement ad hoc data structures, called *dynamic data structures*, on a per-problem basis. In this section, we briefly overview the design of several dynamic data structures for some relatively simple problems and point out some difficulties with the approach.

As a simple example, consider mapping a list to another list. Here is the interface for a `DynamicMap` data structure:

```
signature DynamicMap =
sig
    type (α,β) t
    val map: α list -> (α -> β) -> β list * (α,β) t
    val insert: α * int * (α,β) t -> β list * (α,β) t
end
```

The `map` function performs an "initial map" of the input and generates the output list as well as a data structure (of abstract type (α,β) `t`) that can be used to speedup the subsequent insertions. After `map` is executed, we can modify the input by inserting new elements using the `insert` operation. This operation takes the new element with the position at which is should be inserted and the data structure, and returns the updated output list and data structure.

Having designed the interface, let's consider two possible choices for the auxiliary data structure that is used to speed up the insertions.

1. The auxiliary data structure is the input, the `map` function simply returns the input. The `insert` function inserts the element into the list at the specified position. To update the output we have no choice but to re-execute, which offers no performance gain.

2. The auxiliary data structure represents the input and the output along with pointers linking the input elements to the corresponding output elements. These pointers help in finding the location of the element corresponding to an input element in the output. The `map` function constructs and returns this data structure. The `insert` function inserts the element in the input at the specified position, maps the element to an output element, and using the pointers to the output, finds the position for the output element, and inserts it. Using this approach, we can insert a new element and update the output with expected constant time overhead over the time it takes to map the input element to an output. Note that we can update the input in (expected) constant time by maintaining a mapping between locations and the pointers to update.

As our second example, consider a dynamic data structure for sorting with the following interface.

```
signature DynamicSort =
sig
    type α t
    val sort: α list -> (α * α -> bool) -> α list * α t
    val insert: (α * int) -> α t -> α list * α t
end
```

The sort operation performs an "initial sort" of the input and generates the output list as well as the auxiliary data structure (of abstract type α t). After sort is executed, we can change the input by inserting new elements using the insert operation. This operation takes the new element with the position at which it should be inserted and the data structure, and returns the updated output list and data structure.

As before, there are choices for the auxiliary data structure.

1. The sort function returns the input as the auxiliary data structure. The insert operation simply modifies the input and sorts from scratch to update the output. This is equivalent to a from-scratch execution.
2. The sort function returns both input and the output as the auxiliary data structure. The insert operation inserts the new element into the input and into the output. In this case, the insert operation can be performed in $O(n)$ time.
3. The sort function builds a balanced binary-tree representation of the input list and returns it as the auxiliary data structure. The nodes of the balanced binary search tree point to their place in the output list. The insert operation performs an insertion into the binary search tree and updates the output by splicing the inserted element into the output at the right place. To find the right place in the output, we find the previous and the next elements in the output by performing a search. These operations can be performed in $O(\log n)$ time by careful use of references and data structures.

The first two approaches are not interesting. They improve performance by no more than a logarithmic factor, which would not worth the additional complexity. The third approach, however, improves performance by a linear factor, which is very significant.[2]

As this example suggests, designing an efficient incremental data structure can be difficult even for a relatively simple problem like sorting. In particular, to support efficient incremental updates, we need to use balanced binary search trees, whose design and analysis is significantly more complex than that of a sorting algorithm. This suggests that there is a design-complexity gap between conventional static problems (where computation data is not subject to modifications) and their dynamic version that can respond efficiently to incremental modifications. Indeed, the design and analysis of such dynamic data structures has been an active field in the algorithms community (Section 10.3). We give more examples of this complexity gap in Section 10.3.

In addition to the design-complexity gap, there are difficulties in using dynamic data structures for building large software systems, because they are not composable. To see why this is important note that conventional algorithms are directly composable. For example if we have some function $f : \alpha \rightarrow \beta$ and $g : \beta \rightarrow \gamma$, then we can compose these two algorithms, $g \circ f$, is well defined and has type $\alpha \rightarrow \gamma$. Concretely, if we want to sort a list of objects and then

---

[2] Note that we can support modifications to the input in (expected) constant time by maintaining a mapping between locations and the pointers to update.

apply a map function to the sorted list, then we can achieve this by composing the functions for sorting and mapping. Not so with dynamic data structures. As an example suppose that we wish to compose DynamicSort and DynamicMap so that we can maintain a sorted and mapped list under incremental modifications to the input. For example, we may want sort a set of (one-dimensional) points on a line from left to right and then project them onto some parabola by using a list-map, while we maintain this relationship as the input list is modified with insertions and deletions. Call the dynamic data structure for this purpose DynamicSortMap.

If dynamic data structures were composable, we could easily implement DynamicSortMap by composing DynamicSort and DynamicMap. The difficulty arises when composing the insert functions. When we insert a new element, we want it to be mapped on to the parabola and inserted at the right place in the output. We could update the initial sorting of the points on the line by invoking the insert of DynamicSort but to apply the insertion to DynamicMap we also need to know where in the output the new point appears so that we can modify the input to DynamicMap. In other words, we don't need just the updated output; we also need to know how the output has changed, which DynamicSort does not provide.

In general, for dynamic data structures to be composable, data structures must return a description of how their output has changed as a result of a modification to their input. This description must be in some universal "language" so that any two dynamic data structures can be combined (when possible). We must also develop some way to apply such output-change descriptions to modify the input. This can require converting arbitrary modifications to the output into input-modifications that are acceptable by the composed data structure. For example, a change that replaces the value of an element in the output must be converted into a deletion and an insertion, if the composed data structures do not support replacement directly. The authors are not aware of any concrete proposals for facilitating such composition of dynamic data structures. Another approach could be to compute the difference between the outputs of a consecutive applications of a function and use this difference as an incremental modification. This approach, however, may be difficult to make work optimally. For example, it can require solving the graph isomorphism problem (when comparing two graphs), which is NP hard.

The approach proposed in this tutorial is different: it enables writing programs that can respond to arbitrary modifications to their data. The programs are written in a style similar to conventional programs; in particular, functions are composable.

3   The Programming Model: An Overview

In self-adjusting computation programs are stratified into two components: a *self-adjusting core*, or a *core* for short, and a meta-level *mutator*.

A (self-adjusting) core is written like a conventional program: it takes an input and produces an output, while also performing some effects (i.e., writing

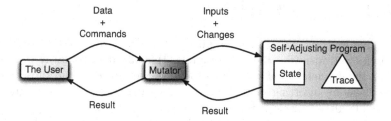

Fig. 2. The self-adjusting computation model

to the screen). Like a conventional program, we can execute the core with an input, performing a a *from-scratch* or an *initial* run. Typically, we execute a core from-scratch only once, hence the name initial run.

After an initial run, the input data or intermediate data, which is generated during the initial run, can be modified and the core can be asked to update its output by performing change propagation. This process of modifying data and propagating the modifications can be repeated as many times as desired. *Change propagation* updates the computation by identifying the parts that are affected by the modifications and re-executing them, while re-using the parts that are unaffected by the changes. Although change propagation re-executes only some parts of the core, it is semantically equivalent to a (from-scratch) run: it is guaranteed to yield the same result as running the core from scratch with the modified input. The asymptotic complexity of change propagation is never slower than a from-scratch run and can be dramatically faster. In a typical use, an initial run is followed by numerous iterations of changing the input data and performing change propagation. We therefore wish change propagation to be fast even if this comes at the expense of slowing down the initial run.

The interaction between the cores initial output and its subsequent inputs may be complex. We therefore embed a core program in a *meta-level mutator* program—the mutator drives the feedback loop between the self-adjusting core and its data. One common kind of core is a program that interacts with the user to obtain the initial input for the core, runs the core with that input to obtain an output, inspects the output, and continues interacting with the user by modifying the data as directed and performing change propagation as necessary. Another common kind of mutator used in motion simulation combines user-interactions with event scheduling. While interacting with the user, such a mutator also maintains an event queue consisting of objects that indicate the comparisons whose outcomes need to be modified and at which time. The mutator performs motion simulation by changing the outcomes of comparisons and performing change propagation. Change propagation updates the event queue and the output. In general, mutators can change computation data in arbitrarily complex ways.

4   An Example: CIRCLES

As a running example, consider an application, called CIRCLES, that displays a set of circles and identifies the pair of circles that are furthest away from each other, i.e., the *diameter*. The user enters the initial set of circles and subsequently modifies them by inserting new circles, deleting existing circles, changing the properties of existing circles, etc.

Figure 3 shows an example interaction between a user and CIRCLES. Initially the user enters some circles, labeled "a" through "g", specifies their color, the position of their center (the top left corner is the origin) and their radii. CIRCLES computes the diameter of this set, namely "c" and "e", and renders these circles as shown on the right. The user is then allowed to modify the set, which s/he does by changing the color of "a" from yellow to blue. CIRCLES responds to this change by re-rendering circle "a". The user then inserts a new circle "h", to which CIRCLES responds by displaying the new circle and updating the new diameter, namely "c" and "h." Finally, the user deletes the new circle "h", to which CIRCLES responds by blanking out "h", and updating and displaying the diameter.

Note that CIRCLES only re-draws the modified circles. Although it is not apparent in this discussion it also updates the diameter efficiently, much faster than re-computing the diameter from scratch.

How can we write such a program? One way would be to design and develop a program that carefully updates the display and the diameter by using efficient algorithms and data structures. We encourage the reader to think about how this could be achieved. Some thought should convince the reader that it is a complex task. Rendering only the affected circles is reasonably simple: we can do this by keeping track of the circle being modified, or inserted/deleted, and rendering only that circle. Updating the diameter efficiently, however, is more difficult. For example, how can we compute the new diameter, when the user deletes one of the circles that is currently part of the diameter? Can this be done more efficiently than recomputing from scratch? This turns out to be a non-trivial question (see Section 10 for some related work). Next, we describe the ΔML language and how we can implement CIRCLES in ΔML.

5   The Delta ML Language

The ΔML language extends the Standard ML language with primitives for self-adjusting computation. The language distinguishes between two function spaces: *conventional functions* and *adaptive functions*. Conventional functions are declared using the conventional ML **fun** syntax for functions. Adaptive functions are declared with the **afun** and **mfun** keywords. The **afun** keyword declares an adaptive, non-memoized function; the **mfun** keyword declares an adaptive, memoized function. Adaptive functions (memoized and non-memoized) have the adaptive-function type τ_1 -\$> τ_2. We use the infix operator \$ for applying adaptive (memoized or non-memoized) functions. An adaptive function must be

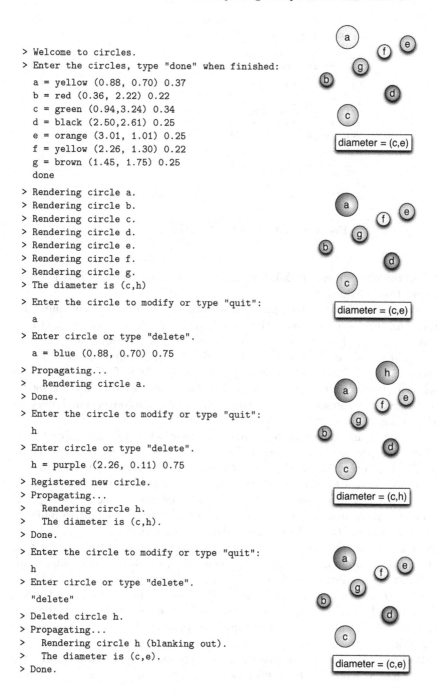

```
> Welcome to circles.
> Enter the circles, type "done" when finished:
  a = yellow (0.88, 0.70) 0.37
  b = red (0.36, 2.22) 0.22
  c = green (0.94,3.24) 0.34
  d = black (2.50,2.61) 0.25
  e = orange (3.01, 1.01) 0.25
  f = yellow (2.26, 1.30) 0.22
  g = brown (1.45, 1.75) 0.25
  done

> Rendering circle a.
> Rendering circle b.
> Rendering circle c.
> Rendering circle d.
> Rendering circle e.
> Rendering circle f.
> Rendering circle g.
> The diameter is (c,h)

> Enter the circle to modify or type "quit":
  a
> Enter circle or type "delete".
  a = blue (0.88, 0.70) 0.75

> Propagating...
>    Rendering circle a.
> Done.
> Enter the circle to modify or type "quit":
  h
> Enter circle or type "delete".
  h = purple (2.26, 0.11) 0.75
> Registered new circle.
> Propagating...
>    Rendering circle h.
>    The diameter is (c,h).
> Done.
> Enter the circle to modify or type "quit":
  h
> Enter circle or type "delete".
  "delete"

> Deleted circle h.
> Propagating...
>    Rendering circle h (blanking out).
>    The diameter is (c,e).
> Done.
```

Fig. 3. An example interaction with circles

```
signature ADAPTIVE = sig
  type 'a box
  val put : 'a -$> 'a box
  val get : 'a box -$> 'a

  val mkPut : unit -$> ('k * 'a -$> 'a box)

  (** Meta operations **)
  val new : 'a -> 'a box
  val deref : 'a box -> 'a
  val change : 'a box * 'a -> unit

  datatype 'a res = Value of 'a | Exn of exn
  val call : ('a -$> 'r) * 'a -> 'r res ref
  val propagate : unit -> unit
end
structure Adaptive :> ADAPTIVE = struct ... end
```

Fig. 4. Signature for the `Adaptive` library

written in the pure subset of SML but can operate on modifiables using the core primitives that we describe below.

An adaptive application can appear only in the body of an adaptive function. We can thus partition a self-adjusting program into a set of adaptive functions, A, that call each other and other (pure) conventional functions, and a set of conventional functions, C, that can only call other (possibly imperative) conventional functions. This distinction helps us statically identify the mutator and the self-adjusting core: the mutator consists of the conventional function set C, the core consists of the set of adaptive functions A and the conventional function called by them.[3]

Except for **afun** and **mfun** keywords, all other self-adjusting computation primitives are provided by a library. Figure 4 shows the interface to this library. The *box type* τ **box** is the type of a modifiable reference and serves as a container for changeable data. The **put**: α -$> α **box** primitive creates a box and places the specified value into the box, while the **get**: α **box** -$> α primitive returns the contents of a box. Since the primitives have adaptive function types, they can only be used within an adaptive function.

The **put** and **get** function are all we need to operate on modifiable references. For the purposes of improving efficiency the library provides an additional primitive: **mkPut**. The **mkPut** operation returns a *putter* that can be used to perform *keyed allocation*. The putter takes a key and a value to be boxed and returns a box (associated with the key) holding that value. Section 7 describes the motivation for **mkPut** and how it can be used to improve the efficiency of change propagation.

To facilitate the mutator to perform initial run and to operate on changeable data, we provide several *meta primitives*. These meta primitives are impure and

---

[3] This distinction also helps improve the efficiency of the compilation mechanisms: we need to treat/compile only adaptive functions specially, other functions are compiled in the conventional manner.

should not be used within adaptive functions; doing otherwise can violate the correctness of change propagation.[4]

To perform an initial run, the interface provides the `call` primitive. At the meta-level the result of an initial run is either an ordinary value or an exception. More concretely, the `call` operation takes an adaptive function and an argument to that function, calls the function, and returns its results or the raised exception in an ordinary reference. Note that the `call` operation is the only means of "applying" an adaptive function outside the body of another adaptive function. The result of the `call` operation is a reference cell containing the output (distinguishing between normal and exceptional termination) of the self-adjusting computation.

The mutator uses the **new**, **change**, and **deref** operations to create and modify inputs, and to inspect outputs of a self-adjusting computation. The **new** operation places a value into box—it is the meta-version of the **put** operation. The **deref** operation returns the contents of a box—it is the meta-version of the **get** operation. The **change** operation takes a value and a box and modifies the contents of the box to the given value by a destructive update.

A typical mutator starts by setting up the input and calling an adaptive function to perform an initial run. Interacting with the environment, it then modifies the input of the adaptive function or other data created by the initial run, and performs change propagation by calling the meta primitive **propagate**. When applied, the **propagate** primitive incorporates the effects of the **change** operations executed since the beginning of the computation or the last call to **propagate**.

6   Implementing CIRCLES

We describe a full implementation of CIRCLES in ΔML. Since self-adjusting computation facilitates interaction with modifications to data via change propagation, we only need to develop a program for the static case where the input list of circles does not change. We then use a mutator to drive the interaction of this program with the user. We first describe the interfaces of libraries for modifiable lists and geometric data structures. We then describe the implementation of the mutator and the core itself. To ensure efficiency, the core uses the quick-hull algorithm for computing convex hulls as a subroutine, which we describe last.

6.1   Lists and Geometric Data Structures

Figure 5 shows the interface of the libraries that we build upon as well as the definitions of some structures implementing them.

Modifiable Lists. We use a list data structure to represent the set of circles. Since we want to insert/delete elements from this list, we want the list to be modifiable, which we achieve by defining

---

[4] Our compiler does not enforce statically this correct-usage principle.

```
datatype α cell = NIL | CONS of α * α modlist
withtype α modlist = α cell box
```

A modifiable list of type α modlist is a linked list of cells of type α cell. A cell is either empty (NIL) or a CONS of an element and a modifiable list. This definition of lists is similar to conventional lists, except that the tail component of a CONS cell is boxed. This enables the mutator to change the contents of a modifiable list by updating the tail modifiables.

As with conventional lists, we can define a number of standard operations on lists, as shown in Figure 5. The lengthLessThan function takes a number and a list and returns a boolean modifiable that indicates whether the length of the

```
signature MOD LIST =
sig
    datatype α cell = NIL | CONS of α * α modlist
    withtype α modlist = α t
    type α t = α modlist

    val lengthLessThan: int -> α t -$> bool box
    val map: (α -> β) -> α t -$> β t
    val filter: (α -> bool) -> α t -$> α t
    val reduce: (α -> α -> α) -> α t -> α -$> β t
end

signature POINT =
sig
  type t
  val fromXY: real * real -> t
  val toXY: t -> real * real
end

signature GEOMETRY =
sig
  structure Point : POINT
  type point
  type line = point * point

  val toLeft : point * point -> bool
  val toRight : point * point -> bool
  val dist : point * point -> real

  val lineSideTest: line * point -> bool
  val distToLine: point * line -> real
end

structure ModList: MOD LIST = ... (see Figure 10)
structure Geom: GEOMETRY = ...
structure L = ModList
structure Point = Geom.Point
type circles = Point.t * (string * string * real)
```

Fig. 5. Modifiable lists, points, and the geometry library

list is less than the specified number. The `map` function takes as arguments a function that can map an element of the list to a new value and a list; it returns the list obtained by applying the function to each element in the list. The `filter` function takes a predicate and a list and returns the list of elements of the input list that satisfies the predicate. The `reduce` function takes as arguments an associative binary operation defined on the elements of the list, a list, and a value to return when the list is empty; it returns the value obtained by combining all elements of the list using the operation.

In our implementation we assume a structure called `ModList` that implements the modifiable lists interface, i.e., `structure ModList:MOD LIST`. For brevity, we abbreviate the name simply as L, i.e., `structure L = ModList`. Section 8 presents and implementation of `ModList`.

Geometric Data Structures and Operations. To operate on circles, we use some geometric data structures. Figure 5 shows the interface for a point data structure and a library of geometric operations. A point supports operations for translation from points into x-y coordinates. The geometry library defines a line as a pair of points and provides some operations on points and lines. The `toLeft` (`toRight`) operation returns `true` if and only if the first point is to the left (right) of the second, i.e., the former's x-coordinate is less (greater) than the latter's. The `dist` operation returns the distance between two points. The `lineSideTest` returns true if the point is above the line, that is the point lies in the upper half-plane defined by the line. The `distToLine` returns the distance between a point and a line.

In our implementation, we assume a structure `Geom` that implement the geometry primitives. For brevity, we define a point structure `Point` as `structure Point = Geom.Point`.

We define a circle type as a tuple consisting of a point (center), and a triple of auxilary information, i.e., a `string` id, a `string` color, and a floating point radius, i.e., `type circle = Point.t * (string * string * real)`.

6.2 Implementing the Mutator

Suppose that we have a self-adjusting function `processCircles` that takes a list of circles, finds their diameter, renders them, and returns the name of the circles on the diameter. The signature of `processCircles` can be written as: `processCircles: ModList.t -> (string * string) box`.

Figure 6 shows a mutator that drives this self-adjusting program by interacting with the user in a style as shown in Figure 3. For brevity, we show here a simplified mutator that only allows the user to modify the properties of an existing circles—it does not support insertion or deletion (the complete mutator is provided in the source distribution). The mutator performs mostly standard tasks, such as prompting the user, reading data from the user, etc.; the self-adjusting computation primitives are underlined to assist with the discussion.

```
fun mutator () =
let
  fun realFromString (str) = ...

  fun prompt target str =
  let val   = print str
      val tokens = String.tokens Char.isSpace (TextIO.input TextIO.stdIn)
  in case tokens of
        t::nil => if t = target then NONE else SOME tokens
      |   => SOME tokens
  end

  fun mkCircle tokens =
  let val [id, color,xs,ys,rs] = tokens
      val (x,y,r) = (realFromString xs,realFromString ys, realFromString rs)
  in (Point.fromXY (x,y),(id,color,r)) end

  fun readCs cs =
    case (prompt "done" ("Enter circle or type 'done' : /n")) of
      NONE => cs
    | SOME tk => let val c = mkCircle tk in readCs (new (L.CONS (c,cs))) end

  fun findAndModify cs id c =
  let fun isId ( ,(id', , )) = id = id'
      fun find f l =
        case deref l of
          L.NIL => raise BadInput
        | L.CONS (h,t) => if f h then SOME l else find f t
      val SOME m = find isId cs
      val L.CONS (h,t) = deref m
  in change (m,L.CONS (c,t)) end

  fun modify cs =
    case (prompt "quit" "Enter the circle to modify or type 'quit'./n") of
      NONE => ()
    | SOME [id] =>
      let val SOME tokens = prompt "" ("Enter circle: /n")
          val c = mkCircle tokens
          val   = findAndModify cs id c
          val   = (print ''Propagating.../n''; propagate (); print ''Done./n'')
      in modify cs end

  fun main () =
  let val   = init ()
      val   = print "Welcome to circles!/n"
      val cs = readCs (new L.NIL)
      val   = call (processCircles, cs)
      val   = modify cs
  in () end

in main () end
```

Fig. 6. A mutator for circles

Let's dissect the mutator in a top down style. The `main` function is the interaction loop. It starts by initializing the self-adjusting computation system, prints a welcome message, and reads the circles from the user. It then calls the adaptive `processCircles` function with the user input to compute the diameter and render the circles on the screen. The computation then proceeds into a modify-propagate loop with function `modify`. The function `modify` asks the user to modify a circle, applies the modifications by calling `findAndModify`, and performs change propagation, which updates the computation. The function `findAndModify` traverses the input list using the meta operation `deref` (used to access the contents of modifiables) and updates the circle by using the `change` meta operation when it finds the circle to modify.[5] The `change` operation destructively updates the contents of the modifiable holding the circle being modified. The upper half of the mutator code, i.e., the functions `realFromString`, `prompt`, `mkCircle`, `readCs` are written using standard techniques. For brevity the code for `realFromString` is omitted.

As this example should make clear, the treatment of modifiables and changeable data at the meta-level (i.e., in the mutator code) is identical to that of references. We process modifiable lists as though modifiables are simple references. We start a self-adjusting computation by calling an adaptive function with the `call` meta operation, and perform change propagation with the `propagate` meta operation when the user changes the computation data.

6.3   Implementing the Core

Figure 7 shows the code for the self-adjusting core of CIRCLES. For the time being, the reader should ignore `mkPut` and read "putM $ (, v)" as "put $ v"; the use of `putM` and `mkPut` is explained in Section 7.

The `circle` function takes the list of circles, renders them (with the `renderCircle` function), and computes their diameter (with the function `findDiameter`).

The `renderCircle` function traverses the list of circles and prints them on the screen. In this implementation, we simply print the properties of the circle—rendering a real image would be structurally identical. Two points about `renderCircle` differ from the same function operating on an ordinary list. First, being a modifiable list, the input is stored in a modifiable, and thus, we use the self-adjusting `get` primitive to access its contents. Second, the function is adaptive function instead of an ordinary function, because it uses a self-adjusting primitive (`get`). Since the function takes more than constant time (it takes linear time in the size of the list), we decided to make it memoized by declaring it with `mfun`.

When deciding what functions to memoize, we observe the following principle: if an adaptive function performs more than constant work excluding the work performed by memoized functions called within its body, then we memoize it.

---

[5] For improved efficiency in finding for the circle to be modified, we may want to use an auxilary search structure such as a hash-table that maps the circle id's to the cons cell that holds that circle.

```
fun map = ... (* See Figure 10 *)
fun reduce = ... (* See Figure 11 *)
fun quick hull l = ... (* See Figure 9 *)


mfun renderCircles l =
let fun printC (c as (p,(id,color,r))) =
    let val (x,y) = Point.toXY p
        val s = id  ^ " : "  ^ color
                    ^ " ("  ^ Real.toString x  ^ ", "  ^ Real.toString y  ^ ")"
                    ^ " "  ^ Real.toString r  ^ "/n"
    in print ("Rendering circle = "  ^ s  ^ "/n"); end

in case get $ l of
        L.NIL => ()
     | L.CONS(h, t) => (printC h ; renderCircles t)
end

afun findDiameter l =
let val putM = mkPut $ ()
    fun maxDist (da as ( ,va),db as ( ,vb)) =
        if (Real.> (va,vb)) then da
        else db

    fun dist (a as (o a, (id a, ,r a))) (b as (o b, (id b, ,r b))) =
        Geom.dist (o a,o b) - r a - r b end

    mfun farthestFrom (c,l) =>
        let val dist = map (dist c) $ l
            val max = reduce maxDist $ dist
        in get $ max end

    mfun findAllDist l =
        let val putM = mkPut $ ()
        in case get $ l of
            L.NIL => putM $ (NONE, L.NIL)
          | L.CONS(h,t) => case get $ t of
                         L.NIL => putM $ (NONE,L.NIL)
                       |  => let val m = farthestFrom $ (h,t)
                                in putM $ (SOME m, L.CONS(m, findAllDist $ t))
                                end
        end

    val hull = quick hull $ l
    val dist = findAllDist $ hull
    val max = reduce maxDist $ dist
    val ((ida,idb), ) = get $ max
    val  = print ("diameter = : "  ^ ida  ^ " x "  ^ idb  ^ "/n")
in putM $ (NONE,(ida,idb)) end

afun processCircles l = (renderCircles l ; findDiameter l)
```

Fig. 7. The code for the core

The function `findDiameter` computes the diameter of the set of circles and prints it on the screen. We define the diameter as the maximum distance between any two circles, where the distance between two circles is the minimum distance between any points belonging to them (we can compute the distance between two circles by as the distance between their center points minus the sum of their radii). The function `dist` computes the distance between two circles. To compute the diameter, we need some auxilary functions.

The function `farthestFrom` takes a circle c and a list of circles l and returns the circle that is farthest away from c. The function computes its result by first calculating the distance between each circle in the list and c (by using `map` over the list of circles) and then selecting the maximum of the list (by using `reduce` on the list). Since the function performs calls to adaptive functions, it itself is an adaptive function. Since it takes more than linear time, we declare it memoized.

The function `findAllDist` computes for each circle in the input, the circle that is farthest away from it among the circles that come after it in the input list. Even `findAllDist` computes only half of all possible distances, it correctly finds the maximum distance because distance function is symmetric. Since the function takes more than constant time (more precisely, $O(m^2)$ time in the size of its input), we declare it memoized.

One way to compute the diameter is to compute the pairwise distances of all circles, using `findAllDist`, and then pick the maximum of these distance. This, however, would not be asymptotically efficient because it requires $\Theta(n^2)$ time in the size of the input list. Instead, we first compute the convex hull of the centers of the circles. We then compute the pairwise distances of the circles whose centers lie on the hull.

The convex hull of a set of points is the smallest polygon enclosing the points. Figure 8 shows the convex hull for our running example. It is a property of the convex hulls that the pair of circles that are farthest away from each other is on the hull. To find the diameter of the circles efficiently, we can therefore first find the circles whose centers lie on the convex hull of the centers and consider only these circles when computing the farthest-apart pair. With this approach, we improve efficiency: computing convex hulls requires $O(n \log n)$ time and computing finding the diameter requires $O(h^2)$ time where h is the number of circles on the hull, which is generally significantly smaller than the input n.

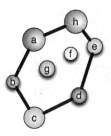

Fig. 8. An example convex hull

In our implementation, we use `quick-hull` to compute the convex hull. This algorithm is not asymptotically optimal but works well in practice.

6.4 Implementing Quickhull

Many algorithms, some optimal, have been proposed for computing convex hulls. In this example, we use the quick-hull algorithm, which is known to perform well in practice, except with some distributions of points. Figure 9 shows the complete code for `quick-hull`. The algorithm uses several geometric primitives. The function `above` returns `true` if and only if the center of the circle c above the line defined by the centers of the circle `cl` and `cr`. The function `distToLine` returns the distance from the center of the circle c to the line defined by the centers of the circles `cl` and `cr`. These functions are standard—they perform no self-adjusting computation.

The `split` function takes two boxed circles, which define the *split-line*, a list of circles, and the partial hull constructed thus far, and it uses the auxiliary `splitM` function to extend the hull. The `splitM` function first eliminates the

```
fun select f (a,b) = if f (a, b) then a else b
fun above (cl as (pl, ), cr as (pr, )) (c as (p, )) =
  Geom.lineSideTest ((pl, pr), p)
fun distToLine (cl as (pl, ), cr as (pr, )) (c as (p, )) =
  Geom.distToLine (p, (pl,pr))

afun split (bcl, bcr, l, hull) =
  let val putM = mkPut $ ()
      mfun splitM (cl, cr, l, hull) =
        let val lf = L.filter (above (cl, cr)) $ l
        in if get $ (L.lengthLessThan 1 $ lf) then
             putM $ (cl, L.CONS (cl, hull))
           else let val dist = distToLine (cl,cr)
                    val selectMax = select (fn (c1,c2) => dist c1 > dist c2)
                    val max = get $ (combine selectMax $ lf)
                in splitM $ (cl, max, lf, splitM $ (max, cr, lf, hull)) end
        end
      val (cl,cr) = (get $ bcl, get $ bcr)
  in splitM $ (cl, cr, l, hull) end

afun quick hull l =
  if get $ (L.lengthLessThan 2 $ l) then l
  else let fun isMin (c1 as (p1, ), c2 as (p2, )) = Geom.toLeft (p1,p2)
           fun isMax (c1 as (p1, ), c2 as (p2, )) = Geom.toRight (p1,p2)
           val min = combine (select isMin) $ l
           val max = combine (select isMax) $ l
           val lower = split $ (max, min, l, put $ L.NIL)
           val hull = split $ (min, max, l, lower)
       in hull end
```

Fig. 9. The code for quick-hull

list of points below the split-line. If the remaining list is empty, then the hull consists of the left circle (cl) alone. If the remaining list is non-empty, then the function finds the circle, max, whose center is furthest away from the line defined by the split-line. The algorithm then recurses with the two split-lines defined by the left circle and the max, and the max and the right circle.

The function quick-hull computes the initial split-line to be the line whose endpoints are the left-most and the right-most circles (based on their centers). Based on this split-line, it then uses split to compute convex hull in two passes. The first pass computes the lower hull, the second pass computes the complete hull.

7 Performance

Self-adjusting computation enables writing programs that can respond to modifications to their data in the style of conventional/non-incremental programs. In this section, we describe how we may analyze the running time of self-adjusting programs for both from-scratch executions and change propagation, and how we may improve the performance for change propagation. Our approach is informal; a precise treatment is out of the scope of this tutorial but the interested reader can find more discussion in Section 10.2 and the papers referenced there.

For the purposes of this tutorial, we consider so-called *monotone* computations only. We define a computation to be monotone if 1) no function is called with the same arguments more than once, and 2) the modifications being considered do not affect the execution order and the ancestor-descendant relationships between function calls. Not all programs are naturally monotone (for interesting classes of input modifications) but all programs can be made so by adding (extra) arguments to function calls.

When analyzing the performance of self-adjusting programs, we consider two different performance metrics: running time of from-scratch execution and running time of change propagation.

7.1 From-Scratch Runs

Analyzing the from-scratch running time of self-adjusting programs is essentially the same as analyzing conventional programs: we treat the program as a conventional program where all (meta and core) self-adjusting computation primitives take expected constant time (the expectation is over internal randomization). More precisely, we can ignore self-adjusting computation primitives when analyzing the from-scratch running time, the actual running time is only slower by an expected constant factor. Thus, analysis of the from-scratch runnning time of self-adjusting programs is standard.

7.2 Stability and Change Propagation

To analyze the running time of change propagation, we first fix the input modification that we want change propagation to handle. For example, we can analyze the running time for change propagation in CIRCLES after inserting (or deleting) a new circle. Considering unit-size modifications (e.g., a single insertion, a single deletion) often suffices, because it is guaranteed that batch modifications never take more time than the sum of their parts. For example, if a the propagation caused by a single application of a modification (e.g., an insertion) requires $O(m)$ time then propagating k applications of that modification (e.g., k insertions) takes no more than $O(k \cdot m)$ time. Additionally, change propagation never takes asymptotically more than a from-scratch run (re-running the program from scratch).

To analyze the time for change propagation, we define a notion of *distance* between computations. Suppose that we run our program with some input I, then we modify the input to I' and perform change propagation to update the output. Intuitively, the time for change propagation will be proportional to the distance between the two runs.

Before defining distance between runs, we need to identify similar subcomputations. We define two calls of the same function to be *similar* if their arguments are the equal and their results are equal. We compare values (arguments and return values) by using structural equality up to modifiables: two values are equal if they are the same non-modifiable value or they are the same modifiable, e.g., the booleans true are true equal, the modifiable l is equal to itself (regardless of the contents), but the (distinct) modifiables l and l' are distinct (regardless of their contents), therefore the tuple (true,l) is equal to itself but distinct from (true,l'). If the values are functions (closures) themselves, then we conservatively assume that they are never equal. Note that when computing the distance, we view modifiables as conventional references.

Next, we define the *difference* $X_1 \setminus X_2$ between executions X_1 and X_2 as the set of function calls in X_1 for which no similar call exists in X_2. We define *distance* between two monotone executions X_1 and X_2 as the size of the symmetric difference between two executions, i.e., $|(X_1 \setminus X_2) \cup (X_2 \setminus X_1)|$. We say that a program is $O(f(n))$-*stable* for some input change, if the distance between two executions of the program with any two inputs related by the change is bounded $O(f(n))$, where n is the maximum input size. Informally, we say that a program is *stable* for some input change, if it is poly-logarithmically stable, i.e., $O(\log^c n)$-stable where c is some constant.

7.3 Programming for Stability

When calculating the stability of a program, we compare modifiables by their identity (i.e., physical location in memory). This makes stability measurements sensitive to the whims of non-deterministic memory allocation: if a program allocates memory in a way that is similar to that of the previous run, then it can be stable, if not, then it will not be stable[6].

---

[6] Since change propagation re-executes only parts of a program, the contrast is less stark in reality. Still, non-determinism in memory allocation can detrimentally affect stability.

To address this unpredictability of non-deterministic memory allocation, we label each modifiable with a unique key and define two modifiables to be equal if they have the same key. We support this memory model by performing memory allocation associatively. In particular, we maintain a hash table that maps keys to allocated locations. When performing an allocation, we first perform a memo lookup to see if there already is a location (from a previous run) associated with the specified key. If so, we re-use it. Otherwise, we allocate a fresh location and insert it into the memo table for re-use in subsequent runs. The idea is that every execution of the an allocation with the same key will return the same modifiable.

The ΔML language relaxes the requirement about keys being unique: different allocations can share the key. In practice, it often seems to suffice for keys to act as a guide for allocation to help improve sharing between computations, but it is not necessary for them to be unique. Requiring that allocations are uniquely keyed, however, simplifies the stability analysis, which we take advantage of in our discussions of stability.

ΔML supports this *keyed allocation* strategy through the mkPut function, which creates a fresh hash table for keyed allocation and returns an associated *putter* function. A putter takes two arguments: a key associated with the modifiable to be allocated and a value to place into the allocated modifiable. We often create putters locally for each function. Since each putter has its own hash function, creating local putters helps eliminate key collision between different functions: allocations performed by different putters can share the same keys without causing a collision.

8 Modifiable Lists

We now turn to the implementation of lists and their asymptotic complexity under change propagation. Figure 10 shows the definition and implementation of modifiable lists and some functions on modifiable lists. A modifiable list of type α modlist is a boxed cell where a cell is either empty or a CONS cell consisting of an element of type α and a modifiable list.

Modifiable lists are defined in a similar way to conventional lists, with the small but crucial difference that the tail of each cell is placed in a modifiable. This enables the mutator to modify the contents of the list by inserting/deleting elements. Thus, we can use modifiable lists to represent a set that changes over time.

As with conventional lists, we can write various primitive list functions. Here we describe how to implement three functions on lists: lengthLessThan, map, and reduce. Omitting the self-adjusting primitives, the first two functions are nearly identical to their conventional counterparts and therefore have comparable asymptotic complexity; the complexity of reduce is discussed below.

In our implementation, we observe the following convention. Each list function creates a putter and defines a locally-scoped *work function* to perform the actual work. When using putters, we key the tail modifiable of a CONS cell by SOME h where h is the head element. This identifies the modifiables by the head item in

```
structure ModList =
struct
    datatype α cell = NIL | CONS of α * α modlist
    withtype α modlist = α cell box
    type α t = α modlist

    afun lengthLessThan (l: 'a modlist) : bool box =
    let putM = mkPut $ g()
        afun len (i,l) =
            if i >= n then false
            else case get $ l of
                    NIL => true
                  | CONS(h,t) => len $ (i+1,t)
    in putM $ (NONE, len $ (0,l)) end

    afun map (f: 'a -> 'b) (l: 'a modlist) : 'b modlist =
    let val putM = mkPut $ ()
        mfun m l =
            case get $ l of
              NIL => NIL
            | CONS(h,t) => CONS (f h, putM $ (SOME h, m t))
    in putM $ (NONE, m l) end
end
```

Fig. 10. Some list primitives

the same CONS cell. In our analysis, we assume that lists contain no duplicates—thus, the tail modifiables are uniquely identified by the head elements. For boxing the head of a list we use the key NONE.

The function lengthLessThan takes an integer and returns a boxed boolean indicating whether the length of the list is less than the supplied integer. Many self-adjusting programs use this function. For example, in quick hull we check whether the input list has two or fewer elements and return the list directly if so. This is often preferable to simply returning the length of the list, because some computations do not directly depend on the length of the list, but rather on whether the length is less than some value. Having this function allows us to express such a dependence more precisely, allowing for more efficient change propagation. The implementation of lengthLessThan follows our description: the outer function allocates a modifiable with putM for the result and calls the work function len with the argument.

The map function takes a function and a list and produces another list by applying the function to the elements of the input list. The outer function creates a putter by using mkPut. The work function m uses the head h of each CONS cell to key the tail modifiable with SOME h. The top-level call to the work function is boxed using the key NONE. This version of map is $O(1)$-stable with respect to single insertions or deletions.

Consider running map with the identity function on lists $[\ldots,1,3,\ldots]$ and $[\ldots,1,2,3,\ldots]$ where each list has no repetitions and both lists are identical except for the element 2 (which occurs at an arbitrary position). Recall that the head of a CONS cell is used to key the tail cell. For example, in the first list the element 1 is used as a key to allocate box l_1, which contains cell CONS$(3,l_3)$. Similarly, the result of map on the first list will have box l_1' holding cell CONS$(3,l_3')$. Therefore the work function on the first list will include calls:

$$\ldots, \text{m } l_0 = \text{CONS}(1,l_1), \text{m } l_1 = \text{CONS}(3,l_3), \qquad\qquad \text{m } l_3 = \cdots, \ldots$$

and the work function on second list will include calls:

$$\ldots, \text{m } l_0 = \text{CONS}(1,l_1), \text{m } l_1 = \text{CONS}(2,l_2), \text{m } l_2 = \text{CONS}(3,l_3), \text{m } l_3 = \cdots, \ldots$$

Therefore, the two runs differ only by three calls: m l_1 = CONS$(3,l_3)$, m l_1 = CONS$(2,l_2)$, and m l_2 = CONS$(3,l_3)$, so map is $O(1)$ stable for single insertions or deletions.

Many programs, e.g., most of those considered in this tutorial, are naturally stable or can be made stable with relatively small changes. When the program is not stable, we often need to choose a different algorithm.

As an example of a program that is not naturally, consider the list function reduce takes a list and an associative binary operator, and produces a single value by applying the operator to the elements of the list, e.g., applying reduce [1,2,3,4] with addition operation yields 10. A typical implementation of reduce (shown below) traverses the list from left to right while maintaining an accumulator of the partial results for the visited prefix.

```
afun reduce f base l =
let mfun red (l,a) =
      case get $ l of NIL => put a
                  | CONS(h,t) => red $ (t,f(h,a))
in red $ (l,base) end
```

This implementation of reduce is not stable. To see why let's consider adding integer elements of a list with inputs that differ by a single key. More precisely consider the case when one list has one extra element at the beginning, e.g., [1,2,3,4,...] and [2,3,4,...]. The function calls performed have the form, red $(l_i,\ a_i)$ where l_i is the modifiable pointing to the ith cons cell and a_i is the sum of the elements in the first $i-1$ cells. With the first input, the accumulators are $a_i = (\ 0, 1, 3, 6, 10, \ldots\ )$. With the second input, the accumulators are one more than the corresponding accumulator in the first case, $a_i = (\ 0, 2, 5, 9, \ldots\ )$. Thus, no two prefix sums are the same and a linear number of operations (in the length of the input) will differ. Consequently, the algorithm is linear stable, i.e., change propagation performs just as good re-computing from scratch.

Figure 11 shows a logarithmic stable solution for reduce. This implementation uses the classic technique of random-sampling to compute the result. The idea is to "halve" the input list into smaller and smaller lists until only a single element remains. To halve the list (halfList), we choose a randomly selected subset of the list and combine the chosen elements to their closest element to

```
fun reduce mkRandSplit f base = afn l =>
let afun halfList l =
    let val putM = mkPut $ ()
        val randSplit = mkRandSplit ()

        afun redRun (v,l) =
            case get $ l of
              NIL => (v, l)
            | CONS (h, t) =>
                  if randSplit h then (f (v,h), t)
                  else redRun $ (f(v,h), t)

        mfun half l =
            case get $ l of
              NIL => NIL
            | CONS (h, t) =>
                  let val (v, tt) = redRun $ (h,t)
                      val ttt = half $ tt
                  in CONS(v, putM $ (SOME h, ttt)) end
    in putM $ (NONE, half $ l) end

  mfun mreduce l =
  let val putM = mkPut $ ()
    if get $ ((lengthLessThan 2) $ l) then
      case get $ l of
        NIL => base
      | CONS(h, ) => h
    else mreduce $ (halfList $ l)

in putM $ (NONE, mreduce $ l) end
```

Fig. 11. The code for list reduce

the left (`redRun`). Note that a deterministic approach, where, for example the elements are combined in pairs, is not stable, because deleting/inserting an element can cause a large change by shifting the positions of many elements by one. Note that we do not require commutativity—associativity alone suffices. For randomization, we use a random hash function that returns 0 or 1 with probability $1/2$.

The approach requires expected linear time because each application of `halfList` reduces the size of the input by a factor of two (in expectation). Thus, we perform a logarithmic number of calls to `halfList` with inputs whose size decreases exponentially.

The approach is $O(\log n)$-stable in expectation (over internal randomization of `mkRandomSplit`). We do not prove this bound here but give some intuition by considering an example. Figure 12 shows executions of `reduce` with lists [0,8,5,3,2,9,6,4,1)] and [0,8,5,3,2,7,9,6,4,1)] to compute the sum of the integers in the lists. The two lists differ by box 7. Comparing two executions, only the function calls that touch the highlighted cells differ. It is not difficult

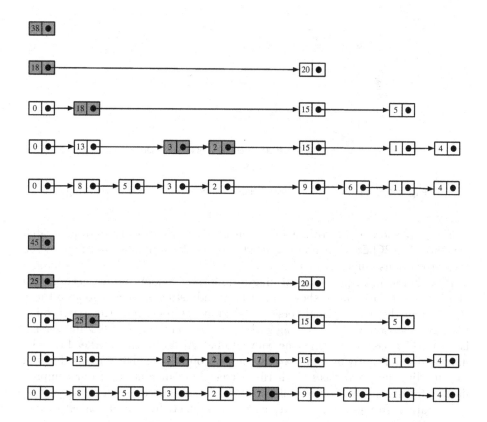

Fig. 12. Example stable list-reduce

to show that there are a constant number of such cells in each level and, based on this, to prove the $O(\log n)$-stability bound.

9   Experimental Results

We present a simple experimental evaluation of CIRCLES. In our evaluations, we compare two versions of CIRCLES: conventional and self-adjusting. The code for self-adjusting version has been presented in this tutorial. The code for the conventional version is automatically derived from the self-adjusting version by removing the primitives on modifiable references and replacing (memoized and non-memoized) adaptive functions with conventional functions.

All of the experiments were performed on a 2.66Ghz dual-core Xeon machine, with 8 GB of memory, running Ubuntu Linux 7.10. We compiled the applications with our compiler with the option "-runtime ram-slop 0.75," directing the runtime system to allocate at most 75% of system memory. Our timings measure the wall-clock time (in seconds).

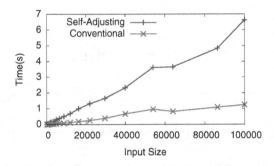

Fig. 13. Time for a from-scratch runs conventional and self-adjusting

Figure 13 shows the run-time for executing the conventional and from-scratch versions of CIRCLES with up to 100,000 circles. We generate the input to the these executions randomly by picking the center of the circle uniformly randomly from within a unit square and picking a uniformly random radius between 0.0 and 1.0. The measurement shows that the self-adjusting version is about 5 times slower than the conventional version. A significant portion of this overhead is garbage collection: when excluding garbage-collection time self-adjusting version is about 3.5 times slower than the conventional. Although the overhead may be improved significantly by more careful compiler optimization techniques directed to self-adjusting programs (which the current implementation of our compiler does not employ), we consider it to be acceptable, because, in self-adjusting computation, from-scratch executions are infrequent. In typical usage, we execute a self-adjusting program from scratch once and then perform all subsequent updates to the input by utilizing change propagation.

Figure 14 shows the average time for change propagation for a single insertion/deletion for varying input sizes. The measurement is performed by repeating an update-step for each circle in order. In each step, we remove the circle from the input and perform change propagation. We then re-insert the circle and perform change propagation. We compute the average time for an insertion/deletion

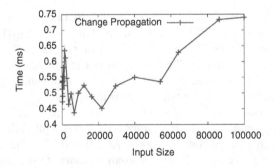

Fig. 14. Time for change propagation

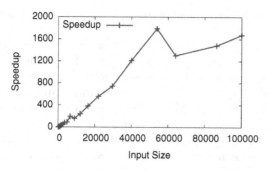

Fig. 15. Speedup of change propagation

as the total time it takes to apply the update step to each element in the list divided by the number of steps, i.e., $2n$ where n is the number of circles in the input. As the figure shows the time for change propagation is rather uneven but increases very slowly over time (less than doubles between the smallest and the largest input sizes). The reason for the unevenness is the input-sensitive nature of CIRCLES: the time to update the diameter critically depends on the number of circles that are on the hull, which also determines the update time for quick-hull.

Figure 15 shows the speedup measured as the time for a from-scratch execution of the conventional version of CIRCLES divided by the time for change propagation. As can be seen, change propagation appears to be faster by an asymptotic linear factor, delivering increasingly significant speedups. The speedups for larger inputs exceed three orders of magnitude. The speedups are significant even with relatively small input sizes.

10   Related Work

The problem of having computation respond to small modifications to their data has been studied extensively in several communities. Earlier work in the programming-languages community, broadly referred to as *incremental computation*, focused on developing techniques for translating static/conventional programs into incremental programs that can respond automatically to modifications to their input. Recent advances on self-adjusting computation generalized these approaches and dramatically improved their effectiveness. In the algorithms community, researchers proposed so called dynamic and kinetic data structures for addressing incremental problems. In this section, we briefly overview the earlier work on incremental computation (Section 10.1), recent work on self-adjusting computation (Section 10.2), and some of the work on algorithms community (Section 10.3).

10.1   Incremental Computation

Incremental computation offers language-centric techniques for developing programs that can automatically respond to modifications to their data. The most effective techniques are based on dependence graphs, memoization, and partial memoization.

Dependence-graph techniques record the dependences between data in a computation and rely on a change-propagation algorithm to update the computation when the input is modified. Demers, Reps, and Teitelbaum [27] and Reps [57] introduced the idea of *static dependence graphs* and presented a change-propagation algorithm for them. Hoover generalized the approach outside the domain of attribute grammars [45]. Yellin and Strom used the dependence graph ideas within the INC language [69], and extended it by having incremental computations within each of its array primitives. Static dependence graphs have been shown to be effective in some applications, e.g., syntax-directed computations. But they are not general-purpose, because they do not permit the change-propagation algorithm to update the dependence structure. For example, the INC language [69], which uses static dependence graphs for incremental updates, does not permit recursion.

The limitations of static dependence graphs motivated researchers to consider alternative approaches. Pugh and Teitelbaum [55] applied memoization (also called function caching) to incremental computation. Memoization, a classic idea that goes back to the late fifties [21,50,51], applies to any purely functional program and therefore is more broadly applicable then static dependence graphs. Since the work of Pugh and Teitelbaum, others have investigated applications of various forms of memoization to incremental computation [1,49,43,61,6]. The idea behind memoization is to remember function calls and their results and re-use them when possible. In the context of incremental computation, memoization can improve efficiency when executions of a program with similar inputs perform similar function calls. Although the reader may expect this to be intuitively the case, it turns out that the effectiveness of memoization critically depends on the structure of the program and the kind of the input modification. For a given computation, it is often possible to find input modifications that prevent a large fraction of function calls from being re-used. Intuitively, the problem is that with memoization all function calls that consume a modified data and all their ancestors in the function call tree need to be re-executed (because these functions will have modified arguments).

Other approaches to incremental computation are based on partial evaluation [65,32]. Sundaresh and Hudak's approach [65] requires the user to fix the partition of the input that the program will be specialized on. The program is then partially evaluated with respect to this partition and the input outside the partition can be modified incrementally. The main limitation of this approach is that it allows input modifications only within a predetermined partition. Field [33], and Field and Teitelbaum [32] present techniques for incremental computation in the context of lambda calculus. Their approach is similar to Hudak and Sundaresh's, but they present formal reduction systems that optimally use partially evaluated results.

10.2   Self-adjusting Computation

Foundations. The first work on self-adjusting computation [5], called Adaptive Functional Programming (AFP), generalized dependence-graph approaches by introducing *dynamic dependence graphs* (*DDGs*), by providing a change propagation algorithm for DDGs, and by offering a technique for constructing DDGs from program executions. Change propagation with DDGs is able to update the dependence structure of the DDG by inserting and deleting dependences as necessary. This makes it possible to apply the approach to any purely functional program. Type-safe linguistic facilities for writing adaptive programs guarantee safety and correctness of change propagation. A prototype implementation in SML was provided but the implementation did not enforce the safety properties statically. Carlsson gave a safe implementation of the proposed linguistic facilities in Haskell [23].

Although DDGs are general purpose, their effectiveness is limited: certain modifications can require as much time as re-computing from scratch. Subsequent work identified a duality between DDGs and memoization and provided linguistic and algorithmic techniques for combining them [4]. The linguistic techniques enable annotating adaptive programs [5] with particular memoization constructs. The algorithms provide efficient re-use of computations (via change propagation) without significantly slowing down a from-scratch run. An experimental evaluation showed that the approach can speedup computations by orders of magnitude (increasing linearly with the input size) while causing the initial run to slowdown by moderate amounts. Follow-up work gave a formal semantics for combining memoization and DDGs and proved it correct with mechanically verified proofs [12].

The aforementioned work on self-adjusting computation assumes a form of purely functional programming. Although modifiables are in fact a form of references, they cannot be updated destructively by self-adjusting programs—only the mutator is allowed to update modifiables destructively. This can limit the applicability of the approach to problems that are suitable for purely functional programs only. Recent work [3] showed that self-adjusting computation may be extended to programs that update memory imperatively by proposing updateable modifiable references, which ΔML supports (we do not discuss updateable references in this tutorial).

The aforementioned approaches to self-adjusting computation rely on specialized linguistic primitives that require a monadic programming style. These primitives enable tracking dependences selectively, i.e., only the dependences on data that can change over time are tracked. If selective dependence tracking is not needed, then it is possible to track all dependences without requiring programmer annotations [2]. The monadic primitives make it cumbersome to write self-adjusting program and also require substantial restructuring of existing code. Recent work developed direct language support self-adjusting computation and provided a compiler for the language [48], which ΔML is based on. Having direct language and compiler support not only simplifies developing self-adjusting programs but also makes it possible to give a precise cost-semantics that enables programmer to analyze the time for change propagation [47].

All of the aforementioned work on self-adjusting computation extends type-safe, high level languages such as Standard ML and Haskell. In an orthogonal line of work, we develop techniques for supporting self-adjusting programs with low-level languages such as C [39]. Low level language present some challenges, because self-adjusting-computation primitives are higher order and they require tracking side effects. They do, however, offer more explicit cost model and some interesting opportunities for improving performance. For example memory management and change propagation may be integrated to support garbage collection without traversing memory [38].

Applications. Self-adjusting computation has been applied to a number of problems from a broad set of application domains such as motion simulation, machine learning, and incremental invariant checking.

Some of these applications are developed and implemented using the linguistic techniques described in earlier work and in this paper. One such class of applications is motion simulators for various geometric properties. In these applications, we employ a mutator that starts with an initial run of a self-adjusting program. The mutator then performs motion simulation by maintaining a simulation time and modifying the outcomes of comparisons performed between moving objects (in accordance with the specified motion plans), updating the computation via change propagation. Using this approach, we obtain motion simulators from purely functional programs by translating them into self-adjusting programs and by combining them with the mutator for motion simulation. Since change propagation is fully general and can handle arbitrary modifications to the input, the approach enables processing a broad range of modifications during motion simulation. It also helps address efficiently some critical robustness issues that arise in motion simulation. Previous work applies the approach to a number of problems from two [10] and three dimensions [8,9]. The solutions on three-dimensional problems made progress on well-known open problems.

Other applications use self-adjusting computation to obtain dynamic algorithms for specific problems. One such application is the tree contraction algorithm of Miller and Reif [52], whose self-adjusting version provides an efficient solution to the problem of dynamic trees [7,11]. We applied the same approach to statistical inference, a classic problem in machine learning, to show that statistical inference can be performed under incremental modifications efficiently [13,14]. These results made progress on open problems related to incremental updating of inferred statistical properties as the underlying models change. In all these applications, the mutators typically perform discrete modifications such as insertions/deletions of edges and nodes into/from a tree, a graph, or a statistical model.

Shankar and Bodik [62] adapted self-adjusting computation techniques (more specifically the approach presented in an earlier paper [4]) for the purposes of incremental invariant checking in Java. In their approach, the Java program acts as a mutator by modifying the contents of memory. Such modifications trigger reevaluation of program invariants, via change propagation, expressed in a separate purely functional language. Instead of tracking dependences selectively, they track all dependences by treating all memory cells as modifiables. This treatment of memory is similar to a formulation of self-adjusting computation proposed in the first author's thesis [2]. They show that the approach can dramatically speedup invariant checking during evaluation.

10.3   Dynamic Algorithms

In the algorithms community, researchers approach the problem of incremental computation from a different perspective. Rather than developing general-purpose techniques for transforming static programs to incremental programs that can respond to modifications to their data, they develop so called *dynamic algorithms* or *dynamic data structures* (e.g., [64,25,30]). Dynamic data structures facilitate the user to modify the data by making small modifications, e.g., inserting/deleting elements. For example a dynamic data structure for computing the diameter (points furthest away from each other) allows the user to insert/delete points into/from a set of points while updating the diameter accordingly. We considered other example dynamic algorithms in Section 2.

By taking advantage of the structure of the particular problem being considered, the algorithmic approach facilitates designing efficient, often optimal algorithms. In fact, previous work shows that there is often a linear-time gap between a dynamic algorithm and its static version in terms of responding to incremental modifications to data. Taking advantage of incrementality, however, often comes at an increased complexity of design, analysis, and implementation. Dynamic algorithms can be significantly more difficult to design, analyze, and implement than their static counterparts. For example, efficient algorithms for computing the convex hull of a set of points in the plane are relatively straightforward. Efficient dynamic algorithms for convex hulls that can respond to incremental modifications (e.g., insertion/deletion of a point), however, are significantly more complicated. In fact this problem has been researched since the late 70's (e.g., [54,53,42,19,24,22,16]). Similarly, computing efficiently the diameter of a point set as the point set changes requires sophisticated algorithms (e.g., [46,28,29,58]). Convex hulls and diameters are not the exception. Another example is Minimum Spanning Trees (MST), whose dynamic version has required more than a decade of research to solve efficiently [34,31,41,40,44], while its static/conventional version is straightforward. Other examples include the problem of dynamic trees, whose various flavors have been studied extensively [63,64,26,56,40,68,17,35,18,67,66].

Because dynamic algorithms are designed to support a particular set of modifications, they are highly specialized (an algorithm may be efficient for some modifications to data but not others), naturally more complex than their static versions, and are not composable (Section 2). These properties make them difficult to adapt to different problems, implement, and use in practice.

Algorithms researchers also study a closely related class of data structures, called *kinetic data structures*, for performing motion simulations efficiently [20]. These data structures take advantage of the incremental nature of continuous motion (Section 2) by updating computed properties efficiently. Many kinetic data structures have been proposed and some have also been implemented (e.g., [15,36] for surveys). These data structures share many characteristics of dynamic data structures. They also pose additional implementation challenges [15,37,60,59], due to difficulties with motion modeling and handling of numerical errors.

11   Conclusion

This tutorial presents a gentle introduction to the ΔML (Delta ML) language. The compiler and the source code for the examples may be reached via the authors web pages.

References

1. Abadi, M., Lampson, B.W., Lévy, J.-J.: Analysis and Caching of Dependencies. In: Proceedings of the International Conference on Functional Programming, pp. 83–91 (1996)
2. Acar, U.A.: Self-Adjusting Computation. PhD thesis, Department of Computer Science. Carnegie Mellon University (May 2005)
3. Acar, U.A., Ahmed, A., Blume, M.: Imperative self-adjusting computation. In: Proceedings of the 25th Annual ACM Symposium on Principles of Programming Languages (2008)
4. Acar, U.A., Blelloch, G.E., Blume, M., Tangwongsan, K.: An experimental analysis of self-adjusting computation. In: Proceedings of the ACM SIGPLAN Conference on Programming Language Design and Implementation (2006)
5. Acar, U.A., Blelloch, G.E., Harper, R.: Adaptive Functional Programming. In: Proceedings of the 29th Annual ACM Symposium on Principles of Programming Languages, pp. 247–259 (2002)
6. Acar, U.A., Blelloch, G.E., Harper, R.: Selective memoization. In: Proceedings of the 30th Annual ACM Symposium on Principles of Programming Languages (2003)
7. Acar, U.A., Blelloch, G.E., Harper, R., Vittes, J.L., Woo, M.: Dynamizing static algorithms with applications to dynamic trees and history independence. In: ACM-SIAM Symposium on Discrete Algorithms (2004)
8. Acar, U.A., Blelloch, G.E., Tangwongsan, K.: Kinetic 3D Convex Hulls via Self-Adjusting Computation (An Illustration). In: Proceedings of the 23rd ACM Symposium on Computational Geometry, SCG (2007)
9. Acar, U.A., Blelloch, G.E., Tangwongsan, K., Türkoğlu, D.: Robust Kinetic Convex Hulls in 3D. In: Proceedings of the 16th Annual European Symposium on Algorithms (September 2008)
10. Acar, U.A., Blelloch, G.E., Tangwongsan, K., Vittes, J.L.: Kinetic Algorithms via Self-Adjusting Computation. In: Proceedings of the 14th Annual European Symposium on Algorithms, September 2006, pp. 636–647 (2006)

11. Acar, U.A., Blelloch, G.E., Vittes, J.L.: An experimental analysis of change propagation in dynamic trees. In: Workshop on Algorithm Engineering and Experimentation (2005)
12. Acar, U.A., Blume, M., Donham, J.: A consistent semantics of self-adjusting computation. In: De Nicola, R. (ed.) ESOP 2007. LNCS, vol. 4421, pp. 458–474. Springer, Heidelberg (2007)
13. Acar, U.A., Ihler, A., Mettu, R., Sümer, Ö.: Adaptive Bayesian Inference. In: Neural Information Processing Systems, NIPS (2007)
14. Acar, U.A., Ihler, A., Mettu, R., Sümer, Ö.: Adaptive Inference on General Graphical Models. In: Uncertainty in Artificial Intelligence, UAI (2008)
15. Agarwal, P.K., Guibas, L.J., Edelsbrunner, H., Erickson, J., Isard, M., Har-Peled, S., Hershberger, J., Jensen, C., Kavraki, L., Koehl, P., Lin, M., Manocha, D., Metaxas, D., Mirtich, B., Mount, D., Muthukrishnan, S., Pai, D., Sacks, E., Snoeyink, J., Suri, S., Wolefson, O.: Algorithmic issues in modeling motion. ACM Comput. Surv. 34(4), 550–572 (2002)
16. Alexandron, G., Kaplan, H., Sharir, M.: Kinetic and dynamic data structures for convex hulls and upper envelopes. In: Dehne, F., López-Ortiz, A., Sack, J.-R. (eds.) WADS 2005. LNCS, vol. 3608, pp. 269–281. Springer, Heidelberg (2005)
17. Alstrup, S., Holm, J., de Lichtenberg, K., Thorup, M.: Minimizing diameters of dynamic trees. In: Automata, Languages and Programming, pp. 270–280 (1997)
18. Alstrup, S., Holm, J., de Lichtenberg, K., Thorup, M.: Maintaining information in fully-dynamic trees with top trees. In: The Computing Research Repository, CoRR (2003), (cs.DS/0310065)
19. Basch, J., Guibas, L.J., Hershberger, J.: Data structures for mobile data. In: Proceedings of the eighth annual ACM-SIAM symposium on Discrete algorithms. Society for Industrial and Applied Mathematics, pp. 747–756 (1997)
20. Basch, J., Guibas, L.J., Hershberger, J.: Data structures for mobile data. Journal of Algorithms 31(1), 1–28 (1999)
21. Bellman, R.: Dynamic Programming. Princeton University Press, Princeton (1957)
22. Brodal, G.S., Jacob, R.: Dynamic planar convex hull. In: Proceedings of the 43rd Annual IEEE Symposium on Foundations of Computer Science, pp. 617–626 (2002)
23. Carlsson, M.: Monads for Incremental Computing. In: Proceedings of the 7th ACM SIGPLAN International Conference on Functional programming, pp. 26–35. ACM Press, New York (2002)
24. Chan, T.M.: Dynamic planar convex hull operations in near-logarithmic amortized time. In: Proceedings of the the 40th Annual IEEE Symposium on Foundations of Computer Science (FOCS), pp. 92–99 (1999)
25. Chiang, Y.-J., Tamassia, R.: Dynamic algorithms in computational geometry. Proceedings of the IEEE 80(9), 1412–1434 (1992)
26. Cohen, R.F., Tamassia, R.: Dynamic expression trees and their applications. In: Proceedings of the 2nd Annual ACM-SIAM Symposium on Discrete Algorithms, pp. 52–61 (1991)
27. Demers, A., Reps, T., Teitelbaum, T.: Incremental Evaluation of Attribute Grammars with Application to Syntax-directed Editors. In: Proceedings of the 8th Annual ACM Symposium on Principles of Programming Languages, pp. 105–116 (1981)

28. Eppstein, D.: Average case analysis of dynamic geometric optimization. In: SODA 1994: Proceedings of the fifth annual ACM-SIAM symposium on Discrete algorithms, Philadelphia, PA, USA. Society for Industrial and Applied Mathematics, pp. 77–86 (1994)

29. Eppstein, D.: Incremental and decremental maintenance of planar width. In: SODA 1999: Proceedings of the tenth annual ACM-SIAM symposium on Discrete algorithms, Philadelphia, PA, USA. Society for Industrial and Applied Mathematics, pp. 899–900 (1999)

30. Eppstein, D., Galil, Z., Italiano, G.F.: Dynamic graph algorithms. In: Atallah, M.J. (ed.) Algorithms and Theory of Computation Handbook, ch. 8. CRC Press, Boca Raton (1999)

31. Eppstein, D., Galil, Z., Italiano, G.F., Nissenzweig, A.: Sparsification—a technique for speeding up dynamic graph algorithms. Journal of the ACM 44(5), 669–696 (1997)

32. Field, J., Teitelbaum, T.: Incremental reduction in the lambda calculus. In: Proceedings of the ACM 1990 Conference on LISP and Functional Programming, June 1990, pp. 307–322 (1990)

33. Field, J.: Incremental Reduction in the Lambda Calculus and Related Reduction Systems. PhD thesis, Department of Computer Science, November 1991. Cornell University (1991)

34. Frederickson, G.N.: Data structures for on-line updating of minimum spanning trees, with applications. SIAM Journal on Computing 14, 781–798 (1985)

35. Frederickson, G.N.: A data structure for dynamically maintaining rooted trees. Journal of Algorithms 24(1), 37–65 (1997)

36. Guibas, L.: Modeling motion. In: Goodman, J., O'Rourke, J. (eds.) Handbook of Discrete and Computational Geometry, 2nd edn., pp. 1117–1134. Chapman and Hall/CRC (2004)

37. Guibas, L., Russel, D.: An empirical comparison of techniques for updating delaunay triangulations. In: SCG 2004: Proceedings of the twentieth annual symposium on Computational geometry, pp. 170–179. ACM Press, New York (2004)

38. Hammer, M.A., Acar, U.A.: Memory management for self-adjusting computation. In: ISMM 2008: Proceedings of the 7th international symposium on Memory management, pp. 51–60 (2008)

39. Hammer, M.A., Acar, U.A., Chen, Y.: CEAL: A C-based language for self-adjusting computation. In: Proceedings of the 2009 ACM SIGPLAN Conference on Programming Language Design and Implementation (June 2009)

40. Henzinger, M.R., King, V.: Randomized fully dynamic graph algorithms with polylogarithmic time per operation. Journal of the ACM 46(4), 502–516 (1999)

41. Henzinger, M.R., King, V.: Maintaining minimum spanning trees in dynamic graphs. In: Degano, P., Gorrieri, R., Marchetti-Spaccamela, A. (eds.) ICALP 1997. LNCS, vol. 1256, pp. 594–604. Springer, Heidelberg (1997)

42. Hershberger, J., Suri, S.: Applications of a semi-dynamic convex hull algorithm. BIT 32(2), 249–267 (1992)

43. Heydon, A., Levin, R., Yu, Y.: Caching Function Calls Using Precise Dependencies. In: Proceedings of the 2000 ACM SIGPLAN Conference on Programming Language Design and Implementation, pp. 311–320 (2000)

44. Holm, J., de Lichtenberg, K., Thorup, M.: Poly-logarithmic deterministic fully-dynamic algorithms for connectivity, minimum spanning tree, 2-edge, and biconnectivity. Journal of the ACM 48(4), 723–760 (2001)

45. Hoover, R.: Incremental Graph Evaluation. PhD thesis, Department of Computer Science. Cornell University (May 1987)
46. Janardan, R.: On maintaining the width and diameter of a planar point-set online. In: Hsu, W.-L., Lee, R.C.T. (eds.) ISA 1991. LNCS, vol. 557, pp. 137–149. Springer, Heidelberg (1991)
47. Ley-Wild, R., Acar, U.A., Fluet, M.: A cost semantics for self-adjusting computation. In: Proceedings of the 26th Annual ACM Symposium on Principles of Programming Languages (2009)
48. Ley-Wild, R., Fluet, M., Acar, U.A.: Compiling self-adjusting programs with continuations. In: Proceedings of the International Conference on Functional Programming (2008)
49. Liu, Y.A., Stoller, S., Teitelbaum, T.: Static Caching for Incremental Computation. ACM Transactions on Programming Languages and Systems 20(3), 546–585 (1998)
50. McCarthy, J.: A Basis for a Mathematical Theory of Computation. In: Braffort, P., Hirschberg, D. (eds.) Computer Programming and Formal Systems, pp. 33–70. North-Holland, Amsterdam (1963)
51. Michie, D.: "Memo" Functions and Machine Learning. Nature 218, 19–22 (1968)
52. Miller, G.L., Reif, J.H.: Parallel tree contraction and its application. In: Proceedings of the 26th Annual IEEE Symposium on Foundations of Computer Science, pp. 487–489 (1985)
53. Overmars, M.H., van Leeuwen, J.: Maintenance of configurations in the plane. Journal of Computer and System Sciences 23, 166–204 (1981)
54. Preparata, F.P.: An optimal real-time algorithm for planar convex hulls. Commun. ACM 22(7), 402–405 (1979)
55. Pugh, W., Teitelbaum, T.: Incremental computation via function caching. In: Proceedings of the 16th Annual ACM Symposium on Principles of Programming Languages, pp. 315–328 (1989)
56. Radzik, T.: Implementation of dynamic trees with in-subtree operations. ACM Journal of Experimental Algorithms 3, Article 9 (1998)
57. Reps, T.: Optimal-time incremental semantic analysis for syntax-directed editors. In: Proceedings of the 9th Annual Symposium on Principles of Programming Languages, pp. 169–176 (1982)
58. Rote, G., Schwarz, C., Snoeyink, J.: Maintaining the approximate width of a set of points in the plane. In: Proceedings of the 5th Canadian Conference on Computational Geometry, pp. 258–263 (1993)
59. Russel, D.: Kinetic Data Structures in Practice. PhD thesis, Department of Computer Science. Stanford University (March 2007)
60. Russel, D., Karavelas, M.I., Guibas, L.J.: A package for exact kinetic data structures and sweepline algorithms. Comput. Geom. Theory Appl. 38(1-2), 111–127 (2007)
61. Saraiva, J., Swierstra, S.D., Kuiper, M.F.: Functional incremental attribute evaluation. In: Watt, D.A. (ed.) CC 2000. LNCS, vol. 1781, pp. 279–294. Springer, Heidelberg (2000)
62. Shankar, A., Bodik, R.: DITTO: Automatic Incrementalization of Data Structure Invariant Checks (in Java). In: Proceedings of the ACM SIGPLAN 2007 Conference on Programming language Design and Implementation (2007)
63. Sleator, D.D., Tarjan, R.E.: A data structure for dynamic trees. Journal of Computer and System Sciences 26(3), 362–391 (1983)
64. Sleator, D.D., Tarjan, R.E.: Self-adjusting binary search trees. Journal of the ACM 32(3), 652–686 (1985)

65. Sundaresh, R.S., Hudak, P.: Incremental compilation via partial evaluation. In: Conference Record of the 18th Annual ACM Symposium on Principles of Programming Languages, pp. 1–13 (1991)
66. Tarjan, R., Werneck, R.: Dynamic trees in practice. In: Demetrescu, C. (ed.) WEA 2007. LNCS, vol. 4525, pp. 80–93. Springer, Heidelberg (2007)
67. Tarjan, R., Werneck, R.: Self-adjusting top trees. In: Proceedings of the Sixteenth Annual ACM-SIAM Symposium on Discrete Algorithms (2005)
68. Tarjan, R.E.: Dynamic trees as search trees via euler tours, applied to the network simplex algorithm. Mathematical Programming 78, 167–177 (1997)
69. Yellin, D.M., Strom, R.E.: INC: A Language for Incremental Computations. ACM Transactions on Programming Languages and Systems 13(2), 211–236 (1991)

Spider Spinning for Dummies

Richard S. Bird

Oxford University Computing Laboratory
Wolfson Building, Parks Road, Oxford, OX1 3QD, UK
bird@comlab.ox.ac.uk

> Oh what a tangled web we weave
> when first we practise to derive.
> (With apologies to Sir Walter Scott)

Abstract. Spider spinning is a snappy name for the problem of listing the ideals of a totally acyclic poset in such a way that each ideal is computed from its predecessor in constant time. Such an algorithm is said to be *loopless*. Our aim in these lectures is to show how to *calculate* a loopless algorithm for spider spinning. The calculation makes use of the fundamental laws of functional programming and the real purpose of the exercise is to show these laws in action.

1 Introduction

Consider the problem of generating all bit strings $a_1 a_2 \ldots a_n$ of length n satisfying given constraints of the form $a_i \leq a_j$ for various i and j. The generation is to be in *Gray path order*, meaning that exactly one bit changes from one bit string to the next. The *transition code* is a list of integers naming the bit that is to be changed at each step.

For example, with $n = 3$, consider the constraints $a_1 \leq a_2$ and $a_3 \leq a_2$. One possible Gray path is 000, 010, 011, 111, 110 with transition code $[2, 3, 1, 3]$ and starting string 000.

The snag is that the problem does not always have a solution. For example, with $n = 4$ and the constraints $a_1 \leq a_2 \leq a_4$ and $a_1 \leq a_3 \leq a_4$, the six possible bit strings, namely

$$0000, \ 0001, \ 0011, \ 0101, \ 0111, \ 1111$$

cannot be permuted into a Gray path.

Exercise 1. Why not?

Constraints of the form $a_i \leq a_j$ on bit strings of length n can be represented by a digraph with n nodes in which a directed edge $i \leftarrow j$ is associated with a constraint $a_i \leq a_j$. Knuth and Ruskey [6] proved that a Gray path exists whenever

P. Koopman and D. Swierstra (Eds.): AFP 2008, LNCS 5832, pp. 39–65, 2009.
© Springer-Verlag Berlin Heidelberg 2009

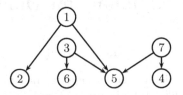

Fig. 1. A three-legged spider

the digraph is *totally acyclic*, meaning that the undirected graph obtained by dropping the directions on the edges is acyclic. They called a connected totally acyclic digraph a *spider* because when an edge $i \leftarrow j$ is drawn with i below j the digraph can be made to look like an arachnid (see Figure 1 for a three-legged spider). They called a totally acyclic digraph a *tad* but, since its connected components are spiders, we will continue the arachnid metaphor and call it a *nest* of spiders.

Knuth called the problem of generating the associated bit strings in Gray path order, *spider squishing*. The more formal rendering of the task is: "generating all ideals[1] of a totally acyclic poset in Gray path order". Since spiders are good for the environment and should never be squished, we will call it *spider spinning* instead.

A useful way to think of the problem of spider spinning is in terms of colourings. Think of the nodes of the spider of Figure 1 as being coloured black if the associated bit is 1, and coloured white if the bit is 0. Thus every descendent of a white node has to be white. For example, if node 1 is white, then nodes 2 and 5 have to be white as well. The problem of spider spinning is then to enumerate all legal colourings by starting with one such colouring and changing the colour of exactly one node at each step. As we will see, the initial colouring cannot in general be chosen to be the all-white or all-black colouring.

Spider spinning has a twist: we want the generation to be *loopless*, meaning that the first transition should be produced in *linear* time in the size of the nest, and each subsequent transition in *constant* time. Note carefully that the idea of a loopless algorithm is defined in terms of the transitions between bit strings, not the bit strings themselves. Writing out a bit string is not possible in constant time.

Knuth and Ruskey gave an algorithm for spider spinning but it wasn't loopless. There is a program, SPIDERS, on Knuth's web site [4] that does perform loopless spider spinning. It is quite complicated, as Knuth readily admits:

"But I apologize at the outset that the algorithm seems to be rather subtle, and I have not been able to think of any way to explain it to dummies".

Hence our title. Our aim in these lectures is to *calculate* a loopless algorithm for spider spinning. I have no idea if my algorithm bears any relationship to Knuth's

---

[1] By an *ideal* of a poset S is meant a subset I of S such that if $x \in I$ and $x \leq y$, then $y \in I$.

algorithm, since I can't explain his algorithm either. What is more, I can't explain my algorithm, even though I can calculate it. While it is generally true in mathematics that calculations are designed to simplify complicated things, in programming it is usually the other way around: simple but inefficient programs are transformed into more efficient programs that can be completely opaque. So it is with loopless spider spinning.

2   Loopless Algorithms

The term *loopless* was first introduced by Ehrlich in [1]. Imagine a program to list all combinatorial patterns of some kind, such as the subsequences or permutations of a list. Suppose each pattern is obtained from its predecessor by a single *transition*. For subsequences a transition i could mean "insert or delete the element at position i". For permutations a transition i could mean "swap the item in position i with the one in position $i-1$". An algorithm for generating all patterns is called *loopless* if the first transition is produced in linear time and there is a constant-time delay between each subsequent transition.

Loopless algorithms were formulated in a procedural setting and many clever techniques and tricks, such as the use of focus pointers, doubly-linked lists, and coroutines, have been used to construct them. See for example [5], which contains references to much of the literature on looplessness. Bear in mind though that loopless algorithms are not necessarily faster than their non-loopless counterparts. To quote again from [4]:

> "The extra contortions that we need to go through in order to achieve looplessness are usually ill-advised, because they actually cause the total execution time to be longer than it would be with a more straightforward algorithm. But hey, looplessness carries an academic cachet. So we might as well treat this task as a challenging exercise that might help us to sharpen our algorithmic wits."

Change the penultimate word to 'calculational' and you will appreciate the real point of these lectures.

2.1   Unfoldr

Being functional rather than procedural programmers, we will formulate the idea of a loopless algorithm in terms of the standard function `unfoldr`. Recall the Haskell standard type `Maybe`:

```
> data Maybe a = Nothing | Just a
```

The function `unfoldr` is defined by

```
> unfoldr :: (b -> Maybe (a,b)) -> b -> [a]
> unfoldr step b
>         = case step b of
>               Nothing     -> []
>               Just (a,b') -> a : unfoldr step b'
```

By definition, a loopless algorithm is one that is expressed in the form

$$\texttt{unfoldr step . prolog}$$

where step takes constant time and prolog x takes $O(n)$ steps, where n some measure of the *size* of x. For instance, if x is a list, we could take n to be the length of x, and if x is a tree, then we could take n to be the number of nodes in the tree. Every loopless algorithm has to be of the above form with these constraints on the ingredients.

There is a slightly tricky problem about our formulation of looplessness. In the framework of a *lazy* functional language such as Haskell, and Haskell is our language of choice for expressing programs, our definition of a loopless program will not in general give a loopless computation with constant delay between each output. In a lazy language the work done by prolog is distributed throughout the computation, and not concentrated all at once at the beginning. Therefore we should really interpret the composition operator (.) between unfoldr step and prolog as being fully strict, meaning that the prolog is evaluated fully the unfolding begins. Although it is not possible to define a general fully-strict composition operator in Haskell, we will take pains to ensure that the step function takes constant time under a strict as well as a lazy semantics.

2.2   Warm-Up 1

By way of warming-up for the spider spinning to come, let us first take a look at some loopless versions of functions that return lists. One obvious place to start is with the identity function on lists. Following the required form of a loopless algorithm to the letter, we have

```
> id :: [a] -> [a]
> id = unfoldr uncons . prolog

> prolog :: [a] -> [a]
> prolog = id

> uncons :: [a] -> Maybe (a,[a])
> uncons []     = Nothing
> uncons (x:xs) = Just (x,xs)
```

That was easy, perhaps too easy, so now let us consider the function reverse that reverses a list. In Haskell this function is defined by

```
> reverse :: [a] -> [a]
> reverse = foldl (flip (:)) []
```

The combinator flip is defined by

```
> flip f x y = f y x
```

A loopless program for reversing a list is now given by

```
> reverse = unfoldr uncons . foldl (flip (:)) []
```

Of course, all the real work is done in the prolog, which reverses a list and does so in linear time.

2.3   Warm-Up 2

For the next warm-up, consider the function `concat` that concatenates a list of lists. Here is a loopless version, discussed below:

```
> concat :: [[a]] -> [a]
> concat = unfoldr step . filter (not . null)

> step :: [[a]] -> Maybe (a,[[a]])
> step []            = Nothing
> step ((x:xs):xss) = Just (x,consList xs xss)

> consList :: [a] -> [[a]] -> [[a]]
> consList xs xss = if null xs then xss else xs : xss
```

The prolog filters out nonempty lists from the input and takes linear time in the length of the list. The function `step` maintains the invariant that it takes and returns a list of *nonempty* lists.

Exercise 2. Why is it necessary to exclude empty lists?

Exercise 3. Would the alternative definition

$$\text{concat = unfoldr uncons . foldr (++) []}$$

also serve as a loopless program?

The answer to the first question is that empty lists have to be filtered out of the input, otherwise `step` would not take constant time. For example, consider an input of the form $[[1],[\,],[\,],\ldots,[\,],[2]]$ in which there are n empty sequences between the first and last singleton lists. After producing the first element 1, it takes n steps to produce the second element 2 of the final list.

The answer to the second question is that it depends on what the notion of size is. The prolog does not take time proportional to the length of the list but it does take time proportional to the total *size* of the list, namely the length of the result of concatenating all its elements together. Ah, but what about the sizes of the elements? Since we are not going to go as far as coding every conceivable input as a string is some finite alphabet, we leave the definition of size informal.

2.4   Warm-Up 3

For the next warm-up consider the preorder traversal of a forest of rose trees:

```
> type Forest a = [Rose a]
> data Rose a   = Node a (Forest a)

> preorder :: Forest a -> [a]
> preorder []           = []
> preorder (Node x ts:us) = x:preorder (ts ++ us)
```

We have `preorder` = `unfoldr step`, where

```
> step :: Forest a -> Maybe (a,Forest a)
> step []            = Nothing
> step (Node x ts:us) = Just (x,ts ++ us)
```

Oh, but `step` is not constant time because `++` isn't.

Exercise 4. How can you make `step` take constant time?

One method is to change the type of `step`. Instead of taking a forest as argument, we can make `step` take a list of *nonempty* forests, revising its definition to read

```
> step :: [Forest a] -> Maybe (a,[Forest a])
> step [] = Nothing
> step ((Node x ts:us):vss)
>           = Just (x,consList ts (consList us vss))
```

This is essentially the same trick as we performed for `concat`. Now we have

```
> preorder   = unfoldr step . wrapList
> wrapList ts = consList ts []
```

This is a loopless program.

2.5   Warm-Up 4

For the final warm-up let us consider the inorder traversal of a binary tree:

```
> data Tree a = Nil | Bin (Tree a) a (Tree a)

> inorder :: Tree a -> [a]
> inorder Nil        = []
> inorder (Bin l x r) = inorder l ++ [x] ++ inorder r
```

How do we make `inorder` loopless?

One answer is to exploit the natural correspondence between binary trees and forests of rose trees. Suppose we convert the binary tree into a forest of rose trees in such a way that the inorder traversal of the former is the preorder traversal of the latter. An example is provided in Figure 2.

The conversion is performed by a function `convert`, defined by

```
> convert Nil        = []
> convert (Bin l x r) = convert l ++ [Node x (convert r)]
```

However, the above definition does not give a linear-time program for `convert`. The way to make it linear time is to introduce an accumulating parameter, defining a new function `addTree` by

$$\text{addTree t rs = convert t ++ rs}$$

Synthesising a direct recursive definition of `addTree` leads to

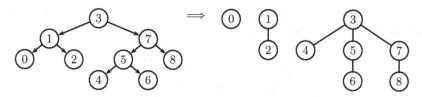

Fig. 2. Converting a binary tree to a forest of rose trees

```
> convert :: Tree a -> [Rose a]
> convert t = addTree t []

> addTree :: Tree a -> [Rose a] -> [Rose a]
> addTree Nil rs       = rs
> addTree (Bin l x r) rs = addTree l (Node x (convert r):rs)
```

Exercise 5. Fill in the details of the synthesis and show that the new definition of convert takes linear time in the size of the tree.

Now we have

```
> inorder = unfoldr step . wrapList . convert
```

where step is as defined for preorder traversal.

Exercise 6. Construct a loopless program for the *postorder* traversal of a forest of rose trees.

3   Spider Spinning with Legless Spiders

Figure 3 shows a picture of some poor legless spiders: The reason for the numbering is that, in analogy with numerals, the least significant spider is on the right. There are no constraints on the nodes in a nest of legless spiders, so we are seeking a method for listing *all* bit strings of given length in such a way that each string differs from its predecessor in just one bit. One possible transition code for the four spiders of Figure 3 is

$$[0,1,0,2,0,1,0,3,0,1,0,2,0,1,0]$$

(3) (2) (1) (0)

Fig. 3. A nest of four legless spiders

This sequence lists the bit strings $a_3 a_2 a_1 a_0$ in the following order (reading columns downwards from left to right):

$$
\begin{array}{cccc}
0000 & 0110 & 1100 & 1010 \\
0001 & 0111 & 1101 & 1011 \\
0011 & 0101 & 1111 & 1001 \\
0010 & 0100 & 1110 & 1000 \\
\end{array}
$$

This particular ordering is called the *Reflected Gray Code*. The least significant bit is on the right and varies the most often. But there are numerous other Gray codes, some of which can are described in [5].

Changing the meaning of transition i to read "insert/delete element a_i", we can also read the transition code as instructions to generate all subsequences of a list of length 4. For example, applying the transitions above to abcd yields

[], a, ab, b, bc, abc, ac, c, cd, acd, abcd, bcd, bd, abd, ad, d

In order to generate all strings $a_n a_{n-1} \ldots a_0$ we can start off with all bits 0 and first generate all bit strings $0 a_{n-1} \ldots a_0$. Then a_n is changed to 1, and again all strings of length n are generated but in reverse order by running through the transitions backwards. This description translates easily into a recursive definition of a function gray for generating transitions:

```
> gray :: Int -> [Int]
> gray 0     = []
> gray (n+1) = gray n ++ [n] ++ reverse (gray n)
```

The first step in making gray loopless is to get rid of the occurrence of reverse.

Exercise 7. How can reverse be eliminated?

The answer to the question is: just remove it! The function gray n returns a *palindrome*, so reverse (gray n) = gray n.

Exercise 8. Prove formally by induction that gray returns a palindrome.

Next, one way to make gray loopless is to observe that the recursive case looks very similar to an instance of the inorder traversal of a certain binary tree:

```
> grayTree :: Int -> Tree Int
> grayTree 0     = Nil
> grayTree (n+1) = Bin t n t  where t = grayTree n
```

We have gray = inorder . grayTree. Here is the proof of the induction step:

```
      gray (n+1)
  =      { definition }
      gray n ++ [n] ++ gray n
  =      { induction }
      inorder (grayTree n) ++ [n] ++  inorder (grayTree n)
  =      { definition of inorder }
      inorder (Bin (grayTree n) n (grayTree n))
  =      { definition of grayTree }
      inorder (grayTree (n+1))
```

Not also that **grayTree n** builds a tree in n steps, even though the resulting tree has an exponential number of nodes. The reason is that the two subtrees of each node are shared.

We know from warm-up 4 how to make **inorder** loopless, so we obtain

```
> gray = unfoldr step . wrapList . convert . grayTree
```

Exercise 9. What is wrong with this 'loopless' definition of **gray**?

The answer is that the prolog takes exponential time! The problem is not with **grayTree**, which – as we have seen – takes linear time, but with **convert**, which takes linear time in the size of the tree. But the tree has exponential size.

What we have to do is construct **convert . grayTree** directly to preserve sharing. Suppose we define

$$\text{grayForest n = convert . grayTree n}$$

and then construct a direct recursive definition of **grayForest**. The base case is easy and the induction step is

```
      grayForest (n+1)
  =      { definitions }
      convert (Bin t n t)  where t = grayTree n
  =      { definition of convert }
      convert t ++ [Node n (convert t)] where t = grayTree n
  =      { definition of grayForest }
      rs ++ [Node n rs] where rs = grayForest n
```

Hence we obtain

```
> grayForest :: Int -> Forest Int
> grayForest 0     = []
> grayForest (n+1) = rs ++ [Node n rs]  where rs = grayforest n
```

Now we have

```
> gray = unfoldr step . wrapList . grayForest
```

where step is as defined in the second warm-up.

Exercise 10. There is still a snag. What is it?

The snag is that grayForest n takes quadratic time because appending an element to the end of a list is a linear-time operation. Quadratic time is much better than exponential time, but not good enough.

Obvious ideas for solving this problem, such as turning appends into cons operations by reversing the forest, or bringing in an accumulating parameter, don't work. The most direct method, and one we will exploit for other purposes below, is to introduce *queues*, redefining a forest to be a *queue* of trees rather than a list. Okasaki's implementation of queues [7] provides a type Queue a for which the following operations all take constant time:

```
insert   :: Queue a -> a -> Queue a
remove   :: Queue a -> (a, Queue a)
empty    :: Queue a
isempty  :: Queue a -> Bool
```

To install queues, we redeclare the type Forest to read

```
> type Forest a = Queue (Tree a)
```

The function grayForest is redefined to read

```
> grayForest 0     = empty
> grayForest (n+1) = insert rq (Node n rq)
>                        where rq = grayForest n
```

Now we have

```
> gray =  unfoldr step . wrapQueue . grayForest
```

where step and wrapQueue are defined as follows:

```
> wrapQueue :: Queue a -> [Queue a]
> wrapQueue xq = consQueue xq []

> consQueue :: Queue a -> [Queue a] -> [Queue a]
> consQueue xq xqs = if isempty xq then xqs else xq:xqs

> step :: [Forest a] -> Maybe (a,[Forest a])
> step []        = Nothing
> step (zq:zqs) = Just (x,consQueue xq (consQueue yq zqs))
>                    where (Fork x xq,yq) = remove zq
```

This is a loopless algorithm for gray.

It is worthwhile summarising the steps that led to this loopless program because we are going to follow exactly the same recipe for the more complicated loopless programs to come. After formulating a recursive program for `gray` we eliminated occurrences of `reverse`, and then expressed the result in terms of the inorder traversal of a particular binary tree. Building the tree and performing an inorder traversal was then made loopless by converting the tree to a forest of rose trees and using a queue to make the necessary append operations constant time.

3.1 Another Loopless Program

Just for completeness, let us briefly sketch another loopless algorithm for `gray`, one that uses a cyclic structure rather than a queue. Consider the forest that arises with `gray 4` and pictured in Figure 4.

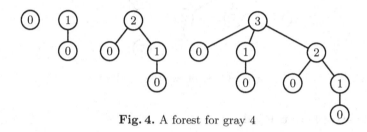

Fig. 4. A forest for gray 4

In general a Gray forest `ts` has the property that a node labelled k has exactly k children; moreover these children are given by the list `take k ts`. Suppose we define `grayCycle` by

```
> grayCycle :: Int -> Forest Int
> grayCycle n = ts  where ts = [Node k ts | k <- [0..n-1]]
```

The result returned by `grayCycle` is a cyclic structure, and building this structure takes linear time.

We can process this cycle of trees by removing the first tree, outputting its label k and adding k subtrees of the cycle to the cycle. Furthermore, we can represent the information about how many trees to take by a pair `(k,ts)`. All this leads to

```
> gray = unfoldr step . wrapPair . grayCycle

> wrapPair ts = [(length ts,ts)]

> step :: [(Int,Forest Int)] -> Maybe (Int,[(Int,Forest Int)])
> step [] = Nothing
> step ((j,Node k ts:us):vss) =
>              Just (k,consPair (k,ts) (consPair (j-1,us) vss))

> consPair (k,ts) kts = if k==0 then kts else (k,ts):kts
```

The function step maintains the invariant that it takes and returns lists of pairs whose first components are nonzero. This is another loopless program for gray.

4   Spider Spinning with Tree Spiders

We now consider spider spinning when each spider is just a tree, so all spiders' legs are directed downwards. A nest of two tree spiders is pictured in Figure 5. This special case of spider spinning was considered by Koda and Ruskey [3]. In the literature, the prefixes of a forest are also known as the "principal sub-forests" and the "ideals of a forest poset". Ingenious loopless algorithms for this problem are described in [3,4,5]. A non-loopless algorithm based on continuations appeared in [2].

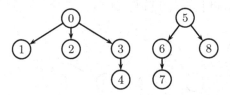

Fig. 5. A nest of two tree spiders

4.1   Boustrophedon Product

One possible transition code for the nest of Figure 5 is given by

586878	0	878685	3	586878	4	878685	2	586878	4
878685	3	586878	1	878685	3	586878	4	878685	2
586878	4	878685	3	586878					

The transitions for the two spiders, x and y say, is formed by weaving together the transitions for x and y. Begin, by going through the transitions for y. Follow this with the first transition for x and then repeat the transitions for y but in reverse order. We saw essentially the same idea in the Gray code problem. Continue in this fashion, weaving single transitions of x with complete transitions of y, alternating forwards and backwards, rather like the shuttle on a loom or an ox ploughing a field. Indeed, Knuth uses the name *boustrophedon product* for essentially this operation. We will call it box because the name is short, pronounceable, and contains an 'ox'.[2] Here is the definition of box:

```
> box :: [a] -> [a] -> [a]
> box [] bs    = bs
> box (a:as) bs = bs ++ [a] ++ box as (reverse bs)
```

For example, box [3,4,5,6] [0,1,2] returns

$$[0,1,2,3,2,1,0,4,0,1,2,5,2,1,0,6,0,1,2]$$

---

[2] There is another reason for the name *box*, but we'll get to that much later on.

Exercise 11. Prove that

```
    box (as ++ [b] ++ bs) cs = box as cs ++ [b] ++ box bs cs'
      where cs' = if even (length as) then reverse cs else cs
```

Exercise 12. Prove that

```
    reverse (box as bs) = box (reverse as) bs'
      where bs' = if even (length as) then reverse bs else bs
```

Exercise 13. Using the result of the two previous exercises, prove that box is associative with unit [].

Just as concat concatenates a list of lists, so the function boxall applies box to a list of lists:

```
> boxall :: [[a]] -> [a]
> boxall = foldr box []
```

Since box is associative with unit [] we could just as well have defined

```
> boxall = foldl box []
```

Exercise 14. Prove this assertion.

For a list of length n of lists each of length m, the output of boxall has length $(m+1)^n - 1$, which is exponential in mn, the total length of the input.

We can now define ncode and scode, the transition codes for a nest of spiders and a single spider, respectively. First we introduce the type declarations

```
> type Nest   = [Spider]
> data Spider = Node Int Nest
```

We will suppose that the labels of nodes in a nest of spiders of size n are the elements of [1..n] in some order. Now we can define

```
> ncode :: Nest -> [Int]
> ncode = boxall . map scode
```

```
> scode :: Spider -> [Int]
> scode (Node a xs) = a : ncode xs
```

The transition code for a single spider consists of an initial transition to change the colour of the root node (in fact, from white to black), followed by a complete list of the transitions for the nest of its subspiders. The definition of ncode is short and sweet, but not loopless.

4.2   Calculating a Loopless Algorithm

So far there has been very little in the way of program calculation. Now we start in earnest. The best advice when faced with the task of calculating a program is to be guided by the form of the definitions under manipulation. In other words, begin by simply taking out the toolbox of functional laws and seeing which tools fit the problem in hand. Another indispensable piece of advice is to begin with a simpler problem, and we did that by starting out with legless spider spinning. Guided by the simpler example we know that at some point we are going to have to eliminate occurrences of reverse and then represent lists by queues of rose trees. But that is in the future.

The first step, dictated solely by the form of the definition of ncode, is an application of the *map-fusion law* for foldr. This law states that

$$\text{foldr f e . map g = foldr (f . g) e}$$

In words, a fold after a map is just a fold. Applying it to ncode gives the alternative definition

```
> ncode = foldr (box . scode) []
```

We now concentrate on the function box . scode and calculate:

```
     box (scode (Node a xs)) bs
=        { definition of scode }
     box (a:ncode xs) bs
=        { definition of box }
     bs ++ [a] ++ box (ncode xs) (reverse bs)
=        { original definition of ncode }
     bs ++ [a] ++ box (boxall (map scode xs)) (reverse bs)
```

The focus now is on the third term, which is an instance of the expression

$$\text{box (foldr box [] ass) cs}$$

in which ass = map scode xs and cs = reverse bs. The form of this expression suggests the use of another fundamental law of functional programming, the *fold-fusion law* of foldr. This law states that

$$\text{f . foldr g a = foldr h b}$$

provided f is strict, f a = b, and f (g x y) = h x (f y) for all x and y. Fold-fusion is one of the fundamental laws of functional programming and crops up in nearly every calculation. Indeed the map-fusion law is a special case of fold-fusion.

Setting f as = box as cs we have that f is strict and f applied to the empty list returns cs since the empty list is the unit of box. Hence the fold-fusion law gives

$$\text{box (foldr box [] ass) cs = foldr h cs ass}$$

provided we can find an h such that

```
box (box as bs) cs = h as (box bs cs)
```

But box is associative, so we can take h = box.

Putting these calculations together, we obtain

```
      box (scode (Node a xs)) bs
```
=   { above }
```
      bs ++ [a] ++ box (boxall (map scode xs)) (reverse bs)
```
=   { fold fusion }
```
      bs ++ [a] ++ foldr box (reverse bs) (map scode xs)
```
=   { map fusion }
```
      bs ++ [a] ++ foldr (box . scode) (reverse bs) xs
```

Hence, setting bop = box . scode[3], we have calculated that

```
> ncode :: [Spider] -> [Int]
> ncode = foldr bop []
> bop (Node a xs) bs = bs ++ [a] ++ foldr bop (reverse bs) xs
```

In this version of ncode the function boxall no longer appears. Neither does scode.

4.3   Eliminating Reverse

Having eliminated boxall, we now eliminate reverse. However, unlike the case of legless spider spinning, this elimination requires a little more work.

First of all, observe that ncode (x:xs) = bop x (ncode xs), and evaluation of bop requires reverse (ncode xs) as well as ncode xs. That suggests it is sensible to construct both sequences at the same time.

To do so we make use of yet a third basic law of functional programming, the *tupling* law of foldr. This law states that

```
fork (foldr f a,foldr g b) = foldr h (a,b)
```

where h x (y,z) = (f x y,g x z).

To apply the tupling law we need a function, pob say (yes, its bop reversed), so that

```
reverse . foldr bop bs = foldr pob (reverse bs)
```

---

[3] We could have introduced this abbreviation earlier, but didn't because of another piece of useful advice about calculation: don't rush into naming things until the moment is ripe, because calculation involving the named thing has both to unpack the name and repackage it again.

This is another instance of the fold-fusion law, the main fusion condition reading

$$\text{reverse (bop x bs)} = \text{pob x (reverse bs)}$$

To discover pob we calculate:

> reverse (bop (Node a xs) bs)
>
> =   { definition of bop }
>
> reverse (bs ++ [a] ++ foldr bop (reverse bs) xs)
>
> =   { property of reverse }
>
> reverse (foldr bop (reverse bs) xs) ++ [a] ++ reverse bs
>
> { putative definition of pob }
>
> foldr pob bs xs ++ [a] ++ reverse bs

Hence we can define

```
> pob (Node a xs) sb = foldr pob (reverse sb) xs ++ [a] ++ sb
```

Now we can apply the tupling law to obtain

$$\text{fork (ncode,reverse . ncode)} = \text{foldr op ([],[])}$$

where

$$\text{op x (bs,sb)} = \text{(bop x bs,pob x sb)}$$

We can simplify op:

> op (Node a xs) (bs,sb)
>
> =   { definition of op }
>
> (bop (Node a xs) bs, pob (Node a xs) sb)
>
> =   { definitions of bop and pob }
>
> (bs ++ [a] ++ foldr bop sb xs, foldr pob bs xs ++ [a] ++ sb)
>
> =   { definition of op }
>
> (bs ++ [a] ++ cs, sc ++ [a] ++ sb)

where (cs,sc) = foldr op (sb,bs) xs. In summary, we have arrived at

```
> ncode = fst . foldr op ([],[])
> op (Node a xs) (bs,sb) = (bs ++ [a] ++ cs, sc ++ [a] ++ sb)
>                         where (cs,sc) = foldr op (sb,bs) xs
```

Occurrences of reverse have been eliminated.

4.4   Trees and Queues

So far, so good. But computation of foldr op ([],[]) takes quadratic time because ++ takes linear time. As with legless spider spinning this problem can be solved by representing lists as the preorder traversals of forests of trees:

```
> type Forest a = Queue (Tree a)
> data Tree a   = Fork a (Tree a)
```

We now have

```
> ncode  = unfoldr step . prolog
> prolog = wrapQueue . fst . foldr op (empty,empty)
> op (Node a xs) (bq,qb)
>           = (insert bq (Fork a cq), insert qc (Fork a qb))
>               where (cq,qc) = foldr op (qb,bq) xs
```

The definitions of step and wrapQueue are exactly the same as in legless spider spinning. This is a loopless algorithm for ncode.

5 Spider Spinning with General Spiders

Finally we tackle the general spider-spinning problem. First, observe that by picking a spider up by one of its nodes we get a tree with directed edges, such as that shown in Figure 6. Different trees arise depending on which node is picked up, but they all represent the same constraints.

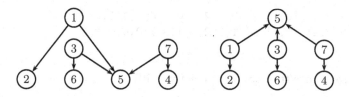

Fig. 6. A spider and an associated tree

It follows that we can model general spiders with the type declarations

```
> type Nest   = [Spider]
> data Spider = Node Int [(Dir,Spider)]
> data Dir    = Dn | Up
```

There is one complication when dealing with general spiders that does not arise with simpler species: the starting bit string is not necessarily a string consisting of all 0s. For example, with $n = 3$ and the constraints $a_1 \geq a_2 \leq a_3$, the five possible bit strings, namely 000, 001, 100, 101, and 111, can only be arranged in Gray path order by starting with one of the odd-weight strings: 001, 100, or 111. However in these lectures we are going to ignore the problem of finding a function seed :: Nest -> [Bit] for determining the starting string.

As with tree spiders we can define

```
> ncode :: Nest -> [Int]
> ncode = boxall . map scode
```

We define `scode` to be the concatenation of two lists, a white code and a black code:

```
> scode :: Spider -> [Int]
> scode (Node a legs) = wcode legs ++ [a] ++ bcode legs
```

The white code, `wcode`, for a spider `Node a legs` is a valid transition sequence when the head node `a` is coloured white (corresponding to a 0 bit), and the black code a valid sequence when `a` is coloured black (corresponding to a 1 bit). Thus `scode` is defined as the sequence that goes through the white code, changes the colour of `a` from white to black, and then goes through the black code. Note that when the spiders are tree spiders, so all legs point downwards, the white code is the empty sequence.

For `scode` to be correct, the final spider colouring generated by executing `wcode legs` has to be the initial colouring on which `bcode legs` starts. In order for the colourings to match up we need to define `wcode` in terms of a variant of `box` which we will call `cox`.[4] The function `cox` is the *conjugate* of `box`:

```
> cox as bs = reverse (box (reverse as) (reverse bs))
```

Whereas `box as bs` begins with `bs` and ends with either `bs` or `reverse bs` depending on whether `as` has even length, `cox as bs` ends with `bs` and begins with either `bs` or `reverse bs`. For example,

```
box [2,3,4] [0,1] = [0,1,2,1,0,3,0,1,4,1,0]
cox [2,3,4] [0,1] = [1,0,2,0,1,3,1,0,4,0,1]
```

Exercise 15. Prove that `cox` is associative with unit `[]`.

Exercise 16. Prove that

```
cox (as ++ [b] ++ bs) cs = cox as cs' ++ [b] ++ cox bs cs
  where cs' = if even (length bs) then reverse cs else cs
```

Exercise 17. Using the result of Exercise 12, prove that

```
box as bs = if even (length as) then cox as bs
            else cox as (reverse bs)
```

Setting `coxall = foldr cox []`, we can now define

```
> wcode, bcode :: [(Dir,Spider)] -> [Int]
> wcode = coxall . map wc
> bcode = boxall . map bc
```

---

[4] By the way, 'to box and cox' means 'to take turns', which is certainly what both operations do and is the real reason for their names. The term comes from the comic play 'Box and Cox - A Romance of Real Life in One Act', by John Maddison Morton. Box and Cox were two lodgers who shared their rooms - one occupying them by day and the other by night.

where wc, bc :: (Dir,Spider) -> [Int]. Use of coxall in the definition of wcode means that the final colouring after executing wcode will be the union of the final colourings generated by the wc transitions, and use of boxall in the definition of bcode means that this colouring will also be the union of the colourings on which the bc transitions start.

It remains to define wc and bc. Given the choices above, the following definitions are forced:

```
> wc (Up,Node a legs) = wcode legs ++ [a] ++ bcode legs
> wc (Dn,Node a legs) = reverse (wcode legs)
> bc (Up,Node a legs) = reverse (bcode legs)
> bc (Dn,Node a legs) = wcode legs ++ [a] ++ bcode legs
```

Look first at wc (Up,x). When the head of the mother spider of x is white and is connected to x by an upwards edge, there are no constraints on wc (Up,x), so we can define it to be either scode x or its reverse. But the subsequent transitions are those in the list bc (Up,x) and the only way to match up the final colouring of the former with the initial colouring of the latter is with the definitions above. The reasoning is dual with bc (Dn,x) and wc (Dn,x).

Finally, we show that ncode can be expressed in terms of bcode:

$$
\begin{aligned}
&\text{ncode xs} \\
=\ &\{\text{ definition of ncode }\} \\
&\text{boxall (map scode xs)} \\
=\ &\{\text{ definition of scode and bc }\} \\
&\text{boxall [bc (Dn,x) | x <- xs]} \\
=\ &\{\text{ definition of bcode }\} \\
&\text{bcode [(Dn,x) | x <- xs]}
\end{aligned}
$$

The complete program is listed in Figure 7. Again, the program is short and sweet but not loopless.

5.1   Calculating a Loopless Algorithm

The transformation to loopless form follows the same path as the simpler problem of a nest of tree spiders. Specifically, we are going to:

1. Eliminate boxall and coxall from the definition of ncode by appeal to map fusion and fold fusion.
2. Eliminate reverse by appeal to tupling.
3. Eliminate the remaining complexity by introducing queues.

It is the appeal to fold fusion in the first step that is the trickiest.

5.2   First Steps

As an easy first step we apply map fusion to the definitions of wcode and bcode, obtaining

```
> ncode :: [Spider] -> [Int]
> ncode xs = bcode [(Dn,x) | x <- xs]

> bcode, wcode :: [(Dir,Spider)] -> [Int]
> bcode = boxall . map bc
> wcode = coxall . map wc

> bc, wc :: (Dir,Spider) -> [Int]
> bc (Up,Node a legs) = reverse (bcode legs)
> bc (Dn,Node a legs) = wcode legs ++ [a] ++ bcode legs
> wc (Up,Node a legs) = wcode legs ++ [a] ++ bcode legs
> wc (Dn,Node a legs) = reverse (wcode legs)
```

Fig. 7. The starting program for ncode

```
> bcode = foldr (box . bc) []
> wcode = foldr (cox . wc) []
```

We now concentrate on the term box . bc. Everything we discover will apply to the second term cox . wc with the obvious changes. We will follow the path of the tree-spider calculation as closely as possible.

There are two clauses in the definition of bc and we consider them in turn. First we have

$$
\begin{aligned}
&\texttt{box (bc (Up,Node a legs)) cs}\\
=\quad &\{\,\text{definition of bc}\,\}\\
&\texttt{box (reverse (bcode legs)) cs}\\
=\quad &\{\,\text{original definition of bcode}\,\}\\
&\texttt{box (reverse (boxall (map bc legs))) cs}
\end{aligned}
$$

As in the case of tree spiders, the next step is an appeal to the fold-fusion law: if a function h can be found so that

$$
\texttt{box (reverse (box as bs)) cs = h as (box (reverse bs) cs)} \qquad (1)
$$

then

$$
\texttt{box (reverse (boxall (map bc ls))) cs = foldr h cs (map bc ls)}
$$

The trouble is that there is no such h to satisfy (1).

Exercise 18. Using Exercise 12, show that if as has even length, then

    box (reverse (box as bs)) = box (reverse as) . box (reverse bs)

while if as has odd length, then

        box (reverse (box as bs)) = box (reverse as) . box bs

In the first case we can define h as = box (reverse as), but in the second case we are stuck: there is no way to compute box bs cs just by knowing the sequence box (reverse bs) cs. For example,

          box "ab" "aaabaaaba" = box "abab" "aaaba"
          box "ba" "aaabaaaba" /= box "baba" "aaaba"

What we can do is find an h such that

    cox (reverse (box as bs)) cs = h as (cox (reverse bs) cs)   (2)

In (2) the first box on each side of (1) has been changed to a cox.
    Here is the way to discover h:

              cox (reverse (box as bs)) cs
        =   { definition of cox }
              cox (cox (reverse as) (reverse bs)) cs
        =   { since cox is associative }
              cox (reverse as) (cox (reverse bs) cs)

Hence we can take h as = cox (reverse as). Appeal to fold-fusion then gives

    cox (reverse (boxall ass)) cs = foldr (cox . reverse) cs ass

But (2) helps only if we can change a box into a cox. Fortunately, Exercise 17 comes to the rescue. Setting

    cs' = if even (length (bcode legs)) then cs else reverse cs

we reason:

              box (bc (Up,Node a legs)) cs
        =   { above }
              box (reverse (boxall (map bc legs))) cs
        =   { Exercise 17 }
              cox (reverse (boxall (map bc legs))) cs'
        =   { fold fusion }
              foldr (cox . reverse) cs' (map bc legs)

We can change cox back into box by another application of fold fusion. Since

$$\text{reverse (cox (reverse as) cs) = box as (reverse cs)}$$

we have

$$\text{reverse . foldr (cox . reverse) cs' = foldr box (reverse cs')}$$

Thus

```
        box (bc (Up,Node a legs)) cs
    =      { above }
        foldr (cox . reverse) cs' (map bc legs)
    =      { fold fusion }
        reverse (foldr box (reverse cs') (map bc legs))
    =      { map fusion }
        reverse (foldr (box . bc) (reverse cs') legs)
```

Hence, introducing bop = box . bc, we have shown

```
> bop (Up,Node a legs) cs = reverse (foldr bop cs' legs)
>   where cs' = if even (length (foldr bop [] legs))
>              then reverse cs else cs
```

Entirely dual reasoning with wop = cox . wc establishes

```
> wop (Dn,Node a legs) cs = reverse (foldr wop cs' legs)
>   where cs' = if even (length (foldr wop [] legs))
>              then reverse cs else cs
```

Exercise 19. Fill in the details of the dual reasoning.

5.3   The Remaining Two Clauses

That was quite a bit of effort but it disposes of only two clauses so more work remains. We now tackle the clause box (bc (Dn,Node a legs)) cs. Setting

```
cs' = if even (length (wcode legs)) then reverse cs else cs
```

we start off by reasoning:

```
        box (bc (Dn,Node a legs)) cs
    =      { definition of bc }
        box (wcode legs ++ [a] ++ bcode legs) cs
    =      { Exercise 11 }
        box (wcode legs) cs ++ [a] ++ box (bcode legs) cs'
```

We tackle each clause in turn. Firstly,

> box (bcode legs) cs'
>
> =   { definition of bcode }
>
> box (foldr box [] (map bc legs)) cs'
>
> =   { fold fusion (exercise) }
>
> foldr box cs' (map bc legs)
>
> =   { map fusion }
>
> foldr bop cs' legs

Secondly,

> box (wcode legs) cs
>
> =   { Exercise 17 }
>
> cox (wcode legs) (reverse cs')
>
> =   { definition of wcode }
>
> cox (foldr cox [] (map wc legs)) (reverse cs')
>
> =   { fold fusion (exercise) }
>
> foldr cox (reverse cs') (map wc legs)
>
> =   { map fusion }
>
> foldr wop (reverse cs') legs

Hence

```
> bop (Dn,Node a legs) cs = foldr wop (reverse cs') legs ++ [a] ++
>                              foldr bop cs' legs
>   where cs' = if even (length (foldr wop [] legs))
>               then reverse cs else cs
```

Dual reasoning establishes

```
> wop (Up,Node a legs) cs = foldr wop cs' legs ++ [a] ++
>                              foldr bop (reverse cs') legs
>   where cs' = if even (length (foldr bop [] legs))
>               then reverse cs else cs
```

This deals with the final two clauses. The program derived so far is summarised in Figure 8. It is not very attractive.

5.4   Parity Spiders

Calculationally speaking, everything so far is tickety-boo[5]. But the result is a mess, mostly owing to the need to compute parity information. Instead of repeatedly computing these values we will install them in a *parity spider*, a spider in which each node is equipped with two boolean values:

[5] tickety-boo: all in order, satisfactory, as it should be.

```
> ncode :: [Spider] -> [Int]
> ncode xs = foldr bop [] [(Dn,x) | x <- xs]

> bop, wop :: (Dir,Spider) -> [Int] -> [Int]
> bop (Up,Node a legs) cs = reverse (foldr bop cs' legs)
>  where cs' = if even (length (foldr bop [] legs))
>             then reverse cs else cs
> bop (Dn,Node a legs) cs = foldr wop (reverse cs') legs ++ [a] ++
>                           foldr bop cs' legs
>  where cs' = if even (length (foldr wop [] legs))
>             then reverse cs else cs
> wop (Up,Node a legs) cs = foldr wop cs' legs ++ [a] ++
>                           foldr bop (reverse cs') legs
>  where cs' = if even (length (foldr bop [] legs))
>             then reverse cs else cs
> wop (Dn,Node a legs) cs = reverse (foldr wop cs' legs)
>  where cs' = if even (length (foldr wop [] legs))
>             then reverse cs else cs
```

Fig. 8. The code after eliminating box and cox

```
> data PSpider = PNode (Bool,Bool) Int [(Dir,PSpider)]
```

The invariant on a parity spider PNode (w,b) a legs is that

```
w = even (length (wcode legs))
b = even (length (bcode legs))
```

Parity information is installed in an ordinary spider by decorating it:

```
> decorate :: Spider -> PSpider
> decorate (Node a legs)
>          = pnode a [(d,decorate x) | (d,x) <- legs]
```

The smart constructor pnode is defined by

```
> pnode a legs = PNode (foldr op (True,True) legs) a legs
```

where

```
> op :: (Dir,PSpider) -> (Bool,Bool) -> (Bool,Bool)
> op (Up,PNode (w,b) _ _) (w',b') = ((w /= b) && w', b && b')
> op (Dn,PNode (w,b) _ _) (w',b') = (w && w', (w /= b) && b')
```

Exercise 20. Justify the above definition of op.

Installing parity information takes linear time in the size of a spider, and leads to the slightly simpler, and much more efficient program of Figure 9.

```
> ncode :: [Spider] -> [Int]
> ncode xs = foldr bop [] [(Dn,decorate x) | x <- xs]

> bop, wop :: (Dir,DSpider) -> [Int] -> [Int]
> bop (Up,PNode (w,b) a legs) cs = reverse (foldr bop (revif b cs) legs)
> bop (Dn,PNode (w,b) a legs) cs = foldr wop (revif (not w) cs) legs ++
>                                  [a] ++
>                                  foldr bop (revif w cs) legs
> wop (Up,PNode (w,b) a legs) cs = foldr wop (revif b cs) legs ++
>                                  [a] ++
>                                  foldr bop (revif (not b) cs) legs
> wop (Dn,PNode (w,b) a legs) cs = reverse (foldr wop (revif w cs) legs)

> revif b cs = if b then reverse cs else cs
```

Fig. 9. Spinning with parity spiders

5.5   Eliminating Reverse

The next step is to eliminate `reverse`. Formally this is done by an appeal to the tupling law for `foldr`, but instead of going into details we will just sketch the reasoning. In effect, every sequence as is represented by a pair of sequences (as,sa) where sa = reverse as. Concatenation of pairs is implemented by

```
> add a (ws,sw) (bs,sb) = (ws ++ [a] ++ bs, sb ++ [a] ++ sw)
```

Reversal is then implemented by swapping the two lists. The result is the program of Figure 10. Ignoring the cost of `add` the computation of `ncode` takes linear time in the size of the nest.

5.6   Queues Again

Now we are ready for looplessness. As in the simpler problem of tree spiders, we represent a list by the preorder traversal of a forest of Rose trees, where a forest is a *queue* of Rose trees:

```
> type Forest a = Queue (Rose a)
> data Rose a   = Fork a (Forest a)
```

We change `add` to be a binary operation on pairs of forests:

```
> add a (wf,fw) (bf,fb) =
>         (insert wf (Fork a bf), insert fb (Fork a fw))
```

We replace the previous definition of `ncode` by

```
> ncode = preorder . fst . foldr bop (empty,empty) . paint
> paint xs = [(Dn,decorate x) | x <- xs]
```

```
> ncode :: [Spider] -> [Int]
> ncode xs = fst (foldr bop ([],[]) [(Dn,decorate x) | x <- xs])

> bop, wop :: (Dir,DSpider) -> ([Int],[Int]) -> ([Int],[Int])
> bop (Up,PNode (w,b) a legs) ps = swap (foldr bop (swapif b ps) legs)
> bop (Dn,PNode (w,b) a legs) ps =
>       add a (foldr wop (swapif (not w) ps) legs)
>             (foldr bop (swapif w ps) legs)
> wop (Up,PNode (w,b) a legs) ps =
>       add a (foldr wop (swapif b ps) legs)
>             (foldr bop (swapif (not b) ps) legs)
> wop (Dn,PNode (w,b) a legs) ps = swap (foldr wop (swapif w ps) legs)

> swap (x,y)     = (y,x)
> swapif b (x,y) = if b then (y,x) else (x,y)
```

Fig. 10. Eliminating reverse

Now all the work is done by preorder, which we can implement just as we did for tree spiders:

```
> preorder :: Forest a -> [a]
> preorder = unfoldr step . wrapQueue
```

The definition of step is the same as it was for the tree spider problem. Summarising, we have

```
> ncode = unfoldr step . prolog
```

where

```
> prolog = wrapQueue . fst . foldr bop (empty,empty) . paint
```

Even though the prolog is now a four-act play, involving characters such as spiders, lists, queues and trees, and strange actions like swapping and folding, it nevertheless takes linear time in the size of the nest, so this finally is a loopless program for spider spinning.

Acknowledgements

I would like to thank participants at the AFP School for feedback during the lectures and two referees who provided a number of insightful comments and suggestions for improving the text. As a result the presentation and style has changed quite a bit, and hopefully is a little less obscure. Without doubt the calculations can be further simplified, but enough is enough.

References

1. Ehrlich, G.: Loopless algorithms for generating permutations, combinations, and other combinatorial configurations. J. ACM 20, 500–513 (1973)
2. Filliâtre, J.-C., Pottier, F.: Producing all ideals of a forest, functionally. Journal of Functional Programming 13(5), 945–956 (2003)
3. Koda, Y., Ruskey, R.: A Gray code for the ideals of a forest poset. Journal of Algorithms 15, 324–340 (1993)
4. Knuth, D.E.: SPIDERS: (2001),
   `http://www-cs-faculty.stanford.edu/~knuth/programs.html`
5. Knuth, D.E.: The Art of Computer Programming, vol. 4, Fascicles 2,3,4. Addison-Wesley, Reading (2005)
6. Knuth, D.E., Ruskey, F.: Efficient Coroutine Generation of Constrained Gray Sequences (aka Deconstructing Coroutines). In: Owe, O., Krogdahl, S., Lyche, T. (eds.) From Object-Orientation to Formal Methods. LNCS, vol. 2635, pp. 183–208. Springer, Heidelberg (2004)
7. Okasaki, C.: Simple and efficient purely functional queues and deques. Journal of Functional Programming 5(4), 583–592 (1995)

From Reduction-Based
to Reduction-Free Normalization

Olivier Danvy

Department of Computer Science, Aarhus University
Aabogade 34, DK-8200 Aarhus N, Denmark
danvy@cs.au.dk
http://www.cs.au.dk/~danvy

Abstract. We document an operational method to construct reduction-free normalization functions. Starting from a reduction-based normalization function from a reduction semantics, i.e., the iteration of a one-step reduction function, we successively subject it to refocusing (i.e., deforestation of the intermediate successive terms in the reduction sequence), equational simplification, refunctionalization (i.e., the converse of defunctionalization), and direct-style transformation (i.e., the converse of the CPS transformation), ending with a reduction-free normalization function of the kind usually crafted by hand. We treat in detail four simple examples: calculating arithmetic expressions, recognizing Dyck words, normalizing lambda-terms with explicit substitutions and call/cc, and flattening binary trees.

The overall method builds on previous work by the author and his students on a syntactic correspondence between reduction semantics and abstract machines and on a functional correspondence between evaluators and abstract machines. The measure of success of these two correspondences is that each of the inter-derived semantic artifacts (i.e., man-made constructs) could plausibly have been written by hand, as is the actual case for several ones derived here.

1   Introduction

Grosso modo, there are two ways to specify the semantics of a programming language, given a specification of its syntax: one uses small steps and is based on a notion of reduction, and the other uses big steps and is based on a notion of evaluation. Plotkin, 30 years ago [64], has connected the two, most notably by showing how two standard reduction orders (namely normal order and applicative order) respectively correspond to two equally standard evaluation orders (namely call by name and call by value). In these lecture notes, we continue Plotkin's program and illustrate how the computational content of a reduction-based normalization function—i.e., a function intensionally defined as the iteration of a one-step reduction function—can pave the way to intensionally constructing a reduction-free normalization function—i.e., a big-step evaluation function:

P. Koopman and D. Swierstra (Eds.): AFP 2008, LNCS 5832, pp. 66–164, 2009.
© Springer-Verlag Berlin Heidelberg 2009

Our starting point: We start from a reduction semantics for a language of terms [40], i.e., an abstract syntax (terms and values), a notion of reduction in the form of a collection of potential redexes and the corresponding contraction function, and a reduction strategy. The reduction strategy takes the form of a grammar of reduction contexts (terms with a hole), its associated recompose function (filling the hole of a given context with a given term), and a decomposition function mapping a term to a value or to a potential redex and a reduction context. Under the assumption that this decomposition is unique, we define a one-step reduction function as a partial function whose fixed points are values and which otherwise decomposes a non-value term into a reduction context and a potential redex, contracts this potential redex if it is an actual one (otherwise the non-value term is stuck), and recomposes the context with the contractum:

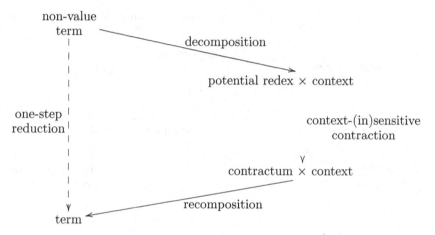

The contraction function is context-insensitive if it maps an actual redex to a contractum regardless of its reduction context. Otherwise, it is context-sensitive and maps an actual redex and its reduction context to a contractum and a reduction context (possibly another one).

A *reduction-based* normalization function is defined as the iteration of this one-step reduction function along the reduction sequence.

A syntactic correspondence: On the way towards a normal form, the reduction-based normalization function repeatedly decomposes, contracts, and recomposes. Observing that most of the time, the decomposition function is applied to the result of the recomposition function [38], Nielsen and the author have suggested to deforest the intermediate term by replacing the composition of the decomposition function and of the recomposition function by a *refocus* function that directly maps a contractum and a reduction context to the next potential redex and reduction context, if there are any in the reduction sequence. Such a refocused normalization function (i.e., a normalization function using a refocus function instead of a decomposition function and a recomposition function) takes the form of a small-step abstract machine. This abstract machine is *reduction-free* because it does not construct any of the intermediate terms in the reduction sequence on the way towards a normal form:

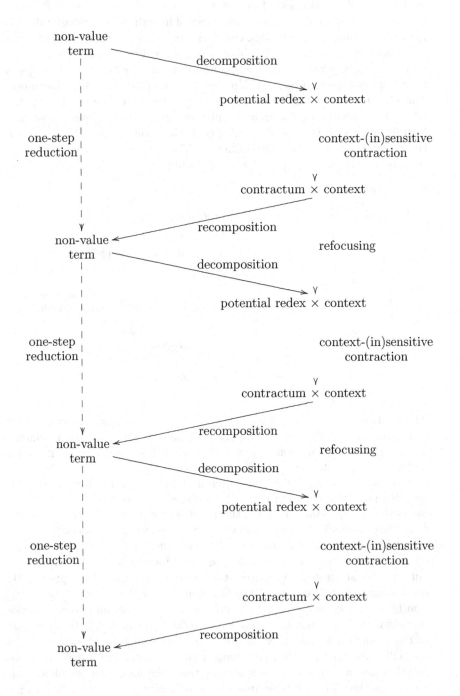

A functional correspondence: A big-step abstract machine is often a defunctionalized continuation-passing program [3,4,5,16,23]. When this is the case, such abstract machines can be refunctionalized [35,37] and transformed into direct style [20,32].

It is our consistent experience that starting from a reduction semantics for a language of terms, we can refocus the corresponding reduction-based normalization function into an abstract machine, and refunctionalize this abstract machine into a reduction-free normalization function of the kind usually crafted by hand. The goal of these lecture notes is to illustrate this method with four simple examples: arithmetic expressions, Dyck words, applicative-order lambda-terms with explicit substitutions, first without and then with call/cc, and binary trees.

Overview: In Section 2, we implement a reduction semantics for arithmetic expressions in complete detail and in Standard ML, and we define the corresponding reduction-based normalization function. In Section 3, we refocus the reduction-based normalization function of Section 2 into a small-step abstract machine, and we present the corresponding compositional reduction-free normalization function. In Sections 4 and 5, we go through the same motions for recognizing Dyck words. In Section 6 and 7, we repeat the construction for lambda-terms applied to integers, and in Section 8 and 9 for lambda-terms applied to integers and call/cc. Finally, in Sections 10 to 13, we turn to flattening binary trees. In Sections 10 and 11, we proceed outside in, whereas in Sections 12 and 13, we proceed inside out. Admittedly at the price of repetitiveness, each of these pairs of sections (i.e., 2 and 3, 4 and 5, etc.) can be read independently. All the other ones have the same structure and narrative and they can thus be given a quicker read.

Structure: Sections 2, 4, 6, 8, 10, and 12 might seem intimidating, but they should not: they describe, in ML, straightforward reduction semantics as have been developed by Felleisen and his co-workers for the last two decades [39,40,73]. For this reason, these sections both have a parallel structure and as similar a narrative as seemed sensible:

1. Abstract syntax
2. Notion of contraction
3. Reduction strategy
4. One-step reduction
5. Reduction-based normalization
6. Summary
7. Exercises

Similarly, to emphasize that the construction of a reduction-free normalization function out of a reduction-based normalization function is systematic, Sections 3, 5, 7, 9, 11, and 13 have also been given a parallel structure and a similar narrative:

1. Decomposition and recomposition
2. Refocusing: from reduction-based to reduction-free normalization
3. Inlining the contraction function
4. Lightweight fusion: from small-step to big-step abstract machine
5. Compressing corridor transitions
6. Renaming transition functions and flattening configurations
7. Refunctionalization
8. Back to direct style
9. Closure unconversion
10. Summary
11. Exercises

We kindly invite the reader to play along and follow this derivational structure, at least for a start.

Prerequisites: We expect the reader to have a very basic familiarity with the programming language Standard ML [59] and to have read John Reynolds's "Definitional Interpreters" [67] at least once (otherwise the reader should start by reading the appendices of the present lecture notes, page 149 and onwards). For the rest, the lecture notes are self-contained.

Concepts: The readers receptive to suggestions will be entertained with the following concepts: reduction semantics [38, 40], including decomposition and its left inverse, recomposition; small-step and big-step abstract machines [65]; lightweight fusion [33, 36, 63] and its left inverse, lightweight fission; defunctionalization [37, 67] and its left inverse, refunctionalization [35]; the CPS transformation [30, 70] and its left inverse, the direct-style transformation [20, 32]; and closure conversion [53] and its left inverse, closure unconversion. In particular, we regularly build on evaluation contexts being the defunctionalized continuations of an evaluation function [22, 26]. To make these lecture notes self-contained, we have spelled out closure conversion, CPS transformation, defunctionalization, lightweight fission, and lightweight fusion in appendix.

Contribution: These lecture notes build on work that was carried out at Aarhus University over the last decade and that gave rise to a number of doctoral theses [2, 10, 15, 24, 57, 58, 62] and MSc theses [48, 61]. The examples of arithmetic expressions and of binary trees were presented at WRS'04 [21]. The example of lambda-terms originates in a joint work with Lasse R. Nielsen [38], Małgorzata Biernacka [12, 13], and Mads Sig Ager, Dariusz Biernacki, and Jan Midtgaard [3, 5]. The term 'lightweight fission' was suggested by Chung-chieh Shan.[1]

Online material: The entire ML code of these lecture notes is available from the home page of the author, at `http://www.cs.au.dk/~danvy/AFP08/`, along with a comprehensive glossary.

---

[1] Personal communication to the author, 30 October 2008, Aarhus, Denmark.

2   A Reduction Semantics for Calculating Arithmetic Expressions

The goal of this section is to define a one-step reduction function for arithmetic expressions and to construct the corresponding reduction-based evaluation function.

To define a reduction semantics for simplified arithmetic expressions (integer literals, additions, and subtractions), we specify their abstract syntax (Section 2.1), their notion of contraction (Section 2.2), and their reduction strategy (Section 2.3). We then define a one-step reduction function that decomposes a non-value term into a potential redex and a reduction context, contracts the potential redex, if it is an actual one, and recomposes the context with the contractum (Section 2.4). We can finally define a reduction-based normalization function that repeatedly applies the one-step reduction function until a value, i.e., a normal form, is reached (Section 2.5).

2.1   Abstract Syntax: Terms and Values

Terms: An arithmetic expression is either a literal or an operation over two terms. In this section, we only consider two operators: addition and subtraction.

```
datatype operator = ADD | SUB
```

```
datatype term = LIT of int | OPR of term * operator * term
```

Values: Values are terms without operations. We specify them with a separate data type, along with an embedding function from values to terms:

```
datatype value = INT of int
```

```
fun embed_value_in_term (INT n)
    = LIT n
```

2.2   Notion of Contraction

A potential redex is an operation over two values:

```
datatype potential_redex = PR_OPR of value * operator * value
```

A potential redex may be an actual one and trigger a contraction, or it may be stuck. Correspondingly, the following data type accounts for a successful or failed contraction:

```
datatype contractum_or_error = CONTRACTUM of term | ERROR of string
```

The string accounts for an error message.

We are now in position to define a contraction function:

```
(*  contract : potential_redex -> contractum_or_error  *)
fun contract (PR_OPR (INT n1, ADD, INT n2))
    = CONTRACTUM (LIT (n1 + n2))
  | contract (PR_OPR (INT n1, SUB, INT n2))
    = CONTRACTUM (LIT (n1 - n2))
```

In the present case, no terms are stuck. Stuck terms would arise if operators were extended to include division, since an integer cannot be divided by 0. (See Exercise 6 in Section 2.7.)

2.3   Reduction Strategy

We seek the left-most inner-most potential redex in a term.

Reduction contexts: The grammar of reduction contexts reads as follows:

```
datatype context = CTX_MT
                 | CTX_LEFT of context * operator * term
                 | CTX_RIGHT of value * operator * context
```

Operationally, a context is a term with a hole, represented inside-out in a zipper-like fashion [47]. (And "MT" is read aloud as "empty.")

Decomposition: A term is a value (i.e., it does not contain any potential redex) or it can be decomposed into a potential redex and a reduction context:

```
datatype value_or_decomposition = VAL of value
                                | DEC of potential_redex * context
```

The decomposition function recursively searches for the left-most inner-most redex in a term. It is usually left unspecified in the literature [40]. We define it here in a form that time and again we have found convenient [26], namely as a big-step abstract machine with two state-transition functions, decompose term and decompose context between two states: a term and a context, and a context and a value.

- decompose term traverses a given term and accumulates the reduction context until it finds a value;
- decompose context dispatches over the accumulated context to determine whether the given term is a value, the search must continue, or a potential redex has been found.

```
(*  decompose_term : term * context -> value_or_decomposition  *)
fun decompose_term (LIT n, C)
    = decompose_context (C, INT n)
  | decompose_term (OPR (t1, r, t2), C)
    = decompose_term (t1, CTX_LEFT (C, r, t2))
```

```
(*  decompose_context : context * value -> value_or_decomposition  *)
and decompose_context (CTX_MT, v)
    = VAL v
  | decompose_context (CTX_LEFT (C, r, t2), v1)
    = decompose_term (t2, CTX_RIGHT (v1, r, C))
  | decompose_context (CTX_RIGHT (v1, r, C), v2)
    = DEC (PR_OPR (v1, r, v2), C)

(*  decompose : term -> value_or_decomposition  *)
fun decompose t
    = decompose_term (t, CTX_MT)
```

Recomposition: The recomposition function peels off context layers and constructs the resulting term, iteratively:

```
(*  recompose : context * term -> term  *)
fun recompose (CTX_MT, t)
    = t
  | recompose (CTX_LEFT (C, r, t2), t1)
    = recompose (C, OPR (t1, r, t2))
  | recompose (CTX_RIGHT (v1, r, C), t2)
    = recompose (C, OPR (embed_value_in_term v1, r, t2))
```

Lemma 1. *A term* t *is either a value or there exists a unique context* C *such that* decompose t *evaluates to* DEC (pr, C), *where* pr *is a potential redex.*

Proof. Straightforward, considering that context and decompose context are a defunctionalized representation. The refunctionalized counterpart of decompose et al. reads as follows:

```
(*  decompose'_term : term * context * (value -> value_or_decomposition)
                    -> value_or_decomposition  *)
fun decompose'_term (LIT n, C, k)
    = k (INT n)
  | decompose'_term (OPR (t1, r, t2), C, k)
    = decompose'_term (t1, CTX_LEFT (C, r, t2), fn v1 =>
        decompose'_term (t2, CTX_RIGHT (v1, r, C), fn v2 =>
          DEC (PR_OPR (v1, r, v2), C)))

(*  decompose' : term -> value_or_decomposition  *)
fun decompose' t
    = decompose'_term (t, CTX_MT, fn v => VAL v)
```

Since decompose' (and its auxiliary function decompose' term) is well typed, it yields a value or a decomposition. Since decompose' term is compositional in its first argument (the term to decompose) and affine in its third (its continuation), it terminates; and since it deterministically traverses its first argument depth first and from left to right, its result is unique. □

2.4   One-Step Reduction

We are now in position to define a one-step reduction function as a function that
(1) decomposes a non-value term into a potential redex and a reduction context,
(2) contracts the potential redex if it is an actual one, and (3) recomposes the
reduction context with the contractum. The following data type accounts for
whether the contraction is successful or the non-value term is stuck:

```
datatype reduct = REDUCT of term
                | STUCK of string


(*  reduce : term -> reduct  *)
fun reduce t
    = (case decompose t
         of (VAL v)
            => REDUCT (embed_value_in_term v)
          | (DEC (pr, C))
            => (case contract pr
                  of (CONTRACTUM t')
                     => REDUCT (recompose (C, t'))
                   | (ERROR s)
                     => STUCK s))
```

2.5   Reduction-Based Normalization

A reduction-based normalization function is one that iterates the one-step reduction function until it yields a value (i.e., a fixed point), if any. The following
data type accounts for whether evaluation yields a value or goes wrong:

```
datatype result = RESULT of value
                | WRONG of string
```

The following definition uses decompose to distinguish between value and non-
value terms:

```
(*  iterate0 : value_or_decomposition -> result  *)
fun iterate0 (VAL v)
    = RESULT v
  | iterate0 (DEC (pr, C))
    = (case contract pr
         of (CONTRACTUM t')
            => iterate0 (decompose (recompose (C, t')))
          | (ERROR s)
            => WRONG s)

(*  normalize0 : term -> result  *)
fun normalize0 t
    = iterate0 (decompose t)
```

2.6 Summary

We have implemented a reduction semantics for arithmetic expressions in complete detail. Using this reduction semantics, we have presented a reduction-based normalization function.

2.7 Exercises

Exercise 1. Define a function embed potential redex in term that maps a potential redex into a term.

Exercise 2. Show that, for any term t, if evaluating decompose t yields DEC (pr, C), then evaluating recompose (C, embed potential redex in term pr) yields t. (Hint: Reason by structural induction over t, using inversion at each step.)

Exercise 3. Write a handful of test terms and specify the expected outcome of their normalization.

Exercise 4. Implement the reduction semantics above in the programming language of your choice (e.g., Haskell or Scheme), and run the tests of Exercise 3.

Exercise 5. Write an unparser from terms to the concrete syntax of your choice, and instrument the normalization function of Section 2.5 so that (one way or another) it displays the successive terms in the reduction sequence.

Exercise 6. Extend the source language with multiplication and division, and adjust your implementation, including the unparser of Exercise 5:

```
datatype operator = ADD | SUB | MUL | DIV

(* contract : potential_redex -> contractum_or_error  *)
fun contract (PR_OPR (INT n1, ADD, INT n2))
    = CONTRACTUM (LIT (n1 + n2))
  | contract (PR_OPR (INT n1, SUB, INT n2))
    = CONTRACTUM (LIT (n1 - n2))
  | contract (PR_OPR (INT n1, MUL, INT n2))
    = CONTRACTUM (LIT (n1 * n2))
  | contract (PR_OPR (INT n1, DIV, INT 0))
    = ERROR "division by 0"
  | contract (PR_OPR (INT n1, DIV, INT n2))
    = CONTRACTUM (LIT (n1 div n2))
```

In addition to the two changes just above (i.e., the definitions of operator and of contract), what else needs to be adjusted in your extended implementation?

Exercise 7. Write test terms that use multiplications and divisions and specify the expected outcome of their evaluation, and run these tests on your extended implementation.

Exercise 8. As a follow-up to Exercise 5, visualize the reduction sequence of a stuck term.

Exercise 9. Write a function mapping a natural number n to a term that normalizes into RESULT (INT n) in n steps. (In other words, the reduction sequence of this term should have length n.)

Exercise 10. Write a function mapping a natural number n to a term that normalizes into RESULT (INT n) in $2 \times n$ steps.

Exercise 11. Write a function mapping an even natural number n to a term that normalizes into RESULT (INT n) in $n/2$ steps.

Exercise 12. Write a function mapping a natural number n to a term that normalizes into RESULT (INT $n!$) (i.e., the factorial of n) in 0 steps.

Exercise 13. Write a function mapping a natural number n to a term whose normalization becomes stuck after 2^n steps.

Exercise 14. Extend the data types reduct and result with not just an error message but also the problematic potential redex:

```
datatype reduct = REDUCT of term
                | STUCK of string * term

datatype result = RESULT of value
                | WRONG of string * term
```

(Hint: The function embed potential redex in term from Exercise 1 will come handy.) Adapt your implementation to this new data type, and test it.

Exercise 15. Write the direct-style counterpart of decompose' and decompose' term in the proof of Lemma 1, using callcc and throw as found in the SMLofNJ.Cont library.

Exercise 16. The following function allegedly distributes multiplications and divisions over additions and subtractions:

```
(* distribute : term -> term *)
fun distribute t
  = let fun visit (LIT n, k)
            = k (LIT n)
          | visit (OPR (t1, ADD, t2), k)
            = OPR (visit (t1, k), ADD, visit (t2, k))
          | visit (OPR (t1, SUB, t2), k)
            = OPR (visit (t1, k), SUB, visit (t2, k))
          | visit (OPR (t1, MUL, t2), k)
            = visit (t1, fn t1' =>
                visit (t2, fn t2' =>
                  k (OPR (t1', MUL, t2'))))
          | visit (OPR (t1, DIV, t2), k)
            = visit (t1, fn t1' =>
                visit (t2, fn t2' =>
                  k (OPR (t1', DIV, t2'))))
    in visit (t, fn t' => t')
    end
```

1. Verify this allegation on a couple of examples.
2. Write a new data type (or more precisely: two) accounting for additions and subtractions of multiplications and divisions, and retarget `distribute` so that it constructs elements of your data type. Run your code on the same couple of examples as just above.
3. What is the type of `visit` now? (To answer this question, you might want to lambda-lift the definition of `visit` outside your definition of `distribute` so that the two definitions coexist in the same scope, and let ML infer their type.)

Exercise 17. It is tempting to see the second parameter of `visit`, in Exercise 16, as a continuation. However, the definition of `visit` is not in continuation-passing style since in the second and third clause, the calls to `visit` are not in tail position. (Technically, the second parameter of `visit` is a 'delimited' continuation [29].)

1. CPS-transform your definition of `visit`, keeping `distribute` in direct style for simplicity. For comparison, CPS-transforming the original definition of `visit` would yield something like the following template:

```
(*  distribute' : term -> term  *)
fun distribute' t
    = let fun visit (..., k, mk)
            = ...
      in visit (t, fn (t', mk) => mk t', fn t' => t')
      end
```

   The result is now in CPS: all calls are tail calls, right up to the initial (meta-) continuation.
2. Defunctionalize the second and third parameters of `visit` (i.e., the delimited continuation `k` and the meta-continuation `mk`). You now have a big-step abstract machine: an iterative state-transition system where each clause specifies a transition.
3. Along the lines of Appendix F, write the corresponding small-step abstract machine.

3   From Reduction-Based to Reduction-Free Normalization

In this section, we transform the reduction-based normalization function of Section 2.5 into a family of reduction-free normalization functions, i.e., ones where no intermediate term is ever constructed. We first refocus the reduction-based normalization function to deforest the intermediate terms, and we obtain a small-step abstract machine implementing the iteration of the refocus function (Section 3.1). After inlining the contraction function (Section 3.2), we transform this small-step abstract machine into a big-step one (Section 3.3). This machine exhibits a number of corridor transitions, and we compress them (Section 3.4). We then flatten its configurations and rename its transition functions into something more intuitive (Section 3.5). The resulting abstract machine is in defunctionalized form, and we refunctionalize it (Section 3.6). The result is in continuation-passing style and we re-express it in direct style (Section 3.7). The resulting direct-style function is a traditional evaluator for arithmetic expressions; in particular, it is compositional and reduction-free.

Modus operandi: In each of the following subsections, we derive successive versions of the normalization function, indexing its components with the number of the subsection. In practice, the reader should run the tests of Exercise 3 in Section 2.7 at each step of the derivation, for sanity value.

3.1 Refocusing: From Reduction-Based to Reduction-Free Normalization

The normalization function of Section 2.5 is reduction-based because it constructs every intermediate term in the reduction sequence. In its definition, decompose is always applied to the result of recompose after the first decomposition. In fact, a vacuous initial call to recompose ensures that in all cases, decompose is applied to the result of recompose:

```
(* normalize0' : term -> result *)
fun normalize0' t
    = iterate0 (decompose (recompose (CTX_MT, t)))
```

Refocusing, extensionally: As investigated earlier by Nielsen and the author [38], the composition of decompose and recompose can be deforested into a 'refocus' function to avoid constructing the intermediate terms in the reduction sequence. Such a deforestation makes the normalization function reduction-free.

Refocusing, intensionally: It turns out that the refocus function can be expressed very simply in terms of the decomposition functions of Section 2.3 (and this is the reason why we chose to specify them precisely like that):

```
(* refocus : term * context -> value_or_decomposition *)
fun refocus (t, C)
    = decompose_term (t, C)
```

The refocused evaluation function therefore reads as follows:

```
(* iterate1 : value_or_decomposition -> result *)
fun iterate1 (VAL v)
    = RESULT v
  | iterate1 (DEC (pr, C))
    = (case contract pr
        of (CONTRACTUM t')
           => iterate1 (refocus (t', C))
         | (ERROR s)
           => WRONG s)
```

```
(*  normalize1 : term -> result  *)
fun normalize1 t
    = iterate1 (refocus (t, CTX_MT))
```

This refocused normalization function is reduction-free because it is no longer based on a (one-step) reduction function. Instead, the refocus function directly maps a contractum and a reduction context to the next redex and reduction context, if there are any in the reduction sequence.

3.2   Inlining the Contraction Function

We first inline the call to contract in the definition of iterate1, and name the resulting function iterate2. Reasoning by inversion, there are two potential redexes and therefore the DEC clause in the definition of iterate1 is replaced by two DEC clauses in the definition of iterate2:

```
(*  iterate2 : value_or_decomposition -> result  *)
fun iterate2 (VAL v)
    = RESULT v
  | iterate2 (DEC (PR_OPR (INT n1, ADD, INT n2), C))
    = iterate2 (refocus (LIT (n1 + n2), C))
  | iterate2 (DEC (PR_OPR (INT n1, SUB, INT n2), C))
    = iterate2 (refocus (LIT (n1 - n2), C))

(*  normalize2 : term -> result  *)
fun normalize2 t
    = iterate2 (refocus (t, CTX_MT))
```

We are now ready to fuse the composition of iterate2 with refocus (shaded just above).

3.3   Lightweight Fusion:
From Small-Step to Big-Step Abstract Machine

The refocused normalization function is small-step abstract machine in the sense that refocus (i.e., decompose term and decompose context) acts as a transition function and iterate1 as a 'trampoline' [43], i.e., a 'driver loop' or again another transition function that keeps activating refocus until a value is obtained. Using Ohori and Sasano's 'lightweight fusion by fixed-point promotion' [33, 36, 63], we fuse iterate2 and refocus (i.e., decompose term and decompose context) so that the resulting function iterate3 is *directly* applied to the result of decompose term and decompose context. The result is a big-step abstract machine [65] consisting of three (mutually tail-recursive) state-transition functions:

- refocus3 term is the composition of iterate2 and decompose term and a clone of decompose term;
- refocus3 context is the composition of iterate2 and decompose context that directly calls iterate3 over a value or a decomposition instead of returning it to iterate2 as decompose context did;
- iterate3 is a clone of iterate2 that calls the fused function refocus3 term.

```
(*  refocus3_term : term * context -> result  *)
fun refocus3_term (LIT n, C)
    = refocus3_context (C, INT n)
  | refocus3_term (OPR (t1, r, t2), C)
    = refocus3_term (t1, CTX_LEFT (C, r, t2))

(*  refocus3_context : context * value -> result  *)
and refocus3_context (CTX_MT, v)
    = iterate3 (VAL v)
  | refocus3_context (CTX_LEFT (C, r, t2), v1)
    = refocus3_term (t2, CTX_RIGHT (v1, r, C))
  | refocus3_context (CTX_RIGHT (v1, r, C), v2)
    = iterate3 (DEC (PR_OPR (v1, r, v2), C))

(*  iterate3 : value_or_decomposition -> result  *)
and iterate3 (VAL v)
    = RESULT v
  | iterate3 (DEC (PR_OPR (INT n1, ADD, INT n2), C))
    = refocus3_term (LIT (n1 + n2), C)
  | iterate3 (DEC (PR_OPR (INT n1, SUB, INT n2), C))
    = refocus3_term (LIT (n1 - n2), C)

(*  normalize3 : term -> result  *)
fun normalize3 t
    = refocus3_term (t, CTX_MT)
```

In this abstract machine, `iterate3` implements the contraction rules of the reduction semantics separately from its congruence rules, which are implemented by `refocus3 term` and `refocus3 context`. This staged structure is remarkable because obtaining this separation for pre-existing abstract machines is known to require non-trivial analyses [44].

3.4   Compressing Corridor Transitions

In the abstract machine above, many of the transitions are 'corridor' ones in that they yield configurations for which there is a unique further transition, and so on. Let us compress these transitions. To this end, we cut-and-paste the transition functions above, renaming their indices from 3 to 4, and consider each of their clauses in turn:

Clause `refocus4 context (CTX MT, v)`:

```
refocus4_context (CTX_MT, v)
= (* by unfolding the call to refocus4_context *)
iterate4 (VAL v)
= (* by unfolding the call to iterate4 *)
RESULT v
```

Clause `iterate4 (DEC (PR OPR (INT n1, ADD, INT n2), C))`:

```
iterate4 (DEC (PR_OPR (INT n1, ADD, INT n2), C))
= (* by unfolding the call to iterate4 *)
refocus4_term (LIT (n1 + n2), C)
= (* by unfolding the call to refocus4_term *)
refocus4_context (C, INT (n1 + n2))
```

Clause `iterate4 (DEC (PR OPR (INT n1, SUB, INT n2), C))`:

```
iterate4 (DEC (PR_OPR (INT n1, SUB, INT n2), C))
= (* by unfolding the call to iterate4 *)
refocus4_term (LIT (n1 - n2), C)
= (* by unfolding the call to refocus4_term *)
refocus4_context (C, INT (n1 - n2))
```

There are two corollaries to the compressions above:

Dead clauses: The clause "`iterate4 (VAL v)`" is dead, and therefore can be implemented as raising a "`DEAD CLAUSE`" exception.

Invariants: All live transitions to `iterate4` are now over `DEC (PR OPR (v1, r, v2), C)`, for some `v1`, `r`, `v2`, and `C`.

3.5   Renaming Transition Functions and Flattening Configurations

The resulting simplified machine is a familiar 'eval/apply/continue' abstract machine [54]. We therefore rename `refocus4 term` to `eval5`, `refocus4 context` to `continue5`, and `iterate4` to `apply5`. We also flatten the configuration `iterate4 (DEC (PR OPR (v1, r, v2), C))` into `apply5 (v1, r, v2, C)`. The result reads as follows:

```
(* eval5 : term * context -> result  *)
fun eval5 (LIT n, C)
    = continue5 (C, INT n)
  | eval5 (OPR (t1, r, t2), C)
    = eval5 (t1, CTX_LEFT (C, r, t2))

(* continue5 : context * value -> result  *)
and continue5 (CTX_MT, v)
    = RESULT v
  | continue5 (CTX_LEFT (C, r, t2), v1)
    = eval5 (t2, CTX_RIGHT (v1, r, C))
  | continue5 (CTX_RIGHT (v1, r, C), v2)
    = apply5 (v1, r, v2, C)

(* apply5 : value * operator * value * context -> result  *)
and apply5 (INT n1, ADD, INT n2, C)
    = continue5 (C, INT (n1 + n2))
  | apply5 (INT n1, SUB, INT n2, C)
    = continue5 (C, INT (n1 - n2))

(* normalize5 : term -> result  *)
fun normalize5 t
    = eval5 (t, CTX_MT)
```

3.6   Refunctionalization

Like many other abstract machines [3, 4, 5, 16, 23], the abstract machine of Section 3.5 is in defunctionalized form [37]: the reduction contexts, together with continue5, are the first-order counterpart of a function. The higher-order counterpart of this abstract machine reads as follows:

```
(*  eval6 : term * (value -> 'a) -> 'a  *)
fun eval6 (LIT n, k)
    = k (INT n)
  | eval6 (OPR (t1, r, t2), k)
    = eval6 (t1, fn v1 =>
        eval6 (t2, fn v2 =>
          apply6 (v1, r, v2, k)))

(*  apply6 : value * operator * value * (value -> 'a) -> 'a  *)
and apply6 (INT n1, ADD, INT n2, k)
    = k (INT (n1 + n2))
  | apply6 (INT n1, SUB, INT n2, k)
    = k (INT (n1 - n2))

(*  normalize6 : term -> result  *)
fun normalize6 t
    = eval6 (t, fn v => RESULT v)
```

The resulting refunctionalized program is a familiar eval/apply evaluation function in CPS.

3.7   Back to Direct Style

The refunctionalized definition of Section 3.6 is in continuation-passing style since it has a functional accumulator and all of its calls are tail calls [30, 20]. Its direct-style counterpart reads as follows:

```
(*  eval7 : term -> value  *)
fun eval7 (LIT n)
    = INT n
  | eval7 (OPR (t1, r, t2))
    = apply7 (eval7 t1, r, eval7 t2)

(*  apply7 : value * operator * value -> value  *)
and apply7 (INT n1, ADD, INT n2)
    = INT (n1 + n2)
  | apply7 (INT n1, SUB, INT n2)
    = INT (n1 - n2)

(*  normalize7 : term -> result  *)
fun normalize7 t
    = RESULT (eval7 t)
```

The resulting program is a traditional eval/apply evaluation function in direct style, à la McCarthy, i.e., a reduction-free normalization function of the kind usually crafted by hand.

3.8   Closure Unconversion

This section is intentionally left blank, since the expressible values in the interpreter of Section 3.7 are first-order.

3.9   Summary

We have refocused the reduction-based normalization function of Section 2 into a small-step abstract machine, and we have exhibited a family of corresponding reduction-free normalization functions. Most of the members of this family are ML implementations of independently known semantic artifacts: abstract machines, big-step operational semantics, and denotational semantics.

3.10   Exercises

Exercise 18. Reproduce the construction above in the programming language of your choice, starting from your solution to Exercise 4 in Section 2.7. At each step of the derivation, run the tests of Exercise 3 in Section 2.7.

Exercise 19. Up to and including the normalization function of Section 3.5, it is simple to visualize the successive terms in the reduction sequence, namely by instrumenting `iterate1`, `iterate2`, `iterate3`, `iterate4`, and `apply5`. Do you agree? What about from Section 3.6 and onwards?

Exercise 20. Would it make sense, in the definition of `normalize6`, to take `fn v => v` as the initial continuation? If so, what would be the definition of `normalize7` and what would be its type?

Exercise 21. Refocus the reduction-based normalization function of Exercise 6 in Section 2.7 and move on until the eval/apply evaluation function in CPS. From then on, to write it in direct style, the simplest is to use a dynamically scoped exception handled at the top level:

```
exception WRONG of string

(*  eval7 : term -> value  *)
fun eval7 (LIT n)
    = INT n
  | eval7 (OPR (t1, r, t2))
    = apply7 (eval7 t1, r, eval7 t2)

(*  apply7 : value * value -> value *)
and apply7 (INT n1, ADD, INT n2)
    = INT (n1 + n2)
  | apply7 (INT n1, SUB, INT n2)
    = INT (n1 - n2)
  | apply7 (INT n1, MUL, INT n2)
    = INT (n1 * n2)
  | apply7 (INT n1, DIV, INT 0)
    = raise (WRONG "division by 0")
```

```
| apply7 (INT n1, DIV, INT n2)
  = INT (n1 div n2)

(* normalize7 : term -> result  *)
fun normalize7 t
  = RESULT (eval7 t)
      handle (WRONG s) => STUCK s
```

In a pinch, of course, a lexically scoped first-class continuation (using `callcc` and `throw` as found in the `SMLofNJ.Cont` library) would do as well:

```
(* normalize7' : term -> result  *)
fun normalize7' t
  = callcc (fn top =>
      let (* eval7 : term -> value  *)
          fun eval7 (LIT n)
              = INT n
          | eval7 (OPR (t1, r, t2))
              = apply7 (eval7 t1, r, eval7 t2)
          (* apply7 : value * value -> value *)
          and apply7 (INT n1, ADD, INT n2)
              = INT (n1 + n2)
          | apply7 (INT n1, SUB, INT n2)
              = INT (n1 - n2)
          | apply7 (INT n1, MUL, INT n2)
              = INT (n1 * n2)
          | apply7 (INT n1, DIV, INT 0)
              = throw top (STUCK "division by 0")
          | apply7 (INT n1, DIV, INT n2)
              = INT (n1 div n2)
      in RESULT (eval7 t)
      end)
```

4   A Reduction Semantics for Recognizing Dyck Words

The goal of this section is to define a one-step reduction function towards recognizing well-parenthesized words, i.e., Dyck words, and to construct the corresponding reduction-based recognition function.

To define a reduction semantics for recognizing Dyck words, we first specify the abstract syntax of parenthesized words (Section 4.1), the associated notion of contraction (Section 4.2), and the reduction strategy (Section 4.3). We then define a one-step reduction function that decomposes a non-empty word into a redex and a reduction context, contracts the redex, and recomposes the context with the contractum if the contraction has succeeded (Section 4.4). We can finally define a reduction-based recognition function that repeatedly applies the one-step reduction function until an empty word is reached, if each contraction has succeeded (Section 4.5).

4.1   Abstract Syntax: Terms and Values

Pre-terms: We start from a string of characters and parse it into a word, i.e., an ML list of parentheses:

```
datatype parenthesis = L of int | R of int

type word = parenthesis list

(*  smurf : string -> word option  *)
fun smurf s
   = let fun loop (~1, ps)
                = SOME ps
            | loop (i, ps)
                = (case String.sub (s, i)
                      of #"("
                          => loop (i - 1, (L 0) :: ps)
                       | #"["
                          => loop (i - 1, (L 1) :: ps)
                       | #"{"
                          => loop (i - 1, (L 2) :: ps)
                       | #"}"
                          => loop (i - 1, (R 2) :: ps)
                       | #"]"
                          => loop (i - 1, (R 1) :: ps)
                       | #")"
                          => loop (i - 1, (R 0) :: ps)
                       | _
                          => NONE)
     in loop ((String.size s) - 1, nil)
     end
```

Terms: A term is a word.
Values: A value is an empty word, i.e., an empty list of parentheses.

4.2   Notion of Contraction

Our notion of contraction consists in removing matching pairs of parentheses in a context. As usual, we represent redexes as a data type and implement their contraction with a function:

```
datatype potential_redex = PR_MATCH of int * int

type contractum_or_error = bool

(*  contract : potential_redex -> contractum_or_error  *)
fun contract (PR_MATCH (l, r))
    = l = r
```

4.3   Reduction Strategy

We seek the left-most pair of matching parentheses in a word.

Reduction contexts: The grammar of reduction contexts reads as follows:

```
type  left_context = int list
type right_context = word

type context = left_context * right_context
```

Decomposition: A term is a value (i.e., it does not contain any potential redex, i.e., here, it is the empty word), it can be decomposed into a potential redex and a reduction context, or it is neither:

```
datatype value_or_decomposition = VAL
                                | DEC of potential_redex * context
                                | NEITHER of string
```

The decomposition function iteratively searches for the left-most potential redex in a word. As in Section 2.3, we define it as a big-step abstract machine with auxiliary functions, decompose word, decompose word paren, and decompose context between three states: a left and a right context; a left context, a left parenthesis, and a right context; and a left context and an optional right parenthesis and right context.

- decompose word dispatches on the right context and defers to decompose word paren, and decompose context;
- decompose word paren dispatches on the current parenthesis, and defers to decompose word or decompose context;
- decompose context determines whether a value has been found, a potential redex has been found, or neither.

```
(*  decompose_word : left_context * right_context
                        -> value_or_decomposition  *)
fun decompose_word (ls, nil)
     = decompose_context (ls, NONE)
  | decompose_word (ls, p :: ps)
     = decompose_word_paren (ls, p, ps)

(*  decompose_word_paren : left_context * parenthesis * right_context
                            -> value_or_decomposition  *)
and decompose_word_paren (ls, L l, ps)
     = decompose_word (l :: ls, ps)
  | decompose_word_paren (ls, R r, ps)
     = decompose_context (ls, SOME (r, ps))

(*  decompose_context:left_context*(parenthesis *right_context)option
                        -> value_or_decomposition  *)
and decompose_context (nil, NONE)
     = VAL
```

```
| decompose_context (nil, SOME (r, ps))
  = NEITHER "unmatched right parenthesis"
| decompose_context (l :: ls, NONE)
  = NEITHER "unmatched left parenthesis"
| decompose_context (l :: ls, SOME (r, ps))
  = DEC (PR_MATCH (l, r), (ls, ps))

(*  decompose : word -> value_or_decomposition  *)
fun decompose w
  = decompose_word (nil, w)
```

Recomposition: The recomposition function peels off the layers of the left context and constructs the resulting term, iteratively:

```
(*  recompose_word : context -> word  *)
fun recompose_word (nil, ps)
  = ps
| recompose_word (l :: ls, ps)
  = recompose_word (ls, (L l) :: ps)

(*  recompose : context * unit -> word  *)
fun recompose ((ls, ps), ())
  = recompose_word (ls, ps)
```

Lemma 2. *A word* w *is either a value, or there exists a unique context* C *such that* decompose w *evaluates to* DEC (pr, C), *where* pr *is a potential redex, or it is stuck.*

Proof. Straightforward (see Exercise 25 in Section 4.7).

4.4   One-Step Reduction

We are now in position to define a one-step reduction function as a function that (1) maps a non-value, non-stuck term into a potential redex and a reduction context, (2) contracts the potential redex if it is an actual one, and (3) recomposes the reduction context with the contractum. The following data type accounts for whether the contraction is successful or the non-value term is stuck:

```
datatype reduct = REDUCT of word
                | STUCK

(*  reduce : word -> reduct  *)
fun reduce w
  = (case decompose w
       of VAL
          => REDUCT nil
        | (DEC (pr, C))
          => if contract pr
             then REDUCT (recompose (C, ()))
             else STUCK
        | (NEITHER s)
          => STUCK)
```

4.5   Reduction-Based Recognition

A reduction-based recognition function is one that iterates the one-step reduction function until it yields a value or finds a mismatch. In the following definition, and as in Section 2.5, we use `decompose` to distinguish between value terms, decomposable terms, and stuck terms:

```
(*  iterate0 : value_or_decomposition -> bool  *)
fun iterate0 VAL
     = true
  | iterate0 (DEC (pr, C))
     = if contract pr
       then iterate0 (decompose (recompose (C, ())))
       else false
  | iterate0 (NEITHER s)
     = false

(*  normalize0 : word -> bool  *)
fun normalize0 w
     = iterate0 (decompose w)
```

The correctness and termination of this definition is simple to establish: each iteration removes the left-most pair of matching parentheses, and the procedure stops if no parentheses are left or if no left-most pair of parentheses exists or if they do not match.

4.6   Summary

We have implemented a reduction semantics for recognizing well-parenthesized words, in complete detail. Using this reduction semantics, we have presented a reduction-based recognition function.

4.7   Exercises

Exercise 22. Write a handful of test words and specify the expected outcome of their recognition.

Exercise 23. Implement the reduction semantics above in the programming language of your choice, and run the tests of Exercise 22.

Exercise 24. Instrument the implementation of Exercise 23 to visualize a reduction sequence.

Exercise 25. In the proof of Lemma 2, do as in the proof of Lemma 1 and write the refunctionalized counterpart of `decompose` et al.

Exercise 26. Let us modify the notion of contraction to match as many left and right parentheses as possible:

```
(*  contract : potential_redex -> contractum_or_error   *)
fun contract (PR_MATCH (l, r), C)
    = let fun visit (l :: ls, (R r) :: ps)
                = if r = l
                  then visit (ls, ps)
                  else NONE
              | visit (ls, ps)
                = SOME (ls, ps)
      in if l = r
         then visit C
         else NONE
      end
```

Use the result of Exercise 24 to visualize a reduction sequence with such a
generalized contraction.

5   From Reduction-Based to Reduction-Free Recognition

In this section, we transform the reduction-based recognition function of Section 4.5 into a family of reduction-free recognition functions, i.e., one where
no intermediate word is ever constructed. We first refocus the reduction-based
recognition function to deforest the intermediate words, and we obtain a small-
step abstract machine implementing the iteration of the refocus function (Section 5.1). After inlining the contraction function (Section 5.2), we transform
this small-step abstract machine into a big-step one (Section 5.3). This abstract
machine exhibits a number of corridor transitions, and we compress them (Section 5.4). We then flatten its configurations and rename its transition functions
into something more intuitive (Section 5.5). The resulting abstract machine is
in defunctionalized form, and we refunctionalize it (Section 5.6). The result is in
continuation-passing style and we re-express it in direct style (Section 5.7). The
resulting direct-style function is compositional and reduction-free.

Modus operandi: In each of the following subsections, and as in Section 3, we
derive successive versions of the recognition function, indexing its components
with the number of the subsection. In practice, the reader should run the tests
of Exercise 22 in Section 4.7 at each step of the derivation, for sanity value.

5.1   Refocusing:
From Reduction-Based to Reduction-Free Recognition

The recognition function of Section 4.5 is reduction-based because it constructs
every intermediate word in the reduction sequence. In its definition, decompose
is always applied to the result of recompose after the first decomposition. In fact,
a vacuous initial call to recompose ensures that in all cases, decompose is applied
to the result of recompose:

```
(* normalize0' : word -> bool *)
fun normalize0' w
   = iterate0 (decompose (recompose ((nil, w), ())))
```

Refocusing, extensionally: The composition of `decompose` and `recompose` can be deforested into a 'refocus' function to avoid constructing the intermediate words in the reduction sequence. Such a deforestation makes the recognition function reduction-free.

Refocusing, intensionally: As in Section 3.1, the `refocus` function can be expressed very simply in terms of the decomposition functions of Section 4.3:

```
(* refocus : context * unit -> value_or_decomposition *)
fun refocus ((ls, ps), ())
   = decompose_word (ls, ps)
```

The refocused evaluation function therefore reads as follows:

```
(* iterate1 : value_or_decomposition -> bool *)
fun iterate1 VAL
     = true
  | iterate1 (DEC (pr, C))
     = if contract pr
       then iterate1 (refocus (C, ()))
       else false
  | iterate1 (NEITHER s)
     = false

(* normalize1 : word -> bool *)
fun normalize1 w
     = iterate1 (refocus ((nil, w), ()))
```

This refocused recognition function is reduction-free because it is no longer based on a (one-step) reduction function. Instead, the refocus function directly maps a contractum and a reduction context to the next redex and reduction context, if there are any in the reduction sequence.

5.2   Inlining the Contraction Function

We first inline the call to `contract` in the definition of `iterate1`, and name the resulting function `iterate2`:

```
(* iterate2 : value_or_decomposition -> bool *)
fun iterate2 VAL
     = true
  | iterate2 (DEC (PR_MATCH (l, r), C))
     = if l = r
       then iterate2 (refocus (C, ()))
       else false
  | iterate2 (NEITHER s)
     = false
```

```
(*  normalize2 : word -> bool  *)
fun normalize2 w
    = iterate2 (refocus  ((nil, w), ()))
```

We are now ready to fuse the composition of `iterate2` with `refocus` (shaded just above).

5.3 Lightweight Fusion:
From Small-Step to Big-Step Abstract Machine

The refocused recognition function is a small-step abstract machine in the sense that `refocus` (i.e., `decompose word`, `decompose word paren`, and `decompose context`) acts as a transition function and `iterate1` as a driver loop that keeps activating `refocus` until a value is obtained. Using Ohori and Sasano's 'lightweight fusion by fixed-point promotion' [33,36,63], we fuse `iterate2` and `refocus` (i.e., `decompose word`, `decompose word paren`, and `decompose context`) so that the resulting function `iterate3` is *directly* applied to the result of `decompose word`, `decompose word paren`, and `decompose context`. The result is a big-step abstract machine [65] consisting of four (mutually tail-recursive) state-transition functions:

- `refocus3 word` is the composition of `iterate2` and `decompose word` and a clone of `decompose word`;
- `refocus3 word paren` is the composition of `iterate2` and `decompose word paren` and a clone of `decompose word paren`;
- `refocus3 context` is the composition of `iterate2` and `decompose context` that directly calls `iterate3` instead of returning to `iterate2` as `decompose context` did;
- `iterate3` is a clone of `iterate2` that calls the fused function `refocus3 word`.

```
(*  refocus3_word : left_context * right_context -> bool  *)
fun refocus3_word (ls, nil)
    = refocus3_context (ls, NONE)
  | refocus3_word (ls, p :: ps)
    = refocus3_word_paren (ls, p, ps)

(*  refocus3_word_paren : left_context * parenthesis * right_context
                          -> bool  *)
and refocus3_word_paren (ls, L l, ps)
    = refocus3_word (l :: ls, ps)
  | refocus3_word_paren (ls, R r, ps)
    = refocus3_context (ls, SOME (r, ps))

(* refocus3_context :left_context *(parenthesis *right_context)option
                          -> bool  *)
and refocus3_context (nil, NONE)
    = iterate3 VAL
  | refocus3_context (nil, SOME (r, ps))
```

```
      = iterate3 (NEITHER "unmatched right parenthesis")
  | refocus3_context (l :: ls, NONE)
      = iterate3 (NEITHER "unmatched left parenthesis")
  | refocus3_context (l :: ls, SOME (r, ps))
      = iterate3 (DEC (PR_MATCH (l, r), (ls, ps)))

(*  iterate3 : value_or_decomposition -> bool  *)
and iterate3 VAL
    = true
  | iterate3 (DEC (PR_MATCH (l, r), C))
    = if l = r
      then refocus3_word C
      else false
  | iterate3 (NEITHER s)
    = false

(*  normalize3 : word -> bool  *)
fun normalize3 w
    = refocus3_word (nil, w)
```

In this abstract machine, `iterate3` implements the contraction rule of the reduction semantics separately from its congruence rules, which are implemented by `refocus3 word`, `refocus3 word paren`, and `refocus3 context`. This staged structure is remarkable because obtaining this separation for pre-existing abstract machines is known to require non-trivial analyses [44].

5.4   Compressing Corridor Transitions

In the abstract machine above, several transitions are 'corridor' ones in that they yield configurations for which there is a unique further transition, and so on. Let us compress these transitions. To this end, we cut-and-paste the transition functions above, renaming their indices from 3 to 4, and consider each of their clauses in turn:

Clause `refocus4 context (nil, NONE)`:

```
refocus4_context (nil, NONE)
= (* by unfolding the call to refocus4_context *)
iterate4 VAL
= (* by unfolding the call to iterate4 *)
true
```

Clause `refocus4 context (nil, SOME (r, ps))`:

```
refocus4_context (nil, SOME (r, ps))
= (* by unfolding the call to refocus4_context *)
iterate4 (NEITHER "unmatched right parenthesis")
= (* by unfolding the call to iterate4 *)
false
```

Clause `refocus4 context (1 :: ls, NONE)`:

```
refocus4_context (l :: ls, NONE)
= (* by unfolding the call to refocus4_context *)
iterate4 (NEITHER "unmatched left parenthesis")
= (* by unfolding the call to iterate4 *)
false
```

Clause `refocus4 context (1 :: ls, SOME (r, ps))`:

```
refocus4_context (l :: ls, SOME (r, ps))
= (* by unfolding the call to refocus4_context *)
iterate4 (DEC (PR_MATCH (l, r), (ls, ps)))
= (* by unfolding the call to iterate4 *)
if l = r
then refocus4_word (ls, ps)
else false
```

There is one corollary to the compressions above:

Dead clauses: All of the calls to `iterate4` have been unfolded, and therefore the definition of `iterate4` is dead.

5.5   Renaming Transition Functions and Flattening Configurations

The resulting simplified machine is an 'eval/dispatch/continue' abstract machine. We therefore rename `refocus4 word` to `eval5`, `refocus4 word paren` to `eval5 paren`, and `refocus4 context` to `continue5`. The result reads as follows:

```
(*  eval5 : left_context * right_context -> bool  *)
fun eval5 (ls, nil)
    = continue5 (ls, NONE)
  | eval5 (ls, p :: ps)
    = eval5_paren (ls, p, ps)

(*  eval5_paren :left_context *parenthesis *right_context -> bool *)
and eval5_paren (ls, L l, ps)
    = eval5 (l :: ls, ps)
  | eval5_paren (ls, R r, ps)
    = continue5 (ls, SOME (r, ps))

(*  continue5 : left_context * (parenthesis * right_context) option
                  -> bool  *)
and continue5 (nil, NONE)
    = true
  | continue5 (nil, SOME (r, ps))
    = false
  | continue5 (l :: ls, NONE)
    = false
  | continue5 (l :: ls, SOME (r, ps))
    = if l = r
      then eval5 (ls, ps)
      else false
```

```
(* normalize5 : word -> bool *)
fun normalize5 w
    = eval5 (nil, w)
```

5.6 Refunctionalization

The above definitions of `eval5` and `continue5` are in defunctionalized form. The reduction contexts, together with `continue5`, are the first-order counterpart of a function. The higher-order counterpart of this abstract machine reads as follows:

```
(*  eval6 : ((parenthesis * right_context) option -> bool)
            * right_context
            -> bool  *)
fun eval6 (k, nil)
    = k NONE
  | eval6 (k, p :: ps)
    = eval6_paren (k, p, ps)

(*  eval6_paren : ((parenthesis * right_context) option -> bool)
                  * parenthesis * right_context
                  -> bool  *)
and eval6_paren (k, L l, ps)
    = eval6 (fn NONE
                  => false
              | (SOME (r, ps))
                  => if l = r
                     then eval6 (k, ps)
                     else false,
             ps)
  | eval6_paren (k, R r, ps)
    = k (SOME (r, ps))

(*  normalize6 : word -> bool  *)
fun normalize6 w
    = eval6 (fn NONE
                  => true
              | (SOME (r, ps))
                  => false,
             w)
```

5.7 Back to Direct Style

The refunctionalized definition of Section 5.6 is in continuation-passing style since it has a functional accumulator and all of its calls are tail calls [30, 20]. Its direct-style counterpart reads as follows:

```
val callcc = SMLofNJ.Cont.callcc
val throw = SMLofNJ.Cont.throw
```

```
(*  normalize7 : word -> bool  *)
fun normalize7 w
    = callcc (fn top =>
        let (*  eval7 : right_context
                        -> (int * right_context) option  *)
            fun eval7 nil
                = NONE
              | eval7 (p :: ps)
                = eval7_paren (p, ps)
            (*  eval7_paren : parenthesis * right_context
                              -> (int * right_context) option  *)
            and eval7_paren (L l, ps)
                = (case eval7 ps
                    of  NONE
                        => throw top false
                      | (SOME (r, ps))
                        => if l = r
                           then eval7 ps
                           else throw top false)
              | eval7_paren (R r, ps)
                = SOME (r, ps)
        in case eval7 w
              of NONE
                 => true
               | (SOME (r, pr))
                 => false
        end)
```

The resulting definition is that of a recursive function that makes as many calls
as it encounters left parentheses and that returns when encountering a right
parenthesis and escapes in case of mismatch.

5.8   Closure Unconversion

This section is intentionally left blank, since the expressible values in the interpreter of Section 5.7 are first-order.

5.9   Summary

We have refocused the reduction-based recognition function of Section 4 into a
small-step abstract machine, and we have exhibited a family of corresponding
reduction-free recognition functions. Most of the members of this family correspond to something one could write by hand.

5.10   Exercises

Exercise 27. Reproduce the construction above in the programming language of
your choice, starting from your solution to Exercise 23 in Section 4.7. At each
step of the derivation, run the tests of Exercise 22 in Section 4.7.

Exercise 28. Continue Exercise 26 and refocus the reduction-based recognition function with generalized contraction. Do you end up with a big-step abstract machine in defunctionalized form?

6   A Reduction Semantics for Normalizing Lambda-Terms with Integers

The goal of this section is to define a one-step reduction function for lambda-terms and to construct the corresponding reduction-based evaluation function.

To define a reduction semantics for lambda-terms with integers (arbitrary literals and a predefined successor function), we specify their abstract syntax (Section 6.1), their notion of contraction (Section 6.2), and their reduction strategy (Section 6.3). We then define a one-step reduction function that decomposes a non-value closure into a potential redex and a reduction context, contracts the potential redex, if it is an actual one, and recomposes the context with the contractum (Section 6.4). We can finally define a reduction-based normalization function that repeatedly applies the one-step reduction function until a value, i.e., a normal form, is reached (Section 6.5).

The abstract syntax of lambda-terms with integer literals reads as follows. It is completely standard:

```
structure Syn
= struct
    datatype term = LIT of int
                  | IDE of string
                  | LAM of string * term
                  | APP of term * term
  end
```

The S combinator (i.e., $\lambda f.\lambda g.\lambda x.f\,x\,(g\,x)$), for example, is represented as follows:

```
local open Syn
in val S = LAM ("f", LAM ("g", LAM ("x",
          APP (APP (IDE "f", IDE "x"),
               APP (IDE "g", IDE "x")))))
end
```

In the course of the development, we will make use of environments to represent the bindings of identifiers to denotable values. Our representation is a canonical association list (i.e., list of pairs associating identifiers and denotable values):

```
structure Env
= struct
    type 'a env = (string * 'a) list

    val empty = []                              (* : 'a env *)
```

```
fun extend (x, v, env)     (*  : string * 'a * 'a env -> 'a env  *)
    = (x, v) :: env


fun lookup (x, env)          (*  : string * 'a env -> 'a option  *)
    = let fun search []
              = NONE
          | search ((x', v) :: env)
              = if x = x' then SOME v else search env
      in search env
      end
end
```

In the initial environment, the identifier succ denotes the successor function.

More about explicit substitutions can be found in Delia Kesner's recent overview of the field [50]. In this section, we consider an applicative order of Curien's calculus of closures [12, 19].

6.1 Abstract Syntax: Closures and Values

A closure can either be an integer, a ground closure pairing a term and an environment, a combination of closures, or the successor function. A value can either be an integer, the successor function, or a ground closure pairing a lambda-abstraction and an environment. Environments bind identifiers to values.

```
datatype  closure = CLO_INT of int
                  | CLO_GND of Syn.term * bindings
                  | CLO_APP of closure * closure
                  | CLO_SUCC
and          value = VAL_INT of int
                   | VAL_SUCC
                   | VAL_FUNC of string * Syn.term * bindings
withtype bindings = value Env.env
```

Values are specified with a separate data type. The corresponding embedding of values in closures reads as follows:

```
fun embed_value_in_closure (VAL_INT n)
    = CLO_INT n
  | embed_value_in_closure (VAL_FUNC (x, t, bs))
    = CLO_GND (Syn.LAM (x, t), bs)
  | embed_value_in_closure VAL_SUCC
    = CLO_SUCC
```

The initial environment binds the identifier succ to the value VAL SUCC:

```
val initial_bindings = Env.extend ("succ", VAL_SUCC, Env.empty)
```

6.2 Notion of Contraction

A potential redex is a ground closure pairing an identifier and an environment, the application of a value to another value, and a ground closure pairing a term application and an environment:

```
datatype potential_redex = PR_IDE of string * bindings
                         | PR_APP of value * value
                         | PR_PROP of Syn.term * Syn.term * bindings
```

A potential redex may be an actual one and trigger a contraction, or it may be stuck. Correspondingly, the following data type accounts for a successful or failed contraction:

```
datatype contractum_or_error = CONTRACTUM of closure
                             | ERROR of string
```

The string accounts for an error message.

We are now in position to define a contraction function:

– A potential redex PR IDE (x, bs) is an actual one if the identifier x is bound in the environment bs. If so, the contractum is the denotation of x in bs.
– A potential redex PR APP (v0, v1) is an actual one if v0 stands for the successor function and if v1 stands for an integer value, or if v0 stands for a functional value that arose from evaluating a ground closure pairing a lambda-abstraction and an environment.
– A ground closure pairing a term application and an environment is contracted into a combination of ground closures.

```
(* contract : potential_redex -> contractum_or_error  *)
fun contract (PR_IDE (x, bs))
    = (case Env.lookup (x, bs)
         of NONE
            => ERROR "undeclared identifier"
          | (SOME v)
            => CONTRACTUM (embed_value_in_closure v))
  | contract (PR_APP (VAL_SUCC, VAL_INT n))
    = CONTRACTUM (embed_value_in_closure (VAL_INT (n + 1)))
  | contract (PR_APP (VAL_SUCC, v))
    = ERROR "non-integer value"
  | contract (PR_APP (VAL_FUNC (x, t, bs), v))
    = CONTRACTUM (CLO_GND (t, Env.extend (x, v, bs)))
  | contract (PR_APP (v0, v1))
    = ERROR "non-applicable value"
  | contract (PR_PROP (t0, t1, bs))
    = CONTRACTUM (CLO_APP (CLO_GND (t0, bs), CLO_GND (t1, bs)))
```

A non-value closure is stuck whenever it(s iterated reduction) gives rise to a potential redex which is not an actual one, which happens when an identifier does not occur in the current environment (i.e., an identifier is used but not declared), or for ill-typed applications of one value to another.

6.3   Reduction Strategy

We seek the left-most inner-most potential redex in a closure.

Reduction contexts: The grammar of reduction contexts reads as follows:

```
datatype context = CTX_MT
                 | CTX_FUN of context * closure
                 | CTX_ARG of value * context
```

Operationally, a context is a closure with a hole, represented inside-out in a zipper-like fashion [47].

Decomposition: A closure is a value (i.e., it does not contain any potential redex) or it can be decomposed into a potential redex and a reduction context:

```
datatype value_or_decomposition = VAL of value
                                | DEC of potential_redex * context
```

The decomposition function recursively searches for the left-most inner-most redex in a closure. It is usually left unspecified in the literature [40]. As usual, we define it here as a big-step abstract machine with two state-transition functions, `decompose closure` and `decompose context` between two states: a closure and a context, and a context and a value.

- `decompose closure` traverses a given closure and accumulates the reduction context until it finds a value;
- `decompose context` dispatches over the accumulated context to determine whether the given closure is a value, the search must continue, or a potential redex has been found.

```
(* decompose_closure : closure * context -> value_or_decomposition *)
fun decompose_closure (CLO_INT n, C)
      = decompose_context (C, VAL_INT n)
  | decompose_closure (CLO_GND (Syn.LIT n, bs), C)
      = decompose_context (C, VAL_INT n)
  | decompose_closure (CLO_GND (Syn.IDE x, bs), C)
      = DEC (PR_IDE (x, bs), C)
  | decompose_closure (CLO_GND (Syn.LAM (x, t), bs), C)
      = decompose_context (C, VAL_FUNC (x, t, bs))
  | decompose_closure (CLO_GND (Syn.APP (t0, t1), bs), C)
      = DEC (PR_PROP (t0, t1, bs), C)
  | decompose_closure (CLO_APP (c0, c1), C)
      = decompose_closure (c0, CTX_FUN (C, c1))
  | decompose_closure (CLO_SUCC, C)
      = decompose_context (C, VAL_SUCC)

(* decompose_context : context * value -> value_or_decomposition *)
and decompose_context (CTX_MT, v)
      = VAL v
  | decompose_context (CTX_FUN (C, c1), v0)
      = decompose_closure (c1, CTX_ARG (v0, C))
  | decompose_context (CTX_ARG (v0, C), v1)
      = DEC (PR_APP (v0, v1), C)
```

```
(*  decompose : closure -> value_or_decomposition  *)
fun decompose c
   = decompose_closure (c, CTX_MT)
```

Recomposition: The recomposition function peels off context layers and constructs the resulting closure, iteratively:

```
(*  recompose : context * closure -> closure  *)
fun recompose (CTX_MT, c)
     = c
  | recompose (CTX_FUN (C, c1), c0)
     = recompose (C, CLO_APP (c0, c1))
  | recompose (CTX_ARG (v0, C), c1)
     = recompose (C, CLO_APP (embed_value_in_closure v0, c1))
```

Lemma 3. *A closure* c *is either a value or there exists a unique context* C *such that* decompose c *evaluates to* DEC (pr, C), *where* pr *is a potential redex.*

Proof. Straightforward (see Exercise 38 in Section 6.7).

6.4   One-Step Reduction

As in Section 2.4, we are now in position to define a one-step reduction function as a function that (1) maps a non-value closure into a potential redex and a reduction context, (2) contracts the potential redex if it is an actual one, and (3) recomposes the reduction context with the contractum. The following data type accounts for whether the contraction is successful or the non-value closure is stuck:

```
datatype reduct = REDUCT of closure
                | STUCK of string

(*  reduce : closure -> reduct  *)
fun reduce c
     = (case decompose c
          of (VAL v)
             => REDUCT (embed_value_in_closure v)
           | (DEC (pr, C))
             => (case contract pr
                   of (CONTRACTUM c')
                      => REDUCT (recompose (C, c'))
                    | (ERROR s)
                      => STUCK s))
```

6.5   Reduction-Based Normalization

As in Section 2.5, a reduction-based normalization function is one that iterates the one-step reduction function until it yields a value (i.e., a fixed point). The following definition uses decompose to distinguish between value and non-value closures:

```
datatype result = RESULT of value
                | WRONG of string

(*  iterate0 : value_or_decomposition -> result  *)
fun iterate0 (VAL v)
    = RESULT v
  | iterate0 (DEC (pr, C))
    = (case contract pr
         of (CONTRACTUM c')
              => iterate0 (decompose (recompose (C, c')))
          | (ERROR s)
              => WRONG s)

(*  normalize0 : term -> result  *)
fun normalize0 t
    = iterate0 (decompose (CLO_GND (t, initial_bindings)))
```

6.6 Summary

We have implemented an applicative-order reduction semantics for lambda-terms
with integers and explicit substitutions in complete detail. Using this reduction
semantics, we have presented a reduction-based applicative-order normalization
function.

6.7 Exercises

Exercise 29. Implement an alternative representation of environments such as

```
type 'a env = string -> 'a option
```

and verify that defunctionalizing this representation yields a representation isomorphic to the one that uses association lists.

Exercise 30. Define a function embed potential redex in closure that maps a
potential redex into a closure.

Exercise 31. Show that, for any closure c, if evaluating decompose c yields DEC
(pr, C), then evaluating recompose (C, embed potential redex in closure pr)
yields c.
(Hint: Reason by structural induction over c, using inversion at each step.)

Exercise 32. Write a handful of test terms and specify the expected outcome of
their normalization.
(Hint: Take a look at Appendix A.2.)

Exercise 33. Implement the reduction semantics above in the programming language of your choice (e.g., Haskell or Scheme), and run the tests of Exercise 32.

Exercise 34. Write an unparser from closures to the concrete syntax of your choice, and instrument the normalization function of Section 6.5 so that (one way or another) it displays the successive closures in the reduction sequence. (Hint: A ground closure can be unparsed as a let expression.) Visualize the reduction sequences of a non-stuck closure and of a stuck closure.

Exercise 35. Extend the source language with curried addition, subtraction, multiplication, and division, and adjust your implementation.

Except for the initial bindings and the contraction function, what else needs to be adjusted in your implementation?

Exercise 36. As a follow-up to Exercise 35, write test terms that use arithmetic operations and specify the expected outcome of their evaluation, and run these tests on your extended implementation.

Exercise 37. Extend the data type `reduct` with not just an error message but also the problematic potential redex:

```
datatype reduct = REDUCT of closure
                | STUCK of string * closure
```

(Hint: A function `embed potential redex in closure` will come handy.) Adapt your implementation to this new data type, and test it.

Exercise 38. In the proof of Lemma 3, do as in the proof of Lemma 1 and write the refunctionalized counterpart of `decompose` et al.

7   From Reduction-Based to Reduction-Free Normalization

In this section, we transform the reduction-based normalization function of Section 6.5 into a family of reduction-free normalization functions, i.e., ones where no intermediate closure is ever constructed. We first refocus the reduction-based normalization function to deforest the intermediate closures, and we obtain a small-step abstract machine implementing the iteration of the refocus function (Section 7.1). After inlining the contraction function (Section 7.2), we transform this small-step abstract machine into a big-step one (Section 7.3). This machine exhibits a number of corridor transitions, and we compress them (Section 7.4). We then flatten its configurations and rename its transition functions into something more intuitive (Section 7.5). The resulting abstract machine is in defunctionalized form, and we refunctionalize it (Section 7.6). The result is in continuation-passing style and we re-express it in direct style (Section 7.7). The resulting direct-style function is in closure-converted form, and we closure-unconvert it (Section 7.8). The result is a traditional call-by-value evaluator for lambda-terms; in particular, it is compositional and reduction-free.

Modus operandi: In each of the following subsections, and as in Section 3, we derive successive versions of the normalization function, indexing its components with the number of the subsection. In practice, the reader should run the tests of Exercise 32 in Section 6.7 at each step of the derivation, for sanity value.

7.1 Refocusing:
From Reduction-Based to Reduction-Free Normalization

The normalization function of Section 6.5 is reduction-based because it constructs every intermediate closure in the reduction sequence. In its definition, decompose is always applied to the result of recompose after the first decomposition. In fact, a vacuous initial call to recompose ensures that in all cases, decompose is applied to the result of recompose:

```
(* normalize0' : term -> result *)
fun normalize0' t
    = iterate0 (decompose (recompose (CTX_MT,
                                      CLO_GND (t, initial_bindings))))
```

Refocusing, extensionally: As in Section 3.1, the composition of decompose and recompose can be deforested into a 'refocus' function to avoid constructing the intermediate closures in the reduction sequence. Such a deforestation makes the normalization function reduction-free.

Refocusing, intensionally: As in Section 3.1, the refocus function can be expressed very simply in terms of the decomposition functions of Section 6.3:

```
(* refocus : closure * context -> value_or_decomposition *)
fun refocus (c, C)
    = decompose_closure (c, C)
```

The refocused evaluation function therefore reads as follows:

```
(* iterate1 : value_or_decomposition -> result *)
fun iterate1 (VAL v)
    = RESULT v
  | iterate1 (DEC (pr, C))
    = (case contract pr
         of (CONTRACTUM c')
            => iterate1 (refocus (c', C))
          | (ERROR s)
            => WRONG s)

(* normalize1 : term -> result *)
fun normalize1 t
    = iterate1 (refocus (CLO_GND (t, initial_bindings), CTX_MT))
```

This refocused normalization function is reduction-free because it is no longer based on a (one-step) reduction function. Instead, the refocus function directly maps a contractum and a reduction context to the next potential redex and reduction context, if there are any in the reduction sequence.

7.2   Inlining the Contraction Function

We first inline the call to contract in the definition of iterate1, and name the resulting function iterate2. Reasoning by inversion, there are six cases and therefore the DEC clause in the definition of iterate1 is replaced by six DEC clauses in the definition of iterate2:

```
(*  iterate2 : value_or_decomposition -> result  *)
fun iterate2 (VAL v)
    = RESULT v
  | iterate2 (DEC (PR_IDE (x, bs), C))
    = (case Env.lookup (x, bs)
         of NONE
            => WRONG "undeclared identifier"
          | (SOME v)
            => iterate2 (refocus (embed_value_in_closure v, C)))
  | iterate2 (DEC (PR_APP (VAL_SUCC, VAL_INT n), C))
   = iterate2 (refocus (embed_value_in_closure(VAL_INT (n + 1)), C))
  | iterate2 (DEC (PR_APP (VAL_SUCC, v), C))
    = WRONG "non-integer value"
  | iterate2 (DEC (PR_APP (VAL_FUNC (x, t, bs), v), C))
    = iterate2 (refocus (CLO_GND (t, Env.extend (x, v, bs)), C))
  | iterate2 (DEC (PR_APP (v0, v1), C))
    = WRONG "non-applicable value"
  | iterate2 (DEC (PR_PROP (t0, t1, bs), C))
  = iterate2(refocus (CLO_APP (CLO_GND (t0, bs), CLO_GND(t1, bs)),C))

(*  normalize2 : term -> result  *)
fun normalize2 t
    = iterate2 (refocus (CLO_GND (t, initial_bindings), CTX_MT))
```

We are now ready to fuse the composition of iterate2 with refocus (shaded just above).

7.3   Lightweight Fusion: From Small-Step to Big-Step Abstract Machine

The refocused normalization function is small-step abstract machine in the sense that refocus (i.e., decompose closure and decompose context) acts as a transition function and iterate1 as a driver loop that keeps activating refocus until a value is obtained. We fuse iterate2 and refocus (i.e., decompose closure and decompose context) so that the resulting function iterate3 is directly applied to the result of decompose closure and decompose context. The result is a big-step abstract machine consisting of three (mutually tail-recursive) state-transition functions:

- refocus3 closure is the composition of iterate2 and decompose closure and a clone of decompose closure;

— refocus3 context is the composition of iterate2 and decompose context that directly calls iterate3 over a value or a decomposition instead of returning it to iterate2 as decompose context did;

— iterate3 is a clone of iterate2 that calls the fused function refocus3 closure.

```
(* refocus3_closure : closure * context -> result  *)
fun refocus3_closure (CLO_INT n, C)
    = refocus3_context (C, VAL_INT n)
  | refocus3_closure (CLO_GND (Syn.LIT n, bs), C)
    = refocus3_context (C, VAL_INT n)
  | refocus3_closure (CLO_GND (Syn.IDE x, bs), C)
    = iterate3 (DEC (PR_IDE (x, bs), C))
  | refocus3_closure (CLO_GND (Syn.LAM (x, t), bs), C)
    = refocus3_context (C, VAL_FUNC (x, t, bs))
  | refocus3_closure (CLO_GND (Syn.APP (t0, t1), bs), C)
    = iterate3 (DEC (PR_PROP (t0, t1, bs), C))
  | refocus3_closure (CLO_APP (c0, c1), C)
    = refocus3_closure (c0, CTX_FUN (C, c1))
  | refocus3_closure (CLO_SUCC, C)
    = refocus3_context (C, VAL_SUCC)

(* refocus3_context : context * value -> result  *)
and refocus3_context (CTX_MT, v)
    = iterate3 (VAL v)
  | refocus3_context (CTX_FUN (C, c1), v0)
    = refocus3_closure (c1, CTX_ARG (v0, C))
  | refocus3_context (CTX_ARG (v0, C), v1)
    = iterate3 (DEC (PR_APP (v0, v1), C))

(* iterate3 : value_or_decomposition -> result  *)
and iterate3 (VAL v)
    = RESULT v
  | iterate3 (DEC (PR_IDE (x, bs), C))
    = (case Env.lookup (x, bs)
         of NONE
             => WRONG "undeclared identifier"
          | (SOME v)
             => refocus3_closure (embed_value_in_closure v, C))
  | iterate3 (DEC (PR_APP (VAL_SUCC, VAL_INT n), C))
    = refocus3_closure (embed_value_in_closure (VAL_INT (n + 1)), C)
  | iterate3 (DEC (PR_APP (VAL_SUCC, v), C))
    = WRONG "non-integer value"
  | iterate3 (DEC (PR_APP (VAL_FUNC (x, t, bs), v), C))
    = refocus3_closure (CLO_GND (t, Env.extend (x, v, bs)), C)
  | iterate3 (DEC (PR_APP (v0, v1), C))
    = WRONG "non-applicable value"
  | iterate3 (DEC (PR_PROP (t0, t1, bs), C))
    = refocus3_closure (CLO_APP (CLO_GND (t0, bs), CLO_GND (t1, bs)),C)

(* normalize3 : term -> result  *)
```

```
fun normalize3 t
  = refocus3_closure (CLO_GND (t, initial_bindings), CTX_MT)
```

In this abstract machine, `iterate3` implements the contraction rules
of the reduction semantics separately from its congruence rules, which are implemented by `refocus3 closure` and `refocus3 context`. This staged structure is
remarkable because obtaining this separation for pre-existing abstract machines
is known to require non-trivial analyses [44].

7.4   Compressing Corridor Transitions

In the abstract machine above, many of the transitions are 'corridor' ones in
that they yield configurations for which there is a unique further transition,
and so on. Let us compress these transitions. To this end, we cut-and-paste the
transition functions above, renaming their indices from 3 to 4, and consider each
of their clauses in turn, making use of the equivalence between `refocus4 closure`
(`embed value in closure v, C`) and `refocus4 context (C, v)`:

Clause `refocus4 closure (CLO GND (Syn.IDE x, bs), C)`:

```
refocus4_closure (CLO_GND (Syn.IDE x, bs), C)
= (* by unfolding the call to refocus4_closure *)
iterate4 (DEC (PR_IDE (x, bs), C))
= (* by unfolding the call to iterate4 *)
(case Env.lookup (x, bs)
   of NONE
      => WRONG "undeclared identifier"
    | (SOME v)
      => refocus4_closure (embed_value_in_closure v, C))
= (* eureka *)
(case Env.lookup (x, bs)
   of NONE
      => WRONG "undeclared identifier"
    | (SOME v)
      => refocus4_context (C, v))
```

Clause `refocus4 closure (CLO GND (Syn.APP (t0, t1), bs), C)`:

```
refocus4_closure (CLO_GND (Syn.APP (t0, t1), bs), C)
= (* by unfolding the call to refocus4_closure *)
iterate4 (DEC (PR_PROP (t0, t1, bs)), C)
= (* by unfolding the call to iterate4 *)
refocus4_closure (CLO_GND (t0, bs), CTX_FUN (C, CLO_GND (t1, bs)))
```

There are two corollaries to the compressions above:

Dead clauses: The clauses for non-ground closures are dead, and so is the
clause "`iterate4 (VAL v).`" They can therefore be implemented as raising a
"`DEAD CLAUSE`" exception.

Invariants: All transitions to `refocus closure` are now over ground closures.
All live transitions to `iterate4` are now over DEC (PR APP (v0, v1), C), for
some v0, v1, and C.

7.5   Renaming Transition Functions and Flattening Configurations

In Section 7.4, the resulting simplified machine is a familiar 'eval/apply/continue' abstract machine [54] operating over ground closures. We therefore rename `refocus4 closure` to `eval5`, `refocus4 context` to `continue5`, and `iterate4` to `apply5`, and flatten the configuration `refocus4 closure (CLO GND (t, bs), C)` into `eval5 (t, bs, C)` and the configuration `iterate4 (DEC (PR APP (v0, v1), C))` into `apply5 (v0, v1, C)`, as well as the definition of values and contexts:

```
datatype     value = VAL_INT of int
                   | VAL_SUCC
                   | VAL_FUNC of string * Syn.term * bindings
withtype bindings = value Env.env

datatype context = CTX_MT
                   | CTX_FUN of context * (Syn.term * bindings)
                   | CTX_ARG of value * context

val initial_bindings = Env.extend ("succ", VAL_SUCC, Env.empty)
```

The result reads as follows:

```
datatype result = RESULT of value
                | WRONG of string

(*  eval5 : term * bindings * context -> result  *)
fun eval5 (Syn.LIT n, bs, C)
    = continue5 (C, VAL_INT n)
  | eval5 (Syn.IDE x, bs, C)
    = (case Env.lookup (x, bs)
         of NONE
            => WRONG "undeclared identifier"
          | (SOME v)
            => continue5 (C, v))
  | eval5 (Syn.LAM (x, t), bs, C)
    = continue5 (C, VAL_FUNC (x, t, bs))
  | eval5 (Syn.APP (t0, t1), bs, C)
    = eval5 (t0, bs, CTX_FUN (C, (t1, bs)))

(*  continue5 : context * value -> result  *)
and continue5 (CTX_MT, v)
    = RESULT v
  | continue5 (CTX_FUN (C, (t1, bs)), v0)
    = eval5 (t1, bs, CTX_ARG (v0, C))
  | continue5 (CTX_ARG (v0, C), v1)
    = apply5 (v0, v1, C)

(*  apply5 : value * value * context -> result  *)
and apply5 (VAL_SUCC, VAL_INT n, C)
    = continue5 (C, VAL_INT (n + 1))
  | apply5 (VAL_SUCC, v, C)
```

```
      = WRONG "non-integer value"
  | apply5 (VAL_FUNC (x, t, bs), v, C)
      = eval5 (t, Env.extend (x, v, bs), C)
  | apply5 (v0, v1, C)
      = WRONG "non-applicable value"

(*  normalize5 : term -> result  *)
fun normalize5 t
      = eval5 (t, initial_bindings, CTX_MT)
```

The resulting abstract machine is the familiar environment-based CEK machine [41].

7.6 Refunctionalization

Like many other big-step abstract machines [3,4,5,16,23], the abstract machine of Section 7.5 is in defunctionalized form [37]: the reduction contexts, together with continue5, are the first-order counterpart of a function. The higher-order counterpart of this abstract machine reads as follows:

```
datatype    value = VAL_INT of int
                  | VAL_SUCC
                  | VAL_FUNC of string * Syn.term * bindings
withtype bindings = value Env.env

val initial_bindings = Env.extend ("succ", VAL_SUCC, Env.empty)

datatype result = RESULT of value
                | WRONG of string

(*  eval6 : term * bindings * (value -> result) -> result  *)
fun eval6 (Syn.LIT n, bs, k)
    = k (VAL_INT n)
  | eval6 (Syn.IDE x, bs, k)
    = (case Env.lookup (x, bs)
         of NONE
             => WRONG "undeclared identifier"
          | (SOME v)
             => k v)
  | eval6 (Syn.LAM (x, t), bs, k)
    = k (VAL_FUNC (x, t, bs))
  | eval6 (Syn.APP (t0, t1), bs, k)
    = eval6 (t0, bs, fn v0 =>
        eval6 (t1, bs, fn v1 =>
          apply6 (v0, v1, k)))

(*  apply6 : value * value * (value -> result) -> result  *)
and apply6 (VAL_SUCC, VAL_INT n, k)
    = k (VAL_INT (n + 1))
  | apply6 (VAL_SUCC, v, k)
```

```
          = WRONG "non-integer value"
      | apply6 (VAL_FUNC (x, t, bs), v, k)
          = eval6 (t, Env.extend (x, v, bs), k)
      | apply6 (v0, v1, k)
          = WRONG "non-applicable value"

  (*  normalize6 : term -> result  *)
  fun normalize6 t
          = eval6 (t, initial_bindings, fn v => RESULT v)
```

The resulting refunctionalized program is a familiar eval/apply evaluation function in CPS.

7.7   Back to Direct Style

The refunctionalized definition of Section 7.6 is in continuation-passing style since it has a functional accumulator and all of its calls are tail calls. Its direct-style counterpart reads as follows:

```
datatype    value = VAL_INT of int
                  | VAL_SUCC
                  | VAL_FUNC of string * Syn.term * bindings
withtype bindings = value Env.env

val initial_bindings = Env.extend ("succ", VAL_SUCC, Env.empty)

exception ERROR of string

(*  eval7 : term * bindings -> value  *)
fun eval7 (Syn.LIT n, bs)
      = VAL_INT n
  | eval7 (Syn.IDE x, bs)
      = (case Env.lookup (x, bs)
           of NONE
              => raise (ERROR "undeclared identifier")
            | (SOME v)
              => v)
  | eval7 (Syn.LAM (x, t), bs)
      = VAL_FUNC (x, t, bs)
  | eval7 (Syn.APP (t0, t1), bs)
      = apply7 (eval7 (t0, bs), eval7 (t1, bs))

(*  apply7 : value * value -> value  *)
and apply7 (VAL_SUCC, VAL_INT n)
      = VAL_INT (n + 1)
  | apply7 (VAL_SUCC, v)
      = raise (ERROR "non-integer value")
  | apply7 (VAL_FUNC (x, t, bs), v)
      = eval7 (t, Env.extend (x, v, bs))
  | apply7 (v0, v1)
      = raise (ERROR "non-applicable value")
```

```
datatype result = RESULT of value
                | WRONG of string

(*  normalize7 : term -> result  *)
fun normalize7 t
    = RESULT (eval7 (t, initial_bindings))
      handle (ERROR s) => WRONG s
```

The resulting program is a traditional eval/apply evaluation function in direct style and using a top-level exception for run-time errors, à la McCarthy, i.e., a reduction-free normalization function of the kind usually crafted by hand.

7.8   Closure Unconversion

The direct-style definition of Section 7.7 is in closure-converted form since its applicable values are introduced with VAL SUCC and VAL FUNC, and eliminated in the clauses of apply7. Its higher-order, closure-unconverted equivalent reads as follows.

Expressible and denotable values. The VAL FUN value constructor is higher-order, and caters both for the predefined successor function and for the value of source lambda-abstractions:

```
datatype value = VAL_INT of int
               | VAL_FUN of value -> value

type bindings = value Env.env
```

The occurrences of VAL FUN are shaded below.
Stuck terms. Run-time errors are still implemented by raising an exception:

```
exception ERROR of string
```

Initial bindings. The successor function is now defined in the initial environment:

```
val val_succ =  VAL_FUN  (fn (VAL_INT n)
                              => VAL_INT (n + 1)
                          | v
                              => raise (ERROR "non-integer value"))

val initial_bindings = Env.extend ("succ", val_succ, Env.empty)
```

The eval/apply component. In eval8, the denotation of an abstraction is now inlined, and in apply8, applicable values are now directly applied:

```
(*  eval8 : term * bindings -> value  *)
fun eval8 (Syn.LIT n, bs)
    = VAL_INT n
  | eval8 (Syn.IDE x, bs)
```

```
            = (case Env.lookup (x, bs)
                of NONE
                    => raise (ERROR "undeclared identifier")
                | (SOME v)
                    => v)
      | eval8 (Syn.LAM (x, t), bs)
          = VAL_FUN (fn v => eval8 (t, Env.extend (x, v, bs)))
      | eval8 (Syn.APP (t0, t1), bs)
          = apply8 (eval8 (t0, bs), eval8 (t1, bs))
  (*  apply8 : value * value -> value  *)
  and apply8 ( VAL_FUN f, v)
        = f v
      | apply8 (v0, v1)
          = raise (ERROR "non-applicable value")
```

The top-level definition. A term t is evaluated in the initial environment. If this evaluation completes, the resulting value is the result of the normalization function. If this evaluation goes wrong, the given term is stuck.

```
datatype result = RESULT of value
                | WRONG of string

(*  normalize8 : term -> result  *)
fun normalize8 t
    = RESULT (eval8 (t, initial_bindings))
      handle (ERROR s) => WRONG s
```

The resulting program is a traditional eval/apply function in direct style that uses a top-level exception for run-time errors. It is also compositional.

7.9   Summary

We have refocused the reduction-based normalization function of Section 6 into a small-step abstract machine, and we have exhibited a family of corresponding reduction-free normalization functions. Most of the members of this family are ML implementations of independently known semantic artifacts and coincide with what one would have independently written by hand.

7.10   Exercises

Exercise 39. Reproduce the construction above in the programming language of your choice, starting from your solution to Exercise 33 in Section 6.7. At each step of the derivation, run the tests of Exercise 32 in Section 6.7.

Exercise 40. Up to and including the normalization function of Section 7.5, it is simple to visualize the successive closures in the reduction sequence, namely by instrumenting iterate1, iterate2, iterate3, iterate4, and apply5. Do you agree? What about from Section 7.6 and onwards?

Exercise 41. Would it make sense, in the definition of `normalize6`, to take `fn v => v` as the initial continuation? If so, what would be the definition of `normalize7` and what would be its type?

Exercise 42. In Section 7.7, we have transformed the evaluator of Section 7.6 into direct style, and then in Section 7.8, we have closure-unconverted it. However, the the evaluator of Section 7.6 is also in closure-converted form:

1. closure-unconvert the evaluator of Section 7.6; the result should be a compositional evaluator in CPS with the following data type of expressible values:

```
datatype value = VAL_INT of int
               | VAL_FUN of value * (value -> result) -> result
     and result = RESULT of value
               | WRONG of string
```

2. transform this compositional evaluator into direct style, and verify that the result coincides with the evaluator of Section 7.8.

Exercise 43. Compare the evaluation functions of Section 7.8 and of Appendix B; of Section 7.7 and of Appendix C; of Section 7.6 and of Appendix D; and of Section 7.5 and of Appendix E. This comparison should explain your feeling of *déjà vu*.

8   A Reduction Semantics for Normalizing Lambda-Terms with Integers and First-Class Continuations

In this section, we extend the source language of Section 6 with one more predefined identifier in the initial environment: `call/cc`. Presentationally, we therefore single out the increment over Section 6 rather than giving a stand-alone reduction semantics.

8.1   Abstract Syntax: Closures, Values, and Contexts

In addition to being an integer, a ground closure pairing a term and an environment, a combination of closures, or the successor function, a closure can also be the call/cc function or a reified context. Correspondingly, in addition to being an integer, the successor function, or a ground closure pairing a lambda-abstraction and an environment, a value can also be the call/cc function or a reified context. Environments bind identifiers to values.

```
datatype  closure = CLO_INT of int
                  | CLO_GND of Syn.term * bindings
                  | CLO_APP of closure * closure
                  | CLO_SUCC
                  | CLO_CWCC
                  | CLO_CONT of context
```

```
and           value = VAL_INT of int
                    | VAL_SUCC
                    | VAL_FUNC of string * Syn.term * bindings
                    | VAL_CWCC
                    | VAL_CONT of context
and         context = CTX_MT
                    | CTX_FUN of context * closure
                    | CTX_ARG of value * context
withtype bindings = value Env.env
```

Values are specified with a separate data type. The corresponding embedding of values in closures reads as follows:

```
fun embed_value_in_closure (VAL_INT n)
    = CLO_INT n
  | embed_value_in_closure (VAL_FUNC (x, t, bs))
    = CLO_GND (Syn.LAM (x, t), bs)
  | embed_value_in_closure VAL_SUCC
    = CLO_SUCC
  | embed_value_in_closure VAL_CWCC
    = CLO_CWCC
  | embed_value_in_closure (VAL_CONT C)
    = CLO_CONT C
```

The initial environment also binds the identifier call/cc to the value VAL CWCC:

```
val initial_bindings = Env.extend ("call/cc", VAL_CWCC,
                         Env.extend ("succ", VAL_SUCC,
                         Env.empty))
```

8.2   Notion of Contraction

A potential redex is as in Section 6.2. The contraction function also accounts for first-class continuations, and is therefore context sensitive in that it maps a potential redex and its reduction context to a contractum and a reduction context (possibly another one):

```
datatype contractum_or_error = CONTRACTUM of closure * context
                             | ERROR of string
```

Compared to Section 6.2, the new clauses are shaded:

```
(*  contract : potential_redex * context -> contractum_or_error  *)
fun contract (PR_IDE (x, bs), C)
    = (case Env.lookup (x, bs)
         of NONE
            => ERROR "undeclared identifier"
          | (SOME v)
            => CONTRACTUM (embed_value_in_closure v, C))
```

```
| contract (PR_APP (VAL_SUCC, VAL_INT n), C)
  = CONTRACTUM (embed_value_in_closure (VAL_INT (n + 1)), C)
| contract (PR_APP (VAL_SUCC, v), C)
  = ERROR "non-integer value"
| contract (PR_APP (VAL_FUNC (x, t, bs), v), C)
  = CONTRACTUM (CLO_GND (t, Env.extend (x, v, bs)), C)
|  contract (PR_APP (VAL_CWCC, v), C)

  =  CONTRACTUM (CLO_APP (embed_value_in_closure v, CLO_CONT C), C)

|  contract (PR_APP (VAL_CONT C', v), C)

  =  CONTRACTUM (embed_value_in_closure v, C')
| contract (PR_APP (v0, v1), C)
  = ERROR "non-applicable value"
| contract (PR_PROP (t0, t1, bs), C)
  = CONTRACTUM (CLO_APP (CLO_GND (t0, bs), CLO_GND (t1, bs)), C)
```

Each of the clauses implements a contraction rule, and all of the rules are context insensitive, except the two shaded ones:

- Applying call/cc to a value leads to this value being applied to a representation of the current context. This context is then said to be "captured" and its representation is said to be "reified."
- Applying a captured context to a value yields a contractum consisting of this value *and the captured context* (instead of the current context, which is discarded).

8.3   Reduction Strategy

We seek the left-most inner-most potential redex in a closure.

Decomposition: The decomposition function is defined as in Section 6.3 but for the following two clauses:

```
fun decompose_closure ...
   = ...
| decompose_closure (CLO_CWCC, C)
  = decompose_context (C, VAL_CWCC)
| decompose_closure (CLO_CONT C', C)
  = decompose_context (C, VAL_CONT C')
```

Recomposition: The recomposition function is defined as in Section 6.3.

Lemma 4. *A closure* c *is either a value or there exists a unique context* C *such that* decompose t *evaluates to* DEC (pr, C), *where* pr *is a potential redex.*

Proof. Straightforward.

8.4   One-Step Reduction

The one-step reduction function is as in Section 6.4, save for the contraction function being context-sensitive, as shaded just below:

```
(*  reduce : closure -> reduct  *)
fun reduce c
    = (case decompose c
         of (VAL v)
             => REDUCT (embed_value_in_closure v)
          | (DEC (pr, C))
             => (case contract (pr, C)
                    of (CONTRACTUM (c', C'))
                        => REDUCT (recompose (C', c'))
                     | (ERROR s)
                        => STUCK s))
```

8.5   Reduction-Based Normalization

The reduction-based normalization function is as in Section 8.5, save for the contraction function being context-sensitive, as shaded just below:

```
(*  iterate0 : value_or_decomposition -> result  *)
fun iterate0 (VAL v)
    = RESULT v
  | iterate0 (DEC (pr, C))
    = (case contract (pr, C)
         of (CONTRACTUM (c', C'))
             => iterate0 (decompose (recompose (C', c')))
          | (ERROR s)
             => WRONG s)

(*  normalize0 : term -> result  *)
fun normalize0 t
    = iterate0 (decompose (CLO_GND (t, initial_bindings)))
```

8.6   Summary

We have minimally extended the applicative-order reduction semantics of Section 6 with call/cc.

8.7   Exercises

As a warmup for Exercise 44, here is an interface to first-class continuations in Standard ML of New Jersey that reifies the current continuation as a function:

```
fun callcc f
    = SMLofNJ.Cont.callcc
        (fn k => f (fn v => SMLofNJ.Cont.throw k v))
```

We also assume that `succ` denotes the successor function.

- Consider the following term:

  `succ (succ (callcc (fn k => succ 10)))`

  In the course of reduction, `k` is made to denote a first-class continuation that is not used. This term is equivalent to one that does not use call/cc, namely

  `succ (succ (succ 10))`

  and evaluating it yields 13.
- Consider now the following term that captures a continuation and then applies it:

  `succ (succ (callcc (fn k => succ (k 10))))`

  In the course of reduction, `k` is made to denote a first-class continuation that is then applied. When it is applied, the current continuation is discarded and replaced by the captured continuation, as if the source term had been

  `succ (succ 10)`

  and the result of evaluation is 12.

  In the reduction semantics of this section, the source term reads as follows:

  ```
  APP (IDE "succ",
      APP (IDE "succ",
          APP (IDE "call/cc",
              LAM ("k", APP (IDE "succ",
                          APP (IDE "k", LIT 10))))))
  ```

  As for the captured continuation, it reads as follows:

  `CLO_CONT (CTX_ARG (VAL_SUCC, CTX_ARG (VAL_SUCC, CTX_MT)))`

  Applying it to `VAL INT 10` has the effect of discarding the current context, and eventually leads to `RESULT (VAL INT 12)`.

Exercise 44. Write a handful of test terms that use call/cc and specify the expected outcome of their normalization.

Exercise 45. Implement the reduction semantics above in the programming language of your choice (e.g., Haskell or Scheme), and run the tests of Exercise 44.

Exercise 46. Extend the unparser of Exercise 34 in Section 6.7 to cater for first-class continuations, and visualize the reduction sequence of a closure that uses call/cc.

9   From Reduction-Based to Reduction-Free Normalization

In this section, we transform the reduction-based normalization function of Section 8.5 into a family of reduction-free normalization functions. Presentationally, we single out the increment over Section 7 rather than giving a stand-alone derivation.

9.1 Refocusing:
From Reduction-Based to Reduction-Free Normalization

As usual, the refocus function is defined as continuing the decomposition in situ:

```
(*  refocus : closure * context -> value_or_decomposition  *)
fun refocus (c, C)
    = decompose_closure (c, C)
```

The refocused evaluation function reads as follows. Except for the context-sensitive contraction function, it is the same as in Section 7.1:

```
(*  iterate1 : value_or_decomposition -> result  *)
fun iterate1 (VAL v)
    = RESULT v
  | iterate1 (DEC (pr, C))
    = (case contract (pr, C)
         of (CONTRACTUM (c', C'))
            => iterate1 (refocus (c', C'))
          | (ERROR s)
            => WRONG s)

(*  normalize1 : term -> result  *)
fun normalize1 ...
    = ...
```

9.2 Inlining the Contraction Function

Compared to Section 7.2, there are two new clauses:

```
(*  iterate2 : value_or_decomposition -> result  *)
fun iterate2 ...
    = ...
  | iterate2 (DEC (PR_APP (VAL_CWCC, v), C))
  = iterate2(refocus(CLO_APP(embed_value_in_closure v, CLO_CONT C),
                C))
  | iterate2 (DEC (PR_APP (VAL_CONT C', v), C))
    = iterate2 (refocus (embed_value_in_closure v, C'))
  | iterate2 ...
    = ...
```

...

9.3 Lightweight Fusion:
From Small-Step to Big-Step Abstract Machine

Compared to Section 7.3, there are two new clauses in refocus3 closure and in iterate3; the definition of refocus3 context is not affected:

```
(*  refocus3_closure : closure * context -> result  *)
fun refocus3_closure ...
     = ...
   | refocus3_closure (CLO_CWCC, C)
     = refocus3_context (C, VAL_CWCC)
   | refocus3_closure (CLO_CONT C', C)
     = refocus3_context (C, VAL_CONT C')

(*  refocus3_context : context * value -> result  *)
fun refocus3_context ...
     = ...

(*  iterate3 : value_or_decomposition -> result  *)
and iterate3 ...
     = ...
   | iterate3 (DEC (PR_APP (VAL_CWCC, v), C))
     = refocus3_closure(CLO_APP(embed_value_in_closure v, CLO_CONT C),
             C)
   | iterate3 (DEC (PR_APP (VAL_CONT C', v), C))
     = refocus3_closure (embed_value_in_closure v, C')
   | iterate3 ...
     = ...
```

9.4   Compressing Corridor Transitions

Compared to Section 7.4, there are two new opportunities to compress corridor transitions:

Clause `iterate4 (DEC (PR APP (VAL CWCC, v), C))`:

```
iterate4 (DEC (PR_APP (VAL_CWCC, v), C))
= (* by unfolding the call to iterate4 *)
refocus4_closure (CLO_APP (embed_value_in_closure v, CLO_CONT C), C)
= (* by unfolding the call to refocus4_closure *)
refocus4_closure (embed_value_in_closure v, CTX_FUN (C, CLO_CONT C))
= (* eureka *)
refocus4_context (CTX_FUN (C, CLO_CONT C), v)
= (* by unfolding the call to refocus4_context *)
refocus4_closure (CLO_CONT C, CTX_ARG (v, C))
= (* by unfolding the call to refocus4_closure *)
refocus4_context (CTX_ARG (v, C), VAL_CONT C)
= (* by unfolding the call to refocus4_context *)
iterate4 (DEC (PR_APP (v, VAL_CONT C), C))
```

Clause `iterate4 (DEC (PR APP (VAL CONT C', v), C))`:

```
iterate4 (DEC (PR_APP (VAL_CONT C', v), C))
= (* by unfolding the call to iterate4 *)
refocus4_closure (embed_value_in_closure v, C')
= (* eureka *)
refocus4_context (C', v)
```

The corollaries to the compressions above are the same as in Section 7.4:

Dead clauses: The clauses for non-ground closures are dead, and so is the clause "`iterate4 (VAL v)`." They can therefore be implemented as raising a "`DEAD CLAUSE`" exception.

Invariants: All transitions to `refocus closure` are now over ground closures. All live transitions to `iterate4` are now over `DEC (PR APP (v0, v1), C)`, for some `v0`, `v1`, and `C`.

9.5   Renaming Transition Functions and Flattening Configurations

The renamed and flattened abstract machine is the familiar CEK machine with call/cc:

```
datatype    value = ...
                  | VAL_CWCC
                  | VAL_CONT of context
and         context = ...
withtype bindings = ...

val initial_bindings = Env.extend ("call/cc", VAL_CWCC,
                          Env.extend ("succ", VAL_SUCC,
                            Env.empty))

(*  eval5 : term * bindings * context -> result  *)
fun eval5 ...
     = ...

(*  continue5 : context * value -> result  *)
and continue5 ...
     = ...

(*  apply5 : value * value * context -> result  *)
and apply5 ...
     = ...
   | apply5 (VAL_CWCC, v, C)
     = apply5 (v, VAL_CONT C, C)
   | apply5 (VAL_CONT C', v, C)
     = continue5 (C', v)
   | apply5 ...
     = ...

(*  normalize5 : term -> result  *)
fun normalize5 ...
     = eval5 ...
```

9.6   Refunctionalization

The higher-order counterpart of the abstract machine of Section 9.5 reads as follows:

```
datatype    value = ...
                  | VAL_CWCC
                  | VAL_CONT of value -> result
withtype bindings = ...

val initial_bindings = Env.extend ("call/cc", VAL_CWCC,
                           Env.extend ("succ", VAL_SUCC,
                               Env.empty))

(* eval6 : term * bindings * (value -> result) -> result  *)
fun eval6 ...
      = ...

(* apply6 : value * value * (value -> result) -> result  *)
and apply6 ...
      = ...
  | apply6 (VAL_CWCC, v, k)
      = apply6 (v, VAL_CONT k, k)
  | apply6 (VAL_CONT k', v, k)
      = k' v
  | apply6 ...
      = ...

(* normalize6 : term -> result  *)
fun normalize6 ...
      = ...
```

The resulting refunctionalized program is a familiar eval/apply evaluation function in CPS [46, Fig. 1, p. 295].

9.7   Back to Direct Style

The direct-style counterpart of the evaluation function of Section 9.6 reads as follows [32]:

```
(* eval7 : term * bindings -> value  *)
fun eval7 ...
      = ...

(* apply7 : value * value -> value  *)
and apply7 ...
      = ...
  | apply7 (VAL_CWCC, v)
      = SMLofNJ.Cont.callcc (fn k => apply7 (v, VAL_CONT k))
  | apply7 (VAL_CONT k', v)
      = SMLofNJ.Cont.throw k' v
  | apply7 ...
      = ...

(* normalize7 : term -> result  *)
fun normalize7 ...
      = ...
```

The resulting program is a traditional eval/apply evaluation function in direct style that uses call/cc to implement call/cc, meta-circularly.

9.8   Closure Unconversion

As in Section 7.8, the direct-style definition of Section 9.7 is in closure-converted form since its applicable values are introduced with VAL SUCC and VAL FUNC, and eliminated in the clauses of apply7. Its higher-order, closure-unconverted equivalent reads as follows.

Expressible and denotable values. The VAL FUN value constructor is higher-order, and caters both for the predefined successor function, for the predefined call/cc function, for the value of source lambda-abstractions, and for captured continuations:

```
datatype value = VAL_INT of int
               | VAL_FUN of value -> value

type bindings = value Env.env
```

Initial bindings. The successor function is now defined in the initial environment:

```
val val_succ = VAL_FUN ...

val val_cwcc = VAL_FUN (fn (VAL_FUN f)
                            => SMLofNJ.Cont.callcc (fn k =>
                                 f (VAL_FUN (fn v =>
                                      SMLofNJ.Cont.throw k v)))
                         | _
                            => raise (WRONG "non-applicable value"))

val initial_bindings = Env.extend ("call/cc", val_cwcc,
                         Env.extend ("succ", val_succ,
                           Env.empty))
```

The eval/apply component. The evaluation function is the same as in Section 7.8:

```
(*  eval8 : term * bindings -> value  *)
fun eval8 ...
    = ...

(*  apply8 : value * value -> value  *)
and apply8 ...
    = ...
```

The top-level definition. The top-level definition is the same as in Section 7.8:

```
(*  normalize8 : term -> result  *)
fun normalize8 ...
    = ...
```

The resulting program is a traditional eval/apply function in direct style that uses a top-level exception for run-time errors. It is also compositional.

9.9   Summary

We have outlined the derivation from the reduction-based normalization function of Section 8 into a small-step abstract machine and into a family of corresponding reduction-free normalization functions. Most of the members of this family are ML implementations of independently known semantic artifacts and coincide with what one usually writes by hand.

9.10   Exercises

Exercise 47. Reproduce the construction above in the programming language of your choice, starting from your solution to Exercise 45 in Section 8.7. At each step of the derivation, run the tests of Exercise 44 in Section 8.7.

Exercise 48. Up to and including the normalization function of Section 9.5, it is simple to visualize the successive closures in the reduction sequence, namely by instrumenting `iterate1`, `iterate2`, `iterate3`, `iterate4`, and `apply5`. Do you agree? What about from Section 9.6 and onwards?

Exercise 49. Would it make sense, in the definition of `normalize6`, to take `fn v => v` as the initial continuation? If so, what would be the definition of `normalize7` and what would be its type?

Exercise 50. In Section 9.7, we have transformed the evaluator of Section 9.6 into direct style, and then in Section 9.8, we have closure-unconverted it. However, the the evaluator of Section 9.6 is also in closure-converted form:

1. closure-unconvert the evaluator of Section 9.6; the result should be a compositional evaluator in CPS with the following data type of expressible values:

```
datatype value = VAL_INT of int
               | VAL_FUN of value * (value -> result) -> result
     and result = RESULT of value
               | WRONG of string
```

2. transform this compositional evaluator into direct style, and verify that the result coincides with the evaluator of Section 9.8.

10   A Reduction Semantics for Flattening Binary Trees Outside In

The goal of this section is to define a one-step flattening function over binary trees, using a left-most outermost strategy, and to construct the corresponding reduction-based flattening function.

   To define a reduction semantics for binary trees, we specify their abstract syntax (Section 10.1), a notion of contraction (Section 10.2), and the left-most outermost reduction strategy (Section 10.3). We then define a one-step reduction function that decomposes a tree which is not in normal form into a redex and a reduction context, contracts the redex, and recomposes the context with the contractum (Section 10.4). We can finally define a reduction-based normalization function that repeatedly applies the one-step reduction function until a value, i.e., a normal form, is reached (Section 10.5).

10.1   Abstract Syntax: Terms and Values

Terms: A tree is either a stub, a leaf holding an integer, or a node holding two subtrees:

```
datatype tree = STUB
              | LEAF of int
              | NODE of tree * tree
```

The flattening rules are as follows: the unit element is neutral on the left and on the right of the node constructor, and the product is associative.

$$\text{NODE (STUB, t)} \longleftrightarrow \text{t}$$
$$\text{NODE (t, STUB)} \longleftrightarrow \text{t}$$
$$\text{NODE (NODE (t1, t2), t3)} \longleftrightarrow \text{NODE (t1, NODE (t2, t3))}$$

Normal forms: Arbitrarily, we pick flat, list-like trees as normal forms. We specify them with the following specialized data type:

```
datatype tree_nf = STUB_nf
                 | NODE_nf of int * tree_nf
```

Values: Rather than defining values as normal forms, as in the previous sections, we choose to represent them as a pair: a term of type `tree` and its isomorphic representation of type `tree nf`:

```
type value = tree * tree_nf
```

This representation is known as "glueing" since Yves Lafont's PhD thesis [52, Appendix A], and is also classically used in the area of partial evaluation [6].

10.2   Notion of Contraction

We introduce a notion of reduction by orienting the conversion rules into contraction rules, and by specializing the second one as mapping a leaf into a flat binary tree:

$$\text{NODE (STUB, t)} \longrightarrow \text{t}$$
$$\text{NODE (LEAF n, STUB)} \longleftarrow \text{LEAF n}$$
$$\text{PROD (PROD (t11, t12), t2)} \longrightarrow \text{PROD (t11, PROD (t12, t2))}$$

We represent redexes as a data type and implement their contraction with the corresponding reduction rules:

```
datatype potential_redex = PR_LEFT_STUB of tree
                         | PR_LEAF of int
                         | PR_ASSOC of tree * tree * tree

datatype contractum_or_error = CONTRACTUM of tree
                             | ERROR of string

(*  contract : potential_redex -> contractum_or_error  *)
fun contract (PR_LEFT_STUB t)
    = CONTRACTUM t
  | contract (PR_LEAF n)
    = CONTRACTUM (NODE (LEAF n, STUB))
  | contract (PR_ASSOC (t11, t12, t2))
    = CONTRACTUM (NODE (t11, NODE (t12, t2)))
```

10.3   Reduction Strategy

We seek the left-most outer-most redex in a tree.

Reduction contexts: The grammar of reduction contexts reads as follows:

```
datatype context = CTX_MT
                 | CTX_RIGHT of int * context
```

Decomposition: A tree is in normal form (i.e., it does not contain any potential redex) or it can be decomposed into a potential redex and a reduction context:

```
datatype value_or_decomposition = VAL of value
                                | DEC of potential_redex * context
```

The decomposition function recursively searches for the left-most outer-most redex in a term. As always, we define it as a big-step abstract machine. This abstract machine has three auxiliary functions, decompose tree, decompose node, and decompose context between three states – a term and a context, two sub-terms and a context, and a context and a value.

  - decompose tree dispatches over the given tree;
  - decompose node dispatches over the left sub-tree of a given tree;
  - decompose context dispatches on the accumulated context to determine whether the given term is a value, a potential redex has been found, or the search must continue.

```
(*  decompose_tree : tree * context -> value_or_decomposition  *)
fun decompose_tree (STUB, C)
    = decompose_context (C, (STUB, STUB_nf))
  | decompose_tree (LEAF n, C)
    = DEC (PR_LEAF n, C)
  | decompose_tree (NODE (t1, t2), C)
    = decompose_node (t1, t2, C)
```

```
(*  decompose_node: tree * tree* context -> value_or_decomposition  *)
and decompose_node (STUB, t2, C)
    = DEC (PR_LEFT_STUB t2, C)
  | decompose_node (LEAF n, t2, C)
    = decompose_tree (t2, CTX_RIGHT (n, C))
  | decompose_node (NODE (t11, t12), t2, C)
    = DEC (PR_ASSOC (t11, t12, t2), C)

(*  decompose_context : context * value -> value_or_decomposition  *)
and decompose_context (CTX_MT, (t', t_nf))
    = VAL (t', t_nf)
  | decompose_context (CTX_RIGHT (n, C), (t', t_nf))
    = decompose_context (C, (NODE (LEAF n, t'), NODE_nf (n, t_nf)))

(*  decompose : tree -> value_or_decomposition  *)
fun decompose t
    = decompose_tree (t, CTX_MT)
```

Recomposition: The recomposition function peels off context layers and constructs the resulting tree, iteratively:

```
(*  recompose : context * tree -> tree  *)
fun recompose (CTX_MT, t)
    = t
  | recompose (CTX_RIGHT (n1, C), t2)
    = recompose (C, NODE (LEAF n1, t2))
```

Lemma 5. *A tree* t *is either in normal form or there exists a unique context* C *such that* decompose t *evaluates to* DEC (pr, C), *where* pr *is a potential redex.*

Proof. Straightforward (see Exercise 56 in Section 10.7).

10.4   One-Step Reduction

We are now in position to define a one-step reduction function as a function that (1) maps a tree that is not in normal form into a potential redex and a reduction context, (2) contracts the potential redex if it is an actual one, and (3) recomposes the reduction context with the contractum. The following data type accounts for whether the contraction is successful or the non-value term is stuck:

```
datatype reduct = REDUCT of tree
                | STUCK of string

(*  reduce : tree -> reduct  *)
fun reduce t
    = (case decompose t
         of (VAL (t', t_nf))
            => REDUCT t'
```

```
      | (DEC (pr, C))
        => (case contract pr
              of (CONTRACTUM t')
                   => REDUCT (recompose (C, t'))
               | (ERROR s)
                   => STUCK s))
```

10.5   Reduction-Based Normalization

The following reduction-based normalization function iterates the one-step reduction function until it yields a normal form:

```
datatype result = RESULT of tree_nf
                | WRONG of string

(*  iterate0 : value_or_decomposition -> result  *)
fun iterate0 (VAL (t', t_nf))
    = RESULT t_nf
  | iterate0 (DEC (pr, C))
    = (case contract pr
         of (CONTRACTUM t')
              => iterate0 (decompose (recompose (C, t')))
          | (ERROR s)
              => WRONG s)

(*  normalize0 : tree -> result  *)
fun normalize0 t
    = iterate0 (decompose t)
```

10.6   Summary

We have implemented a reduction semantics for flattening binary trees, in complete detail. Using this reduction semantics, we have presented a reduction-based normalization function.

10.7   Exercises

Exercise 51. Define a function embed potential redex in tree that maps a potential redex into a tree.

Exercise 52. Show that, for any tree t, if evaluating decompose t yields DEC (pr, C), then evaluating recompose (C, embed potential redex in tree pr) yields t. (Hint: Reason by structural induction over t, using inversion at each step.)

Exercise 53. Write a handful of test trees and specify the expected outcome of their normalization.

Exercise 54. Implement the reduction semantics above in the programming language of your choice, and run the tests of Exercise 53.

Exercise 55. Write an unparser from trees to the concrete syntax of your choice, and instrument the normalization function of Section 10.5 so that (one way or another) it displays the successive trees in the reduction sequence.

Exercise 56. In the proof of Lemma 5, do as in the proof of Lemma 1 and write the refunctionalized counterpart of `decompose` et al.

Exercise 57. Pick another notion of normal form (e.g., flat, list-like trees on the left instead of on the right) and define the corresponding reduction-based normalization function, *mutatis mutandis*.

Exercise 58. Revisit either of the previous pairs of sections using glueing.

11 From Reduction-Based to Reduction-Free Normalization

In this section, we transform the reduction-based normalization function of Section 10.5 into a family of reduction-free normalization functions, i.e., one where no intermediate tree is ever constructed. We first refocus the reduction-based normalization function to deforest the intermediate trees, and we obtain a small-step abstract machine implementing the iteration of the refocus function (Section 11.1). After inlining the contraction function (Section 11.2), we transform this small-step abstract machine into a big-step one (Section 11.3). This abstract machine exhibits a number of corridor transitions, and we compress them (Section 11.4). We then flatten its configurations and rename its transition functions into something more intuitive (Section 11.5). The resulting abstract machine is in defunctionalized form, and we refunctionalize it (Section 11.6). The result is in continuation-passing style and we re-express it in direct style (Section 11.7). The resulting direct-style function is a traditional flatten function that incrementally flattens its input from the top down.

Modus operandi: In each of the following subsections, and as always, we derive successive versions of the normalization function, indexing its components with the number of the subsection. In practice, the reader should run the tests of Exercise 53 in Section 10.7 at each step of the derivation, for sanity value.

11.1 Refocusing:
From Reduction-Based to Reduction-Free Normalization

The normalization function of Section 10.5 is reduction-based because it constructs every intermediate term in the reduction sequence. In its definition, `decompose` is always applied to the result of `recompose` after the first decomposition. In fact, a vacuous initial call to `recompose` ensures that in all cases, `decompose` is applied to the result of `recompose`:

```
(*  normalize0' : tree -> result  *)
fun normalize0' t
   = iterate0 (decompose (recompose (CTX_MT, t)))
```

Refocusing, extensionally: The composition of decompose and recompose can be deforested into a 'refocus' function to avoid constructing the intermediate terms in the reduction sequence. Such a deforestation makes the normalization function reduction-free.

Refocusing, intensionally: As usual, the refocus function can be expressed very simply in terms of the decomposition functions of Section 10.3:

```
(*  refocus : term * context -> value_or_decomposition  *)
fun refocus (t, C)
    = decompose_tree (t, C)
```

The refocused evaluation function therefore reads as follows:

```
(*  iterate1 : value_or_decomposition -> result  *)
fun iterate1 (VAL (t', t_nf))
    = RESULT t_nf
  | iterate1 (DEC (pr, C))
    = (case contract pr
         of (CONTRACTUM t')
            => iterate1 (refocus (t', C))
          | (ERROR s)
            => WRONG s)

(*  normalize1 : tree -> result  *)
fun normalize1 t
    = iterate1 (refocus (t, CTX_MT))
```

This refocused normalization function is reduction-free because it is no longer based on a (one-step) reduction function. Instead, the refocus function directly maps a contractum and a reduction context to the next redex and reduction context, if there are any in the reduction sequence.

11.2   Inlining the Contraction Function

We first inline the call to contract in the definition of iterate1, and name the resulting function iterate2. Reasoning by inversion, there are three potential redexes and therefore the DEC clause in the definition of iterate1 is replaced by three DEC clauses in the definition of iterate2:

```
(*  iterate2 : value_or_decomposition -> result  *)
fun iterate2 (VAL (t', t_nf))
    = RESULT t_nf
  | iterate2 (DEC (PR_LEFT_STUB t, C))
    = iterate2 (refocus (t, C))
  | iterate2 (DEC (PR_LEAF n, C))
    = iterate2 (refocus (NODE (LEAF n, STUB), C))
  | iterate2 (DEC (PR_ASSOC (t11, t12, t2), C))
    = iterate2 (refocus (NODE (t11, NODE (t12, t2)), C))
```

```
(*  normalize2 : tree -> result  *)
fun normalize2 t
    = iterate2 (refocus (t, CTX_MT))
```

We are now ready to fuse the composition of iterate2 with refocus (shaded just above).

11.3   Lightweight Fusion:
From Small-Step to Big-Step Abstract Machine

The refocused normalization function is a small-step abstract machine in the sense that refocus (i.e., decompose tree, decompose node, and decompose context) acts as a transition function and iterate1 as a driver loop that keeps activating refocus until a value is obtained. We fuse iterate2 and refocus (i.e., decompose tree, decompose node, and decompose context) so that the resulting function iterate3 is *directly* applied to the result of decompose tree, decompose node, and decompose context. The result is a big-step abstract machine consisting of four (mutually tail-recursive) state-transition functions:

- refocus3 tree is the composition of iterate2 and decompose tree and a clone of decompose tree that directly calls iterate3 over a leaf instead of returning it to iterate2 as decompose tree did;
- refocus3 node is the composition of iterate2 and decompose node and a clone of decompose node that directly calls iterate3 over a decomposition instead of returning it to iterate2 as decompose node did;
- refocus3 context is the composition of iterate2 and decompose context that directly calls iterate3 over a value or a decomposition instead of returning it to iterate2 as decompose context did;
- iterate3 is a clone of iterate2 that calls the fused function refocus3 tree.

```
(*  refocus3_tree : tree * context -> result  *)
fun refocus3_tree (STUB, C)
    = refocus3_context (C, (STUB, STUB_nf))
  | refocus3_tree (LEAF n, C)
    = iterate3 (DEC (PR_LEAF n, C))
  | refocus3_tree (NODE (t1, t2), C)
    = refocus3_node (t1, t2, C)

(*  refocus3_node : tree * tree * context -> result  *)
and refocus3_node (STUB, t2, C)
    = iterate3 (DEC (PR_LEFT_STUB t2, C))
  | refocus3_node (LEAF n, t2, C)
    = refocus3_tree (t2, CTX_RIGHT (n, C))
  | refocus3_node (NODE (t11, t12), t2, C)
    = iterate3 (DEC (PR_ASSOC (t11, t12, t2), C))

(*  refocus3_context : context * value -> result  *)
and refocus3_context (CTX_MT, (t', t_nf))
    = iterate3 (VAL (t', t_nf))
  | refocus3_context (CTX_RIGHT (n, C), (t', t_nf))
    = refocus3_context (C, (NODE (LEAF n, t'), NODE_nf (n, t_nf)))
```

```
(*  iterate3 : value_or_decomposition -> result  *)
and iterate3 (VAL (t', t_nf))
      = RESULT t_nf
  | iterate3 (DEC (PR_LEFT_STUB t, C))
      = refocus3_tree (t, C)
  | iterate3 (DEC (PR_LEAF n, C))
      = refocus3_tree (NODE (LEAF n, STUB), C)
  | iterate3 (DEC (PR_ASSOC (t11, t12, t2), C))
      = refocus3_tree (NODE (t11, NODE (t12, t2)), C)

(*  normalize3 : tree -> result  *)
fun normalize3 t
      = refocus3_tree (t, CTX_MT)
```

This abstract machine is staged since `iterate3` implements the contraction rules of the reduction semantics separately from its congruence rules, which are implemented by `refocus3 tree`, `refocus3 node` and `refocus3 context`.

11.4 Compressing Corridor Transitions

In the abstract machine above, many of the transitions are 'corridor' ones in that they yield configurations for which there is a unique further transition, and so on. Let us compress these transitions. To this end, we cut-and-paste the transition functions above, renaming their indices from 3 to 4, and consider each of their clauses in turn:

Clause `refocus4 tree (LEAF n, C)`:

```
refocus4_tree (LEAF n, C)
= (* by unfolding the call to refocus4_tree *)
iterate4 (DEC (PR_LEAF n, C))
= (* by unfolding the call to iterate4 *)
refocus4_tree (NODE (LEAF n, STUB), C)
= (* by unfolding the call to refocus4_tree *)
refocus4_node (LEAF n, STUB, C)
= (* by unfolding the call to refocus4_node *)
refocus4_tree (STUB, CTX_RIGHT (n, C))
= (* by unfolding the call to refocus4_tree *)
refocus4_context (CTX_RIGHT (n, C), (STUB, STUB_nf))
= (* by unfolding the call to refocus4_context *)
refocus4_context (C, (NODE (LEAF n, STUB), NODE_nf (n, STUB_nf)))
```

Clause `refocus4 node (STUB, t2, C)`:

```
refocus4_node (STUB, t2, C)
= (* by unfolding the call to refocus4_node *)
iterate4 (DEC (PR_LEFT_STUB t2, C))
= (* by unfolding the call to iterate4 *)
refocus4_tree (t2, C)
```

Clause `refocus4 node (NODE (t11, t12), t2, C)`:

```
refocus4_node (NODE (t11, t12), t2, C)
= (* by unfolding the call to refocus4_node *)
iterate4 (DEC (PR_ASSOC (t11, t12, t2), C))
= (* by unfolding the call to iterate4 *)
refocus4_tree (NODE (t11, NODE (t12, t2)), C)
= (* by unfolding the call to refocus4_tree *)
refocus4_node (t11, NODE (t12, t2), C)
```

Clause `refocus4 context (CTX MT, (t', t nf))`:

```
refocus4_context (CTX_MT, (t', t_nf))
= (* by unfolding the call to refocus4_context *)
iterate4 (VAL (t', t_nf))
= (* by unfolding the call to iterate4 *)
RESULT t_nf
```

There are two corollaries to the compressions above:

Dead clauses: All of the calls to `iterate4` have been unfolded, and therefore the definition of `iterate4` is dead.

Dead component: The term component of the values is now dead. We eliminate it in Section 11.5.

11.5   Renaming Transition Functions and Flattening Configurations

The resulting simplified machine is an 'eval/apply/continue' abstract machine. We therefore rename `refocus4 tree` to `flatten5`, `refocus4 node` to `flatten5 node`, and `refocus4 context` to `continue5`. The result reads as follows:

```
(*  flatten5 : tree * context -> result  *)
fun flatten5 (STUB, C)
    = continue5 (C, STUB_nf)
  | flatten5 (LEAF n, C)
    = continue5 (C, NODE_nf (n, STUB_nf))
  | flatten5 (NODE (t1, t2), C)
    = flatten5_node (t1, t2, C)

(*  flatten5_node : tree * tree * context -> result  *)
and flatten5_node (STUB, t2, C)
    = flatten5 (t2, C)
  | flatten5_node (LEAF n, t2, C)
    = flatten5 (t2, CTX_RIGHT (n, C))
  | flatten5_node (NODE (t11, t12), t2, C)
    = flatten5_node (t11, NODE (t12, t2), C)

(*  continue5 : context * tree_nf -> result  *)
and continue5 (CTX_MT, t_nf)
    = RESULT t_nf
  | continue5 (CTX_RIGHT (n, C), t_nf)
    = continue5 (C, NODE_nf (n, t_nf))
```

```
(* normalize5 : tree -> result  *)
fun normalize5 t
    = flatten5 (t, CTX_MT)
```

11.6 Refunctionalization

The definitions of Section 11.5 are in defunctionalized form. The reduction contexts, together with continue5, are the first-order counterpart of a function. The higher-order counterpart of this abstract machine reads as follows:

```
(* flatten6 : tree * (tree_nf -> 'a) -> 'a  *)
fun flatten6 (STUB, k)
    = k STUB_nf
  | flatten6 (LEAF n, k)
    = k (NODE_nf (n, STUB_nf))
  | flatten6 (NODE (t1, t2), k)
    = flatten6_node (t1, t2, k)

(* flatten6_node : tree * tree * (tree_nf -> 'a) -> 'a  *)
and flatten6_node (STUB, t2, k)
    = flatten6 (t2, k)
  | flatten6_node (LEAF n, t2, k)
    = flatten6 (t2, fn t2_nf => k (NODE_nf (n, t2_nf)))
  | flatten6_node (NODE (t11, t12), t2, k)
    = flatten6_node (t11, NODE (t12, t2), k)

(* normalize6 : tree -> result  *)
fun normalize6 t
    = flatten6 (t, fn t_nf => RESULT t_nf)
```

The resulting refunctionalized program is a familiar eval/apply evaluation function in CPS.

11.7 Back to Direct Style

The refunctionalized definition of Section 11.6 is in continuation-passing style since it has a functional accumulator and all of its calls are tail calls. Its direct-style counterpart reads as follows:

```
(* flatten7 : tree -> tree_nf  *)
fun flatten7 STUB
    = STUB_nf
  | flatten7 (LEAF n)
    = NODE_nf (n, STUB_nf)
  | flatten7 (NODE (t1, t2))
    = flatten7_node (t1, t2)

(* flatten7_node : tree * tree -> tree_nf  *)
and flatten7_node (STUB, t2)
    = flatten7 t2
```

```
  | flatten7_node (LEAF n, t2)
    = NODE_nf (n, flatten7 t2)
  | flatten7_node (NODE (t11, t12), t2)
    = flatten7_node (t11, NODE (t12, t2))
(*  normalize7 : tree -> result  *)
fun normalize7 t
    = RESULT (flatten7 t)
```

The resulting definition is that of an traditional flatten function that iteratively flattens the current left subtree before recursively descending on the current right subtree.

11.8 Closure Unconversion

This section is intentionally left blank, since the tree leaves are integers.

11.9 Summary

We have refocused the reduction-based normalization function of Section 10 into a small-step abstract machine, and we have exhibited a family of corresponding reduction-free normalization functions. Most of the members of this family correspond to something one usually writes by hand.

11.10 Exercises

Exercise 59. Reproduce the construction above in the programming language of your choice, starting from your solution to Exercise 54 in Section 10.7. At each step of the derivation, run the tests of Exercise 53 in Section 10.7.

Exercise 60. Would it make sense, in the definition of `normalize6`, to take `fn v => v` as the initial continuation? If so, what would be the definition of `normalize7` and what would be its type? What about `normalize7'`?

12 A Reduction Semantics for Flattening Binary Trees Inside Out

The goal of this section is to define a one-step flattening function over binary trees, using a right-most innermost strategy, and to construct the corresponding reduction-based flattening function.

To define a reduction semantics for binary trees, we specify their abstract syntax (Section 12.1, which is identical to Section 10.1), a notion of contraction (Section 12.2), and the right-most innermost reduction strategy (Section 12.3). We then define a one-step reduction function that decomposes a tree which is not in normal form into a redex and a reduction context, contracts the redex, and recomposes the context with the contractum (Section 12.4). We can finally define a reduction-based normalization function that repeatedly applies the one-step reduction function until a value, i.e., a normal form, is reached (Section 12.5).

12.1 Abstract Syntax: Terms and Values

This section is is identical to Section 10.1.

12.2 Notion of Contraction

We orient the conversion rules into contraction rules as in Section 10.2. To reflect the inside-out reduction strategy, we represent redexes as another data type:

```
datatype potential_redex = PR_LEFT_STUB of value
                         | PR_LEAF of int
                         | PR_ASSOC of tree * tree * value

datatype contractum_or_error = CONTRACTUM of tree
                             | ERROR of string

(*  contract : potential_redex -> contractum_or_error  *)
fun contract (PR_LEFT_STUB (t, t_nf))
    = CONTRACTUM t
  | contract (PR_LEAF n)
    = CONTRACTUM (NODE (LEAF n, STUB))
  | contract (PR_ASSOC (t11, t12, (t2, t2_nf)))
    = CONTRACTUM (NODE (t11, NODE (t12, t2)))
```

12.3 Reduction Strategy

We seek the right-most inner-most redex in a tree.

Reduction contexts: The grammar of reduction contexts reads as follows:

```
datatype context = CTX_MT
                 | CTX_RIGHT of tree * context
```

Decomposition: A tree is in normal form (i.e., it does not contain any potential redex) or it can be decomposed into a potential redex and a reduction context:

```
datatype value_or_decomposition = VAL of value
                                | DEC of potential_redex * context
```

The decomposition function recursively searches for the right-most inner-most redex in a term. As always, we define it as a big-step abstract machine. This abstract machine has three auxiliary functions, decompose tree, decompose node, and decompose context between three states – a term and a context, two sub-terms and a context, and a context and a value.

- decompose `tree` dispatches over the given tree;
- decompose `node` dispatches over the left sub-tree of a given tree;
- decompose `context` dispatches on the accumulated context to determine whether the given term is a value, a potential redex has been found, or the search must continue.

```
(*  decompose_tree : tree * context -> value_or_decomposition  *)
fun decompose_tree (STUB, C)
    = decompose_context (C, (STUB, STUB_nf))
  | decompose_tree (LEAF n, C)
    = DEC (PR_LEAF n, C)
  | decompose_tree (NODE (t1, t2), C)
    = decompose_tree (t2, CTX_RIGHT (t1, C))

(* decompose_node: tree * value * context -> value_or_decomposition *)
and decompose_node (STUB, v2, C)
    = DEC (PR_LEFT_STUB v2, C)
  | decompose_node (LEAF n, (t2, t2_nf), C)
    = decompose_context (C, (NODE (LEAF n, t2), NODE_nf (n, t2_nf)))
  | decompose_node (NODE (t11, t12), v2, C)
    = DEC (PR_ASSOC (t11, t12, v2), C)

(*  decompose_context : context * value -> value_or_decomposition *  )
and decompose_context (CTX_MT, (t', t_nf))
    = VAL (t', t_nf)
  | decompose_context (CTX_RIGHT (t1, C), (t2', t2_nf))
    = decompose_node (t1, (t2', t2_nf), C)

(*  decompose : tree -> value_or_decomposition  *)
fun decompose t
    = decompose_tree (t, CTX_MT)
```

Recomposition: The recomposition function peels off context layers and constructs the resulting tree, iteratively:

```
fun recompose (CTX_MT, t)
    = t
  | recompose (CTX_RIGHT (t1, C), t2)
    = recompose (C, NODE (t1, t2))
```

Lemma 6. *A tree* t *is either in normal form or there exists a unique context* C *such that* decompose t *evaluates to* DEC (pr, C), *where* pr *is a potential redex.*

Proof. Straightforward (see Exercise 66 in Section 12.7).

12.4   One-Step Reduction

We are now in position to define a one-step reduction function as a function that (1) maps a tree that is not in normal form into a potential redex and a reduction context, (2) contracts the potential redex if it is an actual one, and (3) recomposes the reduction context with the contractum. The following data type accounts for whether the contraction is successful or the non-value term is stuck:

```
datatype reduct = REDUCT of tree
               | STUCK of string

(*  reduce : tree -> reduct  *)
fun reduce t
    = (case decompose t
         of (VAL (t', t_nf))
            => REDUCT t'
          | (DEC (pr, C))
            => (case contract pr
                  of (CONTRACTUM t')
                     => REDUCT (recompose (C, t'))
                   | (ERROR s)
                     => STUCK s))
```

12.5   Reduction-Based Normalization

The following reduction-based normalization function iterates the one-step reduction function until it yields a normal form:

```
datatype result = RESULT of tree_nf
               | WRONG of string

(*  iterate0 : value_or_decomposition -> result  *)
fun iterate0 (VAL (t', t_nf))
    = RESULT t_nf
  | iterate0 (DEC (pr, C))
    = (case contract pr
         of (CONTRACTUM t')
            => iterate0 (decompose (recompose (C, t')))
          | (ERROR s)
            => WRONG s)

(*  normalize0 : tree -> result  *)
fun normalize0 t
    = iterate0 (decompose t)
```

12.6   Summary

We have implemented a reduction semantics for flattening binary trees, in complete detail. Using this reduction semantics, we have presented a reduction-based normalization function.

12.7   Exercises

Exercise 61. Define a function embed potential redex in tree that maps a potential redex into a tree. (This exercise is the same as Exercise 51.)

Exercise 62. Show that, for any tree t, if evaluating `decompose` t yields `DEC` (`pr`, `C`), then evaluating `recompose` (`C`, `embed potential redex in tree pr`) yields t. (Hint: Reason by structural induction over t, using inversion at each step.)

Exercise 63. Write a handful of test trees and specify the expected outcome of their normalization. (This exercise is the same as Exercise 53.)

Exercise 64. Implement the reduction semantics above in the programming language of your choice, and run the tests of Exercise 63.

Exercise 65. Write an unparser from trees to the concrete syntax of your choice, as in Exercise 55, and instrument the normalization function of Section 12.5 so that (one way or another) it displays the successive trees in the reduction sequence.

Exercise 66. In the proof of Lemma 6, do as in the proof of Lemma 1 and write the refunctionalized counterpart of `decompose` et al.

Exercise 67. Pick another notion of normal form (e.g., flat, list-like trees on the left instead of on the right) and define the corresponding reduction-based normalization function, *mutatis mutandis*.

13   From Reduction-Based to Reduction-Free Normalization

In this section, we transform the reduction-based normalization function of Section 12.5 into a family of reduction-free normalization functions, i.e., one where no intermediate tree is ever constructed. We first refocus the reduction-based normalization function to deforest the intermediate trees, and we obtain a small-step abstract machine implementing the iteration of the refocus function (Section 13.1). After inlining the contraction function (Section 13.2), we transform this small-step abstract machine into a big-step one (Section 13.3). This abstract machine exhibits a number of corridor transitions, and we compress them (Section 13.4). We then flatten its configurations and rename its transition functions into something more intuitive (Section 13.5). The resulting abstract machine is in defunctionalized form, and we refunctionalize it (Section 13.6). The result is in continuation-passing style and we re-express it in direct style (Section 13.7). The resulting direct-style function is a traditional flatten function with an accumulator; in particular, it is compositional and reduction-free.

Modus operandi: In each of the following subsections, and as always, we derive successive versions of the normalization function, indexing its components with the number of the subsection. In practice, the reader should run the tests of Exercise 63 in Section 12.7 at each step of the derivation, for sanity value.

13.1 Refocusing:
From Reduction-Based to Reduction-Free Normalization

The normalization function of Section 12.5 is reduction-based because it constructs every intermediate term in the reduction sequence. In its definition, decompose is always applied to the result of recompose after the first decomposition. In fact, a vacuous initial call to recompose ensures that in all cases, decompose is applied to the result of recompose:

```
(*  normalize0' : tree -> result  *)
fun normalize0' t
    = iterate0 (decompose (recompose (CTX_MT, t)))
```

Refocusing, extensionally: The composition of decompose and recompose can be deforested into a 'refocus' function to avoid constructing the intermediate terms in the reduction sequence. Such a deforestation makes the normalization function reduction-free.

Refocusing, intensionally: As usual, the refocus function can be expressed very simply in terms of the decomposition functions of Section 12.3:

```
(*  refocus : term * context -> value_or_decomposition  *)
fun refocus (t, C)
    = decompose_tree (t, C)
```

The refocused evaluation function therefore reads as follows:

```
(*  iterate1 : value_or_decomposition -> result  *)
fun iterate1 (VAL (t', t_nf))
    = RESULT t_nf
  | iterate1 (DEC (pr, C))
    = (case contract pr
         of (CONTRACTUM t')
            => iterate1 (refocus (t', C))
          | (ERROR s)
            => WRONG s)

(*  normalize1 : tree -> result  *)
fun normalize1 t
    = iterate1 (refocus (t, CTX_MT))
```

This refocused normalization function is reduction-free because it is no longer based on a (one-step) reduction function. Instead, the refocus function directly maps a contractum and a reduction context to the next redex and reduction context, if there are any in the reduction sequence.

13.2 Inlining the Contraction Function

We first inline the call to contract in the definition of iterate1, and name the resulting function iterate2. Reasoning by inversion, there are three potential redexes and therefore the DEC clause in the definition of iterate1 is replaced by three DEC clauses in the definition of iterate2:

```
(*  iterate2 : value_or_decomposition -> result  *)
fun iterate2 (VAL (t', t_nf))
    = RESULT t_nf
  | iterate2 (DEC (PR_LEFT_STUB (t, t_nf), C))
    = iterate2 (refocus (t, C))
  | iterate2 (DEC (PR_LEAF n, C))
    = iterate2 (refocus (NODE (LEAF n, STUB), C))
  | iterate2 (DEC (PR_ASSOC (t11, t12, (t2, t2_nf)), C))
    = iterate2 (refocus (NODE (t11, NODE (t12, t2)), C))

(*  normalize2 : tree -> result  *)
fun normalize2 t
    = iterate2 (refocus (t, CTX_MT))
```

We are now ready to fuse the composition of `iterate2` with `refocus` (shaded just above).

13.3   Lightweight Fusion: From Small-Step to Big-Step Abstract Machine

The refocused normalization function is a small-step abstract machine in the sense that `refocus` (i.e., decompose tree, decompose node, and decompose context) acts as a transition function and `iterate1` as a driver loop that keeps activating `refocus` until a value is obtained. We fuse `iterate2` and `refocus` (i.e., decompose tree, decompose node, and decompose context) so that the resulting function `iterate3` is *directly* applied to the result of decompose tree, decompose node, and decompose context. The result is a big-step abstract machine consisting of four (mutually tail-recursive) state-transition functions:

− `refocus3 tree` is the composition of `iterate2` and decompose tree and a clone of decompose tree that directly calls `iterate3` over a leaf instead of returning it to `iterate2` as decompose tree did;
− `refocus3 context` is the composition of `iterate2` and decompose context that directly calls `iterate3` over a value or a decomposition instead of returning it to `iterate2` as decompose context did;
− `refocus3 node` is the composition of `iterate2` and decompose node and a clone of decompose node that directly calls `iterate3` over a decomposition instead of returning it to `iterate2` as decompose node did;
− `iterate3` is a clone of `iterate2` that calls the fused function `refocus3 tree`.

```
(*  refocus3_tree : tree * context -> result  *)
fun refocus3_tree (STUB, C)
    = refocus3_context (C, (STUB, STUB_nf))
  | refocus3_tree (LEAF n, C)
    = iterate3 (DEC (PR_LEAF n, C))
  | refocus3_tree (NODE (t1, t2), C)
    = refocus3_tree (t2, CTX_RIGHT (t1, C))
```

```
(*  refocus3_node : tree * value * context -> result  *)
and refocus3_node (STUB, v2, C)
      = iterate3 (DEC (PR_LEFT_STUB v2, C))
  | refocus3_node (LEAF n, (t2, t2_nf), C)
      = refocus3_context (C, (NODE (LEAF n, t2), NODE_nf (n, t2_nf)))
  | refocus3_node (NODE (t11, t12), v2, C)
      = iterate3 (DEC (PR_ASSOC (t11, t12, v2), C))

(*  refocus3_context : context * value -> result  *)
and refocus3_context (CTX_MT, (t', t_nf))
      = iterate3 (VAL (t', t_nf))
  | refocus3_context (CTX_RIGHT (t1, C), (t2', t2_nf))
      = refocus3_node (t1, (t2', t2_nf), C)

(*  iterate3 : value_or_decomposition -> result  *)
and iterate3 (VAL (t', t_nf))
      = RESULT t_nf
  | iterate3 (DEC (PR_LEFT_STUB (t, t_nf), C))
      = refocus3_tree (t, C)
  | iterate3 (DEC (PR_LEAF n, C))
      = refocus3_tree (NODE (LEAF n, STUB), C)
  | iterate3 (DEC (PR_ASSOC (t11, t12, (t2, t2_nf)), C))
      = refocus3_tree (NODE (t11, NODE (t12, t2)), C)

(*  normalize3 : tree -> result  *)
fun normalize3 t
      = refocus3_tree (t, CTX_MT)
```

This abstract machine is staged since `iterate3` implements the contraction rules of the reduction semantics separately from its congruence rules, which are implemented by `refocus3 tree`, `refocus3 context` and `refocus3 node`.

13.4   Compressing Corridor Transitions

In the abstract machine above, many of the transitions are 'corridor' ones in that they yield configurations for which there is a unique further transition, and so on. Let us compress these transitions. To this end, we cut-and-paste the transition functions above, renaming their indices from 3 to 4, and consider each of their clauses in turn , making use of the equivalence between `refocus4 tree (t, C)` and `refocus4 context (C, t nf)` when t is in normal form (and t nf directly represents this normal form):

Clause `refocus4 tree (LEAF n, C)`:

```
refocus4_tree (LEAF n, C)
= (* by unfolding the call to refocus4_tree *)
iterate4 (DEC (PR_LEAF n, C))
= (* by unfolding the call to iterate4 *)
refocus4_tree (NODE (LEAF n, STUB), C)
```

```
= (* by unfolding the call to refocus4_tree *)
refocus4_tree (STUB, CTX_RIGHT (LEAF n, C))
= (* by unfolding the call to refocus4_tree *)
refocus4_context (CTX_RIGHT (LEAF n, C), (STUB, STUB_nf))
= (* by unfolding the call to refocus4_context *)
refocus4_node (LEAF n, (STUB, STUB_nf), C)
= (* by unfolding the call to refocus4_node *)
refocus4_context (C, (NODE (LEAF n, STUB), NODE_nf (n, STUB_nf)))
```

Clause `refocus4 node (STUB, (t2, t2 nf), C)`:

```
refocus4_node (STUB, (t2, t2_nf), C)
= (* by unfolding the call to refocus4_node *)
iterate4 (DEC (PR_LEFT_STUB (t2, t2_nf), C))
= (* by unfolding the call to iterate4 *)
refocus4_tree (t2, C)
= (* since t2 is in normal form *)
refocus4_context (C, (t2, t2_nf))
```

Clause `refocus4 node (NODE (t11, t12), (t2, t2 nf), C)`:

```
refocus4_node (NODE (t11, t12), (t2, t2_nf), C)
= (* by unfolding the call to refocus4_node *)
iterate4 (DEC (PR_ASSOC (t11, t12, (t2, t2_nf)), C))
= (* by unfolding the call to iterate4 *)
refocus4_tree (NODE (t11, NODE (t12, t2)), C)
= (* by unfolding the call to refocus4_tree *)
refocus4_tree (NODE (t12, t2), CTX_RIGHT (t11, C))
= (* by unfolding the call to refocus4_tree *)
refocus4_tree (t2, CTX_RIGHT (t12, CTX_RIGHT (t11, C)))
= (* since t2 is in normal form *)
refocus4_context (CTX_RIGHT (t12, CTX_RIGHT (t11, C)), (t2, t2_nf))
= (* by unfolding the call to refocus4_context *)
refocus4_node (t12, (t2, t2_nf), CTX_RIGHT (t11, C))
```

There are two corollaries to the compressions above:

Dead clauses: All of the calls to `iterate4` have been unfolded, and therefore the definition of `iterate4` is dead.

Dead component: The term component of the values is now dead. We eliminate it in Section 13.5.

13.5 Renaming Transition Functions and Flattening Configurations

The resulting simplified machine is an 'eval/apply/continue' abstract machine. We therefore rename `refocus4 tree` to `flatten5`, `refocus4 node` to `flatten5 node`, and `refocus4 context` to `continue5`. The result reads as follows:

```
(*  flatten5 : tree * context -> result  *)
fun flatten5 (STUB, C)
      = continue5 (C, STUB_nf)
  | flatten5 (LEAF n, C)
      = continue5 (C, NODE_nf (n, STUB_nf))
  | flatten5 (NODE (t1, t2), C)
      = flatten5 (t2, CTX_RIGHT (t1, C))

(*  flatten5_node : tree * tree_nf * context -> result  *)
and flatten5_node (STUB, t2_nf, C)
      = continue5 (C, t2_nf)
  | flatten5_node (LEAF n, t2_nf, C)
      = continue5 (C, NODE_nf (n, t2_nf))
  | flatten5_node (NODE (t11, t12), t2_nf, C)
      = flatten5_node (t12, t2_nf, CTX_RIGHT (t11, C))

(*  continue5 : context * tree_nf -> result  *)
and continue5 (CTX_MT, t_nf)
      = RESULT t_nf
  | continue5 (CTX_RIGHT (t1, C), t2_nf)
      = flatten5_node (t1, t2_nf, C)

(*  normalize5 : tree -> result  *)
fun normalize5 t
      = flatten5 (t, CTX_MT)
```

13.6 Refunctionalization

The definitions of Section 13.5 are in defunctionalized form. The reduction contexts, together with continue5, are the first-order counterpart of a function. The higher-order counterpart of this abstract machine reads as follows:

```
(*  flatten6 : tree * (tree_nf -> 'a) -> 'a  *)
fun flatten6 (STUB, k)
      = k STUB_nf
  | flatten6 (LEAF n, k)
      = k (NODE_nf (n, STUB_nf))
  | flatten6 (NODE (t1, t2), k)
      = flatten6 (t2, fn t2_nf => flatten6_node (t1, t2_nf, k))

(*  flatten6_node : tree * tree_nf * (tree_nf -> 'a) -> 'a  *)
and flatten6_node (STUB, t2_nf, k)
      = k t2_nf
  | flatten6_node (LEAF n, t2_nf, k)
      = k (NODE_nf (n, t2_nf))
  | flatten6_node (NODE (t11, t12), t2_nf, k)
    = flatten6_node(t12, t2_nf, fn t2_nf =>flatten6_node(t11, t2_nf, k))

(*  normalize6 : tree -> result  *)
fun normalize6 t
      = flatten6 (t, fn t_nf => RESULT t_nf)
```

The resulting refunctionalized program is a familiar eval/apply evaluation function in CPS.

13.7   Back to Direct Style

The refunctionalized definition of Section 13.6 is in continuation-passing style since it has a functional accumulator and all of its calls are tail calls. Its direct-style counterpart reads as follows:

```
(*  flatten7 : tree -> tree_nf  *)
fun flatten7 STUB
    = STUB_nf
  | flatten7 (LEAF n)
    = NODE_nf (n, STUB_nf)
  | flatten7 (NODE (t1, t2))
    = flatten7_node (t1, flatten7 t2)

(*  flatten7_node : tree * tree_nf -> tree_nf  *)
and flatten7_node (STUB, t2_nf)
    = t2_nf
  | flatten7_node (LEAF n, t2_nf)
    = NODE_nf (n, t2_nf)
  | flatten7_node (NODE (t11, t12), t2_nf)
    = flatten7_node (t11, flatten7_node (t12, t2_nf))

(*  normalize7 : tree -> result  *)
fun normalize7 t
    = RESULT (flatten7 t)
```

The resulting definition is that of a flatten function with an accumulator, i.e., an uncurried version of the usual reduction-free normalization function for the free monoid [9, 7, 11, 51]. It also coincides with the definition of the flatten function in Yves Bertot's concise presentation of the Coq proof assistant [8, Section 4.8].

13.8   Closure Unconversion

This section is intentionally left blank, since the tree leaves are integers.

13.9   Summary

We have refocused the reduction-based normalization function of Section 12 into a small-step abstract machine, and we have exhibited a family of corresponding reduction-free normalization functions. Most of the members of this family correspond to something one usually writes by hand.

13.10   Exercises

Exercise 68. Reproduce the construction above in the programming language of your choice, starting from your solution to Exercise 64 in Section 12.7. At each step of the derivation, run the tests of Exercise 63 in Section 12.7.

Exercise 69. Would it make sense, in the definition of `normalize6`, to take `fn v => v` as the initial continuation? If so, what would be the definition of `normalize7` and what would be its type? What about `normalize7'`?

Exercise 70. In Section 13.7, the reduction-free normalization function could be streamlined by skipping `flatten7` as follows:

```
(*  normalize7' : tree -> result  *)
fun normalize7' t
    = RESULT (flatten7_node (t, STUB_nf))
```

This streamlined reduction-free normalization function is the traditional flatten function with an accumulator. It, however, corresponds to another reduction-based normalization function and a slightly different reduction strategy. Which reduction semantics gives rise to this streamlined flatten function?

14   Conclusion

In Jean-Jacques Beineix's movie "Diva," Gorodish shows Postman Jules the Zen aspects of buttering a French baguette. He starts from a small-step description of the baguette that is about as fetching as the one in the more recent movie "Ratatouille" and progressively detaches himself from the bread, the butter and the knife to culminate with a movement, a gesture, big steps. So is it for reduction-free normalization compared to reduction-based normalization: we start from an abstract syntax and a reduction strategy where everything is explicit, and we end up skipping the reduction sequence altogether and reaching a state where everything is implicit, expressed that it is in the meta-language, as in Per Martin Löf's original vision of normalization by evaluation [28, 55]. It is the author's hope that the reader is now in position to butter a French baguette at home with harmony and efficiency, computationally speaking, that is: whether, e.g., calculating an arithmetic expression, recognizing a Dyck word, normalizing a lambda-term with explicit substitutions and possibly call/cc, or flattening a binary tree, one can either use small steps and adopt a notion of reduction and a reduction strategy, or use big steps and adopt a notion of evaluation and an evaluation strategy. Plotkin, 30 years ago [64], extensionally connected the two by showing that for the lambda-calculus, applicative order (resp. normal order) corresponds to call by value (resp. call by name). In these lecture notes, we have shown that this extensional connection also makes sense intensionally: small-step implementations and big-step implementations can be mechanically inter-derived; it is the same elephant.

Acknowledgments. These lecture notes are a revised and substantially expanded version of an invited talk at WRS 2004 [21], for which the author is still grateful to Sergio Antoy and Yoshihito Toyama. Thanks are also due to Rinus Plasmeijer for the opportunity to present this material at AFP 2008; to the other organizers and co-lecturers for a wonderful event; to Alain Crémieux, Diana Fulger and the other AFP 2008 attendees for their interaction and feedback; to Pieter Koopman for his editorship; to Jacob Johannsen, Ian Zerny and the anonymous reviewers and editors for their comments; and to Sivert Bertelsen, Sebastian Erdweg, Alexander Hansen, Dennis Decker Jensen, Finn Rosenbech Jensen and Tillmann Rendel for their extra comments in the spring of 2009.

References

1. Abadi, M., Cardelli, L.: A Theory of Objects. Monographs in Computer Science. Springer, Heidelberg (1996)
2. Ager, M.S.: Partial Evaluation of String Matchers & Constructions of Abstract Machines. PhD thesis, BRICS PhD School, Department of Computer Science, Aarhus University, Aarhus, Denmark (January 2006)
3. Ager, M.S., Biernacki, D., Danvy, O., Midtgaard, J.: A functional correspondence between evaluators and abstract machines. In: Miller, D. (ed.) Proceedings of the Fifth ACM-SIGPLAN International Conference on Principles and Practice of Declarative Programming (PPDP 2003), Uppsala, Sweden, August 2003, pp. 8–19. ACM Press, New York (2003)
4. Ager, M.S., Danvy, O., Midtgaard, J.: A functional correspondence between call-by-need evaluators and lazy abstract machines. Information Processing Letters 90(5), 223–232 (2004); Extended version available as the research report BRICS RS-04-3
5. Ager, M.S., Danvy, O., Midtgaard, J.: A functional correspondence between monadic evaluators and abstract machines for languages with computational effects. Theoretical Computer Science 342(1), 149–172 (2005); Extended version available as the research report BRICS RS-04-28
6. Asai, K.: Binding-time analysis for both static and dynamic expressions. New Generation Computing 20(1), 27–51 (2002); A preliminary version is available in the proceedings of SAS 1999 (LNCS 1694)
7. Balat, V., Danvy, O.: Memoization in type-directed partial evaluation. In: Batory, D., Consel, C., Taha, W. (eds.) GPCE 2002. LNCS, vol. 2487, pp. 78–92. Springer, Heidelberg (2002)
8. Bertot, Y.: Coq in a hurry. CoRR (May 2006), http://arxiv.org/abs/cs/0603118v2
9. Beylin, I., Dybjer, P.: Extracting a proof of coherence for monoidal categories from a proof of normalization for monoids. In: Berardi, S., Coppo, M. (eds.) TYPES 1995. LNCS, vol. 1158, pp. 47–61. Springer, Heidelberg (1996)
10. Biernacka, M.: A Derivational Approach to the Operational Semantics of Functional Languages. PhD thesis, BRICS PhD School, Department of Computer Science, Aarhus University, Aarhus, Denmark (January 2006)
11. Biernacka, M., Biernacki, D., Danvy, O.: An operational foundation for delimited continuations in the CPS hierarchy. Logical Methods in Computer Science 1(2:5), 1–39 (2005); A preliminary version was presented at the Fourth ACM SIGPLAN Workshop on Continuations (CW 2004)
12. Biernacka, M., Danvy, O.: A concrete framework for environment machines. ACM Transactions on Computational Logic 9(1), Article #6, 1–30 (2007); Extended version available as the research report BRICS RS-06-3
13. Biernacka, M., Danvy, O.: A syntactic correspondence between context-sensitive calculi and abstract machines. Theoretical Computer Science 375(1-3), 76–108 (2007); Extended version available as the research report BRICS RS-06-18

14. Biernacka, M., Danvy, O.: Towards compatible and interderivable semantic specifications for the Scheme programming language, Part II: Reduction semantics and abstract machines

15. Biernacki, D.: The Theory and Practice of Programming Languages with Delimited Continuations. PhD thesis, BRICS PhD School, Department of Computer Science, Aarhus University, Aarhus, Denmark (December 2005)

16. Biernacki, D., Danvy, O.: From interpreter to logic engine by defunctionalization. In: Bruynooghe, M. (ed.) LOPSTR 2004. LNCS, vol. 3018, pp. 143–159. Springer, Heidelberg (2004)

17. Church, A.: The Calculi of Lambda-Conversion. Princeton University Press, Princeton (1941)

18. Clinger, W.: 2008 ACM SIGPLAN Workshop on Scheme and Functional Programming, Victoria, British Columbia (September 2008)

19. Curien, P.-L.: An abstract framework for environment machines. Theoretical Computer Science 82, 389–402 (1991)

20. Danvy, O.: Back to direct style. Science of Computer Programming 22(3), 183–195 (1994); A preliminary version was presented at the Fourth European Symposium on Programming (ESOP 1992)

21. Danvy, O.: From reduction-based to reduction-free normalization. In: Antoy, S., Toyama, Y. (eds.) Proceedings of the Fourth International Workshop on Reduction Strategies in Rewriting and Programming (WRS 2004), Aachen, Germany, May 2004. Electronic Notes in Theoretical Computer Science, vol. 124(2), pp. 79–100. Elsevier Science, Amsterdam (2004), Invited talk

22. Danvy, O.: On evaluation contexts, continuations, and the rest of the computation. In: Thielecke, H. (ed.) Proceedings of the Fourth ACM SIGPLAN Workshop on Continuations, CW 2004 (2004); Technical report CSR-04-1, Department of Computer Science, Queen Mary's College, pp. 13–23, Venice, Italy (January 2004), Invited talk

23. Danvy, O.: A rational deconstruction of Landin's SECD machine. In: Grelck, C., Huch, F., Michaelson, G.J., Trinder, P. (eds.) IFL 2004. LNCS, vol. 3474, pp. 52–71. Springer, Heidelberg (2005)

24. Danvy, O.: An Analytical Approach to Program as Data Objects. DSc thesis, Department of Computer Science, Aarhus University, Aarhus, Denmark (October 2006)

25. Danvy, O.: Special Issue on the Krivine Abstract Machine, part I. Higher-Order and Symbolic Computation, vol. 20(3). Springer, Heidelberg (2007)

26. Danvy, O.: Defunctionalized interpreters for programming languages. In: Thiemann, P. (ed.) Proceedings of the 2008 ACM SIGPLAN International Conference on Functional Programming (ICFP 2008), SIGPLAN Notices, Victoria, British Columbia, September 2008, vol. 43(9), pp. 131–142. ACM Press, New York (2008), Invited talk

27. Danvy, O.: Towards compatible and interderivable semantic specifications for the Scheme programming language, Part I: Denotational semantics, natural semantics, and abstract machines

28. Danvy, O., Dybjer, P. (eds.): Proceedings of the 1998 APPSEM Workshop on Normalization by Evaluation (NBE 1998), BRICS Note Series NS-98-8, Gothenburg, Sweden, May 1998. BRICS, Department of Computer Science. Aarhus University (1998), http://www.brics.dk/~nbe98/programme.html

29. Danvy, O., Filinski, A.: Abstracting control. In: Wand, M. (ed.) Proceedings of the 1990 ACM Conference on Lisp and Functional Programming, Nice, France, June 1990, pp. 151–160. ACM Press, New York (1990)

30. Danvy, O., Filinski, A.: Representing control, a study of the CPS transformation. Mathematical Structures in Computer Science 2(4), 361–391 (1992)
31. Danvy, O., Johannsen, J.: Inter-deriving semantic artifacts for object-oriented programming. In: Hodges, W., de Queiroz, R. (eds.) Logic, Language, Information and Computation. LNCS (LNAI), vol. 5110, pp. 1–16. Springer, Heidelberg (2008)
32. Danvy, O., Lawall, J.L.: Back to direct style II: First-class continuations. In: Clinger, W. (ed.) Proceedings of the 1992 ACM Conference on Lisp and Functional Programming, LISP Pointers, San Francisco, California, June 1992, vol. V(1), pp. 299–310. ACM Press, New York (1992)
33. Danvy, O., Millikin, K.: On the equivalence between small-step and big-step abstract machines: a simple application of lightweight fusion. Information Processing Letters 106(3), 100–109 (2008)
34. Danvy, O., Millikin, K.: A rational deconstruction of Landin's SECD machine with the J operator. Logical Methods in Computer Science 4(4:12), 1–67 (2008)
35. Danvy, O., Millikin, K.: Refunctionalization at work. Science of Computer Programming 74(8), 534–549 (2009); Extended version available as the research report BRICS RS-08-04
36. Danvy, O., Millikin, K., Nielsen, L.R.: On one-pass CPS transformations. Journal of Functional Programming 17(6), 793–812 (2007)
37. Danvy, O., Nielsen, L.R.: Defunctionalization at work. In: Søndergaard, H. (ed.) Proceedings of the Third International ACM SIGPLAN Conference on Principles and Practice of Declarative Programming (PPDP 2001), Firenze, Italy, September 2001, pp. 162–174. ACM Press, New York (2001); Extended version available as the research report BRICS RS-01-23
38. Danvy, O., Nielsen, L.R.: Refocusing in reduction semantics. Research Report BRICS RS-04-26, Department of Computer Science, Aarhus University, Aarhus, Denmark (November 2004); A preliminary version appeared in the informal proceedings of the Second International Workshop on Rule-Based Programming (RULE 2001), Electronic Notes in Theoretical Computer Science, vol. 59.4
39. Felleisen, M.: The Calculi of λ-v-CS Conversion: A Syntactic Theory of Control and State in Imperative Higher-Order Programming Languages, PhD thesis. Computer Science Department, Indiana University, Bloomington, Indiana (August 1987)
40. Felleisen, M., Flatt, M.: Programming languages and lambda calculi (1989-2001), http://www.ccs.neu.edu/home/matthias/3810-w02/readings.html (last accessed in April 2008)
41. Felleisen, M., Friedman, D.P.: Control operators, the SECD machine, and the λ-calculus. In: Wirsing, M. (ed.) Formal Description of Programming Concepts III, pp. 193–217. Elsevier Science Publishers B.V (North-Holland), Amsterdam (1986)
42. Friedman, D.P., Wand, M.: Essentials of Programming Languages, 3rd edn. MIT Press, Cambridge (2008)
43. Ganz, S.E., Friedman, D.P., Wand, M.: Trampolined style. In: Lee, P. (ed.) Proceedings of the 1999 ACM SIGPLAN International Conference on Functional Programming, Paris, France, September 1999. SIGPLAN Notices, vol. 34(9), pp. 18–27. ACM Press, New York (1999)
44. Hardin, T., Maranget, L., Pagano, B.: Functional runtime systems within the lambda-sigma calculus. Journal of Functional Programming 8(2), 131–172 (1998)
45. Hatcliff, J., Danvy, O.: Thunks and the λ-calculus. Journal of Functional Programming 7(3), 303–319 (1997)
46. Haynes, C.T., Friedman, D.P., Wand, M.: Continuations and coroutines. In: Steele Jr., G.L. (ed.) Conference Record of the 1984 ACM Symposium on Lisp and Func-

148   O. Danvy

tional Programming, Austin, Texas, August 1984, pp. 293–298. ACM Press, New York (1984)
47. Huet, G.: The zipper. Journal of Functional Programming 7(5), 549–554 (1997)
48. Johannsen, J.: An investigation of Abadi and Cardelli's untyped calculus of objects. Master's thesis, Department of Computer Science, Aarhus University, Aarhus, Denmark (June 2008); BRICS research report RS-08-6
49. Kahn, G.: Natural semantics. In: Brandenburg, F.-J., Vidal-Naquet, G., Wirsing, M. (eds.) STACS 1987. LNCS, vol. 247, pp. 22–39. Springer, Heidelberg (1987)
50. Kesner, D.: The theory of calculi with explicit substitutions revisited. In: Duparc, J., Henzinger, T.A. (eds.) CSL 2007. LNCS, vol. 4646, pp. 238–252. Springer, Heidelberg (2007)
51. Kinoshita, Y.: A bicategorical analysis of E-categories. Mathematica Japonica 47(1), 157–169 (1998)
52. Lafont, Y.: Logiques, Catégories et Machines. PhD thesis, Université de Paris VII, Paris, France (January 1988)
53. Landin, P.J.: The mechanical evaluation of expressions. The Computer Journal 6(4), 308–320 (1964)
54. Marlow, S., Peyton Jones, S.L.: Making a fast curry: push/enter vs. eval/apply for higher-order languages. Journal of Functional Programming 16(4-5), 415–449 (2006); A preliminary version was presented at the 2004 ACM SIGPLAN International Conference on Functional Programming (ICFP 2004) (2004)
55. Martin-Löf, P.: About models for intuitionistic type theories and the notion of definitional equality. In: Proceedings of the Third Scandinavian Logic Symposium (1972). Studies in Logic and the Foundation of Mathematics, vol. 82, pp. 81–109. North-Holland, Amsterdam (1975)
56. McCarthy, J.: Recursive functions of symbolic expressions and their computation by machine, part I. Communications of the ACM 3(4), 184–195 (1960)
57. Midtgaard, J.: Transformation, Analysis, and Interpretation of Higher-Order Procedural Programs. PhD thesis, BRICS PhD School, Aarhus University, Aarhus, Denmark (June 2007)
58. Millikin, K.: A Structured Approach to the Transformation, Normalization and Execution of Computer Programs. PhD thesis, BRICS PhD School, Aarhus University, Aarhus, Denmark (May 2007)
59. Milner, R., Tofte, M., Harper, R., MacQueen, D.: The Definition of Standard ML (Revised). MIT Press, Cambridge (1997)
60. Morris, F.L.: The next 700 formal language descriptions. Lisp and Symbolic Computation 6(3/4), 249–258 (1993); Reprinted from a manuscript dated 1970
61. Munk, J.: A study of syntactic and semantic artifacts and its application to lambda definability, strong normalization, and weak normalization in the presence of state. Master's thesis, Department of Computer Science, Aarhus University, Aarhus, Denmark (May 2007); BRICS research report RS-08-3
62. Nielsen, L.R.: A study of defunctionalization and continuation-passing style. PhD thesis, BRICS PhD School, Department of Computer Science, Aarhus University, Aarhus, Denmark (July 2001), BRICS DS-01-7
63. Ohori, A., Sasano, I.: Lightweight fusion by fixed point promotion. In: Felleisen, M. (ed.) Proceedings of the Thirty-Fourth Annual ACM Symposium on Principles of Programming Languages, Nice, France, January 2007. SIGPLAN Notices, vol. 42(1), pp. 143–154. ACM Press, New York (2007)
64. Plotkin, G.D.: Call-by-name, call-by-value and the λ-calculus. Theoretical Computer Science 1, 125–159 (1975)

65. Plotkin, G.D.: A structural approach to operational semantics. Technical Report FN-19, Department of Computer Science, Aarhus University, Aarhus, Denmark, (September 1981); Reprinted in the Journal of Logic and Algebraic Programming 60-61, 17-139 (2004), with a foreword [66]

66. Plotkin, G.D.: The origins of structural operational semantics. Journal of Logic and Algebraic Programming 60-61, 3–15 (2004)

67. Reynolds, J.C.: Definitional interpreters for higher-order programming languages. In: Proceedings of 25th ACM National Conference, Boston, Massachusetts, pp. 717–740 (1972); Reprinted in Higher-Order and Symbolic Computation, vol. 11(4), pp. 363-397 (1998), with a foreword [68]

68. Reynolds, J.C.: Definitional interpreters revisited. Higher-Order and Symbolic Computation 11(4), 355–361 (1998)

69. Steele Jr., G.L.: Lambda, the ultimate declarative. AI Memo 379, Artificial Intelligence Laboratory, Cambridge, Massachusetts, November 1976. Massachusetts Institute of Technology (1976)

70. Steele Jr., G.L.: Rabbit: A compiler for Scheme. Master's thesis, Artificial Intelligence Laboratory, Cambridge, Massachusetts, May 1978. Massachusetts Institute of Technology (1978); Technical report AI-TR-474

71. Steele Jr., G.L., Sussman, G.J.: Lambda, the ultimate imperative. AI Memo 353, Artificial Intelligence Laboratory. Massachusetts Institute of Technology, Cambridge, Massachusetts (March 1976)

72. Stoy, J.E.: Denotational Semantics: The Scott-Strachey Approach to Programming Language Theory. MIT Press, Cambridge (1977)

73. Xiao, Y., Sabry, A., Ariola, Z.M.: From syntactic theories to interpreters: Automating proofs of unique decomposition. Higher-Order and Symbolic Computation 14(4), 387–409 (2001)

The goal of the following appendices is to review closure conversion, CPS transformation, defunctionalization, lightweight fission, and lightweight fusion. To this end, we retrace John Reynolds's steps from a compositional evaluation function to an abstract machine [67] and then move on to lightweight fission and fusion.

A Lambda-Terms with Integers

We first specify lambda-terms with integers (arbitrary literals and a predefined successor function) and then present a computationally representative sample of lambda-terms.

A.1 Abstract Syntax

A lambda-term is an integer literal, an identifier, a lambda-abstraction or an application:

```
datatype term = LIT of int
              | IDE of string
              | LAM of string * term
              | APP of term * term
```

We assume predefined identifiers, e.g., "succ" to denote the successor function.

A.2   A Sample of Lambda-Terms

Church numerals [17] and mappings between native natural numbers and Church numerals form a good ground to illustrate the expressive power of lambda-terms with integers.

Church numerals. A Church numeral is a functional encoding of a natural number that abstracts a zero value and a successor function:

```
val cn0 = LAM ("s", LAM ("z", IDE "z"))
val cns = LAM ("cn",
              LAM ("s", LAM ("z", APP (APP (IDE "cn", IDE "s"),
                                       APP (IDE "s", IDE "z")))))
```

For example, here is the Church numeral representing the natural number 3:

```
val cn3 = APP (cns, APP (cns, APP (cns, cn0)))
```

Mappings between natural numbers and Church numerals. Given   a natural number n, one constructs the corresponding Church numeral by recursively applying cns n times to cn0. Conversely, applying a Church numeral that represents the natural number n to the native successor function and the native natural number 0 yields a term that reduces to the native representation of n.

```
fun n2cn 0 = cn0
  | n2cn n = APP (cns, n2cn (n - 1))

fun cn2n cn
    = APP (APP (cn, IDE "succ"), LIT 0)
```

Computing with Church numerals. As is well known, applying a Church numeral to another one implements exponentiation. The following term therefore reduces to the native representation of 1024:

```
val n1024 = cn2n (APP (n2cn 10, n2cn 2))
```

B   A Call-by-Value Evaluation Function

Let us write a canonical evaluator for lambda-terms with integers as specified in Section A. The evaluator uses an environment, and proceeds by recursive descent over a given term. It is compositional.

Environments. The environment is a canonical association list (i.e., list of pairs associating identifiers and values):

```
structure Env
= struct
    type 'a env = (string * 'a) list

    val empty = []

    fun extend (x, v, env)
        = (x, v) :: env

    fun lookup (x, env)
        = let fun search []
                   = NONE
               | search ((x', v) :: env)
                   = if x = x' then SOME v else search env
          in search env
          end
  end
```

Values. Values are integers or functions:

```
datatype value = VAL_INT of int
               | VAL_FUN of value -> value
```

Evaluation function. The evaluation function is a traditional, Scott-Tarski one. (Scott because of the reflexive data type of values, and Tarski because of its meta-circular fashion of interpreting a concept in term of the same concept at the meta-level: syntactic lambda-abstractions are interpreted in terms of ML function abstractions, and syntactic applications in terms of ML function applications.) Evaluating a program might go wrong because an undeclared identifier is used, because the successor function is applied to a non-integer, or because a non-function is applied; these events are summarily interpreted by raising an exception to the top level.

```
exception WRONG of string

(* eval0 : term * value Env.env -> value *)
fun eval0 (LIT n, e)
    = VAL_INT n
  | eval0 (IDE x, e)
    = (case Env.lookup (x, e)
         of NONE
            => raise (WRONG "undeclared identifier")
          | (SOME v)
            => v)
  | eval0 (LAM (x, t), e)
    = VAL_FUN (fn v => eval0 (t, Env.extend (x, v, e)))
  | eval0 (APP (t0, t1), e)
    = apply0 (eval0 (t0, e), eval0 (t1, e))
```

```
(*  apply0 : value * value -> value  *)
and apply0 (VAL_FUN f, v)
    = f v
  | apply0 (v0, v1)
    = raise (WRONG "non-applicable value")
```

Initial environment. The initial environment binds, e.g., the identifier `succ` to the successor function:

```
val val_succ = VAL_FUN (fn (VAL_INT n)
                          => VAL_INT (n + 1)
                         | v
                          => raise (WRONG "non-integer value"))

val e_init = Env.extend ("succ", val_succ, Env.empty)
```

Main function. A term is interpreted by evaluating it in the initial environment in the presence of an exception handler. Evaluating a term may diverge; otherwise it either yields a value or an error message if evaluation goes wrong:

```
datatype value_or_error = VALUE of value
                        | ERROR of string

(*  interpret0 : term -> value_or_error  *)
fun interpret0 t
    = VALUE (eval0 (t, e_init))
      handle (WRONG s) => ERROR s
```

C   Closure Conversion

Let us "firstify" the domain of values by defunctionalizing it: the function space, in the data type of values in Appendix B, is inhabited by function values that arise from evaluating two (and only two) function abstractions: one in the `LAM` clause in the definition of `eval0` as the denotation of a syntactic lambda-abstraction, and one in the initial environment as the successor function. We therefore modify the domain of values by replacing the higher-order constructor `VAL FUN` by two first-order constructors `VAL SUCC` and `VAL CLO`:

```
datatype value = VAL_INT of int
               | VAL_SUCC
               | VAL_CLO of string * term * value Env.env
```

The first-order representation tagged by `VAL CLO` is known as a "closure" since Landin's pioneering work [53]: it pairs a lambda-abstraction and its environment of declaration.

Introduction: `VAL SUCC` is produced in the initial environment as the denotation of `succ`; and `VAL CLO` is produced in the `LAM` clause and holds the free variables of `fn v => eval0 (t, Env.extend (x, v, e))`.

Elimination: VAL SUCC and VAL CLO are consumed in new clauses of the apply function, which dispatches over applicable values. As in Appendix B, applying VAL SUCC to an integer yields the successor of this integer and applying it to a non-integer raises an exception; and applying VAL CLO (x, t, e), i.e., the result of evaluating LAM (x, t) in an environment e, to a value v leads t to be evaluated in an extended environment, as in Appendix B.

Compared to Appendix B, the new parts of the following closure-converted interpreter are shaded:

```
val e_init = Env.extend ("succ", VAL_SUCC , Env.empty)

(*  eval1 : term * value Env.env -> value  *)
fun eval1 (LIT n, e)
    = VAL_INT n
  | eval1 (IDE x, e)
    = (case Env.lookup (x, e)
         of NONE
              => raise (WRONG "undeclared identifier")
          | (SOME v)
              => v)
  | eval1 (LAM (x, t), e)
    = VAL_CLO (x, t, e)
  | eval1 (APP (t0, t1), e)
    = apply1 (eval1 (t0, e), eval1 (t1, e))
(*  apply1 : value * value -> value  *)
and apply1 (VAL_SUCC, VAL_INT n)

    = VAL_INT (n + 1)

  | apply1 (VAL_SUCC, v)

    = raise (WRONG "non-integer value")

  | apply1 (VAL_CLO (x, t, e), v)

    = eval1 (t, Env.extend (x, v, e))
  | apply1 (v0, v1)
    = raise (WRONG "non-applicable value")

datatype value_or_error = VALUE of value
                         | ERROR of string

(*  interpret1 : term -> value_or_error  *)
fun interpret1 t
    = VALUE (eval1 (t, e_init))
      handle (WRONG s) => ERROR s
```

The resulting interpreter is a traditional McCarthy-Landin one. (McCarthy because of his original definition of Lisp in Lisp [56] and Landin because of the closures.) It can also be seen as an implementation of Kahn's natural semantics [49].

D   CPS Transformation

Let us transform `eval1` and `apply1`, in Appendix C, into continuation-passing style (CPS). To this end, we name each of their intermediate results, we sequentialize their computation, and we pass them an extra (functional) parameter, the continuation. As a result, the intermediate results are named by the formal parameter of each of the lambda-abstractions that define the continuation (shaded below):

```
(*  eval2 : term * value Env.env * (value -> value_or_error)
               -> value_or_error  *)
fun eval2 (LIT n, e, k)
    = k (VAL_INT n)
  | eval2 (IDE x, e, k)
    = (case Env.lookup (x, e)
         of NONE
            => ERROR "undeclared identifier"
          | (SOME v)
            => k v)
  | eval2 (LAM (x, t), e, k)
    = k (VAL_CLO (x, t, e))
  | eval2 (APP (t0, t1), e, k)
    = eval2 (t0, e, fn v0 =>
        eval2 (t1, e, fn v1 =>
          apply2 (v0, v1, k)))
(*  apply2 : value * value * (value -> value_or_error)
               -> value_or_error  *)
and apply2 (VAL_SUCC, VAL_INT n, k)
    = k (VAL_INT (n + 1))
  | apply2 (VAL_SUCC, v, k)
    = ERROR "non-integer value"
  | apply2 (VAL_CLO (x, t, e), v, k)
    = eval2 (t, Env.extend (x, v, e), k)
  | apply2 (v0, v1, k)
    = ERROR "non-applicable value"

(*  interpret2 : term -> value_or_error  *)
fun interpret2 t
    = eval2 (t, e_init, fn v => VALUE v)
```

The resulting interpreter is a traditional continuation-passing one, as can be found in Morris's early work [60], in Steele and Sussman's lambda-papers [71,69], and in "Essentials of Programming Languages" [42].

E   Defunctionalization

Let us defunctionalize the continuation of Appendix D's interpreter. This function space is inhabited by function values that arise from evaluating three (and only three) function abstractions—those whose formal parameter is shaded above. We therefore partition the function space into three summands and represent it as the following first-order data type:

```
datatype cont = CONT_MT
              | CONT_FUN of cont * term * value Env.env
              | CONT_ARG of value * cont
```

This first-order representation is known as that of an evaluation context [40].

Introduction: CONT MT is produced in the initial call to eval3; CONT FUN is produced in the recursive self-call in eval3; and CONT ARG is produced in the function that dispatches upon the evaluation context, continue3. Each constructor holds the free variables of the function abstraction it represents.

Elimination: The three constructors are consumed in continue3.

Compared to Appendix D, the new parts of the following defunctionalized interpreter are shaded:

```
(*  eval3 : term * value Env.env * cont -> value_or_error  *)
fun eval3 (LIT n, e, C)
      = continue3 (C, VAL_INT n)
  | eval3 (IDE x, e, C)
      = (case Env.lookup (x, e)
           of NONE
              => ERROR "undeclared identifier"
            | (SOME v)
              => continue3 (C, v))
  | eval3 (LAM (x, t), e, C)
      = continue3 (C, VAL_CLO (x, t, e))
  | eval3 (APP (t0, t1), e, C)
      = eval3 (t0, e, CONT_FUN (C, t1, e))

(*  apply3 : value * value * cont -> value_or_error  *)
and apply3 (VAL_SUCC, VAL_INT n, C)
      = continue3 (C, VAL_INT (n + 1))
  | apply3 (VAL_SUCC, v, C)
      = ERROR "non-integer value"
  | apply3 (VAL_CLO (x, t, e), v, C)
      = eval3 (t, Env.extend (x, v, e), C)
  | apply3 (v0, v1, C)
      = ERROR "non-applicable value"

(*  continue3 : context * value -> value_or_error  *)
and continue3 (CONT_MT, v)
      = VALUE v
  | continue3 (CONT_FUN (C, t1, e), v0)
      = eval3 (t1, e, CONT_ARG (v0, C))
  | continue3 (CONT_ARG (v0, C), v1)
      = apply3 (v0, v1, C)
```

```
(*  interpret3 : term -> value_or_error  *)
fun interpret3 t
    = eval3 (t, e_init, CONT_MT )
```

Reynolds pointed at the "machine-like" qualities of this defunctionalized interpreter, and indeed the alert reader will already have recognized that this interpreter implements a big-step version of the CEK abstract machine [41]. Indeed
each (tail-)call implements a state transition.

F   Lightweight Fission

Let us explicitly represent the states of the abstract machine of Appendix E with
the following data type:

```
datatype state = STOP of value
               | WRONG of string
               | EVAL of term * value Env.env * cont
               | APPLY of value * value * cont
               | CONTINUE of cont * value
```

Non-accepting states: The STOP state marks that a value has been computed
    for the given term, and the WRONG state that the given term is a stuck one.
Accepting states: The EVAL, APPLY, and CONTINUE states mark that the machine
    is ready to take a transition corresponding to one (tail-)call in Appendix E,
    as respectively implemented by the following transition functions move eval,
    move apply, and move continue.

```
(*  move_eval : term * value Env.env * cont -> state  *)
fun move_eval (LIT n, e, C)
    = CONTINUE (C, VAL_INT n)
  | move_eval (IDE x, e, C)
    = (case Env.lookup (x, e)
         of NONE
            => WRONG "undeclared identifier"
          | (SOME v)
            => CONTINUE (C, v))
  | move_eval (LAM (x, t), e, C)
    = CONTINUE (C, VAL_CLO (x, t, e))
  | move_eval (APP (t0, t1), e, C)
    = EVAL (t0, e, CONT_FUN (C, t1, e))

(*  move_apply : value * value * cont -> state  *)
fun move_apply (VAL_SUCC, VAL_INT n, C)
    = CONTINUE (C, VAL_INT (n + 1))
  | move_apply (VAL_SUCC, v, C)
    = WRONG "non-integer value"
  | move_apply (VAL_CLO (x, t, e), v, C)
    = EVAL (t, Env.extend (x, v, e), C)
  | move_apply (v0, v1, C)
    = WRONG "non-applicable value"
```

```
(*  move_continue : cont * value -> state  *)
fun move_continue (CONT_MT, v)
     = STOP v
   | move_continue (CONT_FUN (C, t1, e), v0)
     = EVAL (t1, e, CONT_ARG (v0, C))
   | move_continue (CONT_ARG (v0, C), v1)
     = APPLY (v0, v1, C)
```

The following driver loop maps a non-accepting state to a final result or (1) activates the transition corresponding to the current accepting state and (2) iterates:

```
(*  drive : state -> value_or_error  *)
fun drive (STOP v)
     = VALUE v
   | drive (WRONG s)
     = ERROR s
   | drive (EVAL c)
     = drive (move_eval c)
   | drive (APPLY c)
     = drive (move_apply c)
   | drive (CONTINUE c)
     = drive (move_continue c)
```

For a given term t, the initial state of machine is EVAL (t, e init, CONT MT):

```
(*  interpret4 : term -> value_or_error  *)
fun interpret4 t
     = drive (EVAL (t, e_init, CONT_MT))
```

The resulting interpreter is a traditional small-step abstract machine [65], namely the CEK machine [41]. As spelled out in Appendix G, fusing the driver loop and the transition functions yields the big-step abstract machine of Appendix E.

G Lightweight Fusion by Fixed-Point Promotion

Let us review Ohori and Sasano's lightweight fusion by fixed-point promotion [63]. This calculational transformation operates over functional programs in the form of the small-step abstract machine of Appendix F: a (strict) top-level driver function drive activating (total) tail-recursive transition functions. The transformation consists in three steps:

1. Inline the definition of the transition function in the composition.
2. Distribute the tail call to the driver function in the conditional branches.
3. Simplify by inlining the applications of the driver function to known arguments.

One then uses the result of the third step to define new mutually recursive functions that are respectively equal to the compositions obtained in the third step.

Let us consider the following function compositions in turn:

- fn g => drive (move eval g) in Appendix G.1;
- fn g => drive (move apply g) in Appendix G.2; and
- fn g => drive (move continue g) in Appendix G.3.

G.1   Drive o move eval

1. We inline the definition of move eval in the composition:

```
fn g => drive (case g
                of (LIT n, e, C)
                       => CONTINUE (C, VAL_INT n)
                 | (IDE x, e, C)
                       => (case Env.lookup (x, e)
                             of NONE
                                  => WRONG "undeclared identifier"
                              | (SOME v)
                                  => CONTINUE (C, v))
                 | (LAM (x, t), e, C)
                       => CONTINUE (C, VAL_CLO (x, t, e))
                 | (APP (t0, t1), e, C)
                       => EVAL (t0, e, CONT_FUN (C, t1, e)))
```

2. We distribute the tail call to drive in the conditional branches:

```
fn c => case c
          of (LIT n, e, C)
                 => drive (CONTINUE (C, VAL_INT n))
           | (IDE x, e, C)
                 => (case Env.lookup (x, e)
                       of NONE
                            => drive (WRONG "undeclared identifier")
                        | (SOME v)
                            => drive (CONTINUE (C, v)))
           | (LAM (x, t), e, C)
                 => drive (CONTINUE (C, VAL_CLO (x, t, e)))
           | (APP (t0, t1), e, C)
                 => drive (EVAL (t0, e, CONT_FUN (C, t1, e)))
```

Or again, more concisely, with a function declared by cases:

```
fn (LIT n, e, C)
     => drive (CONTINUE (C, VAL_INT n))
 | (IDE x, e, C)
     => (case Env.lookup (x, e)
           of NONE
```

```
                => drive (WRONG "undeclared identifier")
            | (SOME v)
                => drive (CONTINUE (C, v)))
    | (LAM (x, t), e, C)
      => drive (CONTINUE (C, VAL_CLO (x, t, e)))
    | (APP (t0, t1), e, C)
      => drive (EVAL (t0, e, CONT_FUN (C, t1, e)))
```

3. We simplify by inlining the applications of drive to known arguments:

```
fn (LIT n, e, C)
    => drive (move_continue (C, VAL_INT n))
  | (IDE x, e, C)
    => (case Env.lookup (x, e)
          of NONE
              => ERROR "undeclared identifier"
            | (SOME v)
              => drive (move_continue (C, v)))
  | (LAM (x, t), e, C)
    => drive (move_continue (C, VAL_CLO (x, t, e)))
  | (APP (t0, t1), e, C)
    => drive (move_eval (t0, e, CONT_FUN (C, t1, e)))
```

G.2   Drive o move apply

1. We inline the definition of move apply in the composition:

```
fn g => drive (case g
                  of (VAL_SUCC, VAL_INT n, C)
                      => CONTINUE (C, VAL_INT (n + 1))
                    | (VAL_SUCC, v, C)
                      => WRONG "non-integer value"
                    | (VAL_CLO (x, t, e), v, C)
                      => EVAL (t, Env.extend (x, v, e), C)
                    | (v0, v1, C)
                      => WRONG "non-applicable value")
```

2. We distribute the tail call to drive in the conditional branches:

```
fn (VAL_SUCC, VAL_INT n, C)
    => drive (CONTINUE (C, VAL_INT (n + 1)))
  | (VAL_SUCC, v, C)
    => drive (WRONG "non-integer value")
  | (VAL_CLO (x, t, e), v, C)
    => drive (EVAL (t, Env.extend (x, v, e), C))
  | (v0, v1, C)
    => drive (WRONG "non-applicable value")
```

3. We simplify by inlining the applications of **drive** to known arguments:

```
fn (VAL_SUCC, VAL_INT n, C)
   => drive (move_continue (C, VAL_INT (n + 1)))
 | (VAL_SUCC, v, C)
   => ERROR "non-integer value"
 | (VAL_CLO (x, t, e), v, C)
   => drive (move_eval (t, Env.extend (x, v, e), C))
 | (v0, v1, C)
   => ERROR "non-applicable value"
```

G.3   Drive o move continue

1. We inline the definition of move continue in the composition:

```
fn g => drive (case g
                 of (CONT_MT, v)
                    => STOP v
                  | (CONT_FUN (C, t1, e), v0)
                    => EVAL (t1, e, CONT_ARG (v0, C))
                  | (CONT_ARG (v0, C), v1)
                    => APPLY (v0, v1, C))
```

2. We distribute the tail call to **drive** in the conditional branches:

```
fn (CONT_MT, v)
   => drive (STOP v)
 | (CONT_FUN (C, t1, e), v0)
   => drive (EVAL (t1, e, CONT_ARG (v0, C)))
 | (CONT_ARG (v0, C), v1)
   => drive (APPLY (v0, v1, C))
```

3. We simplify by inlining the applications of **drive** to known arguments:

```
fn (CONT_MT, v)
   => VALUE v
 | (CONT_FUN (C, t1, e), v0)
   => drive (move_eval (t1, e, CONT_ARG (v0, C)))
 | (CONT_ARG (v0, C), v1)
   => drive (move_apply (v0, v1, C))
```

G.4   Synthesis

We now use the result of the third steps above to define three new mutually recursive functions **drive move eval**, **drive move apply**, and **drive move continue** that are respectively equal to **drive o move eval**, **drive o move apply**, and **drive o move continue**:

```
fun drive_move_eval (LIT n, e, C)
    = drive_move_continue (C, VAL_INT n)
  | drive_move_eval (IDE x, e, C)
    = (case Env.lookup (x, e)
         of NONE
             => ERROR "undeclared identifier"
          | (SOME v)
             => drive_move_continue (C, v))
  | drive_move_eval (LAM (x, t), e, C)
    = drive_move_continue (C, VAL_CLO (x, t, e))
  | drive_move_eval (APP (t0, t1), e, C)
    = drive_move_eval (t0, e, CONT_FUN (C, t1, e))

and drive_move_apply (VAL_SUCC, VAL_INT n, C)
    = drive_move_continue (C, VAL_INT (n + 1))
  | drive_move_apply (VAL_SUCC, v, C)
    = ERROR "non-integer value"
  | drive_move_apply (VAL_CLO (x, t, e), v, C)
    = drive_move_eval (t, Env.extend (x, v, e), C)
  | drive_move_apply (v0, v1, C)
    = ERROR "non-applicable value"

and drive_move_continue (CONT_MT, v)
    = VALUE v
  | drive_move_continue (CONT_FUN (C, t1, e), v0)
    = drive_move_eval (t1, e, CONT_ARG (v0, C))
  | drive_move_continue (CONT_ARG (v0, C), v1)
    = drive_move_apply (v0, v1, C)

fun interpret5 t
    = drive_move_eval (t, e_init, CONT_MT)
```

Except for the function names (drive move eval instead of eval3, drive move apply instead of apply3, and drive move continue instead of continue3), the fused definition coincides with the definition in Appendix E.

H Exercises

Exercise 71. Implement all the interpreters of this appendix in the programming language of your choice, and verify that each of them maps n1024 (defined in Appendix A.2) to VALUE (VAL INT 1024).

Exercise 72. In Appendices C and D, we closure-converted *and then* CPS-transformed the interpreter of Appendix B. Do the converse, i.e., CPS-transform the interpreter of Appendix B and then closure-convert it. The result should coincide with the interpreter of Appendix D. You will need the following data type of values:

```
datatype value = VAL_INT of int
                | VAL_FUN of value * (value -> value_or_error)
                               -> value_or_error
```

Naturally, your continuation-passing interpreter should not use exceptions. Since it is purely functional and compositional, it can be seen as an implementation of a denotational semantics [72].

Exercise 73. Fold the term and the environment, in either of the abstract machines of Appendix E or F, into the following data type of ground closures:

```
datatype closure = CLO_GND of term * value Env.env
```

- the type of the `eval` transition function should read
```
    closure * cont -> value_or_error
```
- the type of the `move eval` transition function should read
```
    closure * cont -> state
```

In either case, the resulting interpreter is a CK abstract machine [40], i.e., an environment-less machine that operates over ground closures. Conversely, unfolding these closures into a simple pair and flattening the resulting configurations mechanically yields either of the environment-based CEK machines of Appendix E or F.

I   Mini Project: Call by Name

Exercise 74. Write a few lambda-terms that would make a call-by-value evaluation function and a call-by-name evaluation function not yield the same result.

Exercise 75. Modify the code of the evaluation function of Appendix B to make it call by name, using the following data type of values:

```
datatype value = VAL_INT of int
                | VAL_FUN of thunk -> value
withtype thunk = unit -> value
```

Verify that the lambda-terms of Exercise 74 behave as expected.

Exercise 76. In continuation of Exercise 75, closure-convert your call-by-name evaluation function, and verify that the lambda-terms of Exercise 74 behave as expected.

Exercise 77. In continuation of Exercise 76, CPS transform your closure-converted call-by-name evaluation function, and verify that the lambda-terms of Exercise 74 behave as expected.

Exercise 78. For the sake of comparison, CPS-transform *first* the call-by-name evaluation function from Exercise 75, using the optimized data type

```
datatype value = VAL_INT of int
                | VAL_FUN of thunk * (value -> value_or_error)
                             -> value_or_error
withtype thunk = (value -> value_or_error) -> value_or_error
```

(`thunk` would be `unit * (value -> value or error) -> value or error` in an unoptimized version), and then closure-convert it. Do you obtain the same result as in Exercise 77?
(Hint: You should.)

Exercise 79. Defunctionalize the closure-converted, CPS-transformed call-by-name evaluation function of Exercise 77, and compare the result with the Krivine machine [3, 25].

Exercise 80. Using the *call-by-name* CPS transformation [30,64], CPS transform the evaluation function of Appendix C. Do you obtain the same result as in Exercise 77?
(Hint: You should [45].)

Exercise 81. Again, using the *call-by-name* CPS transformation [30, 64], CPS transform the evaluation function of Appendix B. Do you obtain the same interpreter as in Exercise 78 before closure conversion?
(Hint: Again, you should [45].)

Exercise 82. Start from the call-by-name counterpart of Section 6 and, through refocusing, move towards an abstract machine and compare this abstract machine with the Krivine machine.
(Hint: See Section 3 of "A Concrete Framework for Environment Machines" [12].)

J   Further Projects

- The reader interested in other abstract machines is directed to "A Functional Correspondence between Evaluators and Abstract Machines [3].
- For a call-by-need counterpart of Section 6, the reader is directed to "A Functional Correspondence between Call-by-Need Evaluators and Lazy Abstract Machines" [4] and to Section 7 of "A Syntactic Correspondence between Context-Sensitive Calculi and Abstract Machines" [12].
- The reader interested in computational effects is directed to "A Functional Correspondence between Monadic Evaluators and Abstract Machines for Languages with Computational Effects" [5] and "A Syntactic Correspondence between Context-Sensitive Calculi and Abstract Machines" [12].
- The reader interested in the SECD machine is directed to "A Rational Deconstruction of Landin's SECD Machine" [23].
- The reader interested in the SECD machine and the J operator is directed to "A Rational Deconstruction of Landin's SECD Machine with the J Operator" [34].
- The reader interested in delimited continuations and the CPS hierarchy is directed to "An Operational Foundation for Delimited Continuations in the CPS Hierarchy" [11].

- The reader interested in Abadi and Cardelli's untyped calculus of objects [1] is directed to "Inter-deriving Semantic Artifacts for Object-Oriented Programming" [31], the extended version of which also features negational normalization for Boolean formulas.
- The reader interested in the semantics of the Scheme programming language is directed to Parts I and II of "Towards Compatible and Interderivable Semantic Specifications for the Scheme Programming Language" [14, 27].

Libraries for Generic Programming in Haskell

Johan Jeuring, Sean Leather, José Pedro Magalhães,
and Alexey Rodriguez Yakushev

Universiteit Utrecht, The Netherlands

Abstract. These lecture notes introduce libraries for datatype-generic programming in Haskell. We introduce three characteristic generic programming libraries: lightweight implementation of generics and dynamics, extensible and modular generics for the masses, and scrap your boilerplate. We show how to use them to use and write generic programs. In the case studies for the different libraries we introduce generic components of a medium-sized application which assists a student in solving mathematical exercises.

1 Introduction

In the development of software, *structuring data* plays an important role. Many programming methods and software development tools center around creating a datatype (or XML schema, UML model, class, grammar, etc.). Once the structure of the data has been designed, a software developer adds *functionality* to the datatypes. There is always some functionality that is specific for a datatype, and part of the reason why the datatype has been designed in the first place. Other functionality is similar or even the same on many datatypes, following common programming patterns. Examples of such patterns are:

- in a possibly large value of a complicated datatype (for example for representing the structure of a company), applying a given action at all occurrences of a particular constructor (e.g., adding or updating zip codes at all occurrences of street addresses) while leaving the rest of the value unchanged;
- serializing a value of a datatype, or comparing two values of a datatype for equality, functionality that depends only on the *structure* of the datatype;
- adapting data access functions after a datatype has changed, something that often involves modifying large amounts of existing code.

Generic programming addresses these high-level programming patterns. We also use the term datatype-generic programming [Gibbons, 2007] to distinguish the field from Java generics, Ada generic packages, generic programming in C++ STL, etc. Using generic programming, we can easily implement traversals in which a user is only interested in a small part of a possibly large value, functions which are naturally defined by induction on the structure of datatypes, and functions that automatically adapt to a changing datatype. Larger examples of generic programming include XML tools, testing frameworks, debuggers, and data conversion tools.

Often an instance of a datatype-generic program on a particular datatype is obtained by implementing the instance by hand, a boring and error-prone task, which reduces

P. Koopman and D. Swierstra (Eds.): AFP 2008, LNCS 5832, pp. 165–229, 2009.

programmers' productivity. Some programming languages provide standard implementations of basic datatype-generic programs such as equality of two values and printing a value. In this case, the programs are integrated into the language, and cannot be extended or adapted. So, how can we define datatype-generic programs ourselves?

More than a decade ago the first programming languages appeared that supported the definition of datatype-generic programs. Using these programming languages it is possible to define a generic program, which can then be used on a particular datatype without further work. Although these languages allow us to define our own generic programs, they have never grown out of the research prototype phase, and most cannot be used anymore.

The rich type system of Haskell allows us to write a number of datatype-generic programs in the language itself. The power of classes, constructor classes, functional dependencies, generalized algebraic datatypes, and other advanced language constructs of Haskell is impressive, and since 2001 we have seen at least 10 proposals for generic programming libraries in Haskell using one or more of these advanced constructs. Using a library instead of a separate programming language for generic programming has many advantages. The main advantages are that a user does not need a separate compiler for generic programs and that generic programs can be used out of the box. Furthermore, a library is much easier to ship, support, and maintain than a programming language, which makes the risk of using generic programs smaller. A library might be accompanied by tools that depend on non-standard language extensions, for example for generating embedding-projection pairs, but the core is Haskell. The loss of expressiveness compared with a generic programming language such as Generic Haskell is limited.

These lecture notes introduce generic programming in Haskell using generic programming libraries. We introduce several characteristic generic programming libraries, and we show how to write generic programs using these libraries. Furthermore, in the case studies for the different libraries we introduce generic components of a medium-sized application which assists a student in solving mathematical exercises. We have included several exercises in these lecture notes. The answers to these exercises can be found in the technical report accompanying these notes [Jeuring et al., 2008].

These notes are organised as follows. Section 2 puts generic programming into context. It introduces a number of variations on the theme of generics as well as demonstrates how each may be used in Haskell. Section 3 starts our focus on datatype-generic programming by discussing the world of datatypes supported by Haskell and common extensions. In Section 4, we introduce libraries for generic programming and briefly discuss the criteria we used to select the libraries covered in the following three sections. Section 5 starts the discussion of libraries with Lightweight Implementation of Generics and Dynamics (LIGD); however, we leave out the dynamics since we focus on generics in these lecture notes. Section 6 continues with a look at Extensible and Modular Generics for the Masses (EMGM), a library using the same view as LIGD but implemented with a different mechanism. Section 7 examines Scrap Your Boilerplate (SYB), a library implemented with combinators and quite different from LIGD and EMGM. After describing each library individually, we provide an abridged comparison of them in Section 8. In Section 9 we conclude with some suggested reading and some thoughts about the future of generic programming libraries.

2   Generic Programming in Context (and in Haskell)

Generic programming has developed as a technique for increasing the amount and scale of reuse in code while still preserving type safety. The term "generic" is highly overloaded in computer science; however, broadly speaking, most uses involve some sort of parametrisation. A generic program abstracts over the differences in separate but similar programs. In order to arrive at specific programs, one instantiates the parameter in various ways. It is the type of the parameter that distinguishes each variant of generic programming.

Gibbons [2007] lists seven categories of generic programming. In this section, we revisit these with an additional twist: we look at how each may be implemented in Haskell.

Each of the following sections is titled according to the type of the parameter of the generic abstraction. In each, we provide a description of that particular form of generics along with an example of how to apply the technique.

2.1   Value

The most basic form of generic programming is to parametrise a computation by values. The idea goes by various names in programming languages (procedure, subroutine, function, etc.), and it is a fundamental element in mathematics. While a function is not often considered under the definition of "generic," it is perfectly reasonable to model other forms of genericity as functions. The generalization is given by the function $g(x)$ in which a generic component g is parametrised by some entity x. Instantiation of the generic component is then analogous to application of a function.

Functions come naturally in Haskell. For example, here is function that takes two boolean values as arguments and determines their basic equality.

$$eq_{Bool} :: \mathsf{Bool} \rightarrow \mathsf{Bool} \rightarrow \mathsf{Bool}$$
$$eq_{Bool}\ x\ y = (not\ x \wedge not\ y) \vee (x \wedge y)$$

We take this opportunity to introduce a few themes used in these lecture notes. We use a stylized form of Haskell that is not necessarily what one would type into a file. Here, we add a subscript, which can simply be typed, and use the symbols $(\wedge)$ and $(\vee)$, which translate directly to the standard operators (&&) and (||).

As much as possible, we attempt to use the same functions for our examples, so that the similarities or differences are more evident. Equality is one such running example used throughout the text.

2.2   Function

If a function is a first-class citizen in a programming language, parametrisation of one function by another function is exactly the same as parametrisation by value. However, we explicitly mention this category because it enables abstraction over control flow. The full power of function parameters can be seen in the *higher-order functions* of languages such as Haskell and ML.

Suppose we have functions defining the logical conjunction and disjunction of boolean values.

> *and* :: List Bool → Bool
> *and Nil*   = *True*
> *and (Cons p ps)* = *p* ∧ *and ps*

> *or* :: List Bool → Bool
> *or Nil*   = *False*
> *or (Cons p ps)* = *p* ∨ *or ps*

These two functions exhibit the same recursive pattern. To abstract from this pattern, we abstract over the differences between *and* and *or* using a higher-order function. The pattern that is extracted is known in the Haskell standard library as *foldr* ("fold from the right").

> *foldr* :: (a → b → b) → b → List a → b
> *foldr f n Nil*   = *n*
> *foldr f n (Cons x xs)* = *f x (foldr f n xs)*

The *foldr* captures the essence of the recursion in the *and* and *or* by accepting parameters for the *Cons* and *Nil* cases. We can then redefine *and* and *or* in simpler terms using *foldr*.

> *and* = *foldr* (∧) *True*
> *or* = *foldr* (∨) *False*

2.3 Type

Commonly known as *polymorphism*, genericity by type refers to both type abstractions (types parametrised by other types) and polymorphic functions (functions with polymorphic types).

Haskell[1] has excellent support for parametrised datatypes and polymorphic functions. The canonical example of the former is List:

> **data** List a = *Nil* | *Cons* a (List a)

List a is a datatype parametrised by some type a. It is one of a class of datatypes often called "container" types because they provide structure for storing elements of some arbitrary type.

A typical polymorphic function is *length*:

> *length* :: List a → Int
> *length Nil*   = 0
> *length (Cons x xs)* = 1 + *length xs*

---

[1] Specifically, Haskell supports *parametric polymorphism*. There are other flavors of polymorphism such as subtype polymorphism that we elide.

The function *length* can be applied to a value of type List a, and it will return the number of a elements.

An important point to note about parametrised datatypes and polymorphic functions is that they have no knowledge of the parameter. We later discuss other forms of genericity that support increased amounts of information about the parameter.

2.4 Interface

A generic program may abstract over a given set of requirements. In this case, a specific program can only be instantiated by parameters that conform to these requirements, and the generic program remains unaware of any unspecified aspects. Gibbons calls the set of required operations the "structure" of the parameter; however, we think this may easily be confused with generics by the shape of a datatype (in Section 2.7). Instead, we use *interface* as the set of requirements needed for instantiation.

Haskell supports a form of interface using type classes and constraints on functions [Wadler and Blott, 1989], which we illustrate with equality. Equality is not restricted to a single type, and in fact, many different datatypes support equality. But unlike the polymorphic *length*, equality on lists for example requires inspection of the elements. The code below defines the class of types that support equality $((==))$ and inequality $((/=))$.

```
class Eq a where
    (==), (/=) :: a → a → Bool
    a == b = not (a /= b)
    a /= b = not (a == b)
```

This type class definition includes the types of the interface operations and some (optional) default implementations. For a datatype such as List a to support the operations in the class *Eq*, we create an instance of it.

```
instance (Eq a) ⇒ Eq (List a) where
    Nil          == Nil          = True
    (Cons x xs)  == (Cons y ys)  = x == y ∧ xs == ys
                                 = False
```

Notice that our instance for List a requires an instance for a. This is indicated by the context $(Eq\ a) \Rightarrow$.

Methods in type classes and functions that use these methods require a context as well. Consider the observable type of the equality method.

$$(==) :: (Eq\ a) \Rightarrow a \to a \to Bool$$

This function specifies that the type parameter a must be an instance of the *Eq* class. In other words, the type substituted for a must implement the interface specified by *Eq*. This approach is called *ad-hoc polymorphism*. Relatedly, since each recursive call in the definition of the function $(==)$ may have a different type, we also describe the function as having *polymorphic recursion*.

2.5 Property

Gibbons expands the concept of generic programming to include the specifications of programs. These *properties* are "generic" in the sense that they may hold for multiple implementations. Properties may be informally or formally defined, and depending on the language or tool support, they may be encoded into a program, used as part of the testing process, or simply appear as text.

A simple example of a property can be found by looking at the methods of the Eq type class defined in Section 2.4: a programmer with a classical view on logic would expect that $x \quad y \equiv not\ (x\ /\ y)$. This property should hold for all instances of Eq to ensure that an instance only needs to define one or the other. However, Haskell's type system provides no guarantee of this. The functions ( ) and (/) are provided as separate methods to allow for the definition of either (for simplicity) or both (for optimization), and the compiler cannot verify the above relationship. This informal specification relies on programmers implementing the instances of Eq such that the property holds.

There are other examples of properties, such as the well-known monad laws [Wadler, 1990], but many of them cannot be implemented directly in Haskell. It is possible, however, to look at a property as an extension of an interface from Section 2.4 if we allow for evaluation in the interface. This can be done in a language with a more expressive type system such as Coq [Bertot and Castéran, 2004] or Agda [Norell, 2007].

2.6 Program Representation

There are numerous techniques in which one program is parametrised by the representation of another program (or its own). This area includes:

- Code generation, such as the generation of parsers and lexical analysers. Happy [Marlow and Gill, 1997] and Alex [Dornan et al., 2003] are Haskell programs for parser generation and lexical analysis, respectively.
- Reflection or the ability of a program to observe and modify its own structure and behavior. Reflection has been popularized by programming languages that support some dynamic type checking such as Java [Forman and Danforth, 1999], but some attempts have also been made in Haskell [Lämmel and Peyton Jones, 2004].
- Templates in C++ [Alexandrescu, 2001] and multi-stage programming [Taha, 1999] are other techniques.

Gibbons labels these ideas as genericity by stage; however, some techniques such as reflection do not immediately lend themselves to being staged. We think this category of is better described as *metaprogramming* or generic programming in which the parameter is the representation of some program.

Partly inspired by C++ templates and the multi-stage programming language MetaML [Sheard, 1999], Template Haskell provides a metaprogramming extension to Haskell 98 [Sheard and Peyton Jones, 2002].

We introduce the concept with an example of writing selection functions for tuples of different arities. The standard library provides $fst :: (a, b) \rightarrow a$ and $snd :: (a, b) \rightarrow b$ since pairs are the most common form of tuples, but for triples, quadruples, etc., we need to write a new function each time. In other words, we want to automatically generate functions such as these:

$$fst3 \;=\; \lambda(x,\; ,\;)\;\;\; \to x$$
$$snd4 = \lambda(\; ,x,\; ,\;) \to x$$

Using Template Haskell, we can write:

$$fst3 \;=\; \$\, (sel\; 1\; 3)$$
$$snd4 = \$\, (sel\; 2\; 4)$$

This demonstrates the use of the "splice" syntax, $\$(...)$, to evaluate the enclosed expression at compile time. Each call to $\$(sel\; i\; n)$ is expanded to a function that selects the i-th component of a n-tuple. Consider the following implementation[2]:

$$sel :: \mathsf{Int} \to \mathsf{Int} \to \mathsf{ExpQ}$$

$$sel\; i\; n = lamE\; [pat]\; body$$
$$\textbf{where}\; pat\;\; = tupP\; (map\; varP\; vars)$$
$$\qquad\quad body = varE\; (vars \;!!\; (i-1))$$
$$\qquad\quad vars\;\; = [mkName\; (\texttt{"a"} +\!\!+ show\; j)\; |\; j \leftarrow [1\mathinner{.\,.}n]]$$

Function sel creates an abstract syntax recipe of the form $\lambda(a_1, a_2, ..., ai, ..., an) \to ai$ with a lambda expression ($lamE$), a tuple pattern ($tupP$), variable patterns ($varP$), and a variable expression ($varE$).

Template Haskell is type-safe, and a well-typed program will not "go wrong" at run-time [Milner, 1978]. Initially, splice code is type-checked before compilation, and then the entire program is also type-checked after splice insertion. Compiling the example above may fail for reasons such as the function sel not type-checking or the generated code for $\$(sel\; i\; n)$ not type-checking.

Template Haskell has been explored for other uses in generic programming. Most notably, it is possible to prototype datatype-generic extensions to Haskell with Template Haskell [Norell and Jansson, 2004b].

2.7 Shape

Genericity by shape is, in fact, the focus of these notes. The shape parameter refers to the shape or structure of data. Broadly speaking, if all data has a common underlying set of structural elements, we can write functions that work with those elements. Thus, such functions abstract over any values that can be described by the same shape.

We return again to the example of equality. So far, we have seen two different implementations, one for Bool and one for List, while in fact equality can be defined once generically for many datatypes. In Haskell this generic definition is used when a datatype is annotated with **deriving** Eq, but to give you a taste of how this might work in a library, let us look at the shape of some types.

---

[2] The code for sel is derived from the original example [Sheard and Peyton Jones, 2002] with modifications to simplify it and to conform to the *Language.Haskell.TH* library included with GHC 6.8.2.

Intuitively, we can visualize the structural elements by reviewing the syntax for the declaration of the List datatype.

data List a $= Nil \mid Cons$ a (List a)

First, a List value is either a Nil or a $Cons$. This choice between constructors is called a *sum* and denoted by the $+$ symbol in our visualization. Second, each constructor is applied to zero or more arguments. The Nil constructor takes no parameters and has the special designator of *unit* represented by $\mathbb{1}$. $Cons$, on the other hand, is applied to two arguments. We use a *product*, indicated by the symbol $\times$, in this case. The representation for List as a whole appears as follows:

type List° a $= \mathbb{1} + (a \times$ List a$)$

We have now stripped the datatype definition to some basic syntactic elements. Not only can these elements describe the simple List datatype, they also support more complex examples:

data Map k a $= Tip \mid Bin$ Int k a (Map k a) (Map k a)
type Map° k a $= \mathbb{1} + ($Int $\times$ (k $\times$ (a $\times$ (Map k a $\times$ Map k a)))$)$

The Map datatype from the standard libraries introduces a few new aspects of our syntax. Namely, we can reference other types by name (Int), and if a constructor has more than two arguments (Bin), it is represented using a right-associative, nested, product. Furthermore, we reuse the type Map itself in the representation for Map.

The *sum of products* view described above can be used to inductively define functions. We describe the specifics of this for each library in more detail, but for a taste of this process, we define a function in Generic Haskell [Löh, 2004], a language that extends Haskell with syntactic support for datatype-generic programming. Here is equality defined as a generic function:

$$eq\{|a :: \star|\} :: (eq\{|a|\}) \Rightarrow a \rightarrow a \rightarrow \text{Bool}$$

$$
\begin{array}{llll}
eq\{|\text{Int}|\} & x & y & = eq_{Int}\ x\ y \\
eq\{|\text{Char}|\} & c & d & = eq_{Char}\ c\ d \\
eq\{|\text{Unit}|\} & Unit & Unit & = True \\
eq\{|a + b|\} & (Inl\ x) & (Inl\ y) & = eq\{|a|\}\ x\ y \\
eq\{|a + b|\} & (Inr\ x) & (Inr\ y) & = eq\{|b|\}\ x\ y \\
eq\{|a + b|\} & & & = False \\
eq\{|a \times b|\} & (x_1 \times y_1) & (x_2 \times y_2) & = eq\{|a|\}\ x_1\ x_2 \wedge eq\{|b|\}\ y_1\ y_2
\end{array}
$$

Notice how $eq\{|a :: \star|\}$ uses pattern matching on the same structural elements introduced above, which are now types enclosed in $\{||\}$, to perform case analysis. Looking at each case, we see that the type parameter (e.g. a $\times$ b) enables the expansion of the value-level structure of the arguments (e.g. $x_1 \times y_1$), thus permitting us to write a separate test of equality specific to each element (e.g. $eq\{|a|\}\ x_1\ x_2 \wedge eq\{|b|\}\ y_1\ y_2$). We explore these ideas further in the discussion on the libraries LIGD (Section 5) and EMGM (Section 6). For more information on defining generic functions in Generic Haskell, see Löh [2004] and Hinze and Jeuring [2003a,b]. Also note that Generic Haskell is not the only language extension to datatype-generic programming. A comparison of approaches can be found in Hinze et al. [2007].

There are a number of generic views other than the sum of products. For example, we may regard a datatype as a fixed point, allowing us to make all recursion in the datatype explicit. Another example is the spine view that we describe in relation to the SYB library (Section 7). For a more in-depth study of generic views, refer to [Holdermans et al., 2006].

In this section, we introduced a variety of techniques that fall under the heading of generic programming; however, this is assuredly not a complete list. For example, research into types that are parametrised by values, often called dependent types, may be also considered "generic." Instead of a thorough description, however, this background should make clear where these lecture notes fit in the broader context of generic programming.

In the next section, we provide more background on the fundamental component of datatype-generic programming: the datatype.

3   The World of Haskell Datatypes

Datatypes play a central role in programming in Haskell. Solving a problem often consists of designing a datatype, and defining functionality on that datatype. Haskell offers a powerful construct for defining datatypes: **data**. Haskell also offers two other constructs: **type** to introduce type synonyms and **newtype**, a restricted version of **data**.

Datatypes come in many variations: we have finite, regular, nested, and many more kinds of datatypes. This section introduces many of these variations of datatypes by example, and is an updated version of a similar section in Hinze and Jeuring [2003b]. Not all datatypes are pure Haskell 98, some require extensions to Haskell. Many of these extensions are supported by most Haskell compilers, some only by GHC. On the way, we explain kinds and show how they are used to classify types. For most of the datatypes we introduce, we define an equality function. As we will see, the definitions of equality on the different datatypes follow a similar pattern. This pattern will also be used to define generic programs for equality in later sections covering LIGD (Section 5) and EMGM (Section 6).

3.1   Monomorphic Datatypes

We start our journey through datatypes with lists containing values of a particular type. For example, in the previous section we have defined the datatype of lists of booleans:

$$\textbf{data}\ \text{List}_B = \text{Nil}_B \mid \text{Cons}_B\ \text{Bool}\ \text{List}_B$$

We define a new datatype, called List_B, which has two kinds of values: an empty list (represented by the constructor Nil_B), or a list consisting of a boolean value in front of another List_B. This datatype is the same as Haskell's predefined list datatype containing booleans, with $[\,]$ and $(:)$ as constructors. Since the datatype List_B does not take any type parameters, it has base kind $\star$. Other examples of datatypes of kind $\star$ are Int, Char, etc.

Here is the equality function on this datatype:

$$eq_{List_B} :: List_B \rightarrow List_B \rightarrow Bool$$

$$
\begin{aligned}
eq_{List_B} \; Nil_B \qquad\qquad Nil_B &= True \\
eq_{List_B} \; (Cons_B \; b_1 \; l_1) \; (Cons_B \; b_2 \; l_2) &= eq_{Bool} \; b_1 \; b_2 \wedge eq_{List_B} \; l_1 \; l_2 \\
eq_{List_B} \qquad\qquad\qquad\qquad &= False
\end{aligned}
$$

Two empty lists are equal, and two nonempty lists are equal if their head elements are the same (which we check using equality on Bool) and their tails are equal. An empty list and a nonempty list are unequal.

3.2   Parametric Polymorphic Datatypes

We abstract from the datatype of booleans in the type $List_B$ to obtain parametric polymorphic lists.

data List a $= Nil \mid Cons$ a (List a)

Compared with $List_B$, the List a datatype has a different structure: the kind of List is $\star \rightarrow \star$. Kinds classify types, just as types classify values. A kind can either be $\star$ (base kind) or $\kappa \rightarrow \nu$, where κ and ν are kinds. In Haskell, only the base kind is inhabited, which means there are only values of types of kind $\star$. Since List takes a base type as argument, it has the functional kind $\star \rightarrow \star$. The type variable a must be a base type since it appears as a value (as first argument to the $Cons$ constructor). In this way, a type of functional kind (such as List) can be fully-applied to create a type of base kind (such as List Int).

Equality on List is almost the same as equality on $List_B$.

$$eq_{List} :: (a \rightarrow a \rightarrow Bool) \rightarrow List \; a \rightarrow List \; a \rightarrow Bool$$

$$
\begin{aligned}
eq_{List} \; eq_a \; Nil \qquad\qquad Nil &= True \\
eq_{List} \; eq_a \; (Cons \; x_1 \; l_1) \; (Cons \; x_2 \; l_2) &= eq_a \; x_1 \; x_2 \wedge eq_{List} \; eq_a \; l_1 \; l_2 \\
eq_{List} \qquad\qquad\qquad\qquad &= False
\end{aligned}
$$

The only difference with equality on $List_B$ is that we need to have some means of determining equality on the elements of the list, so we need an additional equality function of type $(a \rightarrow a \rightarrow Bool)$ as parameter[3].

3.3   Families and Mutually Recursive Datatypes

A family of datatypes is a set of datatypes that may use each other. We can define a simplified representation of a system of linear equations using a non-recursive family of datatypes. A system of linear equations is a list of equations, each consisting of a pair linear expressions. For example, here is a system of three equations.

---

[3] Using Haskell's type classes, this would correspond to replacing the type of the first argument in the type of eq_{List} by an Eq a $\Rightarrow$ constraint. The class constraint is later transformed by the compiler into an additional argument of type $(a \rightarrow a \rightarrow Bool)$ to the function.

$$x - \quad y \quad\; = 1$$
$$x + \quad y + z = 7$$
$$2\,x + 3\,y + z = 5$$

For simplicity, we assume linear expressions are values of a datatype for arithmetic expressions, Expr a. An arithmetic expression abstracts over the type of constants, typically an instance of the *Num* class, and is a variable, a literal, or the addition, subtraction, multiplication, or division of two arithmetic expressions.

```
type LinearSystem = List LinearExpr
data LinearExpr   = Equation (Expr Int) (Expr Int)
infixl 6 ×, ÷
infixl 5 +, −
data Expr a = Var String
            | Lit a
            | Expr a + Expr a
            | Expr a − Expr a
            | Expr a × Expr a
            | Expr a ÷ Expr a
```

The equality function eq_{Expr} for LinearSystem is straightforward and omitted.

Datatypes in Haskell may also be mutually recursive, as can be seen in the following example. A forest is either empty or a tree followed by a forest, and a tree is either empty or a node of a forest:

```
data Tree a   = Empty | Node a        (Forest a)
data Forest a = Nil    | Cons (Tree a) (Forest a)
```

Defining the equality function for these datatypes amounts to defining the equality function for each datatype separately. The result is a set of mutually recursive functions:

$$eq_{Tree} :: (a \rightarrow a \rightarrow Bool) \rightarrow Tree\ a \rightarrow Tree\ a \rightarrow Bool$$
$$eq_{Tree}\ eq_a\ Empty \qquad\;\; Empty \qquad\;\; = True$$
$$eq_{Tree}\ eq_a\ (Node\ a_1\ f_1)\ (Node\ a_2\ f_2) = eq_a\ a_1\ a_2 \wedge eq_{Forest}\ eq_a\ f_1\ f_2$$
$$eq_{Tree} \qquad\qquad\qquad\qquad\qquad\qquad\;\; = False$$

$$eq_{Forest} :: (a \rightarrow a \rightarrow Bool) \rightarrow Forest\ a \rightarrow Forest\ a \rightarrow Bool$$
$$eq_{Forest}\ eq_a\ Nil \qquad\qquad Nil \qquad\quad = True$$
$$eq_{Forest}\ eq_a\ (Cons\ t_1\ f_1)\ (Cons\ t_2\ f_2) = eq_{Tree}\ eq_a\ t_1\ t_2 \wedge eq_{Forest}\ eq_a\ f_1\ f_2$$
$$eq_{Forest} \qquad\qquad\qquad\qquad\qquad\qquad\; = False$$

Note that although the type LinearSystem defined previously uses several other types, it is not mutually recursive: Expr a is at the end of the hierarchy and is defined only in terms of itself.

3.4 Higher-Order Kinded Datatypes

A datatype uses higher-order kinds if it is parametrized over a variable of functional kind. All the parametric datatypes we've seen previously took parameters of kind $\star$. Consider the following datatype, which represents a subset of logic expressions.

> **data** $Logic_S$ = Lit Bool
> | Not $Logic_S$
> | Or $Logic_S$ $Logic_S$

Suppose we now want to use the fact that disjunction is associative. For this, we can choose to encode sequences of disjunctions by means of a list. We represent our $Logic_S$ datatype as:

> **data** $Logic_L$ = Lit Bool
> | Not $Logic_L$
> | Or (List $Logic_L$)

We can then abstract from the container type List, which contains the subexpressions, by introducing a type argument for it.

> **data** $Logic_F$ f = Lit Bool
> | Not ($Logic_F$ f)
> | Or (f ($Logic_F$ f))

We have introduced a type variable, and so $Logic_F$ does not have kind $\star$ as $Logic_L$. However, its kind is also not $\star \rightarrow \star$, as we have seen previously in, for instance, the List datatype, because the type argument that $Logic_F$ expects is not a base type, but a "type transformer". We can see in the Or constructor that f is applied to an argument. The kind of $Logic_F$ is thus: $(\star \rightarrow \star) \rightarrow \star$. This datatype is a higher-order kinded datatype.

To better understand abstraction over container types, consider the following type:

> **type** $Logic'_L$ = $Logic_F$ List

Modulo undefined values, $Logic'_L$ is isomorphic to $Logic_L$. The type argument of $Logic_F$ describes which "container" will be used for the elements of the Or case.

Defining equality for the $Logic'_L$ datatype is simple:

$$eq_{Logic'_L} :: Logic'_L \rightarrow Logic'_L \rightarrow Bool$$
$$eq_{Logic'_L} (Lit\ x_1)\ (Lit\ x_2) = eq_{Bool}\ x_1\ x_2$$
$$eq_{Logic'_L} (Not\ x_1)\ (Not\ x_2) = eq_{Logic'_L}\ x_1\ x_2$$
$$eq_{Logic'_L} (Or\ l_1)\ (Or\ l_2) =$$
$$\quad length\ l_1 \quad length\ l_2 \wedge and\ (zipWith\ eq_{Logic'_L}\ l_1\ l_2)$$
$$eq_{Logic'_L} \qquad\qquad\qquad = False$$

Note that we use the $zipWith :: (a \rightarrow b \rightarrow c) \rightarrow$ List a $\rightarrow$ List b $\rightarrow$ List c function, because we know the container is the list type.

The $\mathsf{Logic_F}$ type requires a somewhat more complicated equality function.

$$eq_{Logic_F} :: (\;(\mathsf{Logic_F}\ f \rightarrow \mathsf{Logic_F}\ f \rightarrow \mathsf{Bool}) \rightarrow$$
$$f\ (\mathsf{Logic_F}\ f) \rightarrow f\ (\mathsf{Logic_F}\ f) \rightarrow \mathsf{Bool}) \rightarrow$$
$$\mathsf{Logic_F}\ f \rightarrow \mathsf{Logic_F}\ f \rightarrow \mathsf{Bool}$$

$$eq_{Logic_F}\ eq_f\ (Lit\ x_1)\ (Lit\ x_2)\ = eq_{Bool}\ x_1\ x_2$$
$$eq_{Logic_F}\ eq_f\ (Not\ x_1)\ (Not\ x_2) = eq_{Logic_F}\ eq_f\ x_1\ x_2$$
$$eq_{Logic_F}\ eq_f\ (Or\ x_1)\ (Or\ x_2)\ = eq_f\ (eq_{Logic_F}\ eq_f)\ x_1\ x_2$$
$$eq_{Logic_F}\qquad\qquad\qquad\qquad\qquad = False$$

The complexity comes from the need for a higher-order function that itself contains a higher-order function. The function eq_f provides equality on the abstracted container type f, and it needs an equality for its element type $\mathsf{Logic_F}$ f.

We can specialize this to equality on $\mathsf{Logic_F}$ List as follows:

$$eq_{Logic_{F,List}} :: \mathsf{Logic_F}\ \mathsf{List} \rightarrow \mathsf{Logic_F}\ \mathsf{List} \rightarrow \mathsf{Bool}$$
$$eq_{Logic_{F,List}} = eq_{Logic_F}\ (\lambda f\ l_1\ l_2 \rightarrow and\ (zipWith\ f\ l_1\ l_2))$$

3.5 Nested Datatypes

A *regular* data type is a possibly recursive, parametrised type whose recursive occurrences do not involve a change of type parameters. All the datatypes we have introduced so far are regular. However, it is also possible to define so-called nested datatypes [Bird and Meertens, 1998], in which recursive occurrences of the datatype may have other type arguments than the datatype being defined. Perfectly balanced binary trees are an example of such a datatype.

data Perfect a $= Leaf$ a $\mid Node$ (Perfect (a, a))

Any value of this datatype is a full binary tree in which all leaves are at the same depth. This is attained by using the pair constructor in the recursive call for the *Node* constructor. An example of such tree is:

$$perfect = Node\ (Node\ (Node\ (Leaf\ (((1,2),(3,4)),((5,6),(7,8))))))$$

Here is the equality function on Perfect:

$$eq_{Perfect} :: (a \rightarrow a \rightarrow \mathsf{Bool}) \rightarrow \mathsf{Perfect}\ a \rightarrow \mathsf{Perfect}\ a \rightarrow \mathsf{Bool}$$

$$eq_{Perfect}\ eq_a\ (Leaf\ x_1)\ (Leaf\ x_2)\ = eq_a\ x_1\ x_2$$
$$eq_{Perfect}\ eq_a\ (Node\ x_1)\ (Node\ x_2) = eq_{Perfect}\ (eq_{Pair}\ eq_a)\ x_1\ x_2$$
$$eq_{Perfect}\qquad\qquad\qquad\qquad\qquad = False$$

$$eq_{Pair} :: (a \rightarrow a \rightarrow \mathsf{Bool}) \rightarrow (a, a) \rightarrow (a, a) \rightarrow \mathsf{Bool}$$
$$eq_{Pair}\ eq_a\ (x_1, x_2)\ (y_1, y_2) = eq_a\ x_1\ x_2 \wedge eq_a\ y_1\ y_2$$

This definition is again very similar to the equality on datatypes we have introduced before. In our case, the container type is the pair of two values of the same type, so in the *Node* case we use equality on this type (eq_{Pair}).

3.6 Existentially Quantified Datatypes

Many of the datatypes we have seen take arguments, and in the type of the constructors of these datatypes, those type arguments are universally quantified. For example, the constructor *Cons* of the datatype List a has type a → List a → List a for all types a. However, we can also use existential types, which "hide" a type variable that only occurs under a constructor. Consider the following example:

data Dynamic = ∀a . *Dyn* (Rep a) a

The type Dynamic encapsulates a type a and its representation, a value of type Rep a. We will encounter the datatype Rep a later in these lecture notes (Section 5), where it is used to convert between datatypes and their run-time representations. Despite the use of the ∀ symbol, the type variable a is said to be existentially quantified because it is only available inside the constructor—Dynamic has kind ⋆. Existential datatypes are typically used to encapsulate some type with its corresponding actions: in the above example, the only thing we can do with a Dynamic is to inspect its representation. Other important applications of existentially quantified datatypes include the implementation of abstract datatypes, which encapsulate a type together with a set of operations. Existential datatypes are not part of the Haskell 98 standard, but they are a fairly common extension.

Since an existentially quantified datatype may hide the type of some of its components, the definition of equality may be problematic. If we cannot inspect a component, we cannot compare it. Conversely, we can only compare two values of an existentially quantified datatype if the operations provided by the constructor allow us to compare them. For example, if the only operation provided by the constructor is a string representation of the value, we can only compare the string representation of two values, but not the values themselves. Therefore equality can only be defined as the equality of the visible components of the existentially quantified datatype.

3.7 Generalized Algebraic Datatypes

Another powerful extension to the Haskell 98 standard are generalized algebraic datatypes (GADTs). A GADT is a datatype in which different constructors may have related but different result types. Consider the following example, where we combine the datatypes Logic$_s$ and Expr shown before in a datatype for statements:

```
data Stat a where
    Val   :: Expr Int     → Stat (Expr Int)
    Term :: Logicₛ        → Stat Logicₛ
    If    :: Stat Logicₛ → Stat a → Stat a → Stat a
    Write :: Stat a       → Stat ()
    Seq   :: Stat a       → Stat b → Stat b
```

The new aspect here is the ability to give each constructor a different result type of the form Stat x. This has the advantage that we can describe the type of the different constructors more precisely. For example, the type of the *If* constructor now says that the first argument of the *If* returns a logic statement, and the statements returned in the "then" and "else" branches may be of any type, as long as they have the same type.

Defining equality of two statements is still a matter of repeating similar code:

$$eq_{Stat} :: \mathsf{Stat\ a} \rightarrow \mathsf{Stat\ b} \rightarrow \mathsf{Bool}$$

$$
\begin{aligned}
eq_{Stat}\ (Val\ x_1) \quad & (Val\ x_2) && = eq_{Expr}\ (\quad)\ x_1\ x_2 \\
eq_{Stat}\ (Term\ x_1) \quad & (Term\ x_2) && = eq_{Logic}\ x_1\ x_2 \\
eq_{Stat}\ (If\ x_1\ x_2\ x_3) & (If\ x_1'\ x_2'\ x_3') && = eq_{Stat}\ x_1\ x_1' \wedge eq_{Stat}\ x_2\ x_2' \wedge eq_{Stat}\ x_3\ x_3' \\
eq_{Stat}\ (Write\ x_1) \quad & (Write\ x_2) && = eq_{Stat}\ x_1\ x_2 \\
eq_{Stat}\ (Seq\ x_1\ x_2) \quad & (Seq\ x_1'\ x_2') && = eq_{Stat}\ x_1\ x_1' \wedge eq_{Stat}\ x_2\ x_2' \\
eq_{Stat} \quad & && = False
\end{aligned}
$$

We have shown many varieties of datatypes and the example of the equality function, which offers functionality needed on many datatypes. We have seen that we can define the equality functions ourselves, but the code quickly becomes repetitive and tedious. Furthermore, if a datatype changes, the definition of the equality function has to change accordingly. This is not only inefficient and time-consuming but also error-prone. The generic programming libraries introduced in the rest of these lecture notes will solve this problem.

4 Libraries for Generic Programming

Recently, an extensive comparison of generic programming libraries has been performed [Rodriguez et al., 2008b, Rodriguez, 2009]. In these notes we will discuss three of those libraries: a Lightweight Implementation of Generics and Dynamics, Extensible and Modular Generics for the Masses, and Scrap Your Boilerplate. We focus on these three libraries for a number of reasons. First, we think these libraries are representative examples: one library explicitly passes a type representation as argument to a generic function, another relies on the type class mechanism, and the third is traversal- and combinator-based. Furthermore, all three have been used for a number of generic functions, and are relatively easy to use for parts of the lab exercise given in these notes. Finally, all three of them can express many generic functions; the Uniplate library [Mitchell and Runciman, 2007] is also representative and easy to use, but Scrap Your Boilerplate is more powerful.

The example libraries show different ways to implement the essential ingredients of generic programming libraries. Support for generic programming consists of three essential ingredients [Hinze and Löh, 2009]: a run-time type representation, a generic view on data, and support for overloading.

A *type-indexed function* (TIF) is a function that is defined on every type of a family of types. We say that the types in this family index the TIF, and we call the type family a universe. The run-time representation of types determines the universe on which we can pattern match in a type-indexed function. The larger this universe, the more types the function can be applied to.

A type-indexed function only works on the universe on which it is defined. If a new datatype is defined, the type-indexed function cannot be used on this new datatype.

There are two ways to make it work on the new datatype. A non-generic extension of the universe of a TIF requires a type-specific, ad-hoc case for the new datatype. A generic extension (or a generic view) of a universe of a TIF requires to express the new datatype in terms of the universe of the TIF so that the TIF can be used on the new datatype without a type-specific case. A TIF combined with a generic extension is called a *generic function*.

An overloaded function is a function that analyses types to exhibit type-specific behavior. Type-indexed and generic functions are special cases of overloaded functions. Many generic functions even have type-specific behavior: lists are printed in a non-generic way by the generic pretty-printer defined by **deriving** *Show* in Haskell.

In the next sections we will see how to encode these basic ingredients in the three libraries we introduce. For each library, we present its run-time type representation, the generic view on data and how overloading is achieved.

Each of the libraries encodes the basic ingredients in a particular way. However, an encoding of a generic view on datatypes is largely orthogonal to an encoding of overloading, and we can achieve variants of the libraries described in the following sections by combining the basic ingredients differently [Hinze and Löh, 2009].

5   Lightweight Implementation of Generics and Dynamics

In this section, we discuss our first library for datatype-generic programming in Haskell. The library, Lightweight Implementation of Generics and Dynamics [Cheney and Hinze, 2002] or LIGD, serves as a good introduction to many of the concepts necessary for generic programming in a library. For example, it uses a simple encoding of the structural elements for the sum-of-products view that we saw in Section 2.7. Also, LIGD can represent many of the datatypes described in Section 3 with the exceptions being existentially quantified types and generalized algebraic datatypes (GADTs). Cheney and Hinze [2002] demonstrate a method for storing dynamically typed values (such as the one in Section 3.6); however, here we focus only on the generic representation. Lastly, we have updated the representation previously presented to use a GADT for type safety. As a side effect, it provides a good example of the material in Section 3.7.

To initiate our discussion of LIGD in Section 5.1, we first introduce an example function, in this case equality, to give a taste of how the library works. Then, Section 5.2 delves into the most basic representation used for LIGD. Next in Section 5.3, we show the important component necessary to support translating between the representation and Haskell datatypes. In Section 5.4, we describe how to implement a function differently for a certain type using overloading. Finally, Section 5.5 describes a number of useful generic functions (and how the library supports them), and Section 5.6 describes a particular case study using an exercise assistant.

5.1   An Example Function

The equality function in LIGD takes three arguments: the two values for comparison and a representation of the type of these values.

$eq :: \mathsf{Rep}\ a \rightarrow a \rightarrow a \rightarrow \mathsf{Bool}$

The function eq is defined by pattern matching on the type representation type Rep, which contains constructors for type representations, such as $RInt$, $RChar$, etc. It is defined in the following subsection.

$$
\begin{array}{llll}
eq \; (RInt \;\;) & i & j & = eq_{Int} \; i \; j \\
eq \; (RChar) & c & d & = eq_{Char} \; c \; d \\
eq \; (RUnit) & Unit & Unit & = True \\
eq \; (RSum \; r_a \; r_b) \; (L \; a_1) & (L \; a_2) & & = eq \; r_a \; a_1 \; a_2 \\
eq \; (RSum \; r_a \; r_b) \; (R \; b_1) & (R \; b_2) & & = eq \; r_b \; b_1 \; b_2 \\
eq \; (RSum \; r_a \; r_b) & & & = False \\
eq \; (RProd \; r_a \; r_b) \; (a_1 :\times: b_1) & (a_2 :\times: b_2) & = eq \; r_a \; a_1 \; a_2 \wedge eq \; r_b \; b_1 \; b_2
\end{array}
$$

Notice the similarities to the Generic Haskell function defined in Section 2.7. We have unit, sum, and product types, and the function is indexed by a representation of them, in this case the GADT Rep. By pattern matching on the constructors of Rep, the type checker is informed of the types of the remaining arguments, thus allowing us to pattern match on the structural elements.

Let us look at eq on a case-by-case basis. First, we have the primitive types Int and Char. These are not represented generically; rather, their values are stored, and we depend on the primitive functions eq_{Int} and eq_{Char}. Next, we have the collection of generic structural elements: unit, sum, and product. Two $Unit$ values are always equal (ignoring undefined values). A sum presents two alternatives, L and R. If the structure is the same, then we recursively check equality of the contents; otherwise, the alternatives cannot be equal. In the last case, a product is only equal to another product if their components are both equal.

5.2   Run-Time Type Representation

The eq function is a type-indexed function with a run-time type representation as its first argument — it need not appear in that position, but that is standard practice. The representation utilizes a few key types for structure.

```
data Unit  = Unit
data a :+: b = L a | R b
data a :×: b = a :×: b

infixr 5 :+:
infixr 6 :×:
```

These three types represent the values of the unit, sum, and product, and each is isomorphic to a standard Haskell datatype: Unit to $()$, $(:+:)$ to Either, and $(:\times:)$ to $(,)$. We use new datatypes so as to easily distinguish the world of type representations and world of types we want to represent.

The GADT Rep uses the above datatypes to represent the structure of types.

```
data Rep t where
    RInt   ::                     Rep Int
    RChar ::                      Rep Char
    RUnit ::                      Rep Unit
    RSum :: Rep a → Rep b → Rep (a :+: b)
    RProd :: Rep a → Rep b → Rep (a :×: b)
```

The constructors in Rep define the universe of LIGD: the structural elements together with basic types. Of course, there are other basic types such as Float and Double, but their use is similar, and we ignore them for brevity.

Cheney and Hinze [2002] developed the original LIGD before GADTs had been introduced into GHC. They instead used an existentially quantified datatype. Using a GADT has the advantage that case analysis on types can be implemented by pattern matching, a familiar construct to functional programmers.

5.3 Going Generic: Universe Extension

If we define a datatype, how can we use our type-indexed function on this new datatype? In LIGD (and many other generic programming libraries), the introduction of a new datatype does not require redefinition or extension of all existing generic functions. We merely need to describe the new datatype to the library, and all existing and future generic functions will be able to handle it.

In order to add arbitrary datatypes to the LIGD universe, we extend Rep with the *RType* constructor.

```
data Rep t where
    . . .
    RType :: EP d r → Rep r → Rep d
```

The type r provides the structure representation for some datatype d. This indicates that r is isomorphic to d, and the isomorphism is witnessed by an embedding-projection pair.

```
data EP d r = EP{from :: (d → r), to :: (r → d)}
```

The type EP is a pair of functions for converting d values to r values and back. An EP value should preserve the properties (as described in Section 2.5) that $from . to \equiv id$ and $to . from \equiv id$.

As mentioned in Section 2.7, we can represent constructors by nested sums and fields by nested products. To give an example, the isomorphic representation type for List a is:

```
type RList a = Unit :+: a :×: List a
```

The functions for the embedding-projection are:

$$from_{List} :: \text{List a} → \text{RList a}$$
$$from_{List} \ Nil \qquad\qquad = L \ Unit$$

$$from_{List} \; (Cons \; a \; as) \quad = R \; (a :\!\times\!: as)$$

$$to_{List} :: \mathsf{RList} \; a \to \mathsf{List} \; a$$
$$to_{List} \; (L \; Unit) \qquad = Nil$$
$$to_{List} \; (R \; (a :\!\times\!: as)) = Cons \; a \; as$$

The components of the pair are not embedded in the universe. The reason for this is that LIGD does not model recursion explicitly. This is sometimes called a *shallow representation*. In LIGD, a structure representation type is expressed in terms of the basic type representation types Int, Char, Unit, (:+:), and (:×:), and it may refer back to the type that is represented, argument types, and other types that have been represented. As a consequence, it is easy to represent mutually recursive datatypes as introduced in Section 3.3. Some generic programming libraries, such as PolyLib [Norell and Jansson, 2004a], use a *deep representation* of datatypes, in which the arguments of the structure representation types are embedded in the universe as well. This makes it easier to define some generic functions, but much harder to embed families of datatypes and mutually recursive datatypes. However, the very recent generic programming library multirec [Rodriguez et al., 2009] shows how to overcome this limitation.

To extend the universe to lists, we write a type representation using *RType*:

$$r_{List} :: \mathsf{Rep} \; a \to \mathsf{Rep} \; (\mathsf{List} \; a)$$
$$r_{List} \; r_a = RType \; (EP \; from_{List} \; to_{List})$$
$$\qquad\qquad (RSum \; RUnit \; (RProd \; r_a \; (r_{List} \; r_a)))$$

Given the definition of equality in Section 5.1, we can now extend it to support all representable types.

$$eq :: \mathsf{Rep} \; a \to a \to a \qquad \to \mathsf{Bool}$$
$$\dots$$
$$eq \; (RType \; ep \; r_a) \; t_1 \; t_2 = eq \; r_a \; (from \; ep \; t_1) \; (from \; ep \; t_2)$$

This case takes arguments t_1 and t_2 of some type a, transforms them to their structure representation using the embedding-projection pair *ep*, and applies equality to the new values with the representation r_a. Adding this line to the definition of *eq* turns it from a type-indexed function into a generic function.

Note that there are two ways to extend the LIGD universe to a type T. A non-generic extension involves adding a type-specific, ad-hoc constructor to Rep while a generic-extension requires a structure representation for T but no additional function cases. For example, support for Int is non-generic, and support for List is generic. The ability for generic extension is the feature that distinguishes generic functions from type-indexed functions.

Exercise 1. Give the representation of the datatypes Tree and Forest (defined in Section 3.3) for LIGD. ∎

5.4 Support for Overloading

Now that we have seen a very basic generic function, we will explore a few other concepts of generic programming in LIGD. A "show" function — serving the same purpose as the standard *show* function after **deriving** *Show* — illustrates how a library deals with constructor names and how it deals with ad-hoc cases for particular datatypes. First, we look at constructor names.

The type representation as developed so far does not contain any information about constructors, and hence we cannot define a useful generic show function using this representation. To solve this, we add an extra constructor to the structure representation type.

data Rep t **where**
    . . .
      RCon :: String $\rightarrow$ Rep a $\rightarrow$ Rep a

To use this extra constructor, we modify the representation of the datatype List to include the names of the constructors:

r_{List} :: Rep a $\rightarrow$ Rep (List a)

r_{List} r_a = *RType* (EP *from$_{List}$ to$_{List}$*)
                (*RSum* (*RCon* "Nil" *RUnit*)
                     (*RCon* "Cons" (*RProd* r_a (r_{List} r_a))))

Here is a simple definition for a generic show function:

```
show :: Rep t → t → String
show RInt            t          = show t
show RChar           t          = show t
show RUnit           t          = " "
show (RSum ra rb)    (L a)      = show ra a
show (RSum ra rb)    (R b)      = show rb b
show (RProd ra rb)   (a :×: b)  = show ra a ++ " " ++ show rb b
show (RType ep ra)   t          = show ra (from ep t)
show (RCon s RUnit)  t          = s
show (RCon s ra)     t          = "(" ++ s ++ " " ++ show ra t ++ ")"
```

As an example of how *show* works, given an input of (*Cons* 1 (*Cons* 2 *Nil*)), it outputs "(Cons 1 (Cons 2 Nil))". This definition works well generically, but the output for lists seems rather verbose. Suppose we want the list to appear in the comma-delimited fashion of the built-in Haskell lists, e.g. "[1,2]". We can do that with an ad-hoc case for List.

For each type for which we want a generic function to behave in a non-generic way, we extend Rep with a new constructor. For lists, we add *RList*:

data Rep t **where**
    . . .
      RList :: Rep a $\rightarrow$ Rep (List a)

Now we add the following lines to the generic show function to obtain type-specific behavior for the type List a.

$show$ (*RList* r_a) as = *show$_{List}$* (*show* r_a) *True* as

This case uses the following useful higher-order function:

$$show_{List} :: (a \rightarrow String) \rightarrow Bool \rightarrow List\ a \rightarrow String$$
$$show_{List}\ show_a = go$$
$$\textbf{where}\ go\ False\ Nil\qquad\ \ = "\ ]\ "$$
$$\qquad go\ True\ \ Nil\qquad\ \ = "\ [\ ]\ "$$
$$\qquad go\ False\ (Cons\ a\ as) = '\ ,\ '\ :\ rest\ a\ as$$
$$\qquad go\ True\ \ (Cons\ a\ as) = '\ [\ '\ :\ rest\ a\ as$$
$$\qquad rest\ a\ as = show_a\ a\ +\!\!+\ go\ False\ as$$

Now, $show\ (RList\ RInt)\ (Cons\ 1\ (Cons\ 2\ Nil))$ will print a nicely reduced list format. Note that the resulting generic function does not implement all details of **deriving** *Show*, but it does provide the core functionality.

We adapted the type representation Rep to obtain type-specific behavior in the *gshow* function. In general, it is undesirable to change a library in order to obtain special behavior for a single generic function on a particular datatype. Unfortunately, this is unavoidable in LIGD: for any generic function that needs special behavior on a particular datatype, we have to extend the type representation with that datatype. This means that users may decide to construct their own variant of the LIGD library, thus making both the library and the generic functions written using it less portable and reusable. Löh and Hinze [2006] show how to add *open datatypes* to Haskell. A datatype is open if it can be extended in a different module. In a language with open datatypes, the above problem with LIGD disappears.

5.5 Generic Functions in LIGD

This section introduces some more generic functions in LIGD, in particular some functions for which we need different type representations. We start with a simple example of a generic program.

Empty. We can generate an "empty" value for any datatype representable by LIGD. For example, the empty value of Int is 0, and the empty value of List is *Nil*. The *empty* function encodes these choices.

$$empty :: Rep\ a \rightarrow a$$
$$empty\ RInt\qquad\quad = 0$$
$$empty\ RChar\qquad\quad = '\backslash NUL'$$
$$empty\ RUnit\qquad\quad = Unit$$
$$empty\ (RSum\ r_a\ r_b) = L\ (empty\ r_a)$$
$$empty\ (RProd\ r_a\ r_b) = empty\ r_a\ :\times:\ empty\ r_b$$
$$empty\ (RType\ ep\ r_a) = to\ ep\ (empty\ r_a)$$
$$empty\ (RCon\ s\ r_a)\quad = empty\ r_a$$

Note that some of these choices are somewhat arbitrary. We might have used *minBound* for Int or R for sums.

An interesting aspect of this function is that it has a generic value as an output instead of an input. Up to now, we have only seen generic *consumer* functions or functions that accept generic arguments. A *producer* function constructs a generic value.

Exercise 2. Another generic function that constructs values of a datatype is the function *enum* :: Rep a $\rightarrow$ [a], which generates all values of a type. Many datatypes have infinitely many values, so it is important that function *enum* enumerates values fairly. Implement *enum* in LIGD.   ∎

Flatten. We previously introduced container datatypes in Sections 2.3 and 3.4. A useful function on a container datatype is a "flatten" function, which takes a value of the datatype and returns a list containing all values that it contains. For example, on the datatype Tree a, a flatten function would have type Tree a $\rightarrow$ [a]. We explain how to define this generic function in LIGD.

To implement *flatten*, we have to solve a number of problems. The first problem is describing its type. An incorrect attempt would be the following:

flatten :: Rep f $\rightarrow$ f a $\rightarrow$ [a]   -- WRONG!

where f abstracts over types of kind $\star \rightarrow \star$. Since Rep expects arguments of kind $\star$, this gives a kind error. Replacing Rep f by Rep (f a) would solve the kinding problem, but introduce another: how do we split the representation of a container datatype into a representation for f and a representation for a? Type application is implicit in the type representation Rep (f a). We solve this problem by creating a new structure representation type:

data Rep1 g a **where**
RInt1 ::	Rep1 g Int
RChar1 ::	Rep1 g Char
RUnit1 ::	Rep1 g Unit
RSum1 :: Rep1 g a $\rightarrow$ Rep1 g b $\rightarrow$	Rep1 g (a :+: b)
RProd1 :: Rep1 g a $\rightarrow$ Rep1 g b $\rightarrow$	Rep1 g (a :×: b)
RType1 :: EP d r $\rightarrow$ Rep1 g r $\rightarrow$	Rep1 g d
RCon1 :: String $\rightarrow$ Rep1 g a $\rightarrow$	Rep1 g a
RVar1 :: g a $\rightarrow$	Rep1 g a

This datatype is very similar to Rep, but there are two important differences. The first is that Rep1 is now parametrised over two types: a generic function signature g of kind $\star \rightarrow \star$ and a generic type a of kind $\star$. The second change is the addition of the *RVar1* constructor. The combination of the signature, represented by a **newtype**, and the constructor *RVar1* will be used to define the functionality at occurrences of the type argument in constructors.

Our initial challenge for defining *flatten* is to choose a signature (for g above). In general, it should be the most general signature possible, and in our case, we note that our function takes one generic value and produces a list of non-generic elements. Thus, we know the following: it is a function with one argument, that argument is generic, and the return value is a polymorphic list. From this information, we decide on the following **newtype** as our signature:

> **newtype** Flatten b a $=$ *Flatten*{ *selFlatten* :: a $\rightarrow$ [b] }

It is important to notice that the order of the type parameters is significant. Flatten will be used as a type of kind $\star \rightarrow \star$, so the last parameter (a) serves as the generic argument type while the first parameter (b) is simply polymorphic.

Once we have our signature, we can define a type-indexed function (with a type synonym to improve the readability and reduce the visual complexity of types).

> **type** RFlatten b a $=$ Rep1 (Flatten b) a

> *appFlatten* :: RFlatten b a $\rightarrow$ a $\rightarrow$ [b]
> *appFlatten* RInt1   i $=$ [ ]
> *appFlatten* RChar1   c $=$ [ ]
> *appFlatten* RUnit1   Unit $=$ [ ]
> *appFlatten* (RSum1 r_a r_b) (L a) $=$ *appFlatten* r_a a
> *appFlatten* (RSum1 r_a r_b) (R b) $=$ *appFlatten* r_b b
> *appFlatten* (RProd1 r_a r_b) (a :×: b) $=$ *appFlatten* r_a a ++ *appFlatten* r_b b
> *appFlatten* (RType1 ep r_a) x $=$ *appFlatten* r_a (from ep x)
> *appFlatten* (RCon1 r_a) x $=$ *appFlatten* r_a x
> *appFlatten* (RVar1 f)   x $=$ *selFlatten* f x

The function *appFlatten* is not the final result, but it encompasses all of the structural induction on the representation. The primitive types and unit are not important to the structure of the container, so we return empty lists for them. In the sum case, we simply recurse to the appropriate alternative. For products, we append the second list of elements to the first list. In the *RType* case, we convert a Haskell datatype to its representation before recursing. Perhaps the most interesting case is *RVar1*.

The *RVar1* constructor tells us where to apply the function wrapped by our **newtype** signature. Thus, we select the function with the record destructor *selFlatten* and apply it to the value. Since we have not yet defined that signature function, our definition is not yet complete. We can define the signature function and the final result in one go:

> *flatten* :: (RFlatten a a $\rightarrow$ RFlatten a (f a)) $\rightarrow$ f a $\rightarrow$ [a]
> *flatten* rep $=$ *appFlatten* (rep (RVar1 (Flatten (:[]))))

We have added a convenience to the type signature that is perhaps not obvious: it is specialized to take an argument of f a rather than the more general, single-variable type that would be inferred. This change allows us to look at the type and better predict the meaning of the function.

There are a few points worth highlighting in the definition of *flatten*. First, the type signature indicates that its first argument is a representation for a datatype of kind $\star \rightarrow \star$. This is evident from the functional type of the argument. Second, we see a value-level parallel to a type-level operation: the *rep* argument, representative of a type constructor, is applied to the *RVar1* value, itself standing in for the argument of a type constructor. Lastly, our signature function is established by *Flatten* $(:[\,])$, where $(:[\,])$ injects an element into a singleton list. Notice the connection to *appFlatten* in which we use *selFlatten* to apply the signature function in the *RVar1* case.

Now, to see how *flatten* can be used, we create a representation for the List datatype using Rep1. When comparing with the previous representation for Rep, the constructor names and the type require trivial changes.

$r_{List,1} :: \text{Rep1 } g\ a \rightarrow \text{Rep1 } g\ (\text{List } a)$

$r_{List,1}\ r_a = RType1\ (EP\ from_{List}\ to_{List})$
$\qquad\qquad\qquad (RSum1\ (RCon1\ \texttt{"Nil"}\ RUnit1)$
$\qquad\qquad\qquad\qquad (RCon1\ \texttt{"Cons"}\ (RProd1\ r_a\ (r_{List,1}\ r_a))))$

We use this representation to produce a function specialized for lists:

flattenList :: List a $\rightarrow$ [a]
flattenList = *flatten* $r_{List,1}$

Of course, this transformation is isomorphic and not extremely useful, but we can apply the same approach to Tree and Forest for a more productive specialization.

Exercise 3. Many generic functions follow the same pattern of the generic *flatten* function. Examples include a function that sums all the integers in a value of a datatype, and a function that takes the logical "or" of all boolean values in a container. We implement this pattern with *crush*.

The function *crush* abstracts over functionality at occurrences of the type variable. In the definition of *flatten*, this includes the base case $[\,]$ and the binary case $+\!\!+$. The relevant types of *crush* follow.

newtype Crush b a = *Crush*{*gCrush* :: a $\rightarrow$ b}
crush :: Rep1 (Crush b) a $\rightarrow$ (b $\rightarrow$ b $\rightarrow$ b) $\rightarrow$ b $\rightarrow$ a $\rightarrow$ b

Define *crush*. (Attempt to solve it without looking ahead to Section 6 in which *crush* is defined using the EMGM library.)

To test if your function implements the desired behavior, instantiate *crush* with the addition operator, 0, and a value of a datatype containing integers to obtain a generic *sum* function. ∎

Generalised Map. A well-known function is *map* :: (a $\rightarrow$ b) $\rightarrow$ [a] $\rightarrow$ [b] function. It takes a higher-order function and a list as arguments, and applies the function to every element in the list. We can also defined a generic *map* function that applied a function to every element of some container datatype. The *map* function can be viewed as the implementation of **deriving** *Functor*.

As with the generic *flatten*, the generic *map* function needs to know where the occurrences of the type argument of the datatype appear in a constructor. This means that we again need to abstract over type constructors. If we use Rep1 for our representation, the argument function will only return a value of a type that dependent on a or a constant type. Recall that the constructor *RVar1* has type g a $\rightarrow$ Rep1 g a, and thus the signature function g can only specify behavior for a single type variable. A true, generic *map* should be able to change each element type from a to a possibly completely different type b; so, we need a signature function with two type variables.

Our generic *map* will use this new representation datatype.

```
data Rep2 g a b where
    RInt2   ::                                  Rep2 g Int Int
    RChar2 ::                                    Rep2 g Char Char
    RUnit2 ::                                    Rep2 g Unit Unit
    RSum2 :: Rep2 g a b → Rep2 g c d →          Rep2 g (a :+: c) (b :+: d)
    RProd2 :: Rep2 g a b → Rep2 g c d →         Rep2 g (a :×: c) (b :×: d)
    RType2 :: EP a c → EP b d → Rep2 g c d → Rep2 g a b
    RCon2 :: String → Rep2 g a b →              Rep2 g a b
    RVar2  :: g a b →                           Rep2 g a b
```

The significant difference with the representation type Rep1 is the addition of the type variable b in Rep2 g a b and in the signature function g a b argument of *RVar2*. As we would expect, a signature function now has the kind $\star \to \star \to \star$. One other minor but necessary difference from Rep1 (and Rep) is the second EP argument to *RType*. Since we have two generic type parameters, we need an isomorphism for each.

We begin defining the generic function *map* with the signature function type as we did with *flatten*. Analyzing the problem we want to solve, we know that *map* requires a generic input value and a generic output value. There are no polymorphic or known types involved. So, our signature function is as follows:

newtype Map a b = $Map\{selMap :: a \to b\}$

Unlike the *flatten* example, the position of the parameters is not as important.

The type-indexed function appears as so:

type RMap a b = Rep2 Map a b

```
appMap :: RMap a b → a → b
appMap RInt2              i        = i
appMap RChar2             c        = c
appMap RUnit2             Unit     = Unit
appMap (RSum2 ra rb)      (L a)    = L (appMap ra a)
appMap (RSum2 ra rb)      (R b)    = R (appMap rb b)
appMap (RProd2 ra rb)     (a :×: b) = appMap ra a :×: appMap rb b
appMap (RType2 ep1 ep2 ra) x       = (to ep2 . appMap ra . from ep1) x
appMap (RCon2   ra)       x        = appMap ra x
appMap (RVar2 f)          x        = selMap f x
```

Its definition is no real surprise. Since we only apply a change to elements of the container, we only use the signature function *selMap f* in the *RVar2* case. In every other case, we preserve the same structure on the right as on the left. It is also interesting to note the *RType2* case in which we translate *from* a datatype to its structure representation, apply the recursion, and translate the result back *to* the datatype.

The final part of the definition is quite similar to that of *flatten*.

$$map :: (\text{RMap } a\ b \to \text{RMap } (f\ a)\ (f\ b)) \to (a \to b) \to f\ a \to f\ b$$
$$map\ rep\ f = appMap\ (rep\ (RVar2\ (Map\ f)))$$

A major point of difference here is that the signature function f is an argument.

The representation of lists using this new representation type changes in insignificant ways: a second embedding-projection pair and naming updates.

$$r_{List,2}\ r_a = RType2\ (EP\ from_{List}\ to_{List})$$
$$(EP\ from_{List}\ to_{List})$$
$$(RSum2\ (RCon2\ \texttt{"Nil"}\ RUnit2)$$
$$(RCon2\ \texttt{"Cons"}\ (RProd2\ r_a\ (r_{List,2}\ r_a))))$$

Using $r_{List,2}$, we can define *map* on lists as follows:

$$mapList :: (a \to b) \to \text{List } a \to \text{List } b$$
$$mapList = map\ r_{List,2}$$

Since each of the last two generic functions introduced required a new structure representation type, one might wonder if this happens for many generic functions. As far as we have found, the useful extensions stop with three generic type parameters. We could use the datatype Rep3 for all generic functions, but that would introduce many type variables that are never used. We prefer to use the representation type most suitable to the generic function at hand.

Exercise 4. Define the generalised version of function $zipWith :: (a \to b \to c) \to [a] \to [b] \to [c]$ in LIGD. You may need to adapt the structure representation type for this purpose. ∎

5.6   Case Study: Exercise Assistants

In this section, we describe using the LIGD library to define a generic function for a particular case study, an exercise assistant. An exercise assistant supports interactively solving exercises in a certain domain. For example, at the Open University NL and Utrecht University, we are developing exercise assistants for several domains: systems of linear equations [Passier and Jeuring, 2006], disjunctive normal form (DNF) of a logical expression [Lodder et al., 2006], and several kinds of exercises with linear algebra. A screenshot of the assistant that supports calculating a DNF of a logical expression is shown in Figure 1.

The exercise assistants for the different domains are very similar. They need operations such as equality, rewriting, exercise generation, term traversal, selection, and serialization. Each program can be viewed as an instance of a generic exercise assistant. For each generic programming library we discuss in these lecture notes, we also present a case study implementing functionality for an exercise assistant. In this subsection, we show how to implement a generic function for determining the difference between two terms.

Fig. 1. The Exercise Assistant

We have used equality to introduce many concepts in these notes; however, we often want to know whether or not two values differ, and by *how much* or *where*. For example, in the exercise assistant a user can submit a step towards a solution of an exercise. We want to compare the submitted expression against expressions obtained by applying rewrite rules to the previous expression. If none match, we want to find a correctly rewritten expression that is closest in some sense to the expression submitted by the student.

The function *similar* determines a measure of equality between two values. Given two values, the function counts the number of constructors and basic values that are equal. The function traverses its arguments top-down: as soon as it encounters unequal constructors, it does not traverse deeper into the children.

$$similar :: \text{Rep } a \rightarrow a \rightarrow a \rightarrow \text{Int}$$

similar RInt	i	j	$= \text{if } i \quad j \text{ then } 1 \text{ else } 0$
similar RChar	c	d	$= \text{if } c \quad d \text{ then } 1 \text{ else } 0$
similar RUnit			$= 1$
similar $(RSum\ r_a\ r_b)$	$(L\ a)$	$(L\ b)$	$= similar\ r_a\ a\ b$
similar $(RSum\ r_a\ r_b)$	$(R\ a)$	$(R\ b)$	$= similar\ r_b\ a\ b$
similar $(RSum\ r_a\ rA\ )$			$= 0$
similar $(RProd\ r_a\ r_b)$	$(a_1 :\times: b_1)$	$(a_2 :\times: b_2)$	$= similar\ r_a\ a_1\ a_2 + similar\ r_b\ b_1\ b_2$
similar $(RType\ ep\ r_a)$	a	b	$= similar\ r_a\ (from\ ep\ a)\ (from\ ep\ b)$
similar $(RCon\ s\ r_a)$	a	b	$= 1 + similar\ r_a\ a\ b$

Given a definition of a generic function *size* that returns the size of a value by counting all basic values and constructors, we can define the function *diff* by:

$$diff :: \text{Rep } a \rightarrow a \rightarrow a \rightarrow \text{Int}$$
$$diff\ rep\ x\ y = size\ rep\ x - similar\ rep\ x\ y$$

The difference here is reported as the size of the first value minus the similarity of the two. The function *diff* provides a rough estimate. A generic minimum edit distance function [Lempsink et al., 2009] would provide a higher-precision difference.

In this section, we discussed an implementation of datatype-generic programming in the Lightweight Implementation of Generics and Dynamics library. In the next section, we discuss a library that is similar in representation to LIGD but uses type classes instead of GADTs.

6   Extensible and Modular Generics for the Masses

The library "Generics for the Masses" was first introduced by Hinze [2004], and a variant, "Extensible and Modular Generics for the Masses," was later presented by Oliveira et al. [2006]. In this section, we describe latter, EMGM, with a slight twist to ease the extensibility requirements (details in Section 6.6).

Our approach follows much like that of Section 5. We again use equality to introduce generic functions (Section 6.1). We also explain the general mechanics (Section 6.2), the component necessary for extending the universe (Section 6.3), and the support for overloading (Section 6.4). Where EMGM differs from LIGD is the capability for generic functions to be extended with datatype-specific functionality while preserving the modularity of the function definition. We first describe the published approach to solving this problem (Section 6.5) and then introduce our solution to reducing the burden of extensibility (Section 6.6). Next, we define several different generic functions using EMGM (Section 6.7). As with LIGD, these require changes to the representation. Finally, we implement a value generator for the exercise assistant case study (Section 6.8).

6.1   An Example Function

Defining a generic function in the EMGM library involves several steps. First, we declare the type signature of a function in a **newtype** declaration.

$$\textbf{newtype } Eq\ a = Eq\{\ selEq :: a \rightarrow a \rightarrow Bool\}$$

The **newtype** Eq serves a similar purpose to the signature function of LIGD first mentioned when describing the function *flatten* in Section 5.5. Unlike LIGD, however, every generic function in EMGM requires its own **newtype**.

Next, we define the cases of our generic function.

$$
\begin{array}{llll}
selEq_{int} & i & j & = i \quad j \\
selEq_{char} & c & d & = c \quad d \\
selEq_{\mathbb{1}} & Unit & Unit & = True \\
selEq_{+}\ r_a\ r_b\ (L\ a_1) & (L\ a_2) & & = selEq\ r_a\ a_1\ a_2 \\
selEq_{+}\ r_a\ r_b\ (R\ b_1) & (R\ b_2) & & = selEq\ r_b\ b_1\ b_2 \\
selEq_{+} & & & = False \\
selEq_{\times}\ r_a\ r_b\ (a_1 :\times: b_1) & (a_2 :\times: b_2) & & = selEq\ r_a\ a_1\ a_2 \wedge selEq\ r_b\ b_1\ b_2
\end{array}
$$

We can read this in the same fashion as a type-indexed function in LIGD. Indeed, there is a high degree of similarity. However, instead of a single function that uses pattern matching on a type representation, we have many functions, each corresponding to a primitive or structural type. Another major difference with LIGD is that the type representation parameters (e.g. for *RSum*, *RProd*, etc.) are explicit and not embedded in the Rep datatype. Specifically, each function takes the appropriate number of representations according to the arity of the structural element. For example, $selEq_1$ has no representation arguments, and $selEq_+$ and $selEq_\times$ each have two.

These functions are only part of the story, of course. Notice that $selEq_+$ and $selEq_\times$ each call the function *selEq*. We need to tie the recursive knot, so that *selEq* will select the appropriate case. We do this by creating an instance declaration of a type class *Generic* for Eq:

> **instance** *Generic* Eq **where**
> $rint$ $= Eq \; selEq_{int}$
> $rchar$ $= Eq \; selEq_{char}$
> $runit$ $= Eq \; selEq_1$
> $rsum \; r_a \; r_b = Eq \; (selEq_+ \; r_a \; r_b)$
> $rprod \; r_a \; r_b = Eq \; (selEq_\times \; r_a \; r_b)$

The type class has member functions corresponding to primitive and structure types. Each method defines the instance of the type-indexed function for the associated type. The above collection of functions are now used in values of Eq. The EMGM approach uses method overriding instead of the pattern matching used by LIGD, but it still provides an effective case analysis on types. Another difference between the two libraries is that LIGD uses explicit recursion while EMGM's recursion is implicitly implemented by the instance in a fold-like manner.

We now have all of the necessary parts to use the type-indexed function *selEq*.[4]

$$selEq \; (rprod \; rchar \; rint) \; ('Q' :\!\times\! : 42) \; ('Q' :\!\times\! : 42) \rightsquigarrow True$$

On the other hand, we should not need to provide an explicit representation every time. Instead, we introduce a convenient wrapper that determines which type representation we need.

> $eq :: (Rep \; a) \Rightarrow a \rightarrow a \rightarrow$ Bool
> $eq = selEq \; rep$

The type class *Rep* is an interface (Section 2.4) to all known type representations, and its method *rep* statically resolves to a value of the appropriate representation. This mechanism allows us to write a simpler call: $eq \; ('Q' :\!\times\! : 42) \; ('Q' :\!\times\! : 42)$. Note that we might have defined such a class for LIGD (as was done by Cheney and Hinze [2002]); however, that would have only been a convenience. In EMGM, it becomes a necessity for extensibility (Section 6.5).

---

[4] We use the notation $a \rightsquigarrow b$ to mean that, in GHCi, expression a evaluates to b.

6.2   Run-Time Type Representation

In contrast with LIGD's GADT, EMGM makes extensive use of type classes for its run-time type representation. The primary classes are *Generic* and *Rep*, though others may be used to extend the basic concepts of EMGM as we will see later (Section 6.7).

The type class *Generic* serves as the interface for a generic function.

```
class Generic g where
    rint   :: g Int
    rchar :: g Char
    runit :: g Unit
    rsum  :: g a → g b → g (a :+: b)
    rprod :: g a → g b → g (a :×: b)


    infixr 5 'rsum'
    infixr 6 'rprod'
```

The class is parametrised by the type constructor g that serves as the type-indexed function's signature function.

Each method of the class represents a case of the type-indexed function. The function supports the same universe of types as LIGD (e.g. Unit, :+:, :×:, and primitive types). Also like LIGD, the structural induction is implemented through recursive calls, but unlike LIGD, these are polymorphically recursive (see Section 2.4). Thus, in our previous example, each call to *selEq* may have a different type.

The type-indexed function as we have defined it to this point is a destructor for the type g. As such, it requires an value of g, the type representation. In order to alleviate this requirement, we use another type class:

```
class Rep a where
    rep :: (Generic g) ⇒ g a
```

This allows us to replace any value of the type g a with *rep*. This simple but powerful concept uses the type system to dispatch the necessary representation. Representation instances are built inductively using the methods of *Generic*:

```
instance Rep Int where
    rep = rint
instance Rep Char where
    rep = rchar
instance Rep Unit where
    rep = runit
instance (Rep a, Rep b) ⇒ Rep (a :+: b) where
    rep = rsum rep rep
instance (Rep a, Rep b) ⇒ Rep (a :×: b) where
    rep = rprod rep rep
```

As simple as these instances of *Rep* are, they handle an important duty. In the function *eq*, we use *rep* to instantiate the structure of the arguments. For example, it instantiates *rprod rchar rint* given the argument $'Q' :\times: (42 :: \mathsf{Int})$. Now, we may apply *eq* with the same ease of use as with any ad-hoc polymorphic function, even though it is actually datatype-generic.

6.3 Going Generic: Universe Extension

Much like in LIGD, we need to extend our universe to include any new datatypes that we create. We extend our type-indexed functions with a case to support arbitrary datatypes.

class *Generic* g **where**

   . . .

  rtype :: EP b a $\rightarrow$ g a $\rightarrow$ g b

The *rtype* function reuses the embedding-projection pair datatype EP mentioned earlier to witness the isomorphism between the structure representation and the datatype. Note the similarity with the *RType* constructor from LIGD (Section 5.3).

To demonstrate the use of *rtype*, we will once again show how the List datatype may be represented in a value. As mentioned before, we use the same structure types as LIGD, so we can make use of the same pair of functions, $from_{List}$ and to_{List}, in the embedding projection for lists. Using this pair and an encoding of the list structure at the value level, we define a representation of lists:

r_{List} :: (*Generic* g) $\Rightarrow$ g a $\rightarrow$ g (List a)
$r_{List}\ r_a = rtype\ (EP\ from_{List}\ to_{List})\ (runit\ 'rsum'\ r_a\ 'rprod'\ r_{List}\ r_a)$

It is now straightforward to apply a generic function to a list. To make it convenient, we create a new instance of *Rep* for List a with the constraint that the contained type a must also be representable:

instance (*Rep* a) $\Rightarrow$ *Rep* (List a) **where**
  $rep = r_{List}\ rep$

At last, we can transform our type-indexed equality function into a true generic function. For this, we need to add another case for arbitrary datatypes.

$selEq_{type}\ ep\ r_a\ a_1\ a_2 = selEq\ r_a\ (from\ ep\ a_1)\ (from\ ep\ a_2)$

instance *Generic* Eq **where**

   . . .

  rtype ep $r_a = Eq\ (selEq_{type}\ ep\ r_a)$

The function $selEq_{type}$ accepts any datatype for which an embedding-projection pair has been defined. It is very similar to the *RType* case in the LIGD version of equality. The *Generic* instance definition for *rtype* completes the requirements necessary for *eq* to be a generic function.

Exercise 5. Now that you have seen how to define r_{List}, you should be able to define the representation for most other datatypes. Give representations and embedding-projection pairs for $Logic_L$ and $Logic_F$ from Section 3.4. You may need to do the same for other datatypes in the process. Test your results using *eq* as defined above. ∎

6.4   Support for Overloading

In this section, we demonstrate how the EMGM library supports constructor names and ad-hoc cases. As with LIGD in Section 5.4, we illustrate this support using a generic *show* function and lists and strings.

For accessing constructor names in the definition of a generic function, we add another method to our generic function interface.

> **class** *Generic* g **where**
>
>   . . .
>   rcon :: String → g a → g a

We use *rcon* to label other structure components with a constructor name[5]. As an example of using this method, we modify the list type representation with constructor names:

> r_{List} :: (*Generic* g) ⇒ g a → g (List a)
> r_{List} r_a = rtype (EP from$_{List}$ to$_{List}$)
>   (rcon "Nil" runit 'rsum' rcon "Cons" (r_a 'rprod' r_{List} r_a))

Using the capability to display constructor names, we can write a simplified generic show function:

> **newtype** Show a = *Show*{ *selShow* :: a → String }

selShow$_{int}$	i	= *show i*
selShow$_{char}$	c	= *show c*
selShow$_1$	*Unit*	= " "
selShow$_+$	r_a r_b (L a)	= *selShow* r_a a
selShow$_+$	r_a r_b (R b)	= *selShow* r_b b
selShow$_\times$	r_a r_b (a :×: b)	= *selShow* r_a a ++ " " ++ *selShow* r_b b
selShow$_{type}$ ep r_a	a	= *selShow* r_a (*from ep a*)
selShow$_{con}$ s r_a	a	= "(" ++ s ++ " " ++ *selShow* r_a a ++ ")"

> **instance** *Generic* Show **where**
>   rint   = *Show* *selShow*$_{int}$

---

[5] The released EMGM library uses ConDescr instead of String. ConDescr contains a more comprehensive description of a constructor (fixity, arity, etc.). For simplicity's sake, we only use the constructor name in our presentation.

$$rchar \qquad = Show \ selShow_{char}$$
$$runit \qquad = Show \ selShow_1$$
$$rsum \quad r_a \ r_b = Show \ (selShow_+ \ r_a \ r_b)$$
$$rprod \quad r_a \ r_b = Show \ (selShow_\times \ r_a \ r_b)$$
$$rtype \ ep \ r_a \quad = Show \ (selShow_{type} \ ep \ r_a)$$
$$rcon \ s \quad r_a \quad = Show \ (selShow_{con} \ s \ r_a)$$

$$show :: (Rep \ a) \Rightarrow a \rightarrow \text{String}$$
$$show = selShow \ rep$$

Applying this function to a list of integers gives us the expected result:

$$show \ (Cons \ 5 \ (Cons \ 3 \ Nil)) \rightsquigarrow \text{"(Cons 5 (Cons 3 (Nil)))"}$$

As mentioned in Section 5.4, we would prefer to see this list as it natively appears in Haskell: "[5,3]". To this end, just as we added a *RList* constructor to the Rep GADT, it is possible to add a method *rlist* to *Generic*.

class *Generic* g **where**
$$\dots$$
$$rlist :: g \ a \rightarrow g \ (\text{List} \ a)$$

It is then straightforward to define a new case for the generic show function, reusing the $show_{List}$ function from Section 5.4.

instance *Generic* Show **where**
$$\dots$$
$$> rlist \ r_a = Show \ (show_{List} \ (selShow \ r_a) \ True)$$

Our last step is to make these types representable. We replace the previous instance of *Rep* for List a with one using the *rlist* method, and we add a new instance for String.

instance $(Rep \ a) \Rightarrow Rep \ (\text{List} \ a)$ **where**
$$rep = rlist \ rep$$

Now, when applying the example application of *show* above, we receive the more concise output.

In order to extend the generic function representation to support ad-hoc list and string cases, we modified the *Generic* type class. This approach fails when the module containing *Generic* is distributed as a third-party library. Unlike LIGD, there are solutions for preserving modularity while allowing extensibility.

6.5 Making Generic Functions Extensible

Since modifying the type class *Generic* should be considered off-limits, we might consider declaring a hierarchy of classes for extensibility. *Generic* would then be the base class for all generic functions. A user of the library would introduce a subclass for an ad-hoc case on a datatype. To explore this idea, let us revisit the example of defining a special case for *show* on lists.

The subclass for list appears as follows:

> **class** (*Generic* g) ⇒ *GenericList* g **where**
>   *rlist* :: g a → g (List a)
>   *rlist* = r_{List}

This declaration introduces the class *GenericList* encoding a list representation. The default value of *rlist* is the same value that we determined previously, but it can be overridden in an instance declaration. For the ad-hoc case of the generic show function, we would use an instance with the same implementation as before:

> **instance** *GenericList* Show **where**
>   *rlist* r_a = *Show* ($show_{List}$ (*selShow* r_a) *True*)

We have regained some ground on our previous implementation of an ad-hoc case, yet we have lost some as well. We can apply our generic function to a type representation and a value (e.g. (*selShow* (*list rint*) (*Cons* 3 *Nil*))), and it will evaluate as expected. However, we can no longer use the same means of dispatching the appropriate representation with ad-hoc cases. What happens if we attempt to write the following instance of *Rep*?

> **instance** (*Rep* a) ⇒ *Rep* (List a) **where**
>   *rep* = *rlist rep*

GHC returns with this error:

```
Could not deduce (GenericList g)
   from the context (Rep (List a), Rep a, Generic g)
   arising from a use of 'rlist' at ...
Possible fix:
   add (GenericList g) to the context of
      the type signature for 'rep' ...
```

We certainly do not want to follow GHC's advise. Recall that the method *rep* of class *Rep* has the type (*Generic* g, *Rep* a) ⇒ g a. By adding *GenericList* g to its context, we would force all generic functions to support both *Generic* and *GenericList*, thereby ruling out any modularity. In order to use *Rep* as it is currently defined, we must use a type g that is an instance of *Generic*; instances of any subclasses are not valid.

Let us instead abstract over the function signature type g. We subsequently redefine *Rep* as a type class with two parameters.

> **class** *Rep* g a **where**
>   *rep* :: g a

This migrates the parametrisation of the type constructor to the class level and lifts the restriction of the *Generic* context. We now re-define the representative instances.

instance *(Generic* g) ⇒ *Rep* g Int **where**
   rep = *rint*

instance *(Generic* g) ⇒ *Rep* g Char **where**
   rep = *rchar*

instance *(Generic* g) ⇒ *Rep* g Unit **where**
   rep = *runit*

instance *(Generic* g, *Rep* g a, *Rep* g b) ⇒ *Rep* g (a :+: b) **where**
   rep = *rsum rep rep*

instance *(Generic* g, *Rep* g a, *Rep* g b) ⇒ *Rep* g (a :×: b) **where**
   rep = *rprod rep rep*

instance *(GenericList* g, *Rep* g a) ⇒ *Rep* g (List a) **where**
   rep = *rlist rep*

The organization here is very regular. Every instance handled by a method of *Generic* is constrained by *Generic* in its context. For the ad-hoc list instance, we use *GenericList* instead.

Now, we rewrite our generic show function to use the new dispatcher by specialising the type constructor argument g to Show.

show :: (*Rep* Show a) ⇒ a → String
show = *selShow rep*

This approach of using a type-specific class (e.g. *GenericList*) for extensibility as described initially by Oliveira et al. [2006] and demonstrated here by us puts an extra burden on the user. In the next subsection, we explain the problem and how we rectify it.

6.6 Reducing the Burden of Extensibility

Without the change for extensibility (i.e. before Section 6.4), a function such as *show* in EMGM would automatically work with any type that was an instance of *Rep*. When we add Section 6.5, then every generic function must have an instance of every datatype that it will support. In other words, even if we did not want to define an ad-hoc case for Show using *GenericList* as we did earlier, we must provide at least the following (empty) instance to use *show* on lists.

instance *GenericList* Show **where**

This uses the default method for *rlist* and overrides nothing.

As developers of a library, we want to strike a balance between ease of use and flexibility. Since we want to allow for extensibility in EMGM, we cannot provide these instances for each generic function provided by the library. This forces the library user to write one for every unique pair of datatype and generic function that is used, whether or not an ad-hoc case is desired. We can fortunately reduce this burden using an extension to the Haskell language.

Overlapping instances allow more than one instance declaration to match when resolving the class context of a function, provided that there is a most specific one. Using overlapping instances, we no longer need a type-specific class such as GenericList because constraint resolution will choose the list representation as long as List a is the most specific instance.

To continue with our example of specializing Show for lists, we provide the changes needed with respect to Section 6.5. The List instance for *Rep* is the same except for replacing *GenericList* with *Generic*.

> **instance** (*Generic* g, *Rep* g a) ⇒ *Rep* g (List a) **where**
>   *rep* = *rlist rep*

At this point, with overlapping instances enabled, no further work is necessary for lists to be supported by any generic function that uses the *Generic* class. However, since we do want an ad-hoc case, we add an instance for Show:

> **instance** (*Rep* Show a) ⇒ *Rep* Show (List a) **where**
>   *rep* = *Show* (*show*$_{List}$ (*selShow rep*) *True*)

Notice that the **newtype** Show is substituted for the variable g in the first argument of *Rep*.

Exercise 6. The standard *compare* function returns the ordering (less than, equal to, or greater than) between two instances of some type a.

> **data** Ordering = *LT* | *EQ* | *GT*
>
> *compare* :: (*Ord* a) ⇒ a → a → Ordering

This function can be implemented by hand, but more often, it is generated by the compiler using **deriving** *Ord*. The latter uses the syntactic ordering of constructors to determine the relationship. For example, the datatype Ordering derives *Ord* and its constructors have the relationship $LT < EQ < GT$.

Implement an extensible, generic *compare* that behaves like **deriving** *Ord*. It should have a type signature similar to the above, but with a different class context. ∎

6.7   Generic Functions in EMGM

In this section, we discuss the implementation of various generic functions. Some require alternative strategies from the approach described so far.

Empty. As we did with LIGD in Section 5.5, we write the generic producer function *empty* in EMGM as follows:

> **newtype** Empty a = *Empty*{ *selEmpty* :: a }

> **instance** *Generic* Empty **where**
>   *rint*   = *Empty* 0

$$
\begin{array}{ll}
rchar & = Empty \; ' \backslash \text{NUL}' \\
runit & = Empty \; Unit \\
rsum \quad r_a \; r_b & = Empty \; (L \; (selEmpty \; r_a)) \\
rprod \quad r_a \; r_b & = Empty \; (selEmpty \; r_a :\times: selEmpty \; r_b) \\
rtype \; ep \; r_a & = Empty \; (to \; ep \; (selEmpty \; r_a)) \\
rcon \; s \; r_a & = Empty \; (selEmpty \; r_a)
\end{array}
$$

$empty :: (Rep \; \mathsf{Empty} \; \mathsf{a}) \Rightarrow \mathsf{a}$

$empty = selEmpty \; rep$

There are a two noteworthy differences from previous examples. First, since it is a producer function, *empty* outputs a generic value. Unlike *empty* in LIGD, however, the EMGM version takes no arguments at all. In order to use it, we need to specify a concrete type. In the case where this is not inferred, we can give a type annotation.

$empty :: \mathsf{Int} :+: \mathsf{Char} \rightsquigarrow L \; 0$

The second difference lies in the *rtype* definition, where we use *to ep* instead of *from ep*. This is also characteristic of producer functions.

Crush and Flatten. Crush is a fold-like operation over a container datatype [Meertens, 1996]. It is a very flexible function, and many other useful functions can be implemented using crush. As mentioned in Exercise 3, it can be used to implement *flatten*, which we will also demonstrate.

Our goal is a function with a signature similar to the following for datatypes of kind $\star \rightarrow \star$ (see discussion for *flatten* in Section 5.5).

$crushr :: (\mathsf{a} \rightarrow \mathsf{b} \rightarrow \mathsf{b}) \rightarrow \mathsf{b} \rightarrow \mathsf{f} \; \mathsf{a} \rightarrow \mathsf{b}$

The function *crushr* takes three arguments: a "combining" operator that joins a-values with b-values to create new b-values, a "zero" value, and a container f of a-values. *crushr* (sometimes called *reduce*) is a generalization of the standard Haskell *foldr* function. In *foldr*, f is specialized to [ ].

We split the implementation of *crushr* into components, and we begin with the type signature for the combining function.

newtype $\mathsf{Crushr} \; \mathsf{b} \; \mathsf{a} = Crushr \{ selCrushr :: \mathsf{a} \rightarrow \mathsf{b} \rightarrow \mathsf{b} \}$

This function extracts the container's element and combines it with a partial result to produce a final result. The implementation follows[6]:

$$
\begin{array}{ll}
crushr_{int} & e = e \\
crushr_{char} & e = e \\
crushr_{\mathbb{1}} & e = e
\end{array}
$$

---

[6] For brevity, we elide most of the *Generic* instance declaration. It is the same as we have seen before.

$$crushr_+ \quad r_a\ r_b\ (L\ a) \quad e = selCrushr\ r_a\ a\ e$$
$$crushr_+ \quad r_a\ r_b\ (R\ b) \quad e = selCrushr\ r_b\ b\ e$$
$$crushr_\times \quad r_a\ r_b\ (a :\!\times\!: b)\ e = selCrushr\ r_a\ a\ (selCrushr\ r_b\ b\ e)$$
$$crushr_{type}\ ep\ r_a \quad a \qquad e = selCrushr\ r_a\ (from\ ep\ a)\ e$$
$$crushr_{con}\ s\ r_a \quad a \qquad e = selCrushr\ r_a\ a\ e$$

instance *Generic* (Crushr b) **where**
  $rint = Crushr\ crushr_{int}$
  . . .

Note that *selCrushr* is only applied to the parametrised structural type cases: $crushr_+$, $crushr_\times$, $crushr_{type}$, and $crushr_{con}$; it is not applied to the primitive types. Crush only combines the elements of a polymorphic datatype and does not act on non-parametrised types.

We have successfully made it this far, but now we run into a problem. The type for *rep* is $Rep\ g\ a \Rightarrow g\ a$, and type a is the representation type and has kind $\star$. We need a representation for a type of kind $\star \to \star$. To expand *rep* to support type constructors, we define similar class in which the method has a parameter.

class *FRep* g f **where**
  $frep :: g\ a \to g\ (f\ a)$

The class *FRep* (representation for functionally kinded types) takes the same first type argument as *Rep*, but the second is the type constructor f. Notice that the type of *frep* matches the kind of f. This is exactly what we need for types such as Tree or List. The *FRep* instance for List is not too unlike the one for *Rep*:

instance (*Generic* g) $\Rightarrow$ *FRep* g List **where**
  $frep = r_{List}$

Now we can define *crushr*; however, it is a bit of a puzzle to put the pieces together. Let's review what we have to work with.

$Crushr :: (a \to b \to b) \to Crushr\ b\ a$
$frep :: (FRep\ g\ f) \Rightarrow g\ a \to g\ (f\ a)$
$selCrushr :: Crushr\ b\ a \to a \to b \to b$

Applying some analysis of the types (left as an exercise for the reader), we compose these functions to get our result.

$selCrushr . frep . Crushr :: (FRep\ (Crushr\ b)\ f) \Rightarrow (a \to b \to b) \to f\ a \to b \to b$

Finally, we rearrange the arguments to get a final definition with a signature similar to *foldr*.

$crushr :: (FRep\ (Crushr\ b)\ f) \Rightarrow (a \to b \to b) \to b \to f\ a \to b$
$crushr\ f\ z\ x = selCrushr\ (frep\ (Crushr\ f))\ x\ z$

To demonstrate the use of *crushr*, we define the *flattenr* function as a specialization. Recall that flattening involves translating all elements of a structure into a list. The definition of *flattenr* requires only the combining operator, $(:)$, for inserting an element into a list and the zero value, $[\,]$, for starting a new list.

$$flattenr :: (FRep \; (Crushr \; [a]) \; f) \Rightarrow f \; a \to [a]$$
$$flattenr = crushr \; (:) \; [\,]$$

Exercise 7. How is the behavior of the EMGM function *crushr* different from that of the LIGD function *crush*? Why might the *crushr* end with an *r*? What difference would you expect from a function called *crushl*? ∎

Exercise 8. Define two functions using *crushr*:

1. *showElements* takes a container with showable elements and returns a string with the elements printed in a comma-delimited fashion.
2. *sumElements* takes a container with numeric elements and returns the numeric sum of all elements. ∎

Generalised Map. As described in Section 5.5, a generic *map* function gives us the ability to modify the elements of any container type. We aim for a function with this type:

$$map :: (a \to b) \to f \; a \to f \; b$$

Using the same analysis performed to define the signature function for *map* in LIGD, we arrive at the same type.

newtype Map a b = Map$\{selMap :: a \to b\}$

This means we need to abstract over both type arguments in Map. We have not yet seen how that is done in EMGM, but the idea is similar to the change in LIGD's representation.

In order to support abstraction over two types, we need a new class for defining generic functions. One option is to add a type argument to *Generic* and reuse that type class for all previous implementations, ignoring the extra variable. Instead, for simplicity, we choose to create *Generic2* to distinguish generic functions with two type arguments.

```
class Generic2 g where
    rint2   :: g Int Int
    rchar2 :: g Char Char
    runit2 :: g Unit Unit
    rsum2 :: g a₁ a₂ → g b₁ b₂ → g (a₁ :+: b₁) (a₂ :+: b₂)
    rprod2 :: g a₁ a₂ → g b₁ b₂ → g (a₁ :×: b₁) (a₂ :×: b₂)
    rtype2 :: EP a₂ a₁ → EP b₂ b₁ → g a₁ b₁ → g a₂ b₂
```

The major difference from *Generic* is that the signature function type g now has kind $\star \to \star \to \star$. In the case of the primitive types and Unit, this means simply repeating the type twice. In the case of $(:+:)$ and $(:\times:)$, we need to pass two types around instead of one. The method *rtype2*, like the constructor *RType2* now accepts two embedding-projection pairs.

The implementation of the generic function follows:

$$
\begin{aligned}
&map_{int} &i &= i \\
&map_{char} &c &= c \\
&map_\mathbb{1} &Unit &= Unit \\
&map_+ &r_a\ r_b\ (L\ a) &= L\ (selMap\ r_a\ a) \\
&map_+ &r_a\ r_b\ (R\ b) &= R\ (selMap\ r_b\ b) \\
&map_\times &r_a\ r_b\ (a :\times: b) &= selMap\ r_a\ a :\times: selMap\ r_b\ b \\
&map_{type}\ ep_1\ ep_2\ r_a &x &= (to\ ep_2\ .\ selMap\ r_a\ .\ from\ ep_1)\ x
\end{aligned}
$$

> **instance** *Generic2* Map **where**
> $\quad rint2 \qquad\qquad = $ Map map_{int}
> $\quad \dots$
> $\quad rtype2\ ep_1\ ep_2\ r_a = $ Map $(map_{type}\ ep_1\ ep_2\ r_a)$

The explanation for the implementation follows exactly as the one given for LIGD's *appMap* except for the *RVar2* case, which EMGM does not have.

We write the representation for list as:

$$
\begin{aligned}
&r_{List,2} :: (Generic2\ g) \Rightarrow g\ a\ b \to g\ (List\ a)\ (List\ b) \\
&r_{List,2}\ r_a = rtype2\ (EP\ from_{List}\ to_{List})\ (EP\ from_{List}\ to_{List}) \\
&\qquad\qquad\quad (runit2\ 'rsum2'\ r_a\ 'rprod2'\ r_{List,2}\ r_a)
\end{aligned}
$$

We can immediately use the list representation to implement the standard *map* as *mapList*:

$$
\begin{aligned}
&mapList :: (a \to b) \to \text{List } a \to \text{List } b \\
&mapList = selMap\ .\ r_{List,2}\ .\ \text{Map}
\end{aligned}
$$

Of course, our goal is to generalise this, but we need an appropriate dispatcher class. *FRep* will not work because it abstracts over only one type variable. We need to extend it in the same way we extended *Generic* to *Generic2*:

> **class** *FRep2* g f **where**
> $\quad frep2 :: g\ a\ b \to g\ (f\ a)\ (f\ b)$
> **instance** $(Generic2\ g) \Rightarrow FRep2\ g$ List **where**
> $\quad frep2 = r_{List,2}$

The class *FRep2* uses a signature function type g with two argument types. Note, however, that we still expect functionally kinded datatypes: f has kind $\star \to \star$.

Finally, we provide our definition of *map*.

$$map :: (FRep2 \text{ Map } f) \Rightarrow (a \rightarrow b) \rightarrow f\ a \rightarrow f\ b$$
$$map = selMap \cdot frep2 \cdot \text{Map}$$

This definition follows as the expected generalisation of *mapList*.

Exercise 9. Are there other useful generic functions that make use of *Generic2* and/or *FRep2*? Can you define them? ■

Exercise 10. Define a generalisation of the standard function *zipWith* in EMGM. The result should have a type signature similar to this:

$$zipWith :: (a \rightarrow b \rightarrow c) \rightarrow f\ a \rightarrow f\ b \rightarrow f\ c$$

What extensions to the library (as defined) are needed? ■

6.8   Case Study: Generating Values

The exercise assistant offers the possibility to generate a new exercise for a student. This implies that we need a set of exercises for every domain: systems of linear equations, logical expressions, etc. We can create this set either by hand for every domain or generically for an arbitrary domain. The former would likely involve a lot of work, much of which would be duplicated for each domain. For the latter, we need to generically generate exercises. This leads us to defining a generic value generator.

At the simplest, we seek a generic function with this type signature:

$$gen :: \text{Int} \rightarrow a$$

gen takes a (possibly randomly generated) integer and returns a value somehow representative of that number. Suppose that for small Int arguments (e.g. greater than 0 but single-digit), *gen* produces relatively simple values (e.g. with few sums). Then, as the number increases, the output becomes more and more complex. This would lead to an output like QuickCheck [Claessen and Hughes, 2000] typically uses for testing. It would also lead to a set of exercises that progressively get more difficult as they are solved.

One approach to doing this is to enumerate the values of a datatype. We generate a list of all of the values using the following template of a generic function:

newtype Enum a $= Enum\{ selEnum :: [a] \}$
instance *Generic* Enum **where**

$$
\begin{aligned}
rint &&&= Enum\ enum_{int} \\
rchar &&&= Enum\ enum_{char} \\
runit &&&= Enum\ enum_{1} \\
rsum & r_a\ r_b &&= Enum\ (enum_{+} && r_a\ r_b) \\
rprod & r_a\ r_b &&= Enum\ (enum_{\times} && r_a\ r_b) \\
rtype & ep\ r_a &&= Enum\ (enum_{type}\ ep\ r_a) \\
rcon & s\ r_a &&= Enum\ (enum_{con}\ s\ r_a)
\end{aligned}
$$

Now, let us fill in each case of the function. Int values can be positive or negative and cover the range from *minBound* to *maxBound*, the exact values of these being dependent on the implementation. A simple option might be:

$$enum_{int} = [minBound .. maxBound]$$

However, that would lead to a (very long) list of negative numbers followed by another (very long) list of negative numbers. This is an awfully unbalanced sequence while we would prefer to start with the most "basic" value (equivalent to *empty*) and progressively get larger. As a result, we alternate positive and negative numbers.

$$enum_{int} = [0 .. maxBound] \mathbin{||||} [-1, -2 .. minBound]$$

By reversing the negative enumeration, we now begin with 0 and grow larger (in the absolute sense). The interleave operator ($||||$) is defined as follows:

$$
\begin{aligned}
&(||||) :: [a] \rightarrow [a] \rightarrow [a] \\
&[] \qquad ||| \; ys = ys \\
&(x : xs) \; ||| \; ys = x : ys \; ||| \; xs
\end{aligned}
$$

This function is similar to $+\!+$ with the exception of the recursive case, in which xs and ys are swapped. This allows us to interleave the elements of the two lists, thus balancing the positive and negative sides of the Int enumeration. Note that ($||||$) also works if the lists are infinite.

For Char and Unit, the implementations are straightforward.

$$
\begin{aligned}
enum_{char} &= [minBound .. maxBound] \\
enum_{1} &= [Unit]
\end{aligned}
$$

For $enum_{char}$, we enumerate from the first character $'\backslash\text{NUL}'$ to the last, and for $enum_{1}$, we return a singleton list of the only Unit value.

In sums, we have a problem analogous to that of Int. We want to generate L-values and R-values, but we want to choose fairly from each side.

$$enum_{+} \; r_a \; r_b = [L \; x \mid x \leftarrow selEnum \; r_a] \mathbin{||||} [R \; y \mid y \leftarrow selEnum \; r_b]$$

By interleaving these lists, we ensure that there is no preference to either alternative.

We use the Cartesian product for enumerating the pairs of two (possibly infinite) lists.

$$enum_{\times} \; r_a \; r_b = selEnum \; r_a \times selEnum \; r_b$$

The definition of $\times$ is left as Exercise 11 for the reader.

The remaining cases for Enum are $enum_{type}$ and $enum_{con}$. The former requires a *map* to convert a list of generic representations to a list of values. The latter is the same as for Empty (Section 6.7), because constructor information is not used here.

$$enum_{type} \; ep \; r_a = map \; (to \; ep) \; (selEnum \; r_a)$$
$$enum_{con} \; s \; r_a = selEnum \; r_a$$

The final step for a generic enumeration function is to apply it to a representation.

$$enum :: (Rep \; \textsf{Enum} \; a) \Rightarrow [a]$$
$$enum = selEnum \; rep$$

To get to a generic generator, we simply index into the list.

$$gen :: (Rep \; \textsf{Enum} \; a) \Rightarrow \textsf{Int} \to a$$
$$gen = (!!) \; enum$$

The performance of this function is not be optimal; however, we could fuse the indexing operator ($!!$) into the definition of *enum* for a more efficient (and more complicated) function.

Exercise 11. Define a function that takes the diagonalization of a list of lists.

$$diag :: [[a]] \to [a]$$

diag returns a list of all of elements in the inner lists. It will always return at least some elements from every inner list, even if that list is infinite.

We can then use *diag* to define the Cartesian product.

$$(\times) :: [a] \to [b] \to [a :\times: b]$$
$$xs \times ys = diag \; [[x :\times: y \mid y \leftarrow ys] \mid x \leftarrow xs]$$

■

Exercise 12. Design a more efficient generic generator function.   ■

We have provided an introduction to the Extensible and Modular Generics for the Masses library in this section. It relies on similar concepts to LIGD, yet it allows for better extensibility and modularity through the use of type classes. The next section introduces a well-known library using a representation that is completely different from both LIGD and EMGM.

7 Scrap Your Boilerplate

In this section, we describe the Scrap Your Boilerplate (SYB) approach to generic programming [Lämmel and Peyton Jones, 2003, 2004]. The original concept behind SYB is that in contrast to the two approaches discussed previously, the structure of datatypes is not directly exposed to the programmer. Generic functions are built with "primitive" generic combinators, and the combinators in turn can be generated (in GHC) using Haskell's **deriving** mechanism for type classes. We also mention a variation of SYB in which a structure representation is given and used to define functions.

7.1 An Example Function

Recall the Expr datatype from Section 3), and suppose we want to implement a function that increases the value of each literal by one. Here is a simple but incorrect solution:

$inc :: \text{Expr Int} \rightarrow \text{Expr Int}$
$inc\ (Lit\ x) = Lit\ (x + 1)$

This solution is incorrect because we also have to write the "boilerplate" code for traversing the entire expression tree, which just leaves the structure intact and recurses into the arguments. Using SYB, we do not have to do that anymore: we signal that the other cases are uninteresting by saying:

$inc\ x = x$

Now we have the complete definition of function inc: increment the literals and leave the rest untouched. To ensure that this function is applied everywhere in the expression we write:

$increment :: Data\ \text{a} \Rightarrow \text{a} \rightarrow \text{a}$
$increment = everywhere\ (mkT\ inc)$

This is all we need: the $increment$ function increases the value of each literal by one in any Expr. It even works for LinearExprs, or LinearSystems, with no added cost.

We now proceed to explore the internals of SYB to better understand the potential of this approach and the mechanisms involved behind a simple generic function such as $increment$.

7.2 Run-Time Type Representation

Contrary to the approaches to generic programming discussed earlier, SYB does not provide the structure of datatypes to the programmer, but instead offers basic combinators for writing generic programs. At the basis of these combinators is the method $typeOf$ of the type class $Typeable$. Instances of this class can be automatically derived by the GHC compiler, and implement a unique representation of a type, enabling run-time type comparison and type-safe casting.

class $Typeable$ a **where**
    $typeOf :: \text{a} \rightarrow \text{TypeRep}$

An instance of $Typeable$ only provides a TypeRep (type representation) of itself. The automatically derived instances of this class by GHC are guaranteed to provide a unique representation for each type, which is a necessary condition for the type-safe cast, as we will see later. So, providing an instance is as easy as adding **deriving** $Typeable$ at the end of a datatype declaration.

data MyDatatype a = $MyConstructor$ a **deriving** $Typeable$

We will not discuss the internal structure of TypeRep, since instances should not be defined manually. However, the built-in derivation of *Typeable* makes SYB somewhat less portable than the previous two libraries we have seen, and makes it impossible to adapt the type representation.

The *Typeable* class is the "back-end" of SYB. The *Data* class can be considered the "front-end". It is built on top of the *Typeable* class, and adds generic folding, unfolding and reflection capabilities[7].

> **class** *Typeable* d $\Rightarrow$ *Data* d **where**
>   *gfoldl*   :: $(\forall$ a b . *Data* a $\Rightarrow$ c $(a \rightarrow b) \rightarrow a \rightarrow c$ b$)$
> $\rightarrow (\forall$ g . g $\rightarrow$ c g$)$
> $\rightarrow$ d
> $\rightarrow$ c d
>   *gunfold*   :: $(\forall$ b r . *Data* b $\Rightarrow$ c $(b \rightarrow r) \rightarrow c$ r$)$
> $\rightarrow (\forall$ r . r $\rightarrow$ c r$)$
> $\rightarrow$ Constr
> $\rightarrow$ c d
>   *toConstr* :: d $\rightarrow$ Constr
>   *dataTypeOf* :: d $\rightarrow$ DataType

The combinator *gfoldl* is named after the function *foldl* on lists, as it can be considered a "left-associative fold operation for constructor applications," with *gunfold* being the dualizing unfold. The types of these combinators may be a bit intimidating, and they are better understood by looking at specific instances. We will give such instances in the next subsection, since giving an instance of *Data* for a datatype is the way generic functions become available on the datatype.

7.3   Going Generic: Universe Extension

To use the SYB combinators on a particular datatype we have to supply the instances of the datatype for the *Typeable* and the *Data* class. A programmer should not define instances of *Typeable*, but instead rely on the automatically derived instances by the compiler. For *Data*, GHC can also automatically derive instances for a datatype, but we present an instance here to illustrate how SYB works. For example, the instance of *Data* on the List datatype is as follows.

> **instance** $(Typeable$ a, *Data* a$) \Rightarrow$ *Data* $(List$ a$)$ **where**
>   *gfoldl k z Nil*   = z Nil
>   *gfoldl k z* $(Cons$ h t$)$ = z Cons 'k' h 'k' t
>   *gunfold k z l*   = **case** *constrIndex l* **of**
>   1 $\rightarrow$ z Nil
>   2 $\rightarrow$ k $(k$ $(z$ *Cons*$))$

---

[7] The *Data* class has many more methods, but they all have default definitions based on these four basic combinators. They are provided as instance methods so that a programmer can define more efficient versions, specialized to the datatype in question.

Any instance of the *Data* class follows the regular pattern of the above instance: the first argument to *gfoldl* (k) can be seen as an application combinator, and the second argument (z) as the base case generator. Function *gfoldl* differs from the regular *foldl* in two ways: it is not recursive, and the base case takes a constructor as argument, instead of a base case for just the *Nil*. When we apply *gfoldl* to function application and the identity function, it becomes the identity function itself.

$$gfoldl\ (\$)\ id\ x = x$$

We further illustrate the *gfoldl* function with another example.

$$gsize :: Data\ a \Rightarrow a \rightarrow \mathsf{Int}$$
$$gsize = unBox\,.\,gfoldl\ k\ (\lambda\ \ \rightarrow IntBox\ 1)\ \textbf{where}$$
$$\quad k\ (IntBox\ h)\ t = IntBox\ (h + gsize\ t)$$
$$\textbf{newtype}\ \mathsf{IntBox}\ x = IntBox\{\,unBox :: \mathsf{Int}\,\}$$

Function *gsize* returns the number of constructors that appear in a value of any datatype that is an instance of *Data*. For example, if it is applied to a list containing pairs, it will count both the constructors of the datatype List, and of the datatype for pairs. Given the general type of *gfoldl*, we have to use a container type for the result type Int and perform additional boxing and unboxing. The type parameter x of IntBox is a phantom type: it is not used as a value, but is necessary for type correctness.

Function *gunfold* acts as the dual operation of the *gfoldl*: *gfoldl* is a generic consumer, which consumes a datatype value generically to produce some result, and *gunfold* is a generic producer, which consumes a datatype value to produce a datatype value generically. Its definition relies on *constrIndex*, which returns the index of the constructor in the datatype of the argument. It is technically not an unfold, but instead a fold on a different view [Hinze and Löh, 2006].

The two other methods of class *Data* which we have not yet mentioned are *toConstr* and *dataTypeOf*. These functions return, as their names suggest, constructor and datatype representations of the term they are applied to. We continue our example of the *Data* instance for the List datatype.[8]

$$
\begin{array}{lll}
toConstr & Nil & = con_1 \\
toConstr & (Cons\quad) & = con_2 \\
dataTypeOf & & = ty \\
dataCast1\quad f & & = gcast1\ f
\end{array}
$$
$$con_1 = mkConstr\ ty\ \texttt{"Empty\_List"}\ [\,]\ Prefix$$
$$con_2 = mkConstr\ ty\ \texttt{"Cons\_List"}\ [\,]\ Prefix$$
$$ty\ \ = mkDataType\ \texttt{"ModuleNameHere"}\ [con_1, con_2]$$

The functions *mkConstr* and *mkDataType* are provided by the SYB library as means for building Constr and DataType, respectively. *mkConstr* build a constructor representation given the constructor's datatype representation, name, list of field labels and

---

[8] Instead of `"ModuleNameHere"` one should supply the appropriate module name, which is used for unambiguous identification of a datatype.

fixity. *mkDataType* builds a datatype representation given the datatype's name and list of constructor representations. These two methods together form the basis of SYB's type reflection mechanism, allowing the user to inspect and construct types at runtime. Finally, since the List datatype is not of kind $\star$, we have to provide an implementation for the *dataCast1* method in terms of *gcast1*.[9]

SYB supports all datatypes for which we can give a *Data* and *Typeable* instance. This includes all datatypes of Section 3 except GADTs and existentially quantified types, for which we cannot define *gunfold*.

Exercise 13. Write a suitable instance of the *Data* class for the Expr datatype from Section 3.   ■

The basic combinators of SYB are mainly used to define other useful combinators. It is mainly these derived combinators that are used by a generic programmer. Functions like *gunfoldl* appear very infrequently in generic programs. In the next subsection we will show many of the derived combinators in SYB.

7.4   Generic Functions in SYB

We now proceed to show a few generic functions in the SYB approach. In SYB, as in many other approaches, it is often useful to first identify the type of the generic function, before selecting the most appropriate combinators to implement it.

Types of SYB Combinators. Transformations, queries, and builders are some of the important basic combinators of SYB. We discuss the type of each of these.

A transformation transforms an argument value in some way, and returns a value of the same type. It has the following type:

> **type** GenericT $= \forall$a . *Data* a $\Rightarrow$ a $\rightarrow$ a

There is also a monadic variant of transformations, which allows the use of a helper monad in the transformation.

> **type** GenericM m $= \forall$a . *Data* a $\Rightarrow$ a $\rightarrow$ m a

A query function processes an input value to collect information, possibly of another type.

> **type** GenericQ r $= \forall$a . *Data* a $\Rightarrow$ a $\rightarrow$ r

A builder produces a value of a particular type.

> **type** GenericB $= \forall$a . *Data* a $\Rightarrow$ a

---

[9] Datatypes of kind $\star \rightarrow \star$ require the definition of dataCast1, and datatypes of kind $\star \rightarrow \star \rightarrow \star$ require the definition of dataCast2. For datatypes of kind $\star$, the default definition for these methods (*const Nothing*) is appropriate.

A builder that has access to a monad is called a "reader".

$$\textbf{type } \text{GenericR } m = \forall a \, . \, Data \, a \Rightarrow m \, a$$

Note however that the types of both GenericM and GenericR do not require m to be a monad.

Many functions in the SYB library are suffixed with one of the letters T, M, Q, B, or R to help identify their usage. Examples are the functions mkT, mkQ, mkM, $extB$, $extR$, $extQ$, $gmapT$ and $gmapQ$, some of which are defined in the rest of this section.

Basic Examples. Recall the *increment* function with which we started Section 7.1. Its definition uses the higher-order combinators *everywhere* and *mkT*. The former is a traversal pattern for transformations, applying its argument everywhere it can:

$$everywhere :: \text{GenericT} \rightarrow \text{GenericT}$$
$$everywhere \, f = f \, . \, gmapT \, (everywhere \, f)$$

Function $gmapT$ maps a function only to the immediate subterms of an expression. It is defined using $gfoldl$ as follows:

$$gmapT :: Data \, a \Rightarrow (\forall b \, . \, Data \, b \Rightarrow b \rightarrow b) \rightarrow a \rightarrow a$$
$$gmapT \, f \, x = unID \, (gfoldl \, k \, ID \, x)$$
$$\textbf{where}$$
$$k \, (ID \, c) \, y = ID \, (c \, (f \, y))$$
$$\textbf{newtype } \text{ID } x = ID \{ unID :: x \}$$

Exercise 14. Function *everywhere* traverses a (multiway) tree. Define

$$everywhere' :: \text{GenericT} \rightarrow \text{GenericT}$$

as *everywhere* but traversing in the opposite direction.   ∎

Function mkT lifts a (usually type-specific) function to a function that can be applied to a value of any datatype.

$$mkT :: (Typeable \, a, Typeable \, b) \Rightarrow (b \rightarrow b) \rightarrow a \rightarrow a$$

For example, $mkT \, (sin :: \text{Float} \rightarrow \text{Float})$, applies function sin if the input value is of type Float, and the identity function to an input value of any other type. The combination of the two functions *everywhere* and mkT allows us to lift a type-specific function to a generic function and apply it everywhere in a value.

Proceeding from transformations to queries, we define a function that sums all the integers in an expression.

$$total :: \text{GenericQ Int}$$
$$total = everything \, (+) \, (0 \, 'mkQ' \, lit) \, \textbf{where}$$
$$lit :: \text{Expr Int} \rightarrow \text{Int}$$

$$lit\ (Lit\ x) = x$$
$$lit\ x\qquad = 0$$

Queries typically use the *everything* and *mkQ* combinators. Function *everything* applies its second argument everywhere in the argument, and combines results with its first argument. Function *mkQ* lifts a type-specific function of type a $\rightarrow$ b, together with a default value of type b, to a generic a query function of type GenericQ b. If the input value is of type a, then the type-specific function is applied to obtain a b value, otherwise it returns the default value. To sum the literals in an expression, function *total* combines subresults using the addition operator $(+)$, and it keeps occurrences of literals, whereas all other values are replaced by 0.

Generic Maps. Functions such as *increment* and *total* are defined in terms of functions *everywhere*, *everything*, and *mkT*, which in turn are defined in terms of the basic combinators provided by the *Data* and *Typeable* classes. Many generic functions are defined in terms of combinators of the *Data* class directly, as in the examples below. We redefine function *gsize* defined in Section 7.3 using the combinator *gmapQ*, and we define a function *glength*, which determines the number of children of a constructor, also in terms of *gmapQ*.

$$gsize :: Data\ a \Rightarrow a \rightarrow \mathsf{Int}$$
$$gsize\ t = 1 + sum\ (gmapQ\ gsize\ t)$$
$$glength :: \mathsf{GenericQ}\ \mathsf{Int}$$
$$glength = length\ .\ gmapQ\ (const\ ())$$

The combinator *gmapQ* is one of the mapping combinators in *Data* class of the SYB library.

$$gmapQ :: (\forall a\ .\ Data\ a \Rightarrow a \rightarrow u) \rightarrow a \rightarrow [u]$$

It is rather different from the regular list *map* function, in that works on any datatype that is an instance of *Data*, and that it only applies its argument function to the immediate children of the top-level constructor. So for lists, it only applies the argument function to the head of the list and the tail of the list, but it does not recurse into the list. This explains why *gsize* recursively calls itself in *gmapQ*, while *glength*, which only counts immediate children, does not use recursion.

Exercise 15. Define the function:

$$gdepth :: \mathsf{GenericQ}\ \mathsf{Int}$$

which computes the depth of a value of any datatype using *gmapQ*. The depth of a value is the maximum number of constructors on any path to a leaf in the value. For example:

$$gdepth\ [1,2] \rightsquigarrow$$
$$gdepth\ (Lit\ 1 + Lit\ 2 + Var\ "x") \rightsquigarrow$$

■

Exercise 16. Define the function:

    gwidth :: GenericQ Int

which computes the width of a value of any datatype using *gmapQ*. The width of a value is the number of elements that appear at a leaf. For example:

$$gwidth\ () \rightsquigarrow$$
$$gwidth\ (Just\ 1) \rightsquigarrow$$
$$gwidth\ ((1,2),(1,2)) \rightsquigarrow$$
$$gwidth\ (((1,2),2),(1,2)) \rightsquigarrow$$

■

Equality. Defining the generic equality function is a relatively simple task in the libraries we have introduced previously. Defining equality in SYB is not that easy. The reason for this is that the structural representation of datatypes is not exposed directly—in SYB, generic functions are written using combinators like *gfoldl*. To define generic equality we need to generically traverse two values at the same time, and it is not immediately clear how we can do this if *gfoldl* is our basic traversal combinator.

To implement equality, we need a generic zip-like function that can be used to pair together the children of the two argument values. Recall the type of Haskell's *zipWith* function.

    zipWith :: $(a \rightarrow b \rightarrow c) \rightarrow [a] \rightarrow [b] \rightarrow [c]$

However, we need a generic variant that works not only for lists but for any datatype. For this purpose, SYB provides the *gzipWithQ* combinator.

    gzipWithQ :: GenericQ (GenericQ c) $\rightarrow$ GenericQ (GenericQ [c])

The type of *gzipWithQ* is rather intricate, but if we unfold the definition of GenericQ, and omit the occurrences of $\forall$ and *Data*, the argument of *gzipWithQ* has type $a \rightarrow b \rightarrow c$. It would take too much space to explain the details of *gzipWithQ*. Defining equality using *gzipWithQ* is easy:

    geq :: $Data\ a \Rightarrow a \rightarrow a \rightarrow$ Bool
    geq $x\ y = geq'\ x\ y$
        where
          geq' :: GenericQ (GenericQ Bool)
          geq' $x'\ y' = (toConstr\ x' \quad toConstr\ y') \wedge and\ (gzipWithQ\ geq'\ x'\ y')$

The outer function *eq* is used to constrain the type of the function to the type of equality. Function *geq'* has a more general type since it only uses *gzipWithQ* (besides some functions on booleans).

7.5 Support for Overloading

Suppose we want to implement the generic *show* function. Here is a first attempt using the combinators we have introduced in the previous sections.

$$gshow_s :: Data \; a \Rightarrow a \rightarrow String$$
$$gshow_s \; t = "\,(\,"$$
$$+\!\!\!+ showConstr \; (toConstr \; t)$$
$$+\!\!\!+ concat \; (gmapQ \; ((+\!\!\!+) \; "\,\;\," . gshow_s) \; t)$$
$$+\!\!\!+$$
$$"\,)\,"$$

Function *showConstr* :: Constr $\rightarrow$ String is the only function we have not yet introduced. Its behavior is apparent from its type: it returns the string representing the name of the constructor. Function $gshow_s$ returns the string representation of any input value. However, it does not implement **deriving** *Show* faithfully: it inserts too many parentheses, and, what's worse, it treats all types in a uniform way, so both lists and strings are shown using the names of the constructors *Cons* and *Nil*.

$$gshow_s \; "abc" \rightsquigarrow "\,(\,(\,:\,)\;\;(a)\;\;(\,(\,:\,)\;\;(b)\;\;(\,(\,:\,)\;\;(c)\;\;(\,[\,]\,)\,)\,)\,)\,"$$

The problem here is that $gshow_s$ is "too generic": we want its behavior to be non-generic for certain datatypes, such as String. To obtain special behavior for a particular type we use the *ext* combinators of the SYB library. Since function $gshow_s$ has the type of a generic query, we use the *extQ* combinator:

$$extQ :: (Typeable \; a, Typeable \; b) \Rightarrow (a \rightarrow q) \rightarrow (b \rightarrow q) \rightarrow a \rightarrow q$$

This combinator takes an initial generic query and extends it with the type-specific case given in its second argument. It can be seen as a two-way case branch: if the input term (the last argument) is of type b, then the second function is applied. If not, then the first function is applied. Its implementation relies on type-safe cast:

$$extQ \; f \; g \; a = maybe \; (f \; a) \; g \; (cast \; a)$$

Function *cast* relies on the *typeOf* method of the *Typeable* class (the type of which we have introduced in Section 7.2), to guarantee type equality and ultimately uses *unsafeCoerce* to perform the cast.

Using *extQ*, we can now define a better pretty-printer:

$$gshow :: Data \; a \Rightarrow a \rightarrow String$$
$$gshow = (\lambda t \rightarrow$$
$$"\,(\,"$$
$$+\!\!\!+ showConstr \; (toConstr \; t)$$
$$+\!\!\!+ concat \; (gmapQ \; ((+\!\!\!+) \; "\,\;\," . gshow) \; t)$$
$$+\!\!\!+ "\,)\,"$$
$$) \;\, `extQ` \; (show :: String \rightarrow String)$$

Summarizing, the *extQ* combinator (together with its companions *extT*, *extR*, ...) is the mechanism for overloading in the SYB approach.

Exercise 17

1. Check the behavior of function *gshow* on a value of type Char, and redefine it to behave just like the standard Haskell *show*.
2. Check the behavior of *gshow* on standard Haskell lists, and redefine it to behave just like the standard Haskell *show*. Note: since the list datatype has kind $\star \to \star$, using *extQ* will give problems. This problem is solved in SYB by defining combinators for higher kinds. Have a look at the *ext1Q* combinator.
3. Check the behavior of *gshow* on standard Haskell pairs, and redefine it to behave just like the standard Haskell *show*. Note: now the datatype has kind $\star \to \star \to \star$, but *ext2Q* is not defined! Fortunately, you can define it yourself...
4. Make the function more efficient by changing its return type to ShowS and using function composition instead of list concatenation.

■

Exercise 18. Define function *gread* :: $(Data\ a) \Rightarrow String \to [(a, String)]$. Decide for yourself how complete you want your solution to be regarding whitespace, infix operators, etc. Note: you don't have to use *gunfold* directly: *fromConstr*, which is itself defined using *gunfold*, can be used instead. ■

7.6   Making Generic Functions Extensible

The SYB library as described above suffers from a serious drawback: after a generic function is defined, it cannot be extended to have special behavior on a new datatype. We can, as illustrated in Section 7.5 with function *gshow*, define a function with type-specific behavior. But after such function is defined, defining another function to extend the first one with more type-specific behavior is impossible. Suppose we want to extend the *gshow* function with special behavior for a new datatype:

data NewDatatype $=$ *One* String | *Two* [Int] **deriving** (*Typeable, Data*)

gshow' :: *Data* a $\Rightarrow$ a $\to$ String

$gshow' = gshow\ 'extQ'\ showNewDatatype$ **where**
    showNewDatatype :: NewDatatype $\to$ String
    showNewDatatype (*One* s) $=$ "String: " $+\!\!+ s$
    showNewDatatype (*Two* l) $=$ "List: " $+\!\!+ gshow\ l$

Now we have:

$$gshow'\ (One\ "a") \rightsquigarrow "String:\ a"$$

as we expected. However:

$$gshow'\ (One\ "a", One\ "b") \rightsquigarrow "((,)\ (One\ \backslash"a\backslash")\ (One\ \backslash"b\backslash"))"$$

This example illustrates the problem: as soon as *gshow'* calls *gshow*, the type-specific behavior we just defined is never again taken into account, since *gshow* has no knowledge of the existence of *gshow'*.

To make generic functions in SYB extensible, Lämmel and Peyton Jones [2005] extended the SYB library, lifting generic functions to Haskell's type class system. A generic function like *gsize* is now defined as follows:

```
class Size a where
    gsize :: a → Int
```

The default case is written as an instance of the form:

```
instance ... ⇒ Size a where ...
```

Ad-hoc cases are instances of the form (using lists as an example):

```
instance Size a ⇒ Size [a] where ...
```

This requires overlapping instances, since the default case is more general than any type-specific extension. Fortunately, GHC allows overlapping instances. A problem is that this approach also needs to lift generic combinators like *gmapQ* to a type class, which requires abstraction over type classes. Abstraction over type classes is not supported by GHC. The authors then proceed to describe how to circumvent this by encoding an abstraction using dictionaries. This requires the programmer to write the boilerplate code of the proxy for the dictionary type. We do not discuss this extension and refer the reader to [Lämmel and Peyton Jones, 2005] for further information.

7.7   An Explicit View for SYB

Unlike in the two approaches we have seen before, the mechanism for run-time type representation in SYB does not involve an explicit generic view on data. Scrap Your Boilerplate Reloaded [Hinze et al., 2006] presents an alternative interpretation of SYB by replacing the combinator based approach by a tangible representation of the structure of values. The Spine datatype is used to encode the structure of datatypes.

```
data Spine :: ⋆ → ⋆ where
    Con :: a → Spine a
    (◇) :: Spine (a → b) → Typed a → Spine b
```

The Typed representation is given by:

```
data Typed a = (⌃){ typeOf :: Type a, val :: a }
data Type :: ⋆ → ⋆ where
    Int  :: Type Int
    List :: Type a → Type [a]
    ...
```

This approach represents the structure of datatype values by making the application of a constructor to its arguments explicit. For example, the list $[1,2]$ can be represented by[10] $Con\ (:) \diamond (Int \mathbin{\hat{\,}} 1) \diamond (List\ Int \mathbin{\hat{\,}} [2])$. We can define the usual SYB combinators

---

[10] Note the difference between the list constructor (:) and the Typed constructor (⌃).

such as *gfoldl* on the Spine datatype. Function *gunfold* cannot be implemented in the approach. Scrap Your Boilerplate Revolutions [Hinze and Löh, 2006] solves this problem by introducing the "type spine" and "lifted spine" views. These views allow the definition of not only generic readers such as *gunfold*, but even functions that abstract over type constructors, such as *map*, in a natural way. Additionally, functions taking multiple arguments (such as generic equality) also become straightforward to define.

A disadvantage of having the explicit Spine view that generic and non-generic universe extension require recompilation of type representations and generic functions. For this reason, these variants cannot be used as a library, and should be considered a design pattern instead. It is possible to make the variants extensible by using a similar approach as discussed in Section 7.6: abstraction over type classes. We refer the reader to [Hinze et al., 2006, Hinze and Löh, 2006] for further information.

7.8   Case Study: Selections in Exercises Assistants

One of the extensions to the exercise assistants that we are implementing is that a student may select a subexpression and ask for possible rewrite rules for that subexpression. This means that the student selects a range in a pretty-printed expression and chooses a rule to apply to the selection.

Before we can present the possible rewrite rules, we want to check if a selected subexpression is *valid*. Determining the validity of a subexpression may depend on the context. In the general case, a subexpression is valid if it is a typed value that appears in the abstract syntax tree of the original expression. However, in some cases this definition might be too strict. For instance, for arithmetic expressions, the expression $2 + 3$ would not be a subexpression of $1 + 2 + 3$, because the plus operator is left-associative, hence only $1 + 2$ is a valid subexpression. Therefore we consider a subexpression to be valid if it appears in the original expression modulo associative operators and special cases (such as lists).

Checking whether a subexpression is valid or not can be determined in various ways. It is important to realize that the problem is strongly connected to the concrete syntax of the datatype. The validity of a selection depends on how terms are pretty-printed on the screen. Aspects to consider are fixity and associativity of operators, parentheses, etc. Simply parsing the selection will not give an acceptable solution. For instance, in the expression $1 + 2 * 3$, the selection $1 + 2$ parses correctly, but it is not a valid subexpression.

For these reasons, the selection problem depends on parsing and pretty-printing, and the way a datatype is read and shown to the user. Therefore we think that the best way to solve this problem is to devise an extended parser or pretty-printer, which additionally constructs a function that can check the validity of a selection.

However, parsers and pretty-printers for realistic languages are usually not generic. Typically, operator precedence and fixity are used to reduce the number of parentheses and to make the concrete syntax look more natural. Therefore, parsers and pretty-printers are often hand-written, or instances of a generic function with ad-hoc cases.

For conciseness, we will present only a simple solution to this problem, which works for datatypes that are shown with the *gshow* function of the previous section. For simplicity, we do not deal with associativity or infix constructors. We use a state monad transformer with an embedded writer monad. The state monad keeps track of the current position using an Int, while the writer monad gradually builds a Map. Ideally, this would map a selection range (consisting of a pair of Ints) to the type of that selection. This is necessary because an expression might contain subexpressions of different types. However, for simplicity we let Type be singleton.

```
type Range     = (Int, Int)
type Type      = ()
type Selections = Map Range Type

type Pos       = Int
type MyState   = StateT Pos (Writer Selections) ()
```

Using the monad transformer in this way enables us to maintain the position as state while building the output Map at the same time, avoiding manual threading of these values.

The top-level function *selections* runs the monads. Within the monads, we first get the current position (m). Then we calculate the position at the end of the argument expression (n), and add the selection of the complete expression (m, n) to the output Map. The main worker function *selsConstr* calculates the selections within the children of the top-level node. *selsConstr* defines the general behavior, and through overloading pairs and strings are given ad-hoc behavior.

```
selections :: Data a ⇒ a → Selections
selections t' = execWriter (evalStateT (sels' t') 0) where
    sels' :: Data a ⇒ a → MyState
    sels' t = do
                m ← get
                let n = m + length (gshow t)
                tell (M.singleton (m, n) ())
                (selsConstr 'ext2Q' selsPair 'extQ' selsString) t
                put n
```

For the children of the current term we use different functions based on the type. After the children are done we set the current position to the end of this term. This means that the functions that process the children do not need to care about updating the position to reflect finalizing elements (such as a closing bracket, for instance).

Children are dealt with as follows. In case there are no children, the position has to be updated to take into account the opening bracket, the length of the constructor and the closing bracket. If there are children, we recursively apply the worker function to each child. However, the arguments of a constructor are separated by a space, so we have to increment the position in between each child. This is done with *intersperse* (*modify* ($+1$)). Finally the list of resulting monads is sequenced:

```
selsConstr :: Data a ⇒ a → MyState
selsConstr t = do
                when (nrChildren t > 0) $
```

$$modify \ (+(2 + length \ (showConstr \ (toConstr \ t))))$$
$$sequence \ \$ \ intersperse \ (modify \ (+1)) \ \$ \ gmapQ \ sels' \ t$$

The *nrChildren* function returns the number of children of the argument expression, irrespective of their type.

As with function *gshow*, we need different code to handle some specific types. For pairs and Strings we use the following:

$$selsPair :: (Data \ a, Data \ b) \Rightarrow (a, b) \rightarrow MyState$$
$$selsPair \ (a, b) = \textbf{do}$$
$$\qquad\qquad\qquad modify \ (+1)$$
$$\qquad\qquad\qquad sels' \ a$$
$$\qquad\qquad\qquad modify \ (+1)$$
$$\qquad\qquad\qquad sels' \ b$$
$$selsString :: String \rightarrow MyState$$
$$selsString \ t = return \ ()$$

The trivial definition of *selsString* ensures that a String is not seen as a list of characters.

We can check that our function behaves as expected (for the Logic$_s$ type of Section 3.4):

$$map \ fst \ . \ M.to_{List} \ . \ selections \ \$ \ (Or \ (Not \ (Lit \ True)) \ (Lit \ False)) \rightsquigarrow$$
$$[(0, 37), (4, 22), (9, 21), (14, 20), (23, 36), (28, 35)]$$

Indeed we can confirm that

$(0, 37)$ corresponds to $(Or \ (Not \ (Lit \ (True))) \ (Lit \ (False)))$

$(4, 22)$ corresponds to $(Not \ (Lit \ (True)))$

$(9, 21)$ corresponds to $(Lit \ (True))$

$(14, 20)$ corresponds to $(True)$

$(23, 36)$ corresponds to $(Lit \ (False))$

$(28, 35)$ corresponds to $(False)$

As mentioned before, the *selections* function presented in this section has been simplified in many ways. Possible improvements include support for operator fixity and precedence (which change the parentheses), mapping a range to the actual value in the selection, dealing with associative operators and decoupling from a fixed pretty-printer (*gshow* in this case). Additionally, selections of constant types (such as Bool in the example above) are typically not relevant and should not be considered valid.

Exercise 19. Extend the *selections* function with a specific case for lists. Valid selections within a list are every element and the entire list. Additionally, change Type to Dynamic (introduced in Section 3.6). ∎

8 Comparison of the Libraries

In the sections 5, 6, and 7, we introduced three libraries for generic programming in Haskell. There are many other libraries that we exclude for lack of space (see Section 9.1 for a list). The obvious question a Haskell programmer who wants to implement a generic program now asks is: Which library do I use for my project? The answer to this question is, of course, that it depends. In this section, we present an abridged comparison of the three libraries we have seen, focusing mainly on the differences between them. For further study, we refer the reader to a recent, extensive comparison of multiple generic programming libraries and their characteristics [Rodriguez et al., 2008b].

8.1 Differences

There are a few aspects in which the three libraries we have presented differ considerably.

Universe Size. What are the datatypes for which generic universe extension is possible? In Section 3, we saw a variety of Haskell datatypes. The more datatypes a library can support, the more useful that library will be. None of the libraries supports existentially quantified datatypes or GADTs. On the other hand, all libraries support all the other datatypes mentioned.

SYB's automatic derivation does not work for higher-order kinded datatypes, but the programmer can still add the instances manually. Datatypes which are both higher-order kinded and nested are not supported by SYB. Both LIGD and EMGM can support such datatypes, but they cannot be used with EMGM's representation dispatchers.

First-class Generic Functions. If generic functions are first-class, they can be passed as argument to other generic functions. *gmapQ* (as introduced in Section 7.4) is an example of a function which can only be defined if generic functions are first-class.

In LIGD and SYB, a generic function is a polymorphic Haskell function, so it is a first-class value in Haskell implementations that support rank-n polymorphism.

EMGM supports first-class generic functions but in a rather complicated way. The type class instance for a higher-order generic function needs to track calls to a generic function argument. This makes the definition of *gmapQ* in EMGM significantly more complex than other functions.

Ad-hoc Definitions for Datatypes. A library supports ad-hoc definitions for datatypes if it can define functions with specific behavior on a particular datatype while the other datatypes are handled generically. Moreover, the use of ad-hoc cases should not require recompilation of existing code (for instance the type representations).

In LIGD, giving ad-hoc cases requires extending the type representation datatype, and hence recompilation of the module containing type representations. This means the library itself must be changed, so we consider LIGD not to support ad-hoc definitions.

In SYB, ad-hoc cases for queries are supported by means of the *mkQ* and *extQ* combinators. Such combinators are also available for other traversals, for example transformations. The only requirement for ad-hoc cases is that the type being case-analyzed should be an instance of the *Typeable* type class. The new instance does not require recompilation of other modules. In EMGM, ad-hoc cases are given as instances of *Rep*, *FRep*, or one of the other representation dispatchers. Recompilation of the library is not required, because ad-hoc cases are given as type class instances.

Extensibility. If a programmer can extend the universe of a generic function in a different module without the need for recompilation, then the approach is extensible. This is the case for libraries that allow the extension of the generic *show* function with a case for printing lists, for instance. Extensibility is not possible for approaches that do not support ad-hoc cases. For this reason, LIGD is not extensible.

The SYB library supports ad-hoc definitions, but does not support extensible generic functions (as outlined in Section 7.6).

In EMGM, ad-hoc cases are given in instance declarations, which may reside in separate modules; therefore, the library supports extensibility.

Overhead of Library Use. The overhead of library use can be compared in different ways including automatic generation of representations, number of structure representations, and amount of work to define and instantiate a generic function.

SYB is the only library that offers support for automatic generation of representations. It relies on GHC to generate *Typeable* and *Data* instances for new datatypes. This reduces the amount of work for the programmer.

The number of structure representations is also an important factor of overhead. LIGD and EMGM have two sorts of representations: a representation for kind $\star$ types and representations for type constructors, which are arity-based. The latter consists of a number of arity-specific representations. For example, to write the *map* function we have to use a representation of arity two. Since there are useful generic functions requiring a representation of arity three, this makes a total of four type representations for these libraries: one to represent kind $\star$ types, and three for all useful arities. In SYB, the structure representation is given in a *Data* instance. This instance has two methods which are used for generic consumer and transformer functions (*gfoldl*) and generic producer functions (*gunfold*). Therefore, every datatype needs two representations to be used with SYB functions.

Instantiating a generic function should preferably also be simple. Generic functions require a value representing the type to which they are instantiated. This representation may be explicitly supplied by the programmer or implicitly derived. In approaches that use type classes, representations can be derived, thus making instantiation easier for the user. Such is the case for SYB and EMGM. LIGD uses an explicit type representation, which the user has to supply with every generic function call.

Practical Aspects. With practical aspects we mean the availability of a library distribution, quality of documentation, predefined generic functions, etc.

LIGD does not have a distribution online. EMGM recently gained an online status with a website, distribution, and extensive documentation [Utrecht, 2008]. Many generic functions and common datatype representations are provided. SYB is distributed with the GHC compiler. This distribution includes a number of traversal combinators for common generic programming tasks and Haddock documentation. The GHC compiler supports the automatic generation of *Typeable* and *Data* instances.

Portability. The fewer extensions of the Haskell 98 standard (or of the coming Haskell Prime [Haskell Prime list, 2006] standard) an approach requires, the more portable it is across different Haskell compilers.

LIGD, as presented here, relies on GADTs for the type representation. It is not yet clear if GADTs will be included in Haskell Prime. LIGD also requires rank-2 types for the representations of higher-kinded datatypes, but not for other representations or functions. Hence rank-n types are not essential for the LIGD approach, and LIGD is the most portable of the three libraries.

Generics for the Masses as originally introduced [Hinze, 2004] was entirely within Haskell 98; however, EMGM as described in these notes is not as portable. It relies on multiparameter type classes to support implicit type representations and type operators for convenience (both currently slated to become part of Haskell Prime). The features for supporting convenient extensibility (Sections 6.5 and 6.6) also rely on overlapping and undecidable instances, and we do not know if these will become part of Haskell Prime.

SYB requires rank-n polymorphism for the type of the *gfoldl* and *gunfold* combinators, *unsafeCoerce* to implement type safe casts and compiler support for deriving *Data* and *Typeable* instances. Hence, it is the least portable of the three libraries.

8.2   Similarities

There are a couple of aspects in which the libraries are similar.

Abstraction Over Type Constructors. Generic functions like *map* or *crush* require abstraction over type constructors to be defined. Type constructors are types which expect a type argument (and therefore have kind $\star \rightarrow \star$), and represent containers of elements. All libraries support the definition of such functions, although the definition in SYB is rather cumbersome[11].

Separate Compilation. Is generic universe extension modular? A library that can instantiate a generic function to a new datatype without recompiling the function definition or the type/structure representation is modular.

All presented libraries are modular. In LIGD, representation types have a constructor to represent the structure of datatypes, namely *RType*. It follows that generic universe extension requires no extension of the representation datatypes and therefore no recompilation. In EMGM, datatype structure is represented by *rtype*, so a similar argument applies. In SYB, generic universe extension is achieved by defining *Data* and *Typeable* instances for the new datatype, which does not require recompilation of existing code in other modules.

Multiple Arguments. Can a generic programming library support a generic function definition that consumes more than one generic argument? Functions such as generic equality require this. The LIGD and EMGM approaches support the definition of generic

---

[11] This has recently been shown by Reinke [2008] and Kiselyov [2008]. However, the definition is rather intricate, and as such we do not present it in these notes.

equality. Furthermore, equality is not more difficult to define than other consumer functions. Equality can also be defined in SYB, but the definition is not as direct as for other functions such as *gshow*. In SYB, the *gfoldl* combinator processes just one argument at a time. For this reason, the definition of generic equality has to perform the traversal of the arguments in two stages using the generic zip introduced in Section 7.4.

Constructor Names. All generic programming libraries discussed in these notes provide support for constructor names in their structure representations. These names are used by generic show functions.

Consumers, Transformer and Producers. LIGD and EMGM can define consumer, transformer, and producer functions. SYB can also define them, but consumers and producers are written using different combinators.

9   Conclusions

These lecture notes serve as an introduction to generic programming in Haskell. We begin with a look at the context of generics and variations on this theme. The term "generics" usually involves some piece of a program parametrised by some other piece. The most basic form is the function, a computation parametrised by values. A more interesting category is genericity by the shape of a datatype. This has been studied extensively in Haskell, because datatypes plays a central role in program development.

We next explore the world of datatypes. From monomorphic types with no abstraction to polymorphic types with universal quantification to existentially quantified types that can simulate dynamically typed values, there is a wide range of possibilities in Haskell. The importance of datatypes has led directly to a number of attempts to develop methods to increase code reuse when using multiple, different types.

In the last decade, many generic programming approaches have resulted in libraries. Language extensions have also been studied, but libraries have been found to be easier to ship, support, and maintain. We cover three representative libraries in detail: LIGD, EMGM, and SYB. LIGD passes a run-time type representation to a generic function. EMGM relies on type classes to represent structure and dispatching on the appropriate representation. SYB builds generic functions with basic traversal combinators.

Having introduced variants of generic programming libraries in Haskell, we can imagine that the reader wants to explore this area further. For that purpose, we provide a collection of references to help in this regard.

Lastly, we speculate on the future of libraries for generic programming. Given what we have seen in this field, where do we think the research and development work will be next? What are the problems we should focus on, and what advances will help us out?

9.1   Further Reading

We provide several categories for further reading on topics related to generic programming, libraries, programming languages, and similar concepts or background.

Generic Programming Libraries in Haskell. Each of these articles describes a particular generic programming library or approach in Haskell.

LIGD	[Cheney and Hinze, 2002]
SYB	[Lämmel and Peyton Jones, 2003]
	[Lämmel and Peyton Jones, 2004]
PolyLib	[Norell and Jansson, 2004a]
EMGM	[Hinze, 2004, 2006]
	[Oliveira et al., 2006]
SYB with Class	[Lämmel and Peyton Jones, 2005]
Spine	[Hinze et al., 2006]
	[Hinze and Löh, 2006]
RepLib	[Weirich, 2006]
Smash your Boilerplate	[Kiselyov, 2006]
Uniplate	[Mitchell and Runciman, 2007]
Generic Programming, Now!	[Hinze and Löh, 2007]

Generic Programming in Other Programming Languages. We mention a few references for generic programming using language extensions and in programming languages other than Haskell.

Generic Haskell	[Löh, 2004, Hinze and Jeuring, 2003b]
OCaml	[Yallop, 2007]
ML	[Karvonen, 2007]
Java	[Palsberg and Jay, 1998]
Clean	[Alimarine and Plasmijer, 2002]
Maude	[Clavel et al., 2000]
Relational languages	[Backhouse et al., 1991]
	[Bird and Moor, 1997]
Dependently typed languages	[Pfeifer and Ruess, 1999]
	[Altenkirch and McBride, 2003]
	[Benke et al., 2003]

Comparison of Techniques. Here we list some references comparing different techniques of generic programming, whether that be with language extensions, libraries, or between different programming languages.

Approaches in Haskell	[Hinze et al., 2007]
Libraries in Haskell	[Rodriguez et al., 2008b]
	[Rodriguez et al., 2008a]
Language Support	[Garcia et al., 2007]
C++ Concepts and Haskell Type Classes	[Bernardy et al., 2008]

Background. Lastly, we add some sources that explain the background behind generic programming in Haskell. Some of these highlight connections to theorem proving and category theory.

Generic Programs and Proofs	[Hinze, 2000]
An Introduction to Generic Programming	[Backhouse et al., 1999]
ADTs and Program Transformation	[Malcolm, 1990]
Law and Order in Algorithmics	[Fokkinga, 1992]
Functional Programming with Morphisms	[Meijer et al., 1991]

9.2   The Future of Generic Programming Libraries

There has been a wealth of activity on generic programming in the last decade and on libraries for generic programming in Haskell in the last five years. Generic programming is spreading through the community, and we expect the use of such techniques to increase in the coming years. Generic programming libraries are also getting more mature and more powerful, and the number of examples of generic programs is increasing.

We expect that libraries will replace language extensions such as Generic Haskell—and possibly Generic Clean [Alimarine and Plasmijer, 2002]—since they are more flexible, easier to maintain and distribute, and often equally as powerful. In particular, if the community adopts type families and GADTs as common programming tools, there is no reason to have separate language extensions for generic programming. Since each generic programming library comes with some boilerplate code, for example for generating embedding-projection pairs, we expect that generic programming libraries will be accompanied by code-generation tools.

Generic programs are useful in many software packages, but we expect that compilers and compiler-like programs will particularly profit from generic programs. However, to be used in compilers, generic programs must not introduce performance penalties. At the moment, GHC's partial evaluation techniques are not powerful enough to remove the performance penalty caused by transforming values of datatypes to values in type representations, performing the generic functionality, and transforming the result back again to the original datatype. By incorporating techniques for partial evaluation of generic programs [Alimarine and Smetsers, 2004], GHC will remove the performance overhead and make generic programs a viable alternative.

Acknowledgements. This work has been partially funded by the Netherlands Organisation for Scientific Research (NWO), via the Real-life Datatype-Generic programming project, project nr. 612.063.613, and by the Portuguese Foundation for Science and Technology (FCT), via the SFRH/BD/35999/2007 grant.

We are grateful to many people for their comments on these lecture notes. The anonymous referee suggested many improvements to the text. Americo Vargas and students of the Generic Programming course at Utrecht University provided feedback on an early version. The attendees at the 2008 Summer School on Advanced Functional Programming provided further reactions.

References

Alexandrescu, A.: Modern C++ design: generic programming and design patterns applied. Addison-Wesley Longman Publishing Co., Inc., Boston (2001)

Alimarine, A., Plasmijer, R.: A generic programming extension for Clean. In: Arts, T., Mohnen, M. (eds.) IFL 2002. LNCS, vol. 2312, pp. 168–186. Springer, Heidelberg (2002)

Alimarine, A., Smetsers, S.: Optimizing generic functions. In: Kozen, D. (ed.) MPC 2004. LNCS, vol. 3125, pp. 16–31. Springer, Heidelberg (2004)

Altenkirch, T., McBride, C.: Generic programming within dependently typed programming. In: Gibbons, J., Jeuring, J. (eds.) Generic Programming. IFIP, vol. 243, pp. 1–20. Kluwer Academic Publishers, Dordrecht (2003)

Backhouse, R., de Bruin, P., Malcolm, G., Voermans, E., van der Woude, J.: Relational catamorphisms. In: Möller, B. (ed.) Proceedings of the IFIP TC2/WG2.1 Working Conference on Constructing Programs, pp. 287–318. Elsevier Science Publishers B.V, Amsterdam (1991)

Backhouse, R., Jansson, P., Jeuring, J., Meertens, L.: Generic programming—an introduction. In: Swierstra, S.D., Oliveira, J.N. (eds.) AFP 1998. LNCS, vol. 1608, pp. 28–115. Springer, Heidelberg (1999)

Benke, M., Dybjer, P., Jansson, P.: Universes for generic programs and proofs in Sdependent type theory. Nordic Journal of Computing 10(4), 265–289 (2003)

Bernardy, J.-P., Jansson, P., Zalewski, M., Schupp, S., Priesnitz, A.: A comparison of C++ concepts and Haskell type classes. In: ACM SIGPLAN Workshop on Generic Programming. ACM, New York (2008)

Bertot, Y., Castéran, P.: Interactive Theorem Proving and Program Development. In: Coq'Art: The Calculus of Inductive Constructions. Texts in Theoretical Computer Science. EATCS (2004), ISBN 3-540-20854-2

Bird, R., Meertens, L.: Nested datatypes. In: Jeuring, J. (ed.) MPC 1998. LNCS, vol. 1422, pp. 52–67. Springer, Heidelberg (1998)

Bird, R., de Moor, O.: Algebra of programming. Prentice-Hall, Englewood Cliffs (1997)

Cheney, J., Hinze, R.: A lightweight implementation of generics and dynamics. In: Chakravarty, M. (ed.) Proceedings of the 2002 ACM SIGPLAN workshop on Haskell, Haskell 2002, pp. 90–104. ACM, New York (2002)

Claessen, K., Hughes, J.: Quickcheck: a lightweight tool for random testing of Haskell programs. In: Proceedings of the 5th ACM SIGPLAN International Conference on Functional Programming, ICFP 2000, pp. 268–279. ACM, New York (2000)

Clavel, M., Durán, F., Martí-Oliet, N.: Polytypic programming in Maude. Electronic Notes in Theoretical Computer Science, vol. 36, pp. 339–360 (2000)

Dornan, C., Jones, I., Marlow, S.: Alex User Guide (2003),
http://www.haskell.org/alex

Fokkinga, M.M.: Law and Order in Algorithmics, PhD thesis. University of Twente (1992)

Forman, I.R., Danforth, S.H.: Putting metaclasses to work: a new dimension in object-oriented programming. Addison Wesley Longman Publishing Co., Inc., Redwood City (1999)

Garcia, R., Järvi, J., Lumsdaine, A., Siek, J., Willcock, J.: An extended comparative study of language support for generic programming. Journal of Functional Programming 17(2), 145–205 (2007)

Gibbons, J.: Datatype-generic programming. In: Backhouse, R., Gibbons, J., Hinze, R., Jeuring, J. (eds.) SSDGP 2006. LNCS, vol. 4719, pp. 1–71. Springer, Heidelberg (2007)

The Haskell Prime list. Haskell prime (2006),
http://hackage.haskell.org/trac/haskell-prime

Hinze, R.: Generic programs and proofs. Bonn University, Habilitation (2000)

Hinze, R.: Generics for the masses. In: Proceedings of the ACM SIGPLAN International Conference on Functional Programming, ICFP 2004, pp. 236–243. ACM, New York (2004)

Hinze, R.: Generics for the masses. Journal of Functional Programming 16, 451–482 (2006)

Hinze, R., Jeuring, J.: Generic Haskell: applications. In: Backhouse, R., Gibbons, J. (eds.) Generic Programming. LNCS, vol. 2793, pp. 57–96. Springer, Heidelberg (2003)

Hinze, R., Jeuring, J.: Generic Haskell: practice and theory. In: Backhouse, R., Gibbons, J. (eds.) Generic Programming. LNCS, vol. 2793, pp. 1–56. Springer, Heidelberg (2003)

Hinze, R., Löh, A.: Generic programming in 3D. Science of Computer Programming (to appear, 2009)

Hinze, R., Löh, A.: "Scrap Your Boilerplate" revolutions. In: Uustalu, T. (ed.) MPC 2006. LNCS, vol. 4014, pp. 180–208. Springer, Heidelberg (2006)

Hinze, R., Löh, A.: Generic programming, now! In: Backhouse, R., Gibbons, J., Hinze, R., Jeuring, J. (eds.) SSDGP 2006. LNCS, vol. 4719, pp. 150–208. Springer, Heidelberg (2007)

Hinze, R., Löh, A., Oliveira, B.C.d.S.: "Scrap Your Boilerplate" reloaded. In: Hagiya, M., Wadler, P. (eds.) FLOPS 2006. LNCS, vol. 3945, pp. 13–29. Springer, Heidelberg (2006)

Hinze, R., Jeuring, J., Löh, A.: Comparing approaches to generic programming in Haskell. In: Backhouse, R., Gibbons, J., Hinze, R., Jeuring, J. (eds.) SSDGP 2006. LNCS, vol. 4719, pp. 72–149. Springer, Heidelberg (2007)

Holdermans, S., Jeuring, J., Löh, A., Rodriguez, A.: Generic views on data types. In: Uustalu, T. (ed.) MPC 2006. LNCS, vol. 4014, pp. 209–234. Springer, Heidelberg (2006)

Jeuring, J., Leather, S., Magalhães, J.P., Yakushev, A.R.: Libraries for generic programming in Haskell. Technical Report UU-CS-2008-025, Department of Information and Computing Sciences. Utrecht University (2008)

Karvonen, V.A.J.: Generics for the working ML'er. In: Proceedings of the 2007 Workshop on ML, ML 2007, pp. 71–82. ACM, New York (2007)

Kiselyov, O.: Smash your boilerplate without class and typeable (2006), http://article.gmane.org/gmane.comp.lang.haskell.general/14086

Kiselyov, O.: Compositional gmap in SYB1 (2008), http://www.haskell.org/pipermail/generics/2008-July/000362.html

Lämmel, R., Jones, S.P.: Scrap your boilerplate: a practical approach to generic programming. In: Proceedings of the ACM SIGPLAN Workshop on Types in Language Design and Implementation, TLDI 2003, pp. 26–37. ACM, New York (2003)

Lämmel, R., Jones, S.P.: Scrap more boilerplate: reflection, zips, and generalised casts. In: Proceedings of the ACM SIGPLAN International Conference on Functional Programming, ICFP 2004, pp. 244–255. ACM, New York (2004)

Lämmel, R., Jones, S.P.: Scrap your boilerplate with class: extensible generic functions. In: Proceedings of the ACM SIGPLAN International Conference on Functional Programming, ICFP 2005, pp. 204–215. ACM, New York (2005)

Lempsink, E., Leather, S., Löh, A.: Type-safe diff for families of datatypes (submitted for publication, 2009)

Lodder, J., Jeuring, J., Passier, H.: An interactive tool for manipulating logical formulae. In: Manzano, M., Pérez Lancho, B., Gil, A. (eds.) Proceedings of the Second International Congress on Tools for Teaching Logic (2006)

Löh, A.: Exploring Generic Haskell. PhD thesis, Utrecht University (2004)

Löh, A., Hinze, R.: Open data types and open functions. In: Maher, M. (ed.) Proceedings of the 8th ACM SIGPLAN symposium on Principles and practice of declarative programming, PPDP 2006, pp. 133–144. ACM, New York (2006)

Malcolm, G.: Algebraic data types and program transformation. PhD thesis, Department of Computing Science. Groningen University (1990)

Marlow, S., Gill, A.: Happy User Guide (1997), http://www.haskell.org/happy

Meertens, L.: Calculate polytypically! In: Kuchen, H., Swierstra, S.D. (eds.) PLILP 1996. LNCS, vol. 1140, pp. 1–16. Springer, Heidelberg (1996)

Meijer, E., Fokkinga, M., Paterson, R.: Functional programming with bananas, lenses, envelopes and barbed wire. In: Hughes, J. (ed.) FPCA 1991. LNCS, vol. 523, pp. 124–144. Springer, Heidelberg (1991)

Milner, R.: A theory of type polymorphism in programming. Journal of Computer and System Sciences 17, 348–375 (1978)

Mitchell, N., Runciman, C.: Uniform boilerplate and list processing. In: Proceedings of the 2007 ACM SIGPLAN workshop on Haskell, Haskell 2007. ACM, New York (2007)

Norell, U.: Towards a practical programming language based on dependent type theory. PhD thesis, Chalmers University of Technology and Göteborg University (2007)

Norell, U., Jansson, P.: Polytypic programming in Haskell. In: Trinder, P., Michaelson, G.J., Peña, R. (eds.) IFL 2003. LNCS, vol. 3145, pp. 168–184. Springer, Heidelberg (2004)

Norell, U., Jansson, P.: Prototyping generic programming in Template Haskell. In: Kozen, D. (ed.) MPC 2004. LNCS, vol. 3125, pp. 314–333. Springer, Heidelberg (2004)

Bruno C. d. S. Oliveira, Hinze, R., Löh, A.: Extensible and modular generics for the masses. In: Nilsson, H. (ed.) Revised Selected Papers from the Seventh Symposium on Trends in Functional Programming, TFP 2006, vol. 7, pp. 199–216 (2006)

Palsberg, J., Barry Jay, C.: The essence of the visitor pattern. In: Proceedings of the 22nd IEEE Conference on International Computer Software and Applications, COMPSAC 1998, pp. 9–15 (1998)

Passier, H., Jeuring, J.: Feedback in an interactive equation solver. In: Seppälä, M., Xambo, S., Caprotti, O. (eds.) Proceedings of the Web Advanced Learning Conference and Exhibition, WebALT 2006, pp. 53–68. Oy WebALT Inc. (2006)

Pfeifer, H., Ruess, H.: Polytypic proof construction. In: Bertot, Y., Dowek, G., Hirschowitz, A., Paulin, C., Théry, L. (eds.) TPHOLs 1999. LNCS, vol. 1690, pp. 55–72. Springer, Heidelberg (1999)

Reinke, C.: Traversable functor data, or: X marks the spot (2008), http://www.haskell.org/pipermail/generics/2008-June/000343.html

Rodriguez, A.: Towards Getting Generic Programming Ready for Prime Time. PhD thesis, Utrecht University (2009)

Rodriguez, A., Jeuring, J., Jansson, P., Gerdes, A., Kiselyov, O., Oliveira, B.C.d.S.: Comparing libraries for generic programming in haskell. Technical report, Utrecht University (2008a)

Rodriguez, A., Jeuring, J., Jansson, P., Gerdes, A., Kiselyov, O., Oliveira, B.C.d.S.: Comparing libraries for generic programming in haskell. In: Haskell Symposium 2008 (2008b)

Rodriguez, A., Holdermans, S., Löh, A., Jeuring, J.: Generic programming with fixed points for mutually recursive datatypes. In: Proceedings of the ACM SIGPLAN International Conference on Functional Programming, ICFP 2009 (2009)

Sheard, T.: Using MetaML: A staged programming language. In: Revised Lectures of the Third International School on Advanced Functional Programming (1999)

Sheard, T., Jones, S.P.: Template metaprogramming for Haskell. In: Chakravarty, M.M.T. (ed.) ACM SIGPLAN Haskell Workshop 2002, pp. 1–16. ACM, New York (2002)

Taha, W.: Multi-Stage Programming: Its Theory and Applications. PhD thesis, Oregon Graduate Institute of Science and Technology (1999)

Universiteit Utrecht. EMGM (2008), http://www.cs.uu.nl/wiki/GenericProgramming/EMGM

Wadler, P.: Comprehending monads. In: Proceedings of the 1990 ACM conference on LISP and Functional Programming, LFP 1990, pp. 61–78. ACM, New York (1990)

Wadler, P., Blott, S.: How to make ad-hoc polymorphism less ad-hoc. In: Conference Record of the 16th Annual ACM Symposium on Principles of Programming Languages, pp. 60–76. ACM, New York (1989)

Weirich, S.: RepLib: a library for derivable type classes. In: Proceedings of the 2006 ACM SIGPLAN workshop on Haskell, Haskell 2006, pp. 1–12. ACM, New York (2006)

Yallop, J.: Practical generic programming in OCaml. In: Proceedings of the 2007 workshop on Workshop on ML, ML 2007, pp. 83–94. ACM, New York (2007)

Dependently Typed Programming in Agda

Ulf Norell

Chalmers University, Gothenburg

1 Introduction

In Hindley-Milner style languages, such as Haskell and ML, there is a clear separation between types and values. In a dependently typed language the line is more blurry – types can contain (*depend on*) arbitrary values and appear as arguments and results of ordinary functions.

The standard example of a dependent type is the type of lists of a given length: Vec A n. Here A is the type of the elements and n is the length of the list. Many languages allow you to define lists (or arrays) of a given size, but what makes Vec a true dependent type is that the length of the list can be an arbitrary term, which need not be known at compile time.

Since dependent types allows types to talk about values, we can encode properties of values as types whose elements are proofs that the property is true. This means that a dependently typed programming language can be used as a logic. In order for this logic to be consistent we need to require programs to be total, i.e. they are not allowed to crash or non-terminate.

The rest of these notes are structured as follows: Section 2 introduces the dependently typed language Agda and its basic features, and Section 3 explains a couple of programming techniques made possible by the introduction of dependent types.

2 Agda Basics

Agda is a dependently typed language based on intuitionistic type theory developed at Chalmers University in Gothenburg. This section introduces the basic features of Agda and how they can be employed in the construction of dependently typed programs. Information on how to obtain the Agda system and further details on the topics discussed here can be found on the Agda wiki [2].

This section is a literate Agda file which can be compiled by the Agda system. Hence, we need to start at the beginning: Every Agda file contains a single top-level module whose name corresponds to the name of the file. In this case the file is called AgdaBasics.lagda[1].

```
module AgdaBasics where
```

The rest of your program goes inside the top-level module. Let us start by defining some simple datatypes and functions.

---

[1] Literate Agda files have the extension lagda and ordinary Agda files have the extension agda.

P. Koopman and D. Swierstra (Eds.): AFP 2008, LNCS 5832, pp. 230–266, 2009.

2.1   Datatypes and Pattern Matching

Similar to languages like Haskell and ML, a key concept in Agda is pattern matching over algebraic datatypes. With the introduction of dependent types pattern matching becomes even more powerful as we shall see in Section 2.4 and Section 3. But for now, let us start with simply typed functions and datatypes.

Datatypes are introduced by a `data` declaration, giving the name and type of the datatype as well as the constructors and their types. For instance, here is the type of booleans

```
data Bool : Set where
   true  : Bool
   false : Bool
```

The type of `Bool` is `Set`, the type of small[2] types. Functions over `Bool` can be defined by pattern matching in a for Haskell programmers familiar way:

```
not : Bool -> Bool
not true  = false
not false = true
```

Agda functions are not allowed to crash, so a function definition must cover all possible cases. This will be checked by the type checker and an error is raised if there are missing cases.

In Haskell and ML the type of `not` can be inferred from the defining clauses and so in these languages the type signature is not required. However, in the presence of dependent types this is no longer the case and we are forced to write down the type signature of `not`. This is not a bad thing, since by writing down the type signature we allow the type checker, not only to tell us when we make mistakes, but also to guide us in the construction of the program. When types grow more and more precise the dialog between the programmer and the type checker gets more and more interesting.

Another useful datatype is the type of (unary) natural numbers.

```
data Nat : Set where
   zero : Nat
   suc  : Nat -> Nat
```

Addition on natural numbers can be defined as a recursive function.

```
_+_ : Nat -> Nat -> Nat
zero  + m = m
suc n + m = suc (n + m)
```

In the same way as functions are not allowed to crash, they must also be terminating. To guarantee termination recursive calls have to be made on structurally smaller arguments. In this case `_+_` passes the termination checker since the first argument is getting smaller in the recursive call (n < suc n). Let us define multiplication while we are at it

---

[2] There is hierarchy of increasingly large types. The type of `Set` is `Set1`, whose type is `Set2`, and so on.

```
_*_ : Nat -> Nat -> Nat
zero  * m = zero
suc n * m = m + n * m
```

Agda supports a flexible mechanism for mixfix operators. If a name of a function contains underscores (_) it can be used as an operator with the arguments going where the underscores are. Consequently, the function _+_ can be used as an infix operator writing n + m for _+_ n m. There are (almost) no restrictions on what symbols are allowed as operator names, for instance we can define

```
_or_ : Bool -> Bool -> Bool
true  or x = x
false or _ = false

if_then_else_ : {A : Set} -> Bool -> A -> A -> A
if true  then x else y = x
if false then x else y = y
```

In the second clause of the _or_ function the underscore is a wildcard pattern, indicating that we don't care what the second argument is and we can't be bothered giving it a name. This, of course, means that we cannot refer to it on the right hand side. The precedence and fixity of an operator can be declared with an infix declaration:

```
infixl 60 _*_
infixl 40 _+_
infixr 20 _or_
infix  5 if_then_else_
```

There are some new and interesting bits in the type of if_then_else_. For now, it is sufficient to think about {A : Set} -> as declaring a polymorphic function over a type A. More on this in Sections 2.2 and 2.3.

Just as in Haskell and ML datatypes can be parameterised by other types. The type of lists of elements of an arbitrary type is defined by

```
infixr 40 _::_
data List (A : Set) : Set where
    []   : List A
    _::_ : A -> List A -> List A
```

Again, note that Agda is quite liberal about what is a valid name. Both [] and _::_ are accepted as sensible names. In fact, Agda names can contain arbitrary non-whitespace unicode characters, with a few exceptions, such as parenthesis and curly braces. So, if we really wanted (which we don't) we could define the list type as

```
data _⋆ (α : Set) : Set where
    ε : α ⋆
    _◁_ : α -> α ⋆ -> α ⋆
```

This liberal policy of names means that being generous with whitespace becomes important. For instance, not:Bool->Bool would not be a valid type signature for the not function, since it is in fact a valid name.

2.2   Dependent Functions

Let us now turn our attention to dependent types. The most basic dependent type is the dependent function type, where the result type depends on the value of the argument. In Agda we write (x : A) -> B for the type of functions taking an argument x of type A and returning a result of type B, where x may appear in B. A special case is when x itself is a type. For instance, we can define

```
identity : (A : Set) -> A -> A
identity A x = x

zero' : Nat
zero' = identity Nat zero
```

This is a dependent function taking a type argument A and an element of A and returns the element. This is how polymorphic functions are encoded in Agda. Here is an example of a more intricate dependent function; the function which takes a dependent function and applies it to an argument:

```
apply : (A : Set)(B : A -> Set) ->
          ((x : A) -> B x) -> (a : A) -> B a
apply A B f a = f a
```

Agda accepts some short hands for dependent function types:

- (x : A)(y : B) -> C for (x : A) -> (y : B) -> C , and
- (x y : A) -> B for (x : A)(y : A) -> B .

The elements of dependent function types are lambda terms which may carry explicit type information. Some alternative ways to define the identity function above are:

```
identity₂ : (A : Set) -> A -> A
identity₂ = \A x -> x

identity₃ : (A : Set) -> A -> A
identity₃ = \(A : Set)(x : A) -> x

identity₄ : (A : Set) -> A -> A
identity₄ = \(A : Set) x -> x
```

2.3   Implicit Arguments

We saw in the previous section how dependent functions taking types as arguments could be used to model polymorphic types. The thing with polymorphic functions, however, is that you don't have to say at which type you want to apply it – that is inferred by the type checker. However, in the example of the identity function we had to explicitly provide the type argument when applying the function. In Agda this problem is solved by a general mechanism for *implicit arguments.* To declare a function argument implicit we use curly braces instead of parenthesis in the type: {x : A} -> B means the same thing as (x : A) -> B except that when you use a function of this type the type checker will try to figure out the argument for you.

Using this syntax we can define a new version of the identity function, where you don't have to supply the type argument.

```
id : {A : Set} -> A -> A
id x = x

true' : Bool
true' = id true
```

Note that the type argument is implicit both when the function is applied and when it is defined.

There are no restrictions on what arguments can be made implicit, nor are there any guarantees that an implicit argument can be inferred by the type checker. For instance, we could be silly and make the second argument of the identity function implicit as well:

```
silly : {A : Set}{x : A} -> A
silly {_}{x} = x

false' : Bool
false' = silly {x = false}
```

Clearly, there is no way the type checker could figure out what the second argument to `silly` should be. To provide an implicit argument explicitly you use the implicit application syntax `f {v}`, which gives v as the left-most implicit argument to `f`, or as shown in the example above, `f {x = v}`, which gives v as the implicit argument called x. The name of an implicit argument is obtained from the type declaration.

Conversely, if you want the type checker to fill in a term which needs to be given explicitly you can replace it by an underscore. For instance,

```
one : Nat
one = identity _ (suc zero)
```

It is important to note that the type checker will not do any kind of search in order to fill in implicit arguments. It will only look at the typing constraints and perform unification[3].

Even so, a lot can be inferred automatically. For instance, we can define the fully dependent function composition. (Warning: the following type is not for the faint of heart!)

```
_o_ : {A : Set}{B : A -> Set}{C : (x : A) -> B x -> Set}
      (f : {x : A}(y : B x) -> C x y)(g : (x : A) -> B x)
```

---

[3] Miller pattern unification to be precise.

```
        (x : A) -> C x (g x)
 (f ∘ g) x = f (g x)
```

```
plus-two = suc ∘ suc
```

The type checker can figure out the type arguments A, B, and C, when we use _∘_.

We have seen how to define simply typed datatypes and functions, and how to use dependent types and implicit arguments to represent polymorphic functions. Let us conclude this part by defining some familiar functions.

```
map : {A B : Set} -> (A -> B) -> List A -> List B
map f []       = []
map f (x :: xs) = f x :: map f xs
```

```
_++_ : {A : Set} -> List A -> List A -> List A
[]        ++ ys = ys
(x :: xs) ++ ys = x :: (xs ++ ys)
```

2.4   Datatype Families

So far, the only use we have seen of dependent types is to represent polymorphism, so let us look at some more interesting examples. The type of lists of a certain length, mentioned in the introduction, can be defined as follows:

```
data Vec (A : Set) : Nat -> Set where
  []   : Vec A zero
  _::_ : {n : Nat} -> A -> Vec A n -> Vec A (suc n)
```

This declaration introduces a number of interesting things. First, note that the type of Vec A is Nat -> Set. This means that Vec A is a family of types indexed by natural numbers. So, for each natural number n, Vec A n is a type. The constructors are free to construct elements in an arbitrary type of the family. In particular, [] constructs an element in Vec A zero and _::_ an element in Vec A (suc n) for some n.

There is a distinction between *parameters* and *indices* of a datatype. We say that Vec is parameterised by a type A and indexed over natural numbers.

In the type of _::_ we see an example of a dependent function type. The first argument to _::_ is an implicit natural number n which is the length of the tail. We can safely make n implicit since the type checker can infer it from the type of the third argument.

Finally, note that we chose the same constructor names for Vec as for List. Constructor names are not required to be distinct between different datatypes.

Now, the interesting part comes when we start pattern matching on elements of datatype families. Suppose, for instance, that we want to take the head of a non-empty list. With the Vec type we can actually express the type of non-empty lists, so we define head as follows:

```
head : {A : Set}{n : Nat} -> Vec A (suc n) -> A
head (x :: xs) = x
```

This definition is accepted by the type checker as being exhaustive, despite the fact that we didn't give a case for []. This is fortunate, since the [] case would not even be type correct – the only possible way to build an element of Vec A (suc n) is using the _::_ constructor.

The rule for when you have to include a particular case is very simple: *if it is type correct you have to include it.*

Dot Patterns. Here is another function on Vec:

```
vmap : {A B : Set}{n : Nat} -> (A -> B) -> Vec A n -> Vec B n
vmap f []       = []
vmap f (x :: xs) = f x :: vmap f xs
```

Perhaps surprisingly, the definition map on Vec is exactly the same as on List, the only thing that changed is the type. However, something interesting is going on behind the scenes. For instance, what happens with the length argument when we pattern match on the list? To see this, let us define new versions of Vec and vmap with fewer implicit arguments:

```
data Vec₂ (A : Set) : Nat -> Set where
   nil  : Vec₂ A zero
   cons : (n : Nat) -> A -> Vec₂ A n -> Vec₂ A (suc n)

vmap₂ : {A B : Set}(n : Nat) -> (A -> B) -> Vec₂ A n -> Vec₂ B n
vmap₂ .zero    f nil        = nil
vmap₂ .(suc n) f (cons n x xs) = cons n (f x) (vmap₂ n f xs)
```

What happens when we pattern match on the list argument is that we learn things about its length: if the list turns out to be nil then the length argument must be zero, and if the list is cons n x xs then the only type correct value for the length argument is suc n. To indicate that the value of an argument has been deduced by type checking, rather than observed by pattern matching it is prefixed by a dot (.).

In this example we could choose to define vmap by first pattern matching on the length rather than on the list. In that case we would put the dot on the length argument of cons[4]:

```
vmap₃ : {A B : Set}(n : Nat) -> (A -> B) -> Vec₂ A n -> Vec₂ B n
vmap₃ zero    f nil        = nil
vmap₃ (suc n) f (cons .n x xs) = cons n (f x) (vmap₃ n f xs)
```

The rule for when an argument should be dotted is: *if there is a unique type correct value for the argument it should be dotted.*

---

[4] In fact the dot can be placed on any of the ns. What is important is that there is a unique binding site for each variable in the pattern.

In the example above, the terms under the dots were valid patterns, but in general they can be arbitrary terms. For instance, we can define the image of a function as follows:

```
data Image_∋_ {A B : Set}(f : A -> B) : B -> Set where
   im : (x : A) -> Image f ∋ f x
```

Here we state that the only way to construct an element in the image of f is to pick an argument x and apply f to x. Now if we know that a particular y is in the image of f we can compute the inverse of f on y:

```
inv : {A B : Set}(f : A -> B)(y : B) -> Image f ∋ y -> A
inv f .(f x) (im x) = x
```

Absurd Patterns. Let us define another datatype family, name the family of numbers smaller than a given natural number.

```
data Fin : Nat -> Set where
   fzero : {n : Nat} -> Fin (suc n)
   fsuc  : {n : Nat} -> Fin n -> Fin (suc n)
```

Here fzero is smaller than suc n for any n and if i is smaller than n then fsuc i is smaller than suc n. Note that there is no way of constructing a number smaller than zero. When there are no possible constructor patterns for a given argument you can pattern match on it with the absurd pattern ():

```
magic : {A : Set} -> Fin zero -> A
magic ()
```

Using an absurd pattern means that you do not have to give a right hand side, since there is no way anyone could provide an argument to your function. One might think that the clause would not have to be given at all, that the type checker would see that the matching is exhaustive without any clauses, but remember that a case can only be omitted if there is no type correct way of writing it. In the case of magic a perfectly type correct left hand side is magic x.

It is important to note that an absurd pattern can only be used if there are no valid constructor patterns for the argument, it is not enough that there are no closed inhabitants of the type[5]. For instance, if we define

```
data Empty : Set where
   empty : Fin zero -> Empty
```

Arguments of type Empty can not be matched with an absurd pattern, since there is a perfectly valid constructor pattern that would do: empty x. Hence, to define the magic function for Empty we have to write

---

[5] Since checking type inhabitation is undecidable.

```
magic' : {A : Set} -> Empty -> A
magic' (empty ())
-- magic' ()  -- not accepted
```

Now, let us define some more interesting functions. Given a list of length n and a number i smaller than n we can compute the ith element of the list (starting from 0):

```
_!_ : {n : Nat}{A : Set} -> Vec A n -> Fin n -> A
[]        ! ()
(x :: xs) ! fzero   = x
(x :: xs) ! (fsuc i) = xs ! i
```

The types ensure that there is no danger of indexing outside the list. This is reflected in the case of the empty list where there are no possible values for the index.

The _!_ function turns a list into a function from indices to elements. We can also go the other way, constructing a list given a function from indices to elements:

```
tabulate : {n : Nat}{A : Set} -> (Fin n -> A) -> Vec A n
tabulate {zero} f = []
tabulate {suc n} f = f fzero :: tabulate (f ∘ fsuc)
```

Note that tabulate is defined by recursion over the length of the result list, even though it is an implicit argument. There is in general no correspondance between implicit data and computationally irrelevant data.

2.5 Programs as Proofs

As mentioned in the introduction, Agda's type system is sufficiently powerful to represent (almost) arbitrary propositions as types whose elements are proofs of the proposition. Here are two very simple propositions, the true proposition and the false proposition:

```
data   False : Set where
record True  : Set where

trivial : True
trivial = _
```

The false proposition is represented by the datatype with no constructors and the true proposition by the record type with no fields (see Section 2.8 for more information on records). The record type with no fields has a single element which is the empty record. We could have defined True as a datatype with a single element, but the nice thing with the record definition is that the type checker knows that there is a unique element of True and will fill in any implicit arguments of type True with this element. This is exploited in the definition of

trivial where the right hand side is just underscore. If you nevertheless want
to write the element of True, the syntax is record{}.

These two propositions are enough to work with decidable propositions. We
can model decidable propositions as booleans and define

```
isTrue : Bool -> Set
isTrue true  = True
isTrue false = False
```

Now, isTrue b is the type of proofs that b equals true. Using this technique
we can define the safe list lookup function in a different way, working on simply
typed lists and numbers.

```
_<_ : Nat -> Nat -> Bool
_     < zero  = false
zero  < suc n = true
suc m < suc n = m < n

length : {A : Set} -> List A -> Nat
length []        = zero
length (x :: xs) = suc (length xs)

lookup : {A : Set}(xs : List A)(n : Nat) ->
         isTrue (n < length xs) -> A
lookup []        n         ()
lookup (x :: xs) zero      p = x
lookup (x :: xs) (suc n)   p = lookup xs n p
```

In this case, rather than there being no index into the empty list, there is
no proof that a number n is smaller than zero. In this example using indexed
types to capture the precondition is a little bit nicer, since we don't have to pass
around an explicit proof object, but some properties cannot be easily captured
by indexed types, in which case this is a nice alternative.

We can also use datatype families to define propositions. Here is a definition
of the identity relation

```
data _==_ {A : Set}(x : A) : A -> Set where
  refl : x == x
```

For a type A and an element x of A, we define the the family of proofs of "being
equal to x". This family is only inhabited at index x where the single proof is
refl.

Another example is the less than or equals relation on natural numbers. This
could be defined as a boolean function, as we have seen, but we can also define
it inductively

```
data _≤_ : Nat -> Nat -> Set where
  leq-zero : {n : Nat} -> zero ≤ n
  leq-suc  : {m n : Nat} -> m ≤ n -> suc m ≤ suc n
```

One advantage of this approach is that we can pattern match on the proof object. This makes proving properties of $\_\leq\_$ easier. For instance,

```
leq-trans : {l m n : Nat} -> l ≤ m -> m ≤ n -> l ≤ n
leq-trans leq-zero    _             = leq-zero
leq-trans (leq-suc p) (leq-suc q) = leq-suc (leq-trans p q)
```

2.6   More on Pattern Matching

We have seen how to pattern match on the arguments of a function, but sometimes you want to pattern match on the result of some intermediate computation. In Haskell and ML this is done on the right hand side using a case or match expression. However, as we have learned, when pattern matching on an expression in a dependently typed language, you not only learn something about the shape of the expression, but you can also learn things about other expressions. For instance, pattern matching on an expression of type `Vec A n` will reveal information about n. This is not captured by the usual case expression, so instead of a case expression Agda provides a way of matching on intermediate computations on the left hand side.

The *with* Construct. The idea is that if you want to pattern match on an expression e in the definition of a function f, you abstract f over the value of e, effectively adding another argument to f which can then be matched on in the usual fashion. This abstraction is performed by the `with` construct. For instance,

```
min : Nat -> Nat -> Nat
min x y with x < y
min x y | true  = x
min x y | false = y
```

The equations for `min` following the with abstraction have an extra argument, separated from the original arguments by a vertical bar, corresponding to the value of the expression `x < y`. You can abstract over multiple expressions at the same time, separating them by vertical bars and you can nest with abstractions. In the left hand side, with abstracted arguments should be separated by vertical bars.

In this case pattern matching on `x < y` doesn't tell us anything interesting about the arguments of `min`, so repeating the left hand sides is a bit tedious. When this is the case you can replace the left hand side with `...`:

```
filter : {A : Set} -> (A -> Bool) -> List A -> List A
filter p [] = []
filter p (x :: xs) with p x
... | true  = x :: filter p xs
... | false = filter p xs
```

Here is an example when we do learn something interesting. Given two numbers we can compare them to see if they are equal. Rather than returning an uninteresting boolean, we can return a proof that the numbers are indeed equal when this is the case, and an explanation of why they are different when this is the case:

```
data _≠_ : Nat -> Nat -> Set where
  z≠s : {n : Nat} -> zero ≠ suc n
  s≠z : {n : Nat} -> suc n ≠ zero
  s≠s : {m n : Nat} -> m ≠ n -> suc m ≠ suc n

data Equal? (n m : Nat) : Set where
  eq  : n == m -> Equal? n m
  neq : n ≠ m -> Equal? n m
```

Two natural numbers are different if one is `zero` and the other `suc` of something, or if both are successors but their predecessors are different. Now we can define the function `equal?` to check if two numbers are equal:

```
equal? : (n m : Nat) -> Equal? n m
equal? zero    zero    = eq refl
equal? zero    (suc m) = neq z≠s
equal? (suc n) zero    = neq s≠z
equal? (suc n) (suc m) with equal? n m
equal? (suc n) (suc .n) | eq refl = eq refl
equal? (suc n) (suc m)  | neq p   = neq (s≠s p)
```

Note that in the case where both numbers are successors we learn something by pattern matching on the proof that the predecessors are equal. We will see more examples of this kind of informative datatypes in Section 3.1.

When you abstract over an expression using `with`, that expression is abstracted from the entire context. This means that if the expression occurs in the type of an argument to the function or in the result type, this occurrence will be replaced by the with-argument on the left hand side. For example, suppose we want to prove something about the `filter` function. That the only thing it does is throwing away some elements of its argument, say. We can define what it means for one list to be a sublist of another list:

```
infix 20 _⊆_
data _⊆_ {A : Set} : List A -> List A -> Set where
  stop : [] ⊆ []
  drop : forall {xs y ys} -> xs ⊆ ys ->      xs ⊆ y :: ys
  keep : forall {x xs ys} -> xs ⊆ ys -> x :: xs ⊆ x :: ys
```

The intuition is that to obtain a sublist of a given list, each element can either be dropped or kept. When the type checker can figure out the type of an argument in a function type you can use the `forall` syntax:

- `forall {x y} a b -> A` is short for `{x : _}{y : _}(a : _)(b : _) -> A`.

Using this definition we can prove that `filter` computes a sublist of its argument:

```
lem-filter : {A : Set}(p : A -> Bool)(xs : List A) ->
               filter p xs ⊆ xs
lem-filter p []          = stop
lem-filter p (x :: xs) with p x
... | true  = keep (lem-filter p xs)
... | false = drop (lem-filter p xs)
```

The interesting case is the _::_ case. Let us walk through it slowly:

```
-- lem-filter p (x :: xs) = ?
```

At this point the goal that we have to prove is

```
-- (filter p (x :: xs) | p x) ⊆ x :: xs
```

In the goal filter has been applied to its with abstracted argument p x and will not reduce any further. Now, when we abstract over p x it will be abstracted from the goal type so we get

```
-- lem-filter p (x :: xs) with p x
-- ... | px = ?
```

where p x has been replaced by px in the goal type

```
-- (filter p (x :: xs) | px) ⊆ x :: xs
```

Now, when we pattern match on px the call to filter will reduce and we get

```
-- lem-filter p (x :: xs) with p x
-- ... | true  = ?  {- x :: filter p xs ⊆ x :: xs -}
-- ... | false = ?  {-      filter p xs ⊆ x :: xs -}
```

In some cases, it can be helpful to use with to abstract over an expression which you are not going to pattern match on. In particular, if you expect this expression to be instantiated by pattern matching on something else. Consider the proof that n + zero == n:

```
lem-plus-zero : (n : Nat) -> n + zero == n
lem-plus-zero zero = refl
lem-plus-zero (suc n) with n + zero | lem-plus-zero n
... | .n | refl = refl
```

In the step case we would like to pattern match on the induction hypothesis n + zero == n in order to prove suc n + zero == suc n, but since n + zero cannot be unified with n that is not allowed. However, if we abstract over n + zero, calling it m, we are left with the induction hypothesis m == n and the goal suc m == suc n. Now we can pattern match on the induction hypothesis, instantiating m to n.

2.7   Modules

The module system in Agda is primarily used to manage name spaces. In a dependently typed setting you could imagine having modules as first class objects that could be passed around and created on the fly, but in Agda this is not the case.

We have already seen that each file must define a single top-level module containing all the declarations in the file. These declarations can in turn be modules.

```
module Maybe where
  data Maybe (A : Set) : Set where
    nothing : Maybe A
    just    : A -> Maybe A

  maybe : {A B : Set} -> B -> (A -> B) -> Maybe A -> B
  maybe z f nothing  = z
  maybe z f (just x) = f x
```

By default all names declared in a module are visible from the outside. If you want to hide parts of a module you can declare it `private`:

```
module A where
  private
    internal : Nat
    internal = zero

  exported : Nat -> Nat
  exported n = n + internal
```

To access public names from another module you can qualify the name by the name of the module.

```
mapMaybe₁ : {A B : Set} -> (A -> B) -> Maybe.Maybe A -> Maybe.Maybe B
mapMaybe₁ f Maybe.nothing  = Maybe.nothing
mapMaybe₁ f (Maybe.just x) = Maybe.just (f x)
```

Modules can also be opened, locally or on top-level:

```
mapMaybe₂ : {A B : Set} -> (A -> B) -> Maybe.Maybe A -> Maybe.Maybe B
mapMaybe₂ f m = let open Maybe in maybe nothing (just o f) m

open Maybe

mapMaybe₃ : {A B : Set} -> (A -> B) -> Maybe A -> Maybe B
mapMaybe₃ f m = maybe nothing (just o f) m
```

When opening a module you can control which names are brought into scope with the `using`, `hiding`, and `renaming` keywords. For instance, to open the Maybe module without exposing the `maybe` function, and using different names for the type and the constructors we can say

```
open Maybe hiding (maybe)
          renaming (Maybe to _option; nothing to none; just to some)

mapOption : {A B : Set} -> (A -> B) -> A option -> B option
mapOption f none      = none
mapOption f (some x) = some (f x)
```

Renaming is just cosmetic, `Maybe A` and `A option` are interchangable.

```
mtrue : Maybe Bool
mtrue = mapOption not (just false)
```

Parameterised Modules. Modules can be parameterised by arbitrary types[6].

```
module Sort (A : Set)(_<_ : A -> A -> Bool) where
  insert : A -> List A -> List A
  insert y [] = y :: []
  insert y (x :: xs) with x < y
  ... | true  = x :: insert y xs
  ... | false = y :: x :: xs

  sort : List A -> List A
  sort []       = []
  sort (x :: xs) = insert x (sort xs)
```

When looking at the functions in parameterised module from the outside, they take the module parameters as arguments, so

```
sort₁ : (A : Set)(_<_ : A -> A -> Bool) -> List A -> List A
sort₁ = Sort.sort
```

You can apply the functions in a parameterised module to the module parameters all at once, by instantiating the module

```
module SortNat = Sort Nat _<_
```

This creates a new module `SortNat` with functions `insert` and `sort`.

```
sort₂ : List Nat -> List Nat
sort₂ = SortNat.sort
```

Often you want to instantiate a module and open the result, in which case you can simply write

```
open Sort Nat _<_ renaming (insert to insertNat; sort to sortNat)
```

without having to give a name to the instantiated module.

Sometimes you want to export the contents of another module from the current module. In this case you can open the module *publicly* using the `public` keyword:

---

[6] But not by other modules.

```
module Lists (A : Set)(_<_ : A -> A -> Bool) where
  open Sort A _<_ public
  minimum : List A -> Maybe A
  minimum xs with sort xs
  ... | []     = nothing
  ... | y :: ys = just y
```

Now the `Lists` module will contain `insert` and `sort` as well as the `minimum` function.

Importing Modules from Other Files. Agda programs can be split over multiple files. To use definitions from a module defined in another file the module has to be *imported*. Modules are imported by their names, so if you have a module `A.B.C` in a file `/some/local/path/A/B/C.agda` it is imported with the statement `import A.B.C`. In order for the system to find the file `/some/local/path` must be in Agda's search path.[7]

I have a file `Logic.agda` in the same directory as these notes, defining logical conjunction and disjunction. To import it we say

```
import Logic using (_∧_; _∨_)
```

Note that you can use the same namespace control keywords as when opening modules. Importing a module does not automatically open it (like when you say `import qualified` in Haskell). You can either open it separately with an open statement, or use the short form `open import Logic`.

Splitting a program over several files will improve type checking performance, since when you are making changes the type checker only has to type check the files that are influenced by the changes.

2.8 Records

We have seen a record type already, namely the record type with no fields which was used to model the true proposition. Now let us look at record types with fields. A record type is declared much like a datatype where the fields are indicated by the `field` keyword. For instance

```
record Point : Set where
  field x : Nat
        y : Nat
```

This declares a record type `Point` with two natural number fields `x` and `y`. To construct an element of `Point` you write

```
mkPoint : Nat -> Nat -> Point
mkPoint a b = record{ x = a; y = b }
```

[7] The search path can be set from emacs by executing `M-x customize-group agda2`.

To allow projection of the fields from a record, each record type comes with a module of the same name. This module is parameterised by an element of the record type and contains projection functions for the fields. In the point example we get a module

```
-- module Point (p : Point) where
--    x : Nat
--    y : Nat
```

This module can be used as it is or instantiated to a particular record.

```
getX : Point -> Nat
getX = Point.x

abs² : Point -> Nat
abs² p = let open Point p in x * x + y * y
```

At the moment you cannot pattern match on records, but this will hopefully be possible in a later version of Agda.

It is possible to add your own functions to the module of a record by including them in the record declaration after the fields.

```
record Monad (M : Set -> Set) : Set1 where
  field
    return : {A : Set} -> A -> M A
    _>>=_  : {A B : Set} -> M A -> (A -> M B) -> M B

  mapM : {A B : Set} -> (A -> M B) -> List A -> M (List B)
  mapM f [] = return []
  mapM f (x :: xs) = f x        >>= \y ->
                     mapM f xs >>= \ys ->
                     return (y :: ys)

mapM' : {M : Set -> Set} -> Monad M ->
        {A B : Set} -> (A -> M B) -> List A -> M (List B)
mapM' Mon f xs = Monad.mapM Mon f xs
```

2.9   Exercises

Exercise 2.1. Matrix transposition

We can model an $n \times m$ matrix as a vector of vectors:

```
Matrix : Set -> Nat -> Nat -> Set
Matrix A n m = Vec (Vec A n) m
```

The goal of this exercise is to define the transposition of such a matrix.

(a) Define a function to compute a vector containing n copies of an element x.

```
vec : {n : Nat}{A : Set} -> A -> Vec A n
vec {n} x = {! !}
```

(b) Define point-wise application of a vector of functions to a vector of arguments.

```
infixl 90 _$_
_$_ : {n : Nat}{A B : Set} -> Vec (A -> B) n -> Vec A n -> Vec B n
fs $ xs = {! !}
```

(c) Define matrix transposition in terms of these two functions.

```
transpose : forall {A n m} -> Matrix A n m -> Matrix A m n
transpose xss = {! !}
```

Exercise 2.2. Vector lookup

Remember `tabulate` and `!` from Section 2.4. Prove that they are indeed each other's inverses.

(a) This direction should be relatively easy.

```
lem-!-tab : forall {A n} (f : Fin n -> A)(i : Fin n) ->
              tabulate f ! i == f i
lem-!-tab f i = {! !}
```

(b) This direction might be trickier.

```
lem-tab-! : forall {A n} (xs : Vec A n) -> tabulate (_!_ xs) == xs
lem-tab-! xs = {! !}
```

Exercise 2.3. Sublists

Remember the representation of sublists from Section 2.4:

```
data _⊆_ {A : Set} : List A -> List A -> Set where
  stop : [] ⊆ []
  drop : forall {x xs ys} -> xs ⊆ ys ->     xs ⊆ x :: ys
  keep : forall {x xs ys} -> xs ⊆ ys -> x :: xs ⊆ x :: ys
```

(a) Prove the reflexivity and transitivity of ⊆ :

```
⊆-refl : {A : Set}{xs : List A} -> xs ⊆ xs
⊆-refl {xs = xs} = {! !}

⊆-trans : {A : Set}{xs ys zs : List A} ->
          xs ⊆ ys -> ys ⊆ zs -> xs ⊆ zs
⊆-trans p q = {! !}
```

Instead of defining the sublist relation we can define the type of sublists of a given list as follows:

```
infixr 30 _::_
data SubList {A : Set} : List A -> Set where
  []   : SubList []
  _::_ : forall x {xs} -> SubList xs -> SubList (x :: xs)
  skip : forall {x xs} -> SubList xs -> SubList (x :: xs)
```

(b) Define a function to extract the list corresponding to a sublist.

```
forget : {A : Set}{xs : List A} -> SubList xs -> List A
forget s = {! !}
```

(c) Now, prove that a SubList is a sublist in the sense of ⊆ .

```
lem-forget : {A : Set}{xs : List A}(zs : SubList xs) ->
              forget zs ⊆ xs
lem-forget zs = {! !}
```

(d) Give an alternative definition of filter which satisfies the sublist property by construction.

```
filter' : {A : Set} -> (A -> Bool) -> (xs : List A) -> SubList xs
filter' p xs = {! !}
```

(e) Define the complement of a sublist

```
complement : {A : Set}{xs : List A} -> SubList xs -> SubList xs
complement zs = {! !}
```

(f) Compute all sublists of a given list

```
sublists : {A : Set}(xs : List A) -> List (SubList xs)
sublists xs = {! !}
```

3   Programming Techniques

In this section we will describe and exemplify a couple of programming techniques which are made available in dependently typed languages: *views* and *universe constructions*.

3.1   Views

As we have seen pattern matching in Agda can reveal information not only about the term being matched but also about terms occurring in the type of this term. For instance, matching a proof of x == y against the refl constructor we (and the type checker) will learn that x and y are the same.

We can exploit this, and design datatypes whose sole purpose is to tell us something interesting about its indices. We call such a datatype a *view* [?]. To use the view we define a view function, computing an element of the view for arbitrary indices.

This section on views is defined in the file Views.lagda so here is the top-level module declaration:

```
module Views where
```

Natural Number Parity. Let us start with an example. We all know that any natural number n can be written on the form $2k$ or $2k+1$ for some k. Here is a view datatype expressing that. We use the natural numbers defined in the summer school library module `Data.Nat`.

```
open import Data.Nat

data Parity : Nat -> Set where
   even : (k : Nat) -> Parity (k * 2)
   odd  : (k : Nat) -> Parity (1 + k * 2)
```

An element of `Parity` n tells you if n is even or odd, i.e. if $n = 2k$ or $n = 2k+1$, and in each case what k is. The reason for writing `k * 2` and `1 + k * 2` rather than `2 * k` and `2 * k + 1` has to do with the fact that `_+_` and `_*_` are defined by recursion over their first argument. This way around we get a better reduction behaviour.

Now, just defining the view datatype isn't very helpful. We also need to show that any natural number can be viewed in this way. In other words, that given an arbitrary natural number n we can to compute an element of `Parity n`.

```
parity : (n : Nat) -> Parity n
parity zero = even zero
parity (suc n) with parity n
parity (suc .(k * 2))      | even k = odd k
parity (suc .(1 + k * 2)) | odd  k = even (suc k)
```

In the `suc n` case we use the view recursively to find out the parity of n. If `n = k * 2` then `suc n = 1 + k * 2` and if `n = 1 + k * 2` then `suc n = suc k * 2`.

In effect, this view gives us the ability to pattern match on a natural number with the patterns `k * 2` and `1 + k * 2`. Using this ability, defining the function that divides a natural number by two is more or less trivial:

```
half : Nat -> Nat
half n with parity n
half .(k * 2)      | even k = k
half .(1 + k * 2) | odd k  = k
```

Note that k is bound in the pattern for the view, not in the dotted pattern for the natural number.

Finding an Element in a List. Let us turn our attention to lists. First some imports: we will use the definitions of lists and booleans from the summer school library.

```
open import Data.Function
open import Data.List
open import Data.Bool
```

Now, given a predicate P and a list xs we can define what it means for P to hold for all elements of xs:

```
infixr 30 _:all:_
data All {A : Set}(P : A -> Set) : List A -> Set where
  all[]   : All P []
  _:all:_ : forall {x xs} -> P x -> All P xs -> All P (x :: xs)
```

A proof of All P xs is simply a list of proofs of P x for each element x of xs. Note that P does not have to be a decidable predicate. To turn a decidable predicate into a general predicate we define a function satisfies.

```
satisfies : {A : Set} -> (A -> Bool) -> A -> Set
satisfies p x = isTrue (p x)
```

Using the All datatype we could prove the second part of the correctness of the filter function, namely that all the elements of the result of filter satisfies the predicate: All (Sat p) (filter p xs). This is left as an exercise. Instead, let us define some interesting views on lists.

Given a decidable predicate on the elements of a list, we can either find an element in the list that satisfies the predicate, or else all elements satifies the negation of the predicate. Here is the corresponding view datatype:

```
data Find {A : Set}(p : A -> Bool) : List A -> Set where
  found : (xs : List A)(y : A) -> satisfies p y -> (ys : List A) ->
          Find p (xs ++ y :: ys)
  not-found : forall {xs} -> All (satisfies (not ∘ p)) xs ->
              Find p xs
```

We don't specify which element to use as a witness in the found case. If we wanted the view to always return the first (or last) matching element we could force the elements of xs (or ys) to satisfy the negation of p. To complete the view we need to define the view function computing an element of Find p xs for any p and xs. Here is a first attempt:

```
find₁ : {A : Set}(p : A -> Bool)(xs : List A) -> Find p xs
find₁ p [] = not-found all[]
find₁ p (x :: xs) with p x
... | true  = found [] x {! !} xs
... | false = {! !}
```

In the case where p x is true we want to return found (hence, returning the first match), but there is a problem. The type of the hole ({! !}) is isTrue (p x), even though we already matched on p x and found out that it was true. The problem is that when we abstracted over p x we didn't know that we wanted to use the found constructor, so there were no p x to abstract over. Remember that with doesn't remember the connection between the with-term and the patterns. One solution to this problem is to make this connection explicit with a proof object. The idea is to not abstract over the term itself but rather over an arbitrary term of the same type and a proof that it is equal to the original term. Remember the type of equality proofs:

```
data _==_ {A : Set}(x : A) : A -> Set where
  refl : x == x
```

Now we define the type of elements of a type A together with proofs that they are equal to some given x in A.

```
data Inspect {A : Set}(x : A) : Set where
  it : (y : A) -> x == y -> Inspect x
```

There is one obvious way to construct an element of Inspect x, namely to pick x as the thing which is equal to x.

```
inspect : {A : Set}(x : A) -> Inspect x
inspect x = it x refl
```

We can now define find by abstracting over inspect (p x) rather than p x itself. This will provide us with either a proof of p x == true or a proof of p x == false which we can use in the arguments to found and not-found. First we need a couple of lemmas about isTrue and isFalse:

```
trueIsTrue : {x : Bool} -> x == true -> isTrue x
trueIsTrue refl = _

falseIsFalse : {x : Bool} -> x == false -> isFalse x
falseIsFalse refl = _
```

Now we can define find without any problems.

```
find : {A : Set}(p : A -> Bool)(xs : List A) -> Find p xs
find p [] = not-found all[]
find p (x :: xs) with inspect (p x)
... | it true prf = found [] x (trueIsTrue prf) xs
... | it false prf with find p xs
find p (x :: ._) | it false _    | found xs y py ys =
  found (x :: xs) y py ys
find p (x :: xs) | it false prf | not-found npxs =
  not-found (falseIsFalse prf :all: npxs)
```

In the case where p x is true, inspect (p x) matches it true prf where prf : p x == true. Using our lemma we can turn this into the proof of isTrue (p x) that we need for the third argument of found. We get a similar situation when p x is false and find p xs returns not-found.

Indexing into a List. In Sections 2.4 and Section 2.5 we saw two ways of safely indexing into a list. In both cases the type system guaranteed that the index didn't point outside the list. However, sometimes we have no control over the value of the index and it might well be that it is pointing outside the list. One solution in this case would be to wrap the result of the lookup function in a maybe type, but maybe types don't really tell you anything very interesting and we can do a lot better. First let us define the type of proofs that an element x is in a list xs.

```
data _∈_ {A : Set}(x : A) : List A -> Set where
  hd : forall {xs}    -> x ∈ x :: xs
  tl : forall {y xs} -> x ∈ xs -> x ∈ y :: xs
```

The first element of a list is a member of the list, and any element of the tail of a list is also an element of the entire list. Given a proof of x ∈ xs we can compute the index at which x occurs in xs simply by counting the number of tls in the proof.

```
index : forall {A}{x : A}{xs} -> x ∈ xs -> Nat
index hd     = zero
index (tl p) = suc (index p)
```

Now, let us define a view on natural numbers n with respect to a list xs. Either n indexes some x in xs in which case it is of the form index p for some proof p : x ∈ xs, or n points outside the list, in which case it is of the form length xs + m for some m.

```
data Lookup {A : Set}(xs : List A) : Nat -> Set where
  inside  : (x : A)(p : x ∈ xs) -> Lookup xs (index p)
  outside : (m : Nat) -> Lookup xs (length xs + m)
```

In the case that n is a valid index we not only get the element at the corresponding position in xs but we are guaranteed that this is the element that is returned. There is no way a lookup function could cheat and always return the first element, say. In the case that n is indexing outside the list we also get some more information. We get a proof that n is out of bounds and we also get to know by how much.

Defining the lookup function is no more difficult than it would have been to define the lookup function returning a maybe.

```
_!_ : {A : Set}(xs : List A)(n : Nat) -> Lookup xs n
[] ! n = outside n
(x :: xs) ! zero  = inside x hd
(x :: xs) ! suc n with xs ! n
(x :: xs) ! suc .(index p)        | inside y p = inside y (tl p)
(x :: xs) ! suc .(length xs + n) | outside n  = outside n
```

A Type Checker for λ-calculus. To conclude this section on views, let us look at a somewhat bigger example: a type checker for simply typed λ-calculus. This example is due to Conor McBride [4] and was first implemented in Epigram. His version not only guaranteed that when the type checker said ok things were really ok, but also provided a detailed explanation in the case where type checking failed. We will focus on the positive side here and leave the reporting of sensible and guaranteed precise error message as an exercise.

First, let us define the type language. We have one base type ι and a function type.

```
infixr 30 _→_
data Type : Set where
  ι   : Type
  _→_ : Type -> Type -> Type
```

When doing type checking we will inevitably have to compare types for equality, so let us define a view.

```
data Equal? : Type -> Type -> Set where
  yes : forall {τ} -> Equal? τ τ
  no  : forall {σ τ} -> Equal? σ τ

_=?=_ : (σ τ : Type) -> Equal? σ τ
ι             =?= ι          = yes
ι             =?= (_ → _) = no
(_ → _)   =?= ι          = no
(σ₁ → τ₁) =?= (σ₂ → τ₂) with σ₁ =?= σ₂ | τ₁ =?= τ₂
(σ → τ)   =?= (.σ → .τ) | yes | yes = yes
(σ₁ → τ₁) =?= (σ₂ → τ₂) | _   | _   = no
```

Note that we don't give any justification in the no case. The _=?=_ could return no all the time without complaints from the type checker. In the yes case, however, we guarantee that the two types are identical.

Next up we define the type of raw lambda terms. We use unchecked deBruijn indices to represent variables.

```
infixl 80 _$_
data Raw : Set where
  var : Nat -> Raw
  _$_ : Raw -> Raw -> Raw
  lam : Type -> Raw -> Raw
```

We use Church style terms in order to simplify type inference. The idea with our type checker is that it should take a raw term and return a well-typed term, so we need to define the type of well-typed λ-terms with respect to a context Γ and a type τ.

```
Cxt = List Type

data Term (Γ : Cxt) : Type -> Set where
  var : forall {τ} -> τ ∈ Γ -> Term Γ τ
  _$_ : forall {σ τ} -> Term Γ (σ → τ) -> Term Γ σ -> Term Γ τ
  lam : forall σ {τ} -> Term (σ :: Γ) τ -> Term Γ (σ → τ)
```

We represent variables by proofs that a type is in the context. Remember that the proofs of list membership provide us with an index into the list where the element can be found. Given a well-typed term we can erase all the type information and get a raw term.

```
erase : forall {Γ τ} -> Term Γ τ -> Raw
erase (var x)   = var (index x)
erase (t $ u)   = erase t $ erase u
erase (lam σ t) = lam σ (erase t)
```

In the variable case we turn the proof into a natural number using the `index` function.

Now we are ready to define the view of a raw term as either being the erasure of a well-typed term or not. Again, we don't provide any justification for giving a negative result. Since, we are doing type inference the type is not a parameter of the view but computed by the view function.

```
data Infer (Γ : Cxt) : Raw -> Set where
   ok  : (τ : Type)(t : Term Γ τ) -> Infer Γ (erase t)
   bad : {e : Raw} -> Infer Γ e
```

The view function is the type inference function taking a raw term and computing an element of the `Infer` view.

```
infer : (Γ : Cxt)(e : Raw) -> Infer Γ e
```

Let us walk through the three cases: variable, application, and lambda abstraction.

```
infer Γ (var n)    with Γ ! n
infer Γ (var .(length Γ + n)) | outside n  = bad
infer Γ (var .(index x))      | inside σ x = ok σ (var x)
```

In the variable case we need to take case of the fact that the raw variable might be out of scope. We can use the lookup function `_!_` we defined above for that. When the variable is in scope the lookup function provides us with the type of the variable and the proof that it is in scope.

```
infer Γ (e₁ $ e₂)
   with infer Γ e₁
infer Γ (e₁ $ e₂)            | bad     = bad
infer Γ (.(erase t₁) $ e₂)  | ok ı t₁ = bad
infer Γ (.(erase t₁) $ e₂)  | ok (σ → τ) t₁
      with infer Γ e₂
infer Γ (.(erase t₁) $ e₂)  | ok (σ → τ) t₁ | bad = bad
infer Γ (.(erase t₁) $ .(erase t₂)) | ok (σ → τ) t₁ | ok σ' t₂
         with σ =?= σ'
infer Γ (.(erase t₁) $ .(erase t₂))
   | ok (σ → τ) t₁ | ok .σ t₂ | yes = ok τ (t₁ $ t₂)
infer Γ (.(erase t₁) $ .(erase t₂))
   | ok (σ → τ) t₁ | ok σ' t₂ | no = bad
```

The application case is the bulkiest simply because there are a lot of things we need to check: that the two terms are type correct, that the first term has a function type and that the type of the second term matches the argument type of the first term. This is all done by pattern matching on recursive calls to the `infer` view and the type equality view.

```
infer Γ (lam σ e) with infer (σ :: Γ) e
infer Γ (lam σ .(erase t)) | ok τ t  = ok (σ → τ) (lam σ t)
infer Γ (lam σ e)          | bad     = bad
```

Finally, the lambda case is very simple. If the body of the lambda is type correct in the extended context, then the lambda is well-typed with the corresponding function type.

Without much effort we have defined a type checker for simply typed λ-calculus that not only is guaranteed to compute well-typed terms, but also guarantees that the erasure of the well-typed term is the term you started with.

3.2 Universes

The second programming technique we will look at that is not available in non-dependently typed languages is *universe construction*. First the module header.

```
module Universes where
```

A universe is a set of types (or type formers) and a universe construction consists of a type of codes and a decoding function mapping codes to types in the universe. The purpose of a universe construction is to be able to define functions over the types of the universe by inspecting their codes. In fact we have seen an example of a universe construction already.

A Familiar Universe. The universe of decidable propositions consists of the singleton type **True** and the empty type **False**. Codes are booleans and the decoder is the isTrue function.

```
data   False : Set where
record True  : Set where

data Bool : Set where
   true  : Bool
   false : Bool

isTrue : Bool -> Set
isTrue true  = True
isTrue false = False
```

Now functions over decidable propositions can be defined by manipulating the boolean codes. For instance, we can define negation and conjunction as functions on codes and prove some properties of the corresponding propositions.

```
infix  30 not_
infixr 25 _and_

not_ : Bool -> Bool
not true  = false
```

```
not false = true

_and_ : Bool -> Bool -> Bool
true  and x = x
false and _ = false

notNotId : (a : Bool) -> isTrue (not not a) -> isTrue a
notNotId true  p = p
notNotId false ()

andIntro : (a b : Bool) -> isTrue a -> isTrue b -> isTrue (a and b)
andIntro true  _ _ p = p
andIntro false _ () _
```

A nice property of this universe is that proofs of True can be found automatically. This means that if you have a function taking a proof of a precondition as an argument, where you expect the precondition to be trivially true at the point where you are calling the function, you can make the precondition an implicit argument. For instance, if you expect to mostly divide by concrete numbers, division of natural numbers can be given the type signature

```
open import Data.Nat

nonZero : Nat -> Bool
nonZero zero    = false
nonZero (suc _) = true

postulate _div_ : Nat -> (m : Nat){p : isTrue (nonZero m)} -> Nat

three = 16 div 5
```

Here the proof obligation isTrue (nonZero 5) will reduce to True and solved automatically by the type checker. Note that if you tell the type checker that you have defined the type of natural numbers, you are allowed to use natural number literals like 16 and 5. This has been done in the library.

Universes for Generic Programming. Generic programming deals with the problem of defining functions generically over a set of types. We can achieve this by defining a universe for the set of types we are interested in. Here is a simple example of how to program generically over the set of types computed by fixed points over polynomial functors.

First we define a type of codes for polynomial functors.

```
data Functor : Set1 where
  |Id|  : Functor
  |K|   : Set -> Functor
  _|+|_ : Functor -> Functor -> Functor
  _|x|_ : Functor -> Functor -> Functor
```

A polynomial functor is either the identity functor, a constant functor, the disjoint union of two functors, or the cartesian product of two functors. Since codes

for functors can contain arbitrary Sets (in the case of the constant functor) the
type of codes cannot itself be a Set, but lives in Set1.

Before defining the decoding function for functors we define datatypes for
disjoint union and cartesian product.

```
data _⊕_ (A B : Set) : Set where
   inl : A -> A ⊕ B
   inr : B -> A ⊕ B

data _×_ (A B : Set) : Set where
   _,_ : A -> B -> A × B

infixr 50 _|+|_ _⊕_
infixr 60 _|x|_ _×_
```

The decoding function takes a code for a functor to a function on Sets and is
computed recursively over the code.

```
[_] : Functor -> Set -> Set
[ |Id|    ] X = X
[ |K| A   ] X = A
[ F |+| G ] X = [ F ] X ⊕ [ G ] X
[ F |x| G ] X = [ F ] X × [ G ] X
```

Since it's called a functor it ought to support a map operation. We can define
this by recursion over the code.

```
map : (F : Functor){X Y : Set} -> (X -> Y) -> [ F ] X -> [ F ] Y
map |Id|      f x       = f x
map (|K| A)   f c       = c
map (F |+| G) f (inl x) = inl (map F f x)
map (F |+| G) f (inr y) = inr (map G f y)
map (F |x| G) f (x , y) = map F f x , map G f y
```

Next we define the least fixed point of a polynomial functor.

```
data μ_ (F : Functor) : Set where
   <_> : [ F ] (μ F) -> μ F
```

To ensure termination, recursive datatypes must be strictly positive and this
is checked by the type checker. Our definition of least fixed point goes through,
since the type checker can spot that [_] is strictly positive in its second argument.

With this definition we can define a generic fold operation on least fixed points.
Grabbing for the closest category theory text book we might try something like
this

```
-- fold : (F : Functor){A : Set} -> ([ F ] A -> A) -> μ F -> A
-- fold F φ < x > = φ (map F (fold F φ) x)
```

Unfortunately, this definition does not pass the termination checker since the recursive call to `fold` is passed to the higher order function `map` and the termination checker cannot see that `map` isn't applying it to bad things.

To make `fold` pass the termination checker we can fuse `map` and `fold` into a single function `mapFold F G φ x = map F (fold G φ) x` defined recursively over `x`. We need to keep two copies of the functor since `fold` is always called on the same functor, whereas `map` is defined by taking its functor argument apart.

```
mapFold : forall {X} F G -> ([ G ] X -> X) -> [ F ] (μ G) -> [ F ] X
mapFold |Id|           G φ < x >   = φ (mapFold G G φ x)
mapFold (|K| A)        G φ c       = c
mapFold (F₁ |+| F₂) G φ (inl x) = inl (mapFold F₁ G φ x)
mapFold (F₁ |+| F₂) G φ (inr y) = inr (mapFold F₂ G φ y)
mapFold (F₁ |x| F₂) G φ (x , y) = mapFold F₁ G φ x , mapFold F₂ G φ y

fold : {F : Functor}{A : Set} -> ([ F ] A -> A) -> μ F -> A
fold {F} φ < x > = φ (mapFold F F φ x)
```

There is a lot more fun to be had here, but let us make do with a couple of examples. Both natural numbers and lists are examples of least fixed points of polynomial functors:

```
NatF = |K| True |+| |Id|
NAT  = μ NatF

Z : NAT
Z = < inl _ >

S : NAT -> NAT
S n = < inr n >

ListF = \A -> |K| True |+| |K| A |x| |Id|
LIST  = \A -> μ (ListF A)

nil : {A : Set} -> LIST A
nil = < inl _ >

cons : {A : Set} -> A -> LIST A -> LIST A
cons x xs = < inr (x , xs) >
```

To make implementing the argument to fold easier we introduce a few helper functions:

```
[_||_] : {A B C : Set} -> (A -> C) -> (B -> C) -> A ⊕ B -> C
[ f || g ] (inl x) = f x
[ f || g ] (inr y) = g y

uncurry : {A B C : Set} -> (A -> B -> C) -> A × B -> C
uncurry f (x , y) = f x y
```

```
const : {A B : Set} -> A -> B -> A
const x y = x
```

Finally some familiar functions expressed as folds.

```
foldr : {A B : Set} -> (A -> B -> B) -> B -> LIST A -> B
foldr {A}{B} f z = fold [ const z || uncurry f ]

plus : NAT -> NAT -> NAT
plus n m = fold [ const m || S ] n
```

Universes for Overloading. At the moment, Agda does not have a class system like the one in Haskell. However, a limited form of overloading can be achieved using universes. The idea is simply if you know in advance at which types you want to overload a function, you can construct a universe for these types and define the overloaded function by pattern matching on a code.

A simple example: suppose we want to overload equality for some of our standard types. We start by defining our universe:

```
open import Data.List

data Type : Set where
  bool : Type
  nat  : Type
  list : Type -> Type
  pair : Type -> Type -> Type

El : Type -> Set
El nat        = Nat
El bool       = Bool
El (list a)   = List (El a)
El (pair a b) = El a × El b
```

In order to achieve proper overloading it is important that we don't have to supply the code explicitly everytime we are calling the overloaded function. In this case we won't have to since the decoding function computes distinct datatypes in each clause. This means that the type checker can figure out a code from its decoding. For instance, the only code that can decode into Bool is bool, and if the decoding of a code is a product type then the code must be pair of some codes.

Now an overloaded equality function simply takes an implicit code and computes a boolean relation over the semantics of the code.

```
infix 30 _==_
_==_ : {a : Type} -> El a -> El a -> Bool

_==_ {nat} zero     zero    = true
_==_ {nat} (suc _) zero    = false
_==_ {nat} zero     (suc _) = false
```

```
_==_ {nat} (suc n) (suc m) = n == m

_==_ {bool} true  x = x
_==_ {bool} false x = not x

_==_ {list a} [] []        = true
_==_ {list a} (_ :: _) [] = false
_==_ {list a} [] (_ :: _) = false
_==_ {list a} (x :: xs) (y :: ys) = x == y and xs == ys

_==_ {pair a b} (x₁ , y₁) (x₂ , y₂) = x₁ == x₂ and y₁ == y₂
```

In the recursive calls of `_==_` the code argument is inferred automatically. The same happens when we use our equality function on concrete examples:

```
example₁ : isTrue (2 + 2 == 4)
example₁ = _

example₂ : isTrue (not (true :: false :: [] == true :: true :: []))
example₂ = _
```

In summary, universe constructions allows us to define functions by pattern matching on (codes for) types. We have seen a few simple examples, but there are a lot of other interesting possibilities. For example

- XML schemas as codes for the types of well-formed XML documents,
- a universe of tables in a relational database, allowing us to make queries which are guaranteed to be well-typed.

3.3   Exercises

Exercise 3.1. Natural numbers

Here is a view on pairs of natural numbers.

```
data Compare : Nat -> Nat -> Set where
  less : forall {n} k -> Compare n (n + suc k)
  more : forall {n} k -> Compare (n + suc k) n
  same : forall {n} -> Compare n n
```

(a) Define the view function

```
compare : (n m : Nat) -> Compare n m
compare n m = {! !}
```

(b) Now use the view to compute the difference between two numbers

```
difference : Nat -> Nat -> Nat
difference n m = {! !}
```

Exercise 3.2. Type checking λ-calculus

Change the type checker from Section 3.1 to include precise information also in the failing case.

(a) Define inequality on types and change the type comparison to include inequality proofs. Hint: to figure out what the constructors of $\neq$ should be you can start defining the `=?=` function and see what you need from $\neq$.

```
data _≠_ : Type -> Type -> Set where
  -- ...


data Equal? : Type -> Type -> Set where
  yes : forall {τ} -> Equal? τ τ
  no  : forall {σ τ} -> σ ≠ τ -> Equal? σ τ

_=?=_ : (σ τ : Type) -> Equal? σ τ
σ =?= τ = {! !}
```

(b) Define a type of illtyped terms and change `infer` to return such a term upon failure. Look to the definition of `infer` for clues to the constructors of BadTerm.

```
data BadTerm (Γ : Cxt) : Set where
  -- ...


eraseBad : {Γ : Cxt} -> BadTerm Γ -> Raw
eraseBad b = {! !}


data Infer (Γ : Cxt) : Raw -> Set where
  ok  : (τ : Type)(t : Term Γ τ) -> Infer Γ (erase t)
  bad : (b : BadTerm Γ) -> Infer Γ (eraseBad b)


infer : (Γ : Cxt)(e : Raw) -> Infer Γ e
infer Γ e = {! !}
```

Exercise 3.3. Properties of list functions

Remember the following predicates on lists from Section 3.1

```
data _∈_ {A : Set}(x : A) : List A -> Set where
  hd : forall {xs} -> x ∈ x :: xs
  tl : forall {y xs} -> x ∈ xs -> x ∈ y :: xs

infixr 30 _::_
data All {A : Set}(P : A -> Set) : List A -> Set where
  []   : All P []
  _::_ : forall {x xs} -> P x -> All P xs -> All P (x :: xs)
```

(a) Prove the following lemma stating that `All` is sound.

```
lemma-All-∈ : forall {A x xs}{P : A -> Set} ->
              All P xs -> x ∈ xs -> P x
lemma-All-∈ p i = {! !}
```

We proved that filter computes a sublist of its input. Now let's finish the job.

(b) Below is the proof that all elements of `filter p xs` satisfies p. Doing this without any auxiliary lemmas involves some rather subtle use of with-abstraction.

Figure out what is going on by replaying the construction of the program and looking at the goal and context in each step.

```
lem-filter-sound : {A : Set}(p : A -> Bool)(xs : List A) ->
                   All (satisfies p) (filter p xs)
lem-filter-sound p [] = []
lem-filter-sound p (x :: xs) with inspect (p x)
lem-filter-sound p (x :: xs) | it y prf with p x | prf
lem-filter-sound p (x :: xs) | it .true prf  | true  | refl =
  trueIsTrue prf :: lem-filter-sound p xs
lem-filter-sound p (x :: xs) | it .false prf | false | refl =
  lem-filter-sound p xs
```

(c) Finally prove `filter` complete, by proving that all elements of the original list satisfying the predicate are present in the result.

```
lem-filter-complete : {A : Set}(p : A -> Bool)(x : A){xs : List A} ->
                      x ∈ xs -> satisfies p x -> x ∈ filter p xs
lem-filter-complete p x el px = {! !}
```

Exercise 3.4. An XML universe
  Here is simplified universe of XML schemas:

```
Tag = String

mutual
  data Schema : Set where
    tag : Tag -> List Child -> Schema

  data Child : Set where
    text : Child
    elem : Nat -> Nat -> Schema -> Child
```

The number arguments to `elem` specifies the minimum and maximum number of repetitions of the subschema. For instance, `elem 0 1 s` would be an optional child and `elem 1 1 s` would be a child which has to be present.

To define the decoding function we need a type of lists of between n and m elements. This is the `FList` type below.

```
data BList (A : Set) : Nat -> Set where
  []   : forall {n} -> BList A n
  _::_ : forall {n} -> A -> BList A n -> BList A (suc n)

data Cons (A B : Set) : Set where
  _::_ : A -> B -> Cons A B
```

```
FList : Set -> Nat -> Nat -> Set
FList A zero     m        = BList A m
FList A (suc n) zero     = False
FList A (suc n) (suc m) = Cons A (FList A n m)
```

Now we define the decoding function as a datatype XML.

```
mutual
   data XML : Schema -> Set where
     element : forall {kids}(t : Tag) -> All Element kids ->
              XML (tag t kids)

   Element : Child -> Set
   Element text        = String
   Element (elem n m s) = FList (XML s) n m
```

(a) Implement a function to print XML documents. The string concatenation function is +++ .

```
mutual
   printXML : {s : Schema} -> XML s -> String
   printXML xml = {! !}

   printChildren : {kids : List Child} -> All Element kids -> String
   printChildren xs = {! !}
```

4   Compiling Agda Programs

This section deals with the topic of getting Agda programs to interact with the real world. Type checking Agda programs requires evaluating arbitrary terms, ans as long as all terms are pure and normalizing this is not a problem, but what happens when we introduce side effects? Clearly, we don't want side effects to happen at compile time. Another question is what primitives the language should provide for constructing side effecting programs. In Agda, these problems are solved by allowing arbitrary Haskell functions to be imported as axioms. At compile time, these imported functions have no reduction behaviour, only at run time is the Haskell function executed.

4.1   Relating Agda Types to Haskell Types

In order to be able to apply arbitrary Haskell functions to Agda terms we need to ensure that the run time representation of the Agda terms is the same as what the function expects. To do this we have to tell the Agda compiler about the relationships between our user defined Agda types and the Haskell types used by the imported functions. For instance, to instruct the compiler that our Unit type should be compiled to the Haskell unit type () we say

```
data Unit : Set where
  unit : Unit

{-# COMPILED_DATA Unit () () #-}
```

The COMPILED DATA directive takes the name of an Agda datatype, the name of the corresponding Haskell datatype and its constructors. The compiler will check that the given Haskell datatype has precisely the given constructors and that their types match the types of the corresponding Agda constructors. Here is the declaration for the maybe datatype:

```
data Maybe (A : Set) : Set where
  nothing : Maybe A
  just : A -> Maybe A

{-# COMPILED_DATA Maybe Maybe Nothing Just #-}
```

Some types have no Agda representation, simply because they are abstract Haskell types exported by some library that we want to use. An example of this is the IO monad. In this case we simply postulate the existence of the type and use the COMPILED TYPE directive to tell the compiler how it should be interpreted.

```
postulate IO : Set -> Set
{-# COMPILED_TYPE IO IO #-}
```

The first argument to COMPILED TYPE is the name of the Agda type and the second is the corresponding Haskell type.

4.2 Importing Haskell Functions

Once the compiler knows what the Agda type corresponding to a Haskell type is, we can import Haskell functions of that type. For instance, we can import the putStrLn function to print a string[8] to the terminal.

```
open import Data.String

postulate
  putStrLn : String -> IO Unit

{-# COMPILED putStrLn putStrLn #-}
```

Just as for compiled types the first argument to COMPILED is the name of the Agda function and the second argument is the Haskell code it should compile to. The compiler checks that the given code has the Haskell type corresponding to the type of the Agda function.

---

[8] The string library contains the compiler directives for how to compile the string type.

4.3 Our First Program

This is all we need to write our first complete Agda program. Here is the `main` function:

```
main : IO Unit
main = putStrLn "Hello world!"
```

To compile the program simply call the command-line tool with the `--compile` (or `-c`) flag. The compiler will compile your Agda program and any Agda modules it imports to Haskell modules and call the Haskell compiler to generate an executable binary.

4.4 Haskell Module Imports

In the example above, everything we imported was defined in the Haskell prelude so there was no need to import any additional Haskell libraries. This will not be the case in general – for instance, you might write some Haskell code yourself, defining Haskell equivalents of some of your Agda datatypes. To import a Haskell module there is an `IMPORT` directive, which has the same syntax as a Haskell import statement. For instance, to import a function to print a string to standard error, we can write the following:

```
{-# IMPORT System.IO (hPutStrLn, stderr) #-}

postulate printError : String -> IO Unit
{-# COMPILED printError (hPutStrLn stderr) #-}
```

4.5 Importing Polymorphic Functions

As we saw in Section 2.2 in Agda polymorphic functions are modeled by functions taking types as arguments. In Haskell, on the other hand, the type arguments of a polymorphic functions are completely implicit. When importing a polymorphic Haskell function we have to keep this difference in mind. For instance, to import *return* and *bind* of the IO monad we say

```
postulate
  return : {A : Set} -> A -> IO A
  _>>=_  : {A B : Set} -> IO A -> (A -> IO B) -> IO B

{-# COMPILED return (\a -> return) #-}
{-# COMPILED _>>=_  (\a b -> (>>=)) #-}
```

Applications of the Agda functions `return` and `>>=` will include the type arguments, so the generated Haskell code must take this into account. Since the type arguments are only there for the benefit of the type checker, the generated code simply throws them away.

4.6   Exercises

Exercise 4.1. Turn the type checker for λ-calculus from Section 3.1 into a complete program that can read a file containing a raw λ-term and print its type if it's well-typed and an error message otherwise. To simplify things you can write the parser in Haskell and import it into the Agda program.

5   Further Reading

More information on the Agda language and how to obtain the code for these notes can be found on the Agda wiki [2]. If you have any Agda related questions feel free to ask on the Agda mailing list [1].

My thesis [5] contains more of the technical and theoretical details behind Agda, as well as some programming examples. To learn more about dependently typed programming in Agda you can read *The power of Pi* by Oury and Swierstra [6]. For dependently typed programming in general try *The view from the left* by McBride and McKinna [4] and *Why dependent types matter* by Altenkirch, McBride and McKinna [3].

References

1. The Agda mailing list (2008),
   https://lists.chalmers.se/mailman/listinfo/agda
2. The Agda wiki (2008), http://www.cs.chalmers.se/~ulfn/Agda
3. Altenkirch, T., McBride, C., McKinna, J.: Why dependent types matter. Manuscript (April 2005)
4. McBride, C., McKinna, J.: The view from the left. Journal of Functional Programming 14(1), 69–111 (2004)
5. Norell, U.: Towards a practical programming language based on dependent type theory. PhD thesis, Department of Computer Science and Engineering, Chalmers University of Technology, SE-412 96 Göteborg, Sweden (September 2007)
6. Oury, N., Swierstra, W.: The power of pi. In: Accepted for presentation at ICFP (2008)

A Tutorial on Parallel and Concurrent Programming in Haskell

Simon Peyton Jones and Satnam Singh

Microsoft Research Cambridge
simonpj@microsoft.com, satnams@microsoft.com

Abstract. This practical tutorial introduces the features available in Haskell for writing parallel and concurrent programs. We first describe how to write semi-explicit parallel programs by using annotations to express opportunities for parallelism and to help control the granularity of parallelism for effective execution on modern operating systems and processors. We then describe the mechanisms provided by Haskell for writing explicitly parallel programs with a focus on the use of software transactional memory to help share information between threads. Finally, we show how nested data parallelism can be used to write deterministically parallel programs which allows programmers to use rich data types in data parallel programs which are automatically transformed into flat data parallel versions for efficient execution on multi-core processors.

1 Introduction

The introduction of multi-core processors has renewed interest in parallel functional programming and there are now several interesting projects that explore the advantages of a functional language for writing parallel code or implicitly paralellizing code written in a pure functional language. These lecture notes present a variety of techniques for writing concurrent parallel programs which include existing techniques based on semi-implicit parallelism and explicit thread-based parallelism as well as more recent developments in the areas of software transactional memory and nested data parallelism.

We also use the terms *parallel* and *concurrent* with quite specific meanings. A parallel program is one which is written for performance reasons to exploit the potential of a real parallel computing resource like a multi-core processor. For a parallel program we have the expectation of some genuinely simultaneous execution. Concurrency is a software structuring technique that allows us to model computations as hypothetical independent activities (e.g. with their own program counters) that can communicate and synchronize.

In these lecture notes we assume that the reader is familiar with the pure lazy functional programming language Haskell.

P. Koopman and D. Swierstra (Eds.): AFP 2008, LNCS 5832, pp. 267–305, 2009.

2 Applications of Concurrency and Parallelism

Writing concurrent and parallel programs is more challenging than the already difficult problem of writing sequential programs. However, there are some compelling reasons for writing concurrent and parallel programs:

Performance. We need to write parallel programs to achieve improving performance from each new generation of multi-core processors.

Hiding latency. Even on single-core processors we can exploit concurrent programs to hide the latency of slow I/O operations to disks and network devices.

Software structuring. Certain kinds of problems can be conveniently represented as multiple communicating threads which help to structure code in a more modular manner e.g. by modeling user interface components as separate threads.

Real world concurrency. In distributed and real-time systems we have to model and react to events in the real world e.g. handling multiple server requests in parallel.

All new mainstream microprocessors have two or more cores and relatively soon we can expect to see tens or hundreds of cores. We can not expect the performance of each individual core to improve much further. The only way to achieve increasing performance from each new generation of chips is by dividing the work of a program across multiple processing cores. One way to divide an application over multiple processing cores is to somehow automatically parallelize the sequential code and this is an active area of research. Another approach is for the user to write a semi-explicit or explicitly parallel program which is then scheduled onto multiple cores by the operating systems and this is the approach we describe in these lectures.

3 Compiling Parallel Haskell Programs

To reproduce the results in this paper you will need to use a version of the GHC Haskell compiler *later* than 6.10.1 (which at the time of printing requires building the GHC compiler from the HEAD branch of the source code repository). To compile a parallel Haskell program you need to specify the `-threaded` extra flag. For example, to compile the parallel program contained in the file `Wombat.hs` issue the command:

```
ghc --make -threaded Wombat.hs
```

To execute the program you need to specify how many real threads are available to execute the logical threads in a Haskell program. This is done by specifying an argument to Haskell's run-time system at invocation time. For example, to use three real threads to execute the `Wombat` program issue the command:

```
Wombat +RTS -N3
```

In these lecture notes we use the term *thread* to describe a Haskell thread rather than a native operating system thread.

4   Semi-explicit Parallelism

A pure Haskell program may appear to have abundant opportunities for automatic parallelization. Given the lack of side effects it may seem that we can productively evaluate every sub-expression of a Haskell program in parallel. In practice this does not work out well because it creates far too many small items of work which can not be efficiently scheduled and parallelism is limited by fundamental data dependencies in the source program.

Haskell provides a mechanism to allow the user to control the granularity of parallelism by indicating what computations may be usefully carried out in parallel. This is done by using functions from the Control.Parallel module. The interface for Control.Parallel is shown below:

```
1   par :: a -> b -> b
2   pseq :: a -> b -> b
```

The function par indicates to the Haskell run-time system that it may be beneficial to evaluate the first argument in parallel with the second argument. The par function returns as its result the value of the second argument. One can always eliminate par from a program by using the following identity without altering the semantics of the program:

```
1   par a b = b
```

The Haskell run-time system does not necessarily create a thread to compute the value of the expression a. Instead, the run-time system creates a *spark* which has the potential to be executed on a different thread from the parent thread. A sparked computation expresses the possibility of performing some speculative evaluation. Since a thread is not necessarily created to compute the value of a this approach has some similarities with the notion of a *lazy future* [15].

Sometimes it is convenient to write a function with two arguments as an infix function and this is done in Haskell by writing quotes around the function:

```
1   a 'par' b
```

An example of this expression executing in parallel is shown in Figure1.

We call such programs semi-explicitly parallel because the programmer has provided a hint about the appropriate level of granularity for parallel operations and the system implicitly creates threads to implement the concurrency. The user does not need to explicitly create any threads or write any code for inter-thread communication or synchronization.

To illustrate the use of par we present a program that performs two compute intensive functions in parallel. The first compute intensive function we use is the notorious Fibonacci function:

```
1 fib :: Int -> Int
2 fib 0 = 0
3 fib 1 = 1
4 fib n = fib (n-1) + fib (n-2)
```

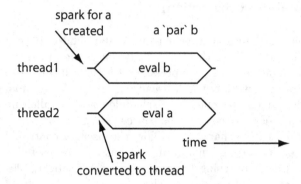

Fig. 1. Semi-explicit execution of a in parallel with the main thread b

The second compute intensive function we use is the sumEuler function [20]:

```
1 mkList :: Int −> [Int]
2 mkList n = [1..n−1]
3
4 relprime :: Int −> Int −> Bool
5 relprime x y = gcd x y == 1
6
7 euler :: Int −> Int
8 euler n = length (filter (relprime n) (mkList n))
9
10 sumEuler :: Int −> Int
11 sumEuler = sum . (map euler) . mkList
```

The function that we wish to parallelize adds the results of calling fib and sumEuler:

```
1 sumFibEuler :: Int −> Int −> Int
2 sumFibEuler a b = fib a + sumEuler b
```

As a first attempt we can try to use par the speculatively spark off the computation of fib while the parent thread works on sumEuler:

```
1 parSumFibEuler :: Int −> Int −> Int
2 parSumFibEuler a b
3     = f 'par' (f + e)
4     where
5       f = fib a
6       e = sumEuler b
```

To help measure how long a particular computation is taking we use the Sytem.Time module and define a function that returns the difference between two time samples as a number of seconds:

```
1 secDiff :: ClockTime −> ClockTime −> Float
2 secDiff (TOD secs1 psecs1) (TOD secs2 psecs2)
3     = fromInteger (psecs2 − psecs1) / 1e12 + fromInteger (secs2 − secs1)
```

The main program calls the sumFibEuler function with suitably large arguments and reports the value

```
1 r1 :: Int
2 r1 = sumFibEuler 38 5300
3
4 main :: IO ()
5 main
6  = do t0 <- getClockTime
7        pseq r1 (return ())
8        t1 <- getClockTime
9        putStrLn ("sum: " ++ show r1)
10       putStrLn ("time: " ++ show (secDiff t0 t1) ++ " seconds")
```

The calculations fib 38 and sumEuler 5300 have been chosen to have roughly the same execution time.

If we were to execute this code using just one thread we would observe the sequence of evaluations shown in Figure 2. Although a spark is created for the evaluation of f there is no other thread available to instantiate this spark so the program first computes f (assuming the + evaluates its left argument first) and then computes e and finally the addition is performed. Making an assumption about the evaluation order of the arguments of + is unsafe and another valid execution trace for this program would involve first evaluating e and then evaluating f.

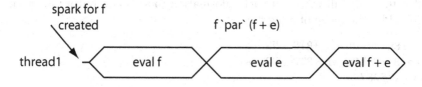

Fig. 2. Executing f 'par' (e + f) on a single thread

The compiled program can now be run on a multi-core computer and we can see how it performs when it uses one and then two real operating system threads:

```
$ ParSumFibEuler +RTS -N1
sum: 47625790
time: 9.274 seconds

$ ParSumFibEuler +RTS -N2
sum: 47625790
time: 9.223 seconds
```

The output above shows that the version run with two cores did not perform any better than the sequential version. Why is this? The problem lies in line 3 of the parSumFibEuler function. Although the work of computing fib 38 is

sparked off for speculative evaluation the parent thread also starts off by trying
to compute fib 38 because this particular implementation of the program used
a version of + that evaluates its left and side before it evaluates its right hand
side. This causes the main thread to *demand* the evaluation of fib 38 so the
spark never gets instantiated onto a thread. After the main thread evaluates fib
38 it goes onto evaluate sumEuler 5300 which results in a performance which is
equivalent to the sequential program. A sample execution trace for this version
of the program is shown in Figure 3. We can obtain further information about

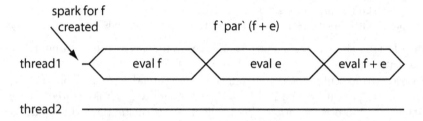

Fig. 3. A spark that does not get instantiated onto a thread

what happened by asking the run-time system to produce a log which contains
information about how many sparks were created and then actually evaluated
as well as information about how much work was performed by each thread. The
-s flag by itself will write out such information to standard output or it can be
followed by the name of a log file.

```
$ ParSumFibEuler +RTS -N2 -s
.\ParSumFibEuler +RTS -N2 -s
sum: 47625790
time: 9.223 seconds
...
  SPARKS: 1 (0 converted, 0 pruned)

  INIT  time    0.00s (  0.01s elapsed)
  MUT   time    8.75s (  8.79s elapsed)
  GC    time    0.42s (  0.43s elapsed)
  EXIT  time    0.00s (  0.00s elapsed)
  Total time    9.17s (  9.23s elapsed)
...
```

This report shows that although a spark was created it was never actually taken
up for execution on a thread. This behaviour is also reported when we view
the execution trace using the ThreadScope thread profiler as shown in Figure 4
which shows one thread busy all the time but the second thread performs no
work at all. Purple (or black) indicates that a thread is running and orange (or
gray) indicates garbage collection.

Fig. 4. A ThreadScope trace showing lack of parallelism

A tempting fix is to reverse the order of the arguments to +:

```
1 parSumFibEuler :: Int −> Int −> Int
2 parSumFibEuler a b
3   = f 'par' (e + f)
4   where
5     f = fib a
6     e = sumEuler b
```

Here we are sparking off the computation of fib for speculative evaluation with respect to the parent thread. The parent thread starts off by computing sumEuler and hopefully the run-time will convert the spark for computing fib and execute it on a thread located on a different core in parallel with the parent thread. This does give a respectable speedup:

```
$ ParFibSumEuler2 +RTS −N1
sum: 47625790
time: 9.158 seconds

$ ParFibSumEuler2 +RTS −N2
sum: 47625790
time: 5.236 seconds
```

A sample execution trace for this version of the program is shown in Figure 5

We can confirm that a spark was created and productively executed by looking at the log output using the -s flag:

```
$ .\ParFibSumEuler2 +RTS −N2 -s
.\ParSumFibEuler2 +RTS −N2 -s
. . .
  SPARKS: 1 (1 converted, 0 pruned)

  INIT  time    0.00s (  0.01s elapsed)
  MUT   time    8.92s (  4.83s elapsed)
  GC    time    0.39s (  0.41s elapsed)
  EXIT  time    0.00s (  0.00s elapsed)
  Total time    9.31s (  5.25s elapsed)
. . .
```

Here we see that one spark was created and converted into work for a real thread. A total of 9.31 seconds worth of work was done in 5.25 seconds of wall clock time

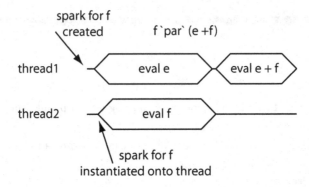

Fig. 5. A lucky parallelization (bad dependency on the evaluation order of +)

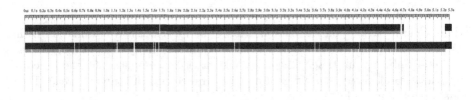

Fig. 6. A ThreadScope trace showing a lucky parallelization

indicating a reasonable degree of parallel execution. A ThreadScope trace of this execution is shown in Figure 6 which clearly indicates parallel activity on two threads.

However, it is a Very Bad Idea to rely on the evaluation order of + for the performance (or correctness) of a program. The Haskell language does not define the evaluation order of the left and right hand arguments of + and the compiler is free to transform a + b to b + a. What we really need to be able to specify what work the main thread should do first. We can use the pseq function from the Control.Monad module for this purpose. The expression a 'pseq' b evaluates a and then returns b. We can use this function to specify what work the main thread should do first (as the first argument of pseq) and we can then return the result of the overall computation in the second argument without worrying about things like the evaluation order of +. This is how we can re-write ParFibSumEuler with pseq:

```
1 parSumFibEuler :: Int -> Int -> Int
2 parSumFibEuler a b
3   = f 'par' (e 'pseq' (e + f))
4     where
5     f = fib a
6     e = sumEuler b
```

This program still gives a roughly 2X speedup as does the following version which has the arguments to + reversed but the use of pseq still ensures that the main thread works on sumEuler before it computes fib (which will hopefully have been computed by a speculatively created thread):

```
1 parSumFibEuler :: Int -> Int -> Int
2 parSumFibEuler a b
3   = f 'par' (e 'pseq' (f + e))
4     where
5     f = fib a
6     e = sumEuler b
```

An execution trace for this program is shown in Figure 7.

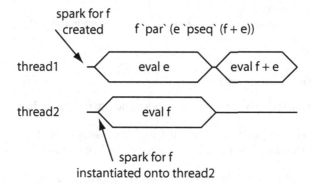

Fig. 7. A correct parallelization which is not dependent on the evaluation order of +

4.1 Weak Head Normal Form (WHNF)

The program below is a variant of the fib-Euler program in which each parallel workload involves mapping an operation over a list.

```
1 module Main
2 where
3 import System.Time
4 import Control.Parallel
5
6 fib :: Int -> Int
7 fib 0 = 0
8 fib 1 = 1
9 fib n = fib (n−1) + fib (n−2)
10
11 mapFib :: [Int]
12 mapFib = map fib [37, 38, 39, 40]
13
14 mkList :: Int -> [Int]
15 mkList n = [1..n−1]
```

```
16
17 relprime :: Int -> Int -> Bool
18 relprime x y = gcd x y == 1
19
20 euler :: Int -> Int
21 euler n = length (filter (relprime n) (mkList n))
22
23 sumEuler :: Int -> Int
24 sumEuler = sum . (map euler) . mkList
25
26 mapEuler :: [Int]
27 mapEuler = map sumEuler [7600, 7600]
28
29 parMapFibEuler :: Int
30 parMapFibEuler = mapFib 'par'
31                      (mapEuler 'pseq' (sum mapFib + sum mapEuler))
32
33 main :: IO ()
34 main
35   = putStrLn (show parMapFibEuler)
```

The intention here is to compute two independent functions in parallel:

- mapping the fib function over a list and then summing the result
- mapping the sumEuler function over a list and the summing the result

The main program then adds the two sums to produce the final result. We have chosen arguments which result in a similar run-time for mapFib and mapEuler.

However, when we run this program with one and then two cores we observe no speedup:

```
satnams@MSRC-LAGAVULIN ~/papers/afp2008/whnf
$ time WHNF2 +RTS -N1
263935901


real    0m48.086s
user    0m0.000s
sys     0m0.015s

satnams@MSRC-LAGAVULIN ~/papers/afp2008/whnf
$ time WHNF2 +RTS -N2
263935901


real    0m47.631s
user    0m0.000s
sys     0m0.015s
```

What went wrong? The problem is that the function mapFib does not return a list with four values each fully evaluated to a number. Instead, the expression is

fib 37   map fib [38, 39, 40]

Fig. 8. parFib evaluated to weak head normal form (WHNF)

reduced to weak head normal form which only return the top level cons cell with the head and the tail elements unevaluated as shown in Figure 8. This means that almost no work is done in the parallel thread. the root of the problem here is Haskell's lazy evaluation strategy which comes into conflict with our desire to control what is evaluated when to help gain performance through parallel execution.

To fix this problem we need to somehow force the evaluation of the list. We can do this by defining a function that iterates over each element of the list and then uses each element as the first argument to pseq which will cause it to be evaluated to a number:

```
1 forceList :: [a] −> ()
2 forceList [] = ()
3 forceList (x:xs) = x 'pseq' forceList xs
```

Using this function we can express our requirement to evaluate the mapFib function fully to a list of numbers rather than to just weak head normal form:

```
1 module Main
2 where
3 import Control.Parallel
4
5 fib :: Int −> Int
6 fib 0 = 0
7 fib 1 = 1
8 fib n = fib (n−1) + fib (n−2)
9
10 mapFib :: [Int]
11 mapFib = map fib [37, 38, 39, 40]
12
13 mkList :: Int −> [Int]
14 mkList n = [1..n−1]
15
16 relprime :: Int −> Int −> Bool
17 relprime x y = gcd x y == 1
18
19 euler :: Int −> Int
20 euler n = length (filter (relprime n) (mkList n))
21
22 sumEuler :: Int −> Int
23 sumEuler = sum . (map euler) . mkList
24
```

```
25 mapEuler :: [Int]
26 mapEuler = map sumEuler [7600, 7600]
27
28 parMapFibEuler :: Int
29 parMapFibEuler = (forceList mapFib) `par`
30                    (forceList mapEuler `pseq` (sum mapFib + sum mapEuler))
31
32 forceList :: [a] -> ()
33 forceList [] = ()
34 forceList (x:xs) = x `pseq` forceList xs
35
36 main :: IO ()
37 main
38   = putStrLn (show parMapFibEuler)
```

This gives the desired performance which shows the work of mapFib is done in parallel with the work of mapEuler:

```
satnams@MSRC-LAGAVULIN ~/papers/afp2008/whnf
$ time WHNF3 +RTS -N1
263935901

real    0m47.680s
user    0m0.015s
sys     0m0.000s

satnams@MSRC-LAGAVULIN ~/papers/afp2008/whnf
$ time WHNF3 +RTS -N2
263935901

real    0m28.143s
user    0m0.000s
sys     0m0.000s
```

Question. What would be the effect on performance if we omitted the call of forceList on mapEuler?

An important aspect of how pseq works is that it evaluates its first argument to weak head normal formal. This does not fully evaluate an expression e.g. for an expression that constructs a list out of a head and a tail expression (a CONS expression) pseq will not evaluate the head and tail sub-expressions.

Haskell also defines a function called seq but the compiler is free to swap the arguments of seq which means the user can not control evaluation order. The compiler has primitive support for pseq and ensures the arguments are never swapped and this function should always be preferred over seq for parallel programs.

4.2   Divide and Conquer

Exercise 1: Parallel quicksort. The program below shows a sequential implementation of a quicksort algorithm. Use this program as a template to write a
parallel quicksort function. The main body of the program generates a pseudo-
random list of numbers and then measures the time taken to build the input list
and then to perform the sort and then add up all the numbers in the list.

```
1  module Main
2  where
3  import System.Time
4  import Control.Parallel
5  import System.Random
6
7  -- A sequential quicksort
8  quicksort :: Ord a => [a] -> [a]
9  quicksort [] = []
10 quicksort (x:xs) = losort ++ x : hisort
11                    where
12                      losort = quicksort [y | y <- xs, y < x]
13                      hisort = quicksort [y | y <- xs, y >= x]
14
15 secDiff :: ClockTime -> ClockTime -> Float
16 secDiff (TOD secs1 psecs1) (TOD secs2 psecs2)
17   = fromInteger (psecs2 - psecs1) / 1e12 + fromInteger (secs2 - secs1)
18
19 main :: IO ()
20 main
21   = do t0 <- getClockTime
22        let input = (take 20000 (randomRs (0,100) (mkStdGen 42)))::[Int]
23        seq (forceList input) (return ())
24        t1 <- getClockTime
25        let r = sum (quicksortF input)
26        seq r (return ()) -- Force evaluation of sum
27        t2 <- getClockTime
28        -- Write out the sum of the result.
29        putStrLn ("Sum of sort: " ++ show r)
30        -- Write out the time taken to perform the sort.
31        putStrLn ("Time to sort: " ++ show (secDiff t1 t2))
```

The performance of a parallel Haskell program can sometimes be improved by
reducing the number of garbage collections that occur during execution and a
simple way of doing this is to increase the heap size of the program. The size
of the heap is specified has an argument to the run-time system e.g. -K100M
specifies a 100MB stack and -H800M means use a 800MB heap.

```
satnams@msrc-bensley /cygdrive/l/papers/afp2008/quicksort
$ QuicksortD +RTS -N1 -H800M
Sum of sort: 50042651196
Time to sort: 4.593779
```

```
satnams@msrc-bensley /cygdrive/l/papers/afp2008/quicksort
$ QuicksortD +RTS -N2 -K100M -H800M
Sum of sort: 50042651196
Time to sort: 2.781196
```

You should consider using par and pseq to try and compute the sub-sorts in parallel. This in itself may not lead to any performance improvement and you should then ensure that the parallel sub-sorts are indeed doing all the work you expect them to do (e.g. consider the effect of lazy evaluation). You may need to write a function to *force* the evaluation of sub-expressions.

You can get some idea of how well a program has been parallelized and how much time is taken up with garbage collection by using the runtime -s flag to dump some statistics to the standard output. We can also enable GHC's parallel garbage collection and disable load balancing for better cache behaviour with the flags -qg0 -qb.

```
$ ./QuicksortD.exe +RTS -N2 -K100M -H300M -qg0 -qb -s
```

After execution of a parallel version of quicksort you can look at the end of the file n2.txt to see what happened:

```
.\QuicksortD.exe +RTS -N2 -K100M -H300M -qg0 -qb -s
   1,815,932,480 bytes allocated in the heap
     242,705,904 bytes copied during GC
      55,709,884 bytes maximum residency (4 sample(s))
       8,967,764 bytes maximum slop
             328 MB total memory in use (2 MB lost due to fragmentation)

  Generation 0:  10 collections,  9 parallel, 1.62s, 0.83s elapsed
  Generation 1:   4 collections,  4 parallel, 1.56s, 0.88s elapsed

  Parallel GC work balance: 1.29 (60660834 / 46891587, ideal 2)

  Task  0 (worker) :  MUT time:   2.34s  (  3.55s elapsed)
                      GC  time:   0.91s  (  0.45s elapsed)

  Task  1 (worker) :  MUT time:   1.55s  (  3.58s elapsed)
                      GC  time:   0.00s  (  0.00s elapsed)

  Task  2 (worker) :  MUT time:   2.00s  (  3.58s elapsed)
                      GC  time:   2.28s  (  1.25s elapsed)

  Task  3 (worker) :  MUT time:   0.00s  (  3.59s elapsed)
                      GC  time:   0.00s  (  0.00s elapsed)

  SPARKS: 7 (7 converted, 0 pruned)
```

```
INIT  time    0.00s  (  0.03s elapsed)
MUT   time    5.89s  (  3.58s elapsed)
GC    time    3.19s  (  1.70s elapsed)
EXIT  time    0.00s  (  0.02s elapsed)
Total time    9.08s  (  5.31s elapsed)

%GC time      35.1%  (32.1% elapsed)

Alloc rate    308,275,009 bytes per MUT second

Productivity  64.9% of total user, 110.9% of total elapsed
```

This execution of quicksort spent 35.1% of its time in garbage collection. The work of the sort was shared out amongst two threads although not evenly. The MUT time gives an indication of how much time was spent performing computation. Seven sparks were created and each of them was evaluated.

5   Explicit Concurrency

Writing semi-implicitly parallel programs can sometimes help to parallelize pure functional programs but it does not work when we want to parallelize stateful computations in the IO monad. For that we need to write explicitly threaded programs. In this section we introduce Haskell's mechanisms for writing explicitly concurrent programs. Haskell presents explicit concurrency features to the programmer via a collection of library functions rather than adding special syntactic support for concurrency and all the functions presented in this section are exported by this module.

5.1   Creating Haskell Threads

The basic functions for writing explicitly concurrent programs are exported by the Control.Concurrent which defines an abstract type ThreadId to allow the identification of Haskell threads (which should not be confused with operating system threads). A new thread may be created for any computation in the IO monad which returns an IO unit result by calling the forkIO function:

```
1 forkIO :: IO () -> IO ThreadId
```

Why does the forkIO function take an expression in the IO monad rather than taking a pure functional expression as its argument? The reason for this is that most concurrent programs need to communicate with each other and this is done through shared synchronized state and these stateful operations have to be carried out in the IO monad.

One important thing to note about threads that are created by calling forkIO is that the main program (the parent thread) will not automatically wait for the child threads to terminate.

Sometimes it is necessary to use a real operating system thread and this can be achieved using the forkOS function:

```
1 forkOS :: IO () -> IO ThreadId
```

Threads created by this call are bound to a specific operating system thread and this capability is required to support certain kinds of foreign calls made by Haskell programs to external code.

5.2   MVars

To facilitate communication and synchronization between threads Haskell provides MVars ("mutable variables") which can be used to atomically communicate information between threads. MVars and their associated operations are exported by the module Control.Concurrent.MVar. The run-time system ensures that the operations for writing to and reading from MVars occur atomically. An MVar may be empty or it may contain a value. If a thread tries to write to an occupied MVar it is blocked and it will be rewoken when the MVar becomes empty at which point it can try again to atomically write a value into the MVar. If more than one thread is waiting to write to an MVar then the system uses a first-in first-out scheme to wake up just the longest waiting thread. If a thread tries to read from an empty MVar it is blocked and rewoken when a value is written into the MVar when it gets a chance to try and atomically read the new value. Again, if more than one thread is waiting to read from an MVar the run-time system will only wake up the longest waiting thread.

Operations are provided to create an empty MVar, to create a new MVar with an initial value, to remove a value from an MVar, to observe the value in an MVar (plus non-blocking variants) as well as several other useful operations.

```
 1 data MVar a
 2
 3 newEmptyMVar :: IO (MVar a)
 4 newMVar :: a -> IO (MVar a)
 5 takeMVar :: MVar a -> IO a
 6 putMVar :: MVar a -> a -> IO ()
 7 readMVar :: MVar a -> IO a
 8 tryTakeMVar :: MVar a -> IO (Maybe a)
 9 tryPutMVar :: MVar a -> a -> IO Bool
10 isEmptyMVar :: MVar a -> IO Bool
11 -- Plus other functions
```

One can use a pair of MVars and the blocking operations putMVar and takeMVar to implement a *rendezvous* between two threads.

```
1 module Main
2 where
3 import Control.Concurrent
4 import Control.Concurrent.MVar
5
6 threadA :: MVar Int -> MVar Float -> IO ()
```

```
 7 threadA valueToSendMVar valueReceiveMVar
 8   = do —— some work
 9        —— now perform rendezvous by sending 72
10        putMVar valueToSendMVar 72 —— send value
11        v <— takeMVar valueReceiveMVar
12        putStrLn (show v)
13
14 threadB :: MVar Int —> MVar Float —> IO ()
15 threadB valueToReceiveMVar valueToSendMVar
16   = do —— some work
17        —— now perform rendezvous by waiting on value
18        z <— takeMVar valueToReceiveMVar
19        putMVar valueToSendMVar (1.2 * z)
20        —— continue with other work
21
22 main :: IO ()
23 main
24   = do aMVar <— newEmptyMVar
25        bMVar <— newEmptyMVar
26        forkIO (threadA aMVar bMVar)
27        forkIO (threadB aMVar bMVar)
28        threadDelay 1000 —— wait for threadA and threadB to finish (sleazy)
```

Exercise 2: Re-write this program to remove the use of threadDelay by using some other more robust mechanism to ensure the main thread does not complete until all the child threads have completed.

```
 1 module Main
 2 where
 3 import Control.Parallel
 4 import Control.Concurrent
 5 import Control.Concurrent.MVar
 6
 7 fib :: Int —> Int
 8 —— As before
 9
10 fibThread :: Int —> MVar Int —> IO ()
11 fibThread n resultMVar
12   = putMVar resultMVar (fib n)
13
14 sumEuler :: Int —> Int
15 —— As before
16
17 s1 :: Int
18 s1 = sumEuler 7450
19
20 main :: IO ()
21 main
22   = do putStrLn "explicit SumFibEuler"
23        fibResult <— newEmptyMVar
24        forkIO (fibThread 40 fibResult)
```

```
25        pseq s1 (return ())
26        f <- takeMVar fibResult
27        putStrLn ("sum: " ++ show (s1+f))
```

The result of running this program with one and two threads is:

```
satnams@MSRC-1607220 ~/papers/afp2008/explicit
$ time ExplicitWrong +RTS -N1
explicit SumFibEuler
sum: 119201850

real    0m40.473s
user    0m0.000s
sys     0m0.031s

satnams@MSRC-1607220 ~/papers/afp2008/explicit
$ time ExplicitWrong +RTS -N2
explicit SumFibEuler
sum: 119201850

real    0m38.580s
user    0m0.000s
sys     0m0.015s
```

To fix this problem we must ensure the computation of fib fully occurs inside the fibThread thread which we do by using pseq.

```
1 module Main
2 where
3 import Control.Parallel
4 import Control.Concurrent
5 import Control.Concurrent.MVar
6
7 fib :: Int -> Int
8 -- As before
9
10 fibThread :: Int -> MVar Int -> IO ()
11 fibThread n resultMVar
12   = do pseq f (return ()) -- Force evaluation in this thread
13        putMVar resultMVar f
14   where
15     f = fib n
16
17 sumEuler :: Int -> Int
18 -- As before
19
20 s1 :: Int
21 s1 = sumEuler 7450
22
23 main :: IO ()
```

```
24 main
25    = do putStrLn "explicit SumFibEuler"
26         fibResult <− newEmptyMVar
27         forkIO (fibThread 40 fibResult)
28         pseq s1 (return ())
29         f <− takeMVar fibResult
30         putStrLn ("sum: " ++ show (s1+f))
```

Writing programs with MVars can easily lead to deadlock e.g. when one thread is waiting for a value to appear in an MVar but no other thread will ever write a value into that MVar. Haskell provides an alternative way for threads to synchronize without using explicit locks through the use of *software transactional memory* (STM) which is accessed via the module Control.Concurrent.STM. A subset of the declarations exposed by this module are shown below.

```
1 data STM a −− A monad supporting atomic memory transactions
2 atomically :: STM a −> IO a −− Perform a series of STM actions atomically
3 retry :: STM a −− Retry current transaction from the beginning
4 orElse :: STM a −> STM a −> STM a −− Compose two transactions
5 data TVar a −− Shared memory locations that support atomic memory operations
6 newTVar :: a −> STM (TVar a) −− Create a new TVar with an initial value
7 readTVar :: TVar a −> STM a −− Return the current value stored in a TVar
8 writeTVar :: TVar a −> a −> STM () −− Write the supplied value into a TVar
```

Software transactional memory works by introducing a special type of shared variable called a TVar rather like a MVar which is used only inside *atomic blocks*. Inside an atomic block a thread can write and read TVars however outside an atomic block TVars can only be created and passed around around but not read or written. These restrictions are enforced by providing read and write operations that work in the *STM* monad. The code inside an atomic block is executed as if it were an atomic instruction. One way to think about atomic blocks is to assume that there is one special global lock available and every atomic block works by taking this lock, executing the code in the atomic block, and then releasing this lock. Functionally, it should appear as if no other thread is running in parallel (or no other code is interleaved) with the code in an atomic block. In reality the system does allow such parallel and interleaved execution through the use of a log which is used to roll back the execution of blocks that have conflicting views of shared information.

To execute an atomic block the function atomically takes a computation in the STM monad and executes it in the IO monad.

To help provide a model for how STM works in Haskell an example is shown in Figures 9 and 10 which illustrates how two threads modify a shared variable using Haskell STM. It is important to note that this is just a *model* and an actual implementation of STM is much more sophisticated.

Thread 1 tries to atomically increment a shared TVar:

```
1    atomically (do v <− readTVar bal
2                   writeTVar bal (v+1)
3              )
```

Thread 2 tries to atomically subtract three from a shared TVar:

```
1    atomically (do v <- readTVar bal
2                    writeTVar bal (v-3)
3                )
```

Figure 9(a) shows a shared variable bal with an initial value of 7 and two threads which try to atomically read and update the value of this variable. Thread 1 has an atomic block which atomically increments the value represented by bal. Thread 2 tries to atomically subtract 3 from the value represented by bal. Examples of valid executions include the case where (a) the value represented by bal is first incremented and then has 3 subtracted yielding the value 5; or (b) the case where bal has 3 subtracted and then 1 added yielding the value 6.

Figure 9(b) shows each thread entering its atomic block and a transaction log is created for each atomic block to record the initial value of the shared variables that are read and to record deferred updates to the shared variable which succeed at commit time if the update is consistent.

Figure 9(c) shows thread 2 reading a value of 7 from the shared variable and this read is recorded its local transaction log.

Figure 9(d) shows that thread 1 also observes a value of 7 from the shared variable which is stored in its transaction log.

Figure 9(e) shows thread 1 updating its view of the shared variable by incrementing it by 1. This update is made to the local transaction log and not to the shared variable itself. The actual update is deferred until the transaction tries to commit when either it will succeed and the shared variable will be updated or it may fail in which case the log is reset and the transaction is re-run.

Figure 9(f) shows thread 2 updating its view of the shared variable to 4 (i.e. 7-3). Now the two threads have inconsistent views of what the value of the shared variable should be.

Figure 9(g) shows thread 1 successfully committing its changes. At commit time the run-time system checks to see if the log contains a consistent value for bal i.e. is the value that has been read in the log the same as the value of the actual bal shared variable? In this case it is i.e. both are 7 so the updated value 8 is written in the shared value. These sequence of events occur atomically. Once the commit succeeds the transaction log is discarded and the program moves onto the next statement after the atomic block.

Figure 9(h) shows how the commit attempt made by thread 2 fails. This is because thread 2 has recorded a value of 7 for bal but the actual value of bal is 8. This causes the run-time system to erase the values in the log and restart the transaction which will cause it to see the updated value of bal.

Figure 10(i) shows how thread 2 re-executes its atomic block but this time observing the value of 8 for bal.

Figure 10(j) shows thread 2 subtracting 3 from the recorded value of bal to yield an updated value of 5.

Figure 10(k) shows that thread 2 can now successfully commit with an update of 5 to the shared variable bal. Its transaction log is discarded.

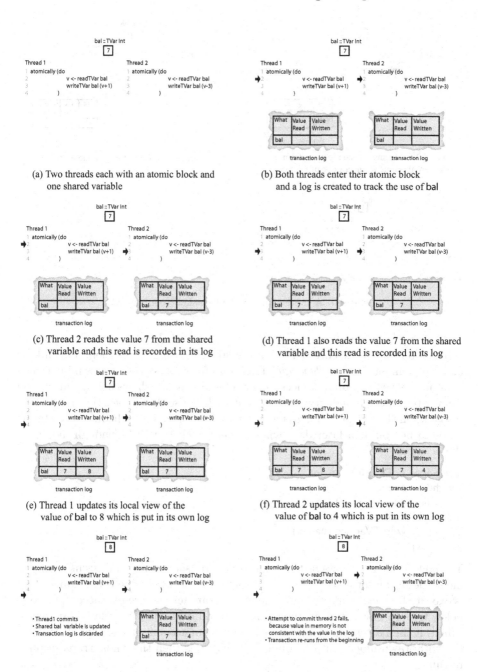

(a) Two threads each with an atomic block and one shared variable

(b) Both threads enter their atomic block and a log is created to track the use of bal

(c) Thread 2 reads the value 7 from the shared variable and this read is recorded in its log

(d) Thread 1 also reads the value 7 from the shared variable and this read is recorded in its log

(e) Thread 1 updates its local view of the value of bal to 8 which is put in its own log

(f) Thread 2 updates its local view of the value of bal to 4 which is put in its own log

(g) Thread 1 finoshes and updates the shared bal variable and discards its log.

(h) Thread 2 tries to commit its changes which are now inconsistent with the updated value of bal

Fig. 9. A model for STM in Haskell

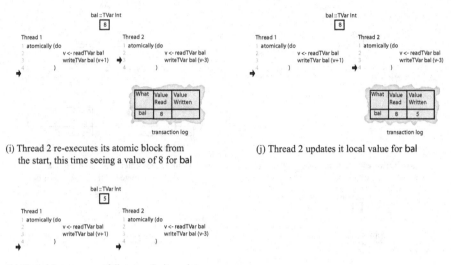

(i) Thread 2 re-executes its atomic block from the start, this time seeing a value of 8 for bal

(j) Thread 2 updates it local value for bal

(k) Thread 2 now successfully commits its updates

Fig. 10. A model for STM in Haskell (continued)

The retry function allows the code inside an atomic block to abort the current transaction and re-execute it from the beginning using a fresh log. This allows us to implement *modular blocking*. This is useful when one can determine that a transaction can not commit successfully. The code below shows how a transaction can try to remove money from an account with a case that makes the transaction re-try when there is not enough money in the account. This schedules the atomic block to be run at a later date when hopefully there will be enough money in the account.

```
1 withdraw :: TVar Int -> Int -> STM ()
2 withdraw acc n
3    = do { bal <- readTVar acc;
4         if bal < n then retry;
5         writeTVar acc (bal−n)
6       }
```

The orElse function allows us to compose two transactions and allows us to implement the notion of *choice*. If one transaction aborts then the other transaction is executed. If it also aborts then the whole transaction is re-executed. The code below tries to first withdraw money from account a1 and if that fails (i.e. retry is called) it then attempts to withdraw money from account a2 and then it deposits the withdrawn money into account b. If that fails then the whole transaction is re-run.

```
1 atomically (do { withdraw a1 3
2                  'orElse'
3                  withdraw a2 3;
4                  deposit b 3 }
5             )
```

To illustrate the use of software transaction memory we outline how to represent a queue which can be shared between Haskell threads. We shall represent a shared queue with a fixed sized array. A thread that writes to a queue that is full (i.e. the array is full) is blocked and a thread that tries to read from a queue that is empty (i.e. the array is empty) is also blocked. The data-type declaration below for an STM-based queue uses transactional variables to record the head element, the tail element, the empty status and the elements of the array that is used to back to queue.

```
1 data Queue e
2   = Queue
3     { shead :: TVar Int,
4       stail :: TVar Int,
5       empty :: TVar Bool,
6       sa :: Array Int (TVar e)
7     }
```

A picture of an empty queue using this representation is shown in Figure 11.

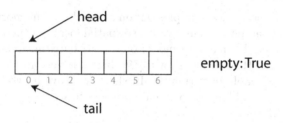

Fig. 11. An empty queue

Exercise. Implement the following operations on this STM-based queue representation.

- Create a new empty queue by defining a function with the type:

  ```
  1 newQueue :: IO (Queue a)
  ```

- Add an element to the queue by defining a function with the type:

  ```
  enqueue :: Queue a -> a -> IO ()
  ```

  If the queue is full the caller should block until space becomes available and the value can be successfully written into the queue.
- Remove an element from the queue and return its value:

  ```
  dequeue :: Queue a -> IO a
  ```

  If the queue is empty the caller should block until there is an item available in the queue for removal.
- Attempt to read a value from a queue and if it is empty then attempt to read a value from a different queue. The caller should block until a value can be obtained from one of the two queues.

  ```
  dequeueEither :: Queue a -> Queue a -> IO a
  ```

6   Nested Data Parallelism

This chapter was written in collaboration with Manuel Chakravarty, Gabriele Keller, and Roman Leshchinskiy (University of New South Wales, Sydney).

The two major ways of exploiting parallelism that we have seen so far each have their disadvantages:

- The `par/seq` style is semantically transparent, but it is hard to ensure that the granularity is consistently large enough to be worth spawning new threads.
- Explicitly-forked threads, communicating using `MVars` or STM give the programmer precise control over granularity, but at the cost of a new layer of semantic complexity: there are now many threads, each mutating shared memory. Reasoning about all the inter leavings of these threads is hard, especially if there are a lot of them.

Furthermore, neither is easy to implement on a distributed-memory machine, because any pointer can point to any value, so spatial locality is poor. It is possible to support this anarchic memory model on a distributed-memory architecture, as Glasgow Parallel Haskell has shown [19], but it is very hard to get reliable, predictable, and scalable performance. In short, we have no good *performance model*, which is a Bad Thing if your main purpose in writing a parallel program is to improve performance.

In this chapter we will explore another parallel programming paradigm: *data parallelism*. The basic idea of data parallelism is simple:

Do the same thing, in parallel, to every element of a large collection of values.

Not every program can be expressed in this way, but data parallelism is very attractive for those that can, because:

- Everything remains purely functional, like `par/seq`, so there is no new semantic complexity.
- Granularity is very good: to a first approximation, we get just one thread (with its attendant overheads) for each physical processor, rather than one thread for each data item (of which there are zillions).
- Locality is very good: the data can be physically partitioned across the processors without random cross-heap pointers.

As a result, we get an excellent performance model.

6.1   Flat Data Parallelism

Data parallelism sounds good doesn't it? Indeed, data-parallel programming is widely and successfully used in mainstream languages such as High-Performance

Fortran. However, there's a catch: the application has to fit the data-parallel programming paradigm, and only a fairly narrow class of applications do so. But this narrow-ness is largely because mainstream data-parallel technology only supports so-called *flat* data parallelism. Flat data parallelism works like this

> Apply the same *sequential* function f, in parallel, to every element of a large collection of values a. Not only is f sequential, but it has a similar run-time for each element of the collection.

Here is how we might write such a loop in Data Parallel Haskell:

```
sumSq :: [: Float :] -> Float
sumSq a = sumP [: x*x | x <- a :]
```

The data type [: Float :] is pronounced "parallel vector of Float". We use a bracket notation reminiscent of lists, because parallel vectors are similar to lists in that consist of an sequence of elements. Many functions available for lists are also available for parallel vectors. For example

```
mapP     :: (a -> b) -> [:a:] -> [:b:]
zipWithP :: (a -> b -> c) -> [:a:] -> [:b:] -> [:c:]
sumP     :: Num a => [:a:] -> a

(+:+)    :: [:a:] -> [:a:] -> [:a:]
filterP  :: (a -> Bool) -> [:a:] -> [:a:]
anyP     :: (a -> Bool) -> [:a:] -> Bool
concatP  :: [:[:a:]:] -> [:a:]
nullP    :: [:a:] -> Bool
lengthP  :: [:a:] -> Int
(!:)     :: [:a:] -> Int -> a    -- Zero-based indexing
```

These functions, and many more, are exported by Data.Array.Parallel. Just as we have list comprehensions, we also have parallel-array comprehensions, of which one is used in the above example. But, just as with list comprehensions, array comprehensions are syntactic sugar, and we could just as well have written

```
sumSq :: [: Float :] -> Float
sumSq a = sumP (mapP (\x -> x*x) a)
```

Notice that there is no forkIO, and no par. The parallelism comes implicitly from use of the primitives operating on parallel vectors, such as mapP, sumP, and so on.

Flat data parallelism is not restricted to consuming a single array. For example, here is how we might take the product of two vectors, by multiplying corresponding elements and adding up the results:

```
vecMul :: [:Float:] -> [:Float:] -> Float
vecMul a b = sumP [: x*y | x <- a | y <- b :]
```

The array comprehension uses a second vertical bar "|" to indicate that we interate over **b** in lockstep with **a**. (This same facility is available for ordinary list comprehensions too.) As before the comprehension is just syntactic sugar, and we could have equivalently written this:

```
vecMul :: [:Float:] -> [:Float:] -> Float
vecMul a b = sumP (zipWithP (*) a b)
```

6.2   Pros and Cons of Flat Data Parallelism

If you can express your program using flat data parallelism, we can implement it really well on a N-processor machine:

- Divide **a** into N chunks, one for each processor.
- Compile a sequential loop that applies **f** successively to each element of a chunk
- Run this loop on each processor
- Combine the results.

Notice that the granularity is good (there is one large-grain thread per processor); locality is good (the elements of **a** are accessed successively); load-balancing is good (each processor does $1/N$ of the work). Furthermore the algorithm works well even if **f** itself does very little work to each element, a situation that is a killer if we spawn a new thread for each invocation of **f**.

In exchange for this great implementation, the programming model is horrible: *all the parallelism must come from a single parallel loop*. This restriction makes the programming model is very non-compositional. If you have an existing function **g** written using the data-parallel **mapP**, you can't call **g** from another data-parallel map (e.g. **mapP g a**), because the argument to **mapP** must be a *sequential* function.

Furthermore, just as the control structure must be flat, so must the data structure. We cannot allow **a** to contain rich nested structure (e.g. the elements of **a** cannot themselves be vectors), or else similar-run-time promise of **f** could not be guaranteed, and data locality would be lost.

6.3   Nested Data Parallelism

In the early 90's, Guy Blelloch described *nested* data-parallel programming. The idea is similar:

> Apply the same function **f**, in parallel, to every element of a large collection of values **a**. However, **f** may *itself* be a (nested) data-parallel function, and does not need to have a similar run-time for each element of **a**.

For example, here is how we might multiply a matrix by a vector:

```
type Vector = [:Float:]
type Matrix = [:Vector:]

matMul :: Matrix -> Vector -> Vector
matMul m v = [: vecMul r v | r <- m :]
```

That is, for each row of the matrix, multiply it by the vector v using vecMul. Here we are calling a data-parallel function vecMul from inside a data-parallel operation (the comprehension in matMul).

In very regular examples like this, consisting of visible, nested loops, modern FORTRAN compilers can collapse a loop nest into one loop, and partition the loop across the processors. It is not entirely trivial to do this, but it is well within the reach of compiler technology. But the flattening process only works for the simplest of cases. A typical complication is the matrices may be *sparse*.

A sparse vector (or matrix) is one in which almost all the elements are zero. We may represent a sparse vector by a (dense) vector of pairs:

```
type SparseVector = [: (Int, Float) :]
```

In this representation, only non-zero elements of the vector are represented, by a pair of their index and value. A sparse matrix can now be represented by a (dense) vector of rows, each of which is a sparse vector:

```
type SparseMatrix = [: SparseVector :]
```

Now we may write vecMul and matMul for sparse arguments thus[1]:

```
sparseVecMul :: SparseVector -> Vector -> Float
sparseVecMul sv v = sumP [: x * v!:i | (i,x) <- sv :]

sparseMatMul :: SparseMatrix -> Vector -> Vector
sparseMatMul sm v = [: sparseVecMul r v | r <- sm :]
```

We use the indexing operator (!:) to index the dense vector v. In this code, the control structure is the same as before (a nested loop, with both levels being data-parallel), but now the data structure is much less regular, and it is *much* less obvious how to flatten the program into a single data-parallel loop, in such a way that the work is evenly distributed over N processors, regardless of the distribution of non-zero data in the matrix.

Blelloch's remarkable contribution was to show that it is possible to take *any* program written using nested data parallelism (easy to write but hard to implement efficiently), and transform it systematically into a program that uses flat data parallelism (hard to write but easy to implement efficiently). He did this for a special-purpose functional language, NESL, designed specifically to demonstrate nested data parallelism.

As a practical programming language, however, NESL is very limited: it is a first-order language, it has only a fixed handful of data types, it is implemented using an interpreter, and so on. Fortunately, in a series of papers, Manuel Chakravarty, Gabriele Keller and Roman Leshchinskiy have generalized Blelloch's transformation to a modern, higher order functional programming language with user-defined algebraic data types – in other words, Haskell. Data

---

[1] Incidentally, although these functions are very short, they are important in some applications. For example, multiplying a sparse matrix by a dense vector (i.e. sparseMatMul) is the inner loop of the NAS Conjugate Gradient benchmark, consuming 95% of runtime [17].

Parallel Haskell is a research prototype implementation of all these ideas, in the Glasgow Haskell Compiler, GHC.

The matrix-multiply examples may have suggested to you that Data Parallel Haskell is intended primarily for scientific applications, and that the nesting depth of parallel computations is statically fixed. However the programming paradigm is much more flexible than that. In the rest of this chapter we will give a series of examples of programming in Data Parallel Haskell, designed to help you gain familiarity with the programming style.

Most (in due course, all) of these examples can be found at in the Darcs repository http://darcs.haskell.org/packages/ndp, in the sub-directory examples/. You can also find a dozen or so other examples of data-parallel algorithms written in NESL at http://www.cs.cmu.edu/~scandal/nesl/algorithms.html.

6.4   Word Search

Here is a tiny version of a web search engine. A Document is a vector of words, each of which is a string. The task is to find all the occurrences of a word in a large collection of documents, returning the matched documents and the matching word positions in those documents. So here is the type signature for search:

```
type Document = [: String :]
type DocColl  = [: Document :]
search :: DocColl -> String -> [: (Document, [:Int:]) :]
```

We start by solving an easier problem, that of finding all the occurrences of a word in a single document:

```
wordOccs :: Document -> String -> [:Int:]
wordOccs d s = [: i | (i,s2) <- zipP [:1..lengthP d:] d
                    , s == s2 :]
```

Here we use a *filter* in the array comprehension, that selects just those pairs (i,s2) for which s==s2. Because this is an array comprehension, the implied filtering is performed in data parallel. The (i,s2) pairs are chosen from a vector of pairs, itself constructed by zipping the document with the vector of its indices. The latter vector [: 1..lengthP d :] is again analogous to the list notation [1..n], which generate the list of values between 1 and n. As you can see, in both of these cases (filtering and enumeration) Data Parallel Haskell tries hard to make parallel arrays and vectors as notationally similar as possible.

With this function in hand, it is easy to build search:

```
search :: [: Document :] -> String -> [: (Document, [:Int:]) :]
search ds s = [: (d,is) | d <- ds
                        , let is = wordOccs d s
                        , not (nullP is) :]
```

6.5 Prime Numbers

Let us consider the problem of computing the prime numbers up to a fixed number n, using the sieve of Erathosthenes. You may know the cunning solution using lazy evaluation, thus:

```
primes :: [Int]
primes = 2 : [x | x <- [3..]
                , not (any ('divides' x) (smallers x))]
           where
               smallers x = takeWhile (\p -> p*p <= x) primes

divides :: Int -> Int -> Bool
divides a b = b 'mod' a == 0
```

(In fact, this code is *not* the sieve of Eratosthenes, as Melissa O'Neill's elegant article shows [16], but it will serve our purpose here.) Notice that when considering a candidate prime x, we check that is is not divisible by any prime smaller than the square root of x. This test involves using primes, the very list the definition produces.

How can we do this in parallel? In principle we want to test a whole batch of numbers in parallel for prime factors. So we must specify how big the batch is:

```
primesUpTo :: Int -> [: Int :]
primesUpTo 1 = [: :]
primesUpTo 2 = [: 2 :]
primesUpTo n = smallers +:+
               [: x | x <- [: ns+1..n :]
                    , not (anyP ('divides' x) smallers) :]
    where
      ns       = intSqrt n
      smallers = primesUpTo ns
```

As in the case of wordOccs, we use a boolean condition in a comprehension to filter the candidate primes. This time, however, computing the condition itself is a nested data-parallel computation (as it was in search). used here to filter candidate primes x.

To compute smallers we make a recursive call to primesUpTo. This makes primesUpTo unlike all the previous examples: the depth of data-parallel nesting is determined *dynamically*, rather than being statically fixed to depth two. It should be clear that the structure of the parallelism is now much more complicated than before, and well out of the reach of mainstream flat data-parallel systems. But it has abundant data parallelism, and will execute with scalable performance on a parallel processor.

6.6 Quicksort

In all the examples so far the "branching factor" has been large. That is, each data-parallel operations has worked on a large collection. What happens if the collection is much smaller? For example, a divide-and-conquer algorithm usually divides a problem into a handful (perhaps only two) sub-problems, solves them, and combines the results. If we visualize the tree of tasks for a divide-and-conquer algorithm, it will have a small branching factor at each node, and may be highly un-balanced.

Is this amenable to nested data parallelism? Yes, it is. Quicksort is a classic divide-and-conquer algorithm, and one that we have already studied. Here it is, expressed in Data Parallel Haskell:

```
qsort :: [: Double :] -> [: Double :]
qsort xs | lengthP xs <=  1 = xs
         | otherwise        = rs!:0 +:+ eq +:+ rs!:1
      where
         p = xs !: (lengthP xs 'div' 2)
     lt = [:x | x <- xs, x < p :]
         eq = [:x | x <- xs, x == p:]
     gr = [:x | x <- xs, x > p :]
     rs = mapP qsort [: lt, gr :]
```

The crucial step here is the use of `mapP` on a *two-element* array `[: lt, gr :]`. This says "in data-parallel, apply `qsort` to `lt` and `gr`". The fact that there are only two elements in the vector does not matter. If you visualize the binary tree of sorting tasks that quicksort generates, then each horizontal layer of the tree is done in data-parallel, even though each layer consists of many unrelated sorting tasks.

6.7   Barnes Hut

All our previous examples worked on simple flat or nested collections. Let's now have a look at an algorithm based on a more complex structure, in which the elements of a parallel array come from a *recursive* and *user-defined* algebraic data type.

In the following, we present an implementation[2] of a simple version of the Barnes-Hut n-body algorithm[1], which is a representative of an important class of parallel algorithms covering applications like simulation and radiocity computations. These algorithms consist of two main steps: first, the data is clustered in a hierarchical tree structure; then, the data is traversed according to the hierarchical structure computed in the first step. In general, we have the situation that the computations that have to be applied to data on the same level of the tree can be executed in parallel. Let us first have a look at the Barnes-Hut algorithm and the data structures that are required, before we discuss the actual implementation in parallel Haskell.

An n-body algorithm determines the interaction between a set of particles by computing the forces which act between each pair of particles. A precise solution therefore requires the computations of n^2 forces, which is not feasible for large

---

[2] Our description here is based heavily on that in [5].

numbers of particles. The Barnes-Hut algorithm minimizes the number of force calculations by grouping particles hierarchically into *cells* according to their spatial position. The hierarchy is represented by a tree. This allows approximating the accelerations induced by a group of particles on distant particles by using the centroid of that group's cell. The algorithm has two phases: (1) The tree is constructed from a particle set, and (2) the acceleration for each particle is computed in a down-sweep over the tree. Each particle is represented by a value of type `MassPoint`, a pair of position in the two dimensional space and mass:

```
type Vec       = (Double, Double)
type Area      = (Vec, Vec)
type Mass      = Double
type MassPoint = (Vec, Mass)
```

We represent the tree as a node which contains the centroid and a parallel array of subtrees:

```
data Tree = Node MassPoint [:Tree:]
```

Notice that a `Tree` contains a parallel array of `Tree`.

Each iteration of `bhTree` takes the current particle set and the area in which the particles are located as parameters. It first splits the area into four subareas `subAs` of equal size. It then subdivides the particles into four subsets according to the subarea they are located in. Then, `bhTree` is called recursively for each subset and subarea. The resulting four trees are the subtrees of the tree representing the particles of the area, and the centroid of their roots is the centroid of the complete area. Once an area contains only one particle, the recursion terminates. Figure 12 shows such a decomposition of an area for a given set of particles, and Figure 13 displays the resulting tree structure.

```
bhTree :: [:MassPnt:] -> Area -> Tree
bhTree p    area = Node p [::]
bhTree ps area =
   let
       subAs = splitArea area
       pgs   = splitParticles ps subAs
```

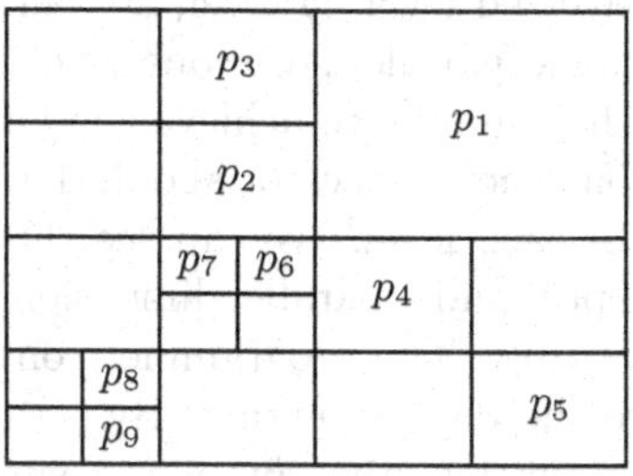

Fig. 12. Hierarchical division of an area into subareas

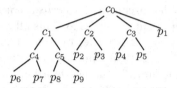

Fig. 13. Example of a Barnes-Hut tree

```
   subts = [: bhTree pg a| pg <- pgs | a <- subAs :]
   cd    = centroid [:mp | Node mp _ <- subts :]
in Node cd subts
```

The tree computed by `bhTree` is then used to compute the forces that act on each particle by a function `accels`. It first splits the set of particles into two subsets: `fMps`, which contains the particles far away (according to a given criteria), and `cMps`, which contains those close to the centroid stored in the root of the tree. For all particles in `fMps`, the acceleration is approximated by computing the interaction between the particle and the centroid. Then, `accels` is called recursively for with `cMps` and each of the subtrees. The computation terminates once there are no particles left in the set.

```
accels:: Tree -> [:MassPoint:] -> [:Vec:]
accels _                 [::] = [::]
accels (Node cd subts)  mps  =
  let
     (fMps, cMps) = splitMps mps
     fAcs         = [:accel  cd mp | mp <- fMps:]
     cAcs         = [:accels t cMps| t <- subts:]
  in combine farAcs closeAcs

accel :: MassPoint -> MassPoint -> Vec
-- Given two particles, the function accel computes the
-- acceleration that one particle exerts on the other
```

The tree is both built and traversed level by level, i.e., all nodes in one level of the tree are processed in a single parallel step, one level after the other. This information is important for the compiler to achieve good data locality and load balance, because it implies that each processor should have approximately the same number of masspoints of each level. We can see the tree as having a sequential dimension to it, its depth, and a parallel dimension, the breadth, neither of which can be predicted statically. The programmer conveys this information to the compiler by the choice the data structure: By putting all subtrees into a parallel array in the type definition, the compiler assumes that all subtrees are going to be processed in parallel. The depth of the tree is modeled by the recursion in the type, which is inherently sequential.

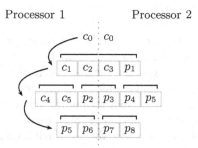

Fig. 14. Distribution of the values of the flattened tree

6.8 A Performance Model

One of the main advantages of the data parallel programming model is that it comes with a *performance model* that lets us make reasonable predictions about the behavior of the program on a parallel machine, including its *scalability* – that is, how performance changes as we add processors. So what is this performance model?

First, we must make explicit something we have glossed over thus far: data-parallel arrays are strict. More precisely, if any element of a parallel array diverges, then all elements diverge[3]. This makes sense, because if we demand any element of a parallel array then we must compute them all in data parallel; and if that computation diverges we are justified in not returning any of them. The same constraint means that we can represent parallel arrays very efficiently. For example, an array of floats, [:Float:], is represented by a contiguous array of unboxed floating-point numbers. There are no pointers, and iterating over the array has excellent spatial locality.

In reasoning about performance, Blelloch [3] characterizes the *work* and *depth* of the program:

- The *work*, W, of the program is the time it would take to execute on a single processor.
- The *depth*, D, of the program is the time it would take to execute on an infinite number processors, under the assumption that the additional processors leap into action when (but only when) a `mapP`, or other data-parallel primitive, is executed.

If you think of the unrolled data-flow diagram for the program, the work is the number of nodes in the data-flow diagram, while the depth is the longest path from input to output.

Of course, we do not have an infinite number of processors. Suppose instead that we have P processors. Then if everything worked perfectly, the work be precisely evenly balanced across the processors and the execution time T would be W/P. That will not happen if the depth D is very large. So in fact, we have

---

[3] What if the elements are pairs? See Leshchinskiy's thesis for the details [12].

$$W/P \leq T \leq W/P + L * D$$

where L is a constant that grows with the latency of communication in the machine. Even this is a wild approximation, because it takes no account of bandwidth limitations. For example, between each of the recursive calls in the Quicksort example there must be some data movement to bring together the elements less than, equal to, and greater than the pivot. Nevertheless, if the network bandwidth of the parallel machine is high (and on serious multiprocessors it usually is) the model gives a reasonable approximation.

$$\mathcal{D}[\![k]\!] = 0 \qquad \text{where } k \text{ is a constant}$$
$$\mathcal{D}[\![x]\!] = 0 \qquad \text{where } x \text{ is a variable}$$
$$\mathcal{D}[\![e_1 + e_2]\!] = 1 + \mathcal{D}[\![e_1]\!] + \mathcal{D}[\![e_2]\!]$$

$$\mathcal{D}[\![\text{if } e_1 \text{ then } e_2 \text{ else } e_3]\!] = \mathcal{D}[\![e_1]\!] + \mathcal{D}[\![e_2]\!] \qquad \text{if } e_1 = \text{True}$$
$$= \mathcal{D}[\![e_1]\!] + \mathcal{D}[\![e_3]\!] \qquad \text{if } e_1 = \text{False}$$
$$\mathcal{D}[\![\text{let } x=e \text{ in } b]\!] = \mathcal{D}[\![b[e/x]]\!]$$

$$\mathcal{D}[\![e_1 \text{ +:+ } e_2]\!] = 1 + \mathcal{D}[\![e_1]\!] + \mathcal{D}[\![e_2]\!]$$
$$\mathcal{D}[\![\text{concatP } e]\!] = 1 + \mathcal{D}[\![e]\!]$$
$$\mathcal{D}[\![\text{mapP } f \ e]\!] = 1 + \mathcal{D}[\![e]\!] + \max_{x \in e} \mathcal{D}[\![f \ x]\!]$$
$$\mathcal{D}[\![\text{filterP } f \ e]\!] = 1 + \mathcal{D}[\![e]\!] + \mathcal{D}[\![f]\!]$$

$$\mathcal{D}[\![\text{sumP } e]\!] = 1 + \mathcal{D}[\![e]\!] + log(length(e))$$

Fig. 15. Depth model for closed expressions

How can we compute work and depth? It is much easier to reason about the work of a program in a strict setting than in a lazy one, because all subexpressions are evaluated. This is why the performance model of the data-parallel part of DPH is more tractable than for Haskell itself.

The computation of depth is where we take account of data parallelism. Figure 15 shows the equations for calculating the depth of a closed expression e, where $\mathcal{D}[\![e]\!]$ means "the depth of e". These equations embody the following ideas:

- By default execution is sequential. Hence, the depth of an addition is the sum of the depths of its arguments.
- The parallel primitive mapP, and its relatives such as filterP, can take advantage of parallelism, so the depth is the worst depth encountered for any element.
- The parallel reduction primitive sumP, and its relatives, take time logarithmic in the length of the array.

The rule for mapP dirctly embodies the idea that nested data parallelism is flattened. For example, suppose e :: [:[:Float:]:]. Then, applying the rules we see that

$$\mathcal{D}[\![\text{mapP } f \ (\text{concatP } e)]\!] = 1 + \mathcal{D}[\![\text{concatP } e]\!] + \max_{x \in \text{concatP } e} \mathcal{D}[\![f \ x]\!]$$

$$= 1 + 1 + \mathcal{D}[\![e]\!] + \max_{x \in \text{concatP } e} \mathcal{D}[\![f \ x]\!]$$

$$= 2 + \mathcal{D}[\![e]\!] + \max_{xs \in e} \max_{x \in xs} \mathcal{D}[\![f \ x]\!]$$

$$\mathcal{D}[\![\text{mapP } (\text{mapP } f) \ e]\!] = 1 + \mathcal{D}[\![e]\!] + \max_{xs \in e} \mathcal{D}[\![\text{mapP } f \ xs]\!]$$

$$= 1 + \mathcal{D}[\![e]\!] + 1 + \max_{xs \in e} \max_{x \in xs} \mathcal{D}[\![f \ x]\!]$$

$$= 2 + \mathcal{D}[\![e]\!] + \max_{xs \in e} \max_{x \in xs} \mathcal{D}[\![f \ x]\!]$$

Notice that although the second case is a *nested* data-parallel computation, it has the same depth expression as the first: the data-parallel nesting is flattened.

These calculations are obviously very approximate, certainly so far as constant factors are concerned. For example, in the inequality for execution time,

$$W/P \leq T \leq W/P + L * D$$

we do not know the value of the latency-related constant L. However, what we are primarily looking for is the *Asymptotic Scalability* (AS) property:

A program has the Asymptotic Scalability property if D grows asymptotically more slowly than W, as the size of the problem increases.

If this is so then, for a sufficiently large problem and assuming sufficient network bandwidth, performance should scale linearly with the number of processors.

For example, the functions sumSq and search both have constant depth, so both have the AS property, and (assuming sufficient bandwidth) performance should scale linearly with the number of processors after some fairly low threshold.

For Quicksort, an inductive argument shows that the depth is logarithmic in the size of the array, assuming the pivot is not badly chosen. So $W = O(n \log n)$ and $D = O(\log n)$, and Quicksort has the AS property.

For computing primes, the depth is smaller: $D = O(\log \log n)$. Why? Because at every step we take the square root of n, so that at depth d we have $n = 2^{2^d}$. Almost all the work is done at the top level. The work at each level involves comparing all the numbers between $\sqrt{n}$ and n with each prime smaller than $\sqrt{n}$. There are approximately $\sqrt{n}/\log n$ primes smaller than $\sqrt{n}$, so the total work is roughly $W = O(n^{3/2}/\log n)$. So again we have the AS property.

Leshchinskiy *et al* [13] give further details of the cost model.

6.9   How It Works

NESL's key insight is that it is possible to transform a program that uses *nested* data-parallelism into one that uses only *flat* data parallelism. While this little miracle happens behind the scenes, it is instructive to have some idea how it works, just as a car driver may find some knowledge of internal combustion engines even if he is not a skilled mechanic. The description here is necessarily brief, but the reader may find a slightly more detailed overview in [7], and in the papers cited there.

We call the nested-to-flat transformation the *vectorization* transform. It has two parts:

- Transform the *data* so that all parallel arrays contain only primitive, flat data, such as Int, Float, Double.
- Transform the *code* to manipulate this flat data.

To begin with, let us focus on the first of these topics. We may consider it as the driving force, because nesting of data-parallel operations is often driven by nested data structures.

Transforming the Data. As we have already discussed, a parallel array of Float is represented by a contiguous array of honest-to-goodness IEEE floating point numbers; and similarly for Int and Double. It is as if we could define the parallel-array type by cases, thus:

```
data instance [: Int    :] = PI Int ByteArray
data instance [: Float  :] = PF Int ByteArray
data instance [: Double :] = PD Int ByteArray
```

In each case the Int field is the size of the array. These data declarations are unusual because they are *non-parametric*: the representation of an array depends on the type of the elements[4].

Matters become even more interesting when we want to represent a parallel array of pairs. We must not represent it as a vector of pointers to heap-allocated pairs, scattered randomly around the address space. We get much better locality if we instead represent it as a *pair of arrays* thus:

```
data instance [: (a,b) :] = PP [:a:] [:b:]
```

Note that elements of vectors are *hyperstrict*. What about a parallel array of parallel arrays? Again, we must avoid a vector of pointers. Instead, the natural representation is obtained by literally concatenating the (representation of) the sub-vectors into one giant vector, together with a vector of indices to indicate where each of the sub-vectors begins.

```
data instance [: [:a:] :] = PA [:Int:] [:a:]
```

By way of example, recall the data types for sparse matrices:

---

[4] None of this is visible to the programmer, but the **data instance** notation is in fact available to the programmer in recent versions of GHC [18,6]. Why? Because GHC has a typed intermediate language so we needed to figure out how to give a *typed* account of the vectorization transformation, and once that is done it seems natural to offer it to the programmer. Furthermore, much of the low-level support code for nested data parallelism is itself written in Haskell, and operates directly on the post-vectorization array representation.

```
type SparseMatrix = [: SparseVector :]
type SparseVector = [: (Int, Float) :]
```

Now consider this tiny matrix, consisting of two short documents:

```
m :: SparseMatrix
m = [: [:(1,2.0), (7,1.9):], [:(3,3.0):] :]
```

This would be represented as follows:

```
PA [:0,2:] (PP [:1,   7,   3  :]
               [:1.0, 1.9, 3.0:])
```

The array (just like the leaves) are themselves represented as byte arrays:

```
PA (PI 2 #<0x0,0x2>)
   (PP (PI 3 #<0x1,     0x7,      0x3>)
       (PF 3 #<0x9383, 0x92818, 0x91813>))
```

Here we have invented a fanciful notation for literal ByteArrays (not supported by GHC, let alone Haskell) to stress the fact that in the end everything boils down to literal bytes. (The hexadecimal encodings of floating point numbers are also made up because the real ones have many digits!)

We have not discussed how to represent arrays of sum types (such as Bool, Maybe, or lists), nor of function types — see [8] and [12] respectively.

Vectorising the Code. As you can see, data structures are transformed quite radically by the vectorisation transform, and it follows that the code must be equally radically transformed. Space precludes proper treatment here; a good starting point is Keller's thesis [11].

A data-parallel program has many array-valued sub-expressions. For example, in sumSq we see

```
sumSq a = sumP [: x*x | x <- a :]
```

However, if a is a big array, it would be silly to compute a new, equally big array of squares, only to immediately consume it with sumP. It would be much better for each processor to zip down its chunk of a, adding the square of each element into a running total, and for each processor's total to be combined.

The elimination of intermediate arrays is called *fusion* and is crucial to improve the constant factor of Data Parallel Haskell. It turns out that vectorisation introduces many *more* intermediate arrays, which makes fusion even more important. These constant factors are extremely important in practice: if there is a slow-down of a factor of 50 relative to C, then even if you get linear speedup by adding processors, Data Parallel Haskell is unlikely to become popular.

6.10   Running Data Parallel Haskell

GHC 6.6 and 6.8 come with support for Data Parallel Haskell syntax, and a *purely sequential* implementation of the operations. So you can readily try out all of the examples in this paper, and ones of your own devising thus:

- Use ghc or ghci version 6.6.x or 6.8.x.
- Use flags -fparr and -XParallelListComp.
- Import module GHC.PArr.

Some support for genuinely-parallel Data Parallel Haskell, including the all-important vectorisation transformation, will be in GHC 6.10 (planned release: autumn 2008). It is not yet clear just how complete the support will be at that time. At the time of writing, for example, type classes are not vectorized, and neither are lists. Furthermore, in a full implementation we will need support for partial vectorisation [9], among other things.

As a result, although all the examples in this paper should work when run sequentially, they may not all vectorise as written, even in GHC 6.10.

A good source of working code is in the Darcs repository http://darcs.haskell.org/packages/ndp, whose sub-directory examples/ contains many executable examples.

6.11   Further Reading

Blelloch and Sabot originated the idea of compiling nested data parallelism into flat data parallelism [4], but an easier starting point is probably Blelloch sub-sequence CACM paper "Programming parallel algorithms" [3], and the NESL language manual [2].

Keller's thesis [11] formalized an intermediate language that models the central aspects of data parallelism, and formalized the key vectorisation transformation. She also studied array *fusion*, to eliminate unnecessary intermediate arrays. Leshchinskiy's thesis [12] extended this work to cover higher order languages ([14] gives a paper-sized summary), while Chakravarty and Keller explain a further generalization to handle user-defined algebraic data types [8].

Data Parallel Haskell is an ongoing research project [7]. The Manticore project at Chicago shares similar goals [10].

References

1. Barnes, J., Hut, P.: A hierarchical $O(n \log n)$ force calculation algorithm. Nature 324 (December 1986)
2. Blelloch, G.: NESL: A nested data-parallel language (3.1). Technical Report CMU-CS-95-170, Carnegie Mellon University (September 1995)
3. Blelloch, G.: Programming parallel algorithms. Commun. ACM 39(3), 85–97 (1996)
4. Blelloch, G., Sabot, G.: Compiling collection-oriented languages onto massively parallel computers. Journal of Parallel and Distributed Computing 8, 119–134 (1990)
5. Chakravarty, M., Keller, G., Lechtchinsky, R., Pfannenstiel, W.: Nepal – nested data-parallelism in haskell. In: Sakellariou, R., Keane, J.A., Gurd, J.R., Freeman, L. (eds.) Euro-Par 2001. LNCS, vol. 2150, pp. 524–534. Springer, Heidelberg (2001)
6. Chakravarty, M., Keller, G., Peyton Jones, S.: Associated type synonyms. In: ACM SIGPLAN International Conference on Functional Programming (ICFP 2005), Tallinn, Estonia (2005)

7. Chakravarty, M., Leshchinskiy, R., Jones, S.P., Keller, G.: Data Parallel Haskell: a status report. In: ACM Sigplan Workshop on Declarative Aspects of Multicore Programming, Nice (January 2007)
8. Chakravarty, M.M., Keller, G.: More types for nested data parallel programming. In: ACM SIGPLAN International Conference on Functional Programming (ICFP 2000), Montreal, pp. 94–105. ACM Press, New York (2000)
9. Chakravarty, M.M., Leshchinskiy, R., Jones, S.P., Keller, G.: Partial vectorisation of Haskell programs. In: Proc. ACM Workshop on Declarative Aspects of Multicore Programming. ACM Press, San Francisco (2008)
10. Fluet, M., Rainey, M., Reppy, J., Shaw, A., Xiao, Y.: Manticore: A heterogeneous parallel language. In: ACM Sigplan Workshop on Declarative Aspects of Multicore Programming, Nice (January 2007)
11. Keller, G.: Transformation-based Implementation of Nested Data Parallelism for Distributed Memory Machines. PhD thesis, Technische Universite at Berlin, Fachbereich Informatik (1999)
12. Leshchinskiy, R.: Higher-order nested data parallelism: semantics and implementation. PhD thesis, Technical University of Berlin (2006)
13. Leshchinskiy, R., Chakravarty, M., Keller, G.: Costing nested array codes. Parallel Processing Letters 12, 249–266 (2002)
14. Leshchinskiy, R., Chakravarty, M.M., Keller, G.: Higher order flattening. In: Alexandrov, V.N., van Albada, G.D., Sloot, P.M.A., Dongarra, J.J. (eds.) ICCS 2006, Part II. LNCS, vol. 3992, pp. 920–928. Springer, Heidelberg (2006)
15. Mohr, E., Kranz, D.A., Halstead, R.H.: Lazy task creation – a technique for increasing the granularity of parallel programs. IEEE Transactions on Parallel and Distributed Systems 2(3) (July 1991)
16. O'Neill, M.: The genuine sieve of Eratosthenes. In: Submitted to JFP (2007)
17. Prins, J., Chatterjee, S., Simons, M.: Irregular computations in fortran: Expression and implementation strategies. Scientific Programming 7, 313–326 (1999)
18. Schrijvers, T., Jones, S.P., Chakravarty, M., Sulzmann, M.: Type checking with open type functions. In: Submitted to ICFP 2008 (2008)
19. Trinder, P., Loidl, H.-W., Barry, E., Hammond, K., Klusik, U., Peyton Jones, S., Rebón Portillo, Á.J.: The Multi-Architecture Performance of the Parallel Functional Language GPH. In: Bode, A., Ludwig, T., Karl, W.C., Wismüller, R. (eds.) Euro-Par 2000. LNCS, vol. 1900, p. 739. Springer, Heidelberg (2000)
20. Trinder, P., Loidl, H.-W., Pointon, R.F.: Parallel and Distributed Haskells. Journal of Functional Programming 12(5), 469–510 (2002)

An iTask Case Study:
A Conference Management System

Rinus Plasmeijer, Peter Achten, Pieter Koopman,
Bas Lijnse, and Thomas van Noort

Radboud University Nijmegen, Netherlands
{rinus,P.Achten,pieter,b.lijnse,thomas}@cs.ru.nl

Abstract. Workflow systems are automated systems in which tasks are coordinated by assigning them to either humans or computers. Contemporary workflow systems are static and not very flexible. In these lecture notes, we discuss the iTask system: a combinator library for specifying workflows in the functional language Clean. This system offers several advantages when compared to commercial systems: tasks are statically typed, tasks can be higher order, the combinators are fully compositional, and dynamic and recursive workflow can be specified. Moreover, the specification is an executable specification offering a web-based multi-user workflow system. In this paper we describe the iTask system using a conference management system as the running example to illustrate the expressive power of functional and generic programming in a real-world domain.

1 Introduction

Workflow systems are automated systems that coordinate *tasks*. Parts of these tasks need to be performed by humans, other parts by computers. Automation of tasks in this way can increase the quality of the process, as the system keeps track of tasks, who or what is performing them, and which tasks are available for execution at any point in time. Many commercial workflow systems exist, such as Business Process Manager, COSA Workflow, FLOWer, i-Flow 6.0, Staffware, Websphere MQ Workflow, and YAWL. When we look at the feautures offered by contemporary workflow systems [1] from the perspective of a modern functional programming language such as Clean or Haskell, there are a number of salient features that functional programmers are accustomed to, and which appear to be missing in workflow systems:

- Functional programmers are keen on abstraction using higher order functions, generic programming techniques, rich type systems, and so on. In commercial workflow systems, workflows are typically specified in a graphical language, instead of a textual language as mostly used in programming languages. By using a graphical representation, a workflow specification is easier to communicate to people in an organization. However, the expressive power of such graphical languages is limited and certainly not comparable to

P. Koopman and D. Swierstra (Eds.): AFP 2008, LNCS 5832, pp. 306–329, 2009.

modern functional languages. Although experiments have been conducted to express functional programs in a graphical way as well (Vital [13], Eros [9]), so far we have to conclude that the expressive power of textual programming languages is hard to beat.

- Workflow systems mainly deal with control flow rather than data flow as in functional languages. As a result, they have focussed less on expressive type systems.
- Within workflow systems, all data is globally known and accessible, and resides in databases. In functional languages, data is passed around between function invocations, and is therefore much more localized.

Given the above observations, we have posed the question which functional programming techniques can contribute to the expressiveness of workflow systems. In these lecture notes we show how web-applications with complex control flow can be constructed by making use of the iTask system: a set of combinators for the specification of interactive multi-user web-based workflow system. The iTask library is built on top of the iData toolkit, and both can be used within the same program. The library covers all *workflow patterns* that can be found in contemporary commercial workflow tools [1]. The iTask toolkit extends these patterns with strong typing, higher-order functions and tasks, lazy evaluation, and a monadic style of programming. Its foundation upon the generic [3,15] features of the iData [19] toolkit yields compact, robust, reusable and understandable code. The workflow which is defined at a high level of abstraction is also an executable specification.

As a running example, we study the architecture of *conference management* (CM) systems, and implement a small prototype in Section 2. This proves to be a good case study of a workflow since it controls the activities of people with various roles, such as program chairs and program committee members. It is also challenging because many of these activities run in parallel, and the system should not hamper the activities of the users of the system. We continue in Section 3 with the semantics of the iTask system. We discuss related work in Section 4 and conclude in Section 5.

In these lecture notes, we assume that the reader is familiar with the functional programming language Clean. For Haskell programmers a short introduction to Clean is given in [2].

2 Defining Workflow

In this section we present the main concepts of the iTask system by means of a number of examples. Where applicable, we use code fragments from the CM prototype. We start out by giving an overview of the CM prototype structure in Section 2.1. We do not cover the entire iTask system. A much more detailed explanation of the iTask system, including the complete API, can be found elsewhere [20].

Exercise

1. *Getting started*

To get started quickly we have compiled a convenient distribution package[1] which contains the latest Clean system for windows, all the additional iTask libraries and the examples and exercises for these lecture notes.

Unpack this zip archive and follow the instructions in the *"iTasks - Do Read This Read Me.doc"* file that can be found in the root folder of the archive. Then, start the Clean IDE and open the project file of the CM system case study, named CM.prj. The project window is now filled with all module names that the CM system uses. Then, compile and run the application. This should give you a console window that asks you to open your browser and direct it to the given address. Follow this instruction, and you are presented with the welcome screen of the CM system, as shown in Figure 1.

Fig. 1. The welcome screen of the CM prototype

2.1 The CM Prototype

The CM prototype allows authors to provide information about their paper at the welcome screen, as depicted in Figure 1. Only the programme chair and registered programme committee members can enter the CM system via the login procedure. After the login procedure, the CM system provides a user with a number of optional tasks, depending on her role.

A programme committee member can:

 − View the list of users, i.e., the programme committee members.
 − View the list of commited papers.

[1] See clean.cs.ru.nl/download/clean22/windows/Clean2.2-iTasks-AFP2008.zip

- Mark the papers, indicating a preference, a conflict of interest, or her level of knowledge of the domain.

In addition to this, the programme chair can:

- Add new users, i.e., new programme committee members or chairs.
- Assign reviewers to papers, based on the marks of each programme committee member.
- Judge reviewed papers.

The code of the CM prototype is organized in a number of modules:

CM: defines the top-level workflow of the CM prototype and is also the main module.
CMCombinators: defines a number of additional convenient combinator functions for the CM application that are used throughout the project, see also Section 2.6 and Section 2.7.
CMDatabase: defines all database access functions, see also Section 2.4.
CMMessages: defines all messages that are used in the CM prototype such that dialogues can be adapted and localized.
CMTypes: defines all used data types which play a pivotal role in the generic programming paradigm, as explained in Section 2.2.
CMUtilities: defines several utility functions.
CMVisualization: defines a number of model-view transformer functions.

2.2   Tasks and Types

With the iTask system, the workflow engineer specifies a workflow by using workflow combinators. This specification is then interpreted by the system which presents a web browser interface to the user. The iTask system makes extensive use of generic programming, and hence, promotes a type directed style of programming. As an example of this style, consider the following definition of two data types that represent CM users and their roles:

```
:: User = { login :: Login
          , email :: TextInput
          , role  :: Role
          }
:: Role = Chair | PC
```

The Login type is predefined and when presented on the screen it allows the user to enter an account name and corresponding password. The type TextInput is also predefined and allows the user to enter basic data (integers, reals, strings).

We create a simple workflow that consists of a single form for editing User values with the following, complete code:

```
module example

import StdEnv, StdiTasks, iTaskUtil

Start :: *World → *World
Start world =
  singleUserTask [] user world

user :: Task User
user = editTask "Done" createDefault

:: User = { login :: Login
          , email :: TextInput
          , role  :: Role
          }
:: Role = Chair | PC

derive gForm  User, Role, Login
derive gUpd   User, Role, Login
derive gPrint User, Role, Login
derive gParse User, Role, Login
```

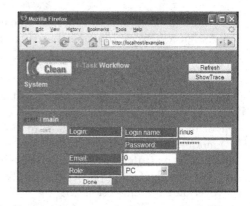

In the code the required modules are imported. The module StdEnv contains the standard functions, data structures, and type classes of Clean. The iTask system is imported by StdiTasks. The module iTaskUtil imports the Login data structure. The expression to be reduced as the main function is always given by the Start function. Because it has an effect on the external world, it is a function of type *World → *World. In Clean, effects on an environment of some type T are usually modeled with environment transformer functions of type $(\ldots *T \to (\ldots ,*T))$. The *uniqueness attribute* * indicates that the environment is to be passed along in a singly threaded way, violations are captured by the type system. In the iTask toolkit, tasks that produce values of some type a have type Task a:

```
:: Task a :== *TSt → (a,*TSt)
```

Here, *TSt is the unique and opaque environment containing the global information maintained by all tasks.

The library function singleUserTask takes a workflow specification (user in this example) and provides the user with a single user infrastructure. It starts out by computing the HTML page that reflects the initial state of the workflow system. The infrastructure provides a tracing option, accessible through a button displayed at the top of the window, which displays a column containing the main tasks of the current user. The current task of the user is displayed next to this column. In Section 2.9 we discuss how to dress up multi-user workflow specifications.

The example workflow is given by the function user. It creates a single task using the library function editTask which has the following type:

```
editTask :: String a → Task a | iData a
```

Its first argument is the label of the push button that the user can press to tell the system that this task is finished. Its second argument is the initial value that the task displays. When the user finished editing, i.e., after pressing the push button, the edited value is returned by editTask. Note that the type of editTask is overloaded. The type class iData collects all generic functions that are required for the iTask library to derive the proper instances:

```
class iData           a | gForm {|*|}, iCreateAndPrint, iParse, iSpecialStore a
class iCreateAndPrint a | iCreate, iPrint a
class iCreate         a | gUpd  {|*|} a
class iPrint          a | gPrint{|*|} a
class iParse          a | gParse{|*|} a
class iSpecialStore   a | TC a
```

These generic functions can be applied to values of *any* type as to automatically create an HTML form (gForm), to handle the effect of any edit action in the browser, including the creation of default values (gUpd); to print or serialize any value (gPrint); to parse or de-serialize any value (gParse); or to serialize and de-serialize values and functions in a Dynamic value (using the compiler generated TC class).

In order to generate the required instances, one has to explicitly request their generation in the code:

```
derive gForm  User, Role, Login
derive gUpd   User, Role, Login
derive gPrint User, Role, Login
derive gParse User, Role, Login
```

If these **derive** statements are omitted the compiler will complain about missing instances of the above generic type classes.

Note that in the example, the type of user is more restrictive than that of editTask. This is because it uses the createDefault function which has signature:

```
createDefault :: a | gUpd{|*|} a
```

This function returns a value for any type for which an instance of the generic gUpd function has been derived. Consequently, the most general type of user is:

```
user :: Task a | iData a
```

which is an overloaded type (in Clean the |-symbol is used to mark the start of a type context restriction). Therefore, the type of Start is overloaded as well, which is not allowed in Clean. By providing user with a specialized type signature, we can directly and concisely create an editor task for any data structure that we like, and start with its default value.

Exercise

2. *Playing with a type of your own*

Create a new directory. Copy the *"exercise1.icl"* file into the new directory, and rename it to *"exercise2.icl"*. Within the Clean IDE, open *"exercise2.icl"* and create a new project. Set the Environment to *"iTasks"*.

Define a new (set of) type(s), such as the User and Role given in Section 2.2, and create a simple editing task for it.

2.3 Task Attributes

In the previous example an extremely simple, single-user, workflow was created. Even for such simple systems, we need to decide where to store the state of the application, and whether it should respond to every user editing action or only after an explicit submit action of the user. These aspects can be controlled via task *attributes*, which are set using the overloaded infix operator <<@:

```
class    (<<@) infixl 3 b :: (Task a) b → Task a
instance <<@ Lifespan, Mode, GarbageCollect, StorageFormat

:: Lifespan       = Database | TxtFile | TxtFileRO | Session
                  | Page     | DataFile | Temp      | Client
:: Mode           = Edit | Submit | Display | NoForm
:: GarbageCollect = Collect | NoCollect
:: StorageFormat  = PlainString | StaticDynamic
```

The Lifespan attribute controls where to store the state of a task: it can be stored persistently on the server side on disk in a relational database (Database), in a file (TxtFile with RO read-only), locally at the client side in the web page (Session (default) and Page), or one can decide not to store it at all (Temp). A novel attribute is to enforce *client side evaluation*, with the Client attribute. Storage and retrieval of data is done automatically by the system. The Mode attribute controls the *rendering* of the iTask: it can be edited (Edit (default)) which means that every change made in the form is communicated to the server, one can choose for the more traditional handling of forms where local changes can be made that are all sent back to the server together when the Submit button is pressed. It can also be displayed (Display) as a constant, or it is not rendered at all (NoForm). The GarbageCollect attribute controls whether the task tree should be garbage collected (Collect (default)) or not (NoCollect). Finally, the StorageFormat attribute determines the way data is stored: either as a string (PlainString (default)) or as a dynamic (StaticDynamic).

As an example, consider attributing the user function of Section 2.2 as follows (see Figure 2):

```
user :: Task User
user = editTask "Done" createDefault <<@ Submit <<@ TxtFile
```

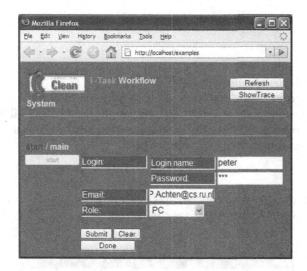

Fig. 2. A `User` iTask attributed to be a 'classic' form editor

With these attributes, the application only responds to user actions after she has pressed the "Submit" button. The value is stored in a text file.

Editor tasks created with `editTask` allow the user to enter any value, provided it corresponds to the type of the editor. For many cases, this is sufficient. Sometimes, however, you wish to impose constraints on the edited values that cannot be expressed via the type system of `Clean`. Examples are editor tasks for even `Int` values, `User` values in which sensible values have been entered, and so on. For this purpose a predicate of type `a → (Bool, HtmlCode)` can be used to test the value of type `a` that is produced by the user. If the test succeeds, the predicate returns `True`, otherwise it returns `False` and an explanation in the form of `HtmlCode`. This is defined by the function `editTaskPred`:

```
editTaskPred :: a (a → (Bool, HtmlCode)) → Task a | iData a
```

The user can edit values as usual, but these are verified using the predicate when the user submits the value. If the predicate does not hold, then the error message is displayed. Only if it holds, then the editor task is completed, and the new value is returned. Consider the following example from the case study:

```
user :: Task User
user = editTaskPred {createDefault & User.email = emptyTextInput} checkUser

checkUser :: User → (Bool, HtmlCode)
checkUser {User | login = {loginName,password}, email}
| loginName == ""           = (False, [Txt "You need to enter a login name"])
| password == PasswordBox "" = (False, [Txt "You need to enter a password"])
| fromTextInput email == ""  = (False, [Txt "You need to enter an email address"])
| otherwise                 = (True, [])
```

Exercise

3. *A persistent type of your own*
Create a new project for *"exercise3.icl"* as instructed in Exercise 2.

Modify the code in such a way that the application stores all data entered by the user persistently. Meaning, once a user returns to the same application, previously entered data is shown in the form.

In this example, the predicate `checkUser` checks a few simple properties of `User` values. Figure 3 shows this editor task in action.

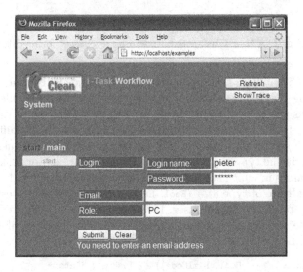

Fig. 3. A `User` iTask, now validating entered values

2.4   Database Access

In the previous section we have shown that the programmer can decide where the state of a task editor is stored. This feature of editors is also used to accommodate simple database access:

```
mkDBid  :: String Lifespan → DBid a
readDB  :: (DBid a)        → Task a | iData a
writeDB :: (DBid a) a      → Task a | iData a
```

The expression `mkDBid name Database` returns a database identifier of type `DBid a` only if the name provided is a proper file name, because the read and write operations are performed on disk. If the second argument is not equal to `Database`, any name is accepted. In either case, an identification value dbid is returned, referring to an existing database if one identified by name already exists, or otherwise to a newly created database. The expression readDB dbid reads the current content of the identified database, or returns a default value otherwise. Finally, the expression writeDB dbid x sets the content of the database identified by dbid to the value x and returns this value for convenience.

Suppose we wish to set up a new User administration. Then, we introduce the following functions for that purpose:

```
usersId :: DBid [User]
usersId = mkDBid "Users" TxtFile

readUsersDB :: Task [User]
readUsersDB = readDB usersId

writeUsersDB :: ([User] → Task [User])
writeUsersDB = writeDB usersId
```

2.5   Sequencing with Monads

In the previous examples, the workflow consisted of a single task. An obvious approach to combining workflow is by means of *sequential composition*. For this the iTask toolkit provides appropriate instances of the *monadic* combinator functions for binding (=>>) and injecting (return_V) values:

```
(=>>) infix 1 :: (Task a) (a → Task b) → Task b | iCreateAndPrint b
return_V     :: b                      → Task b | iCreateAndPrint b
```

The task t =>> λx → u performs task t and makes its result available to task u, which is only activated when required. The only task of the function return_V is to return its argument, i.e. lift it to the Task domain. As usual, a shorthand combinator which ignores the result of the first task is defined in terms of =>>:

```
(#>>) infixl 1 :: (Task a) (Task b) → Task b
(#>>) t u = t =>> const u
```

As an example of sequentially composing tasks, we extend the User adminstration that was given in Section 2.4 with a function to prepend a single user to the administration:

```
addUserDB :: User → Task [User]
addUserDB user =
  readUsersDB =>> λusers →
  writeUsersDB [user:users]
```

2.6   Prompting the User

When a task is in progress, it is useful to provide feedback to the user about what she is supposed to be doing. For this purpose two combinators are introduced:

(?>>) **infix** 5 :: HtmlCode (Task a) → Task a | iCreate a
(!>>) **infix** 5 :: HtmlCode (Task a) → Task a | iCreate a

The task p ?>> t displays prompt p while task t is running, whereas task p !>> t displays prompt p from the moment task t is activated. Hence, a message displayed with !>> remains displayed once it has appeared, and a message displayed with ?>> disappears as soon as its argument task has finished.

The example function user in Section 2.3 defined a User editor task using the predicate checkUser. By adding the following guard just before the otherwise branch, this predicate also verifies that the provided user name does not exist yet:

```
| isMember loginName userNames = (False, [Txt "This login name already exists"])
where
  userNames = [n \\ {User | login = {loginName = n}} ← users]
```

Using this extended predicate, we define a User editor that also verifies that the entered user name does not exist yet:

```
addUserForm :: Task User
addUserForm =
  readUsersDB =>> λusers →
  msg ?>> editTaskPred {createDefault & User.email = emptyTextInput}
                      (checkUser users)
where msg = [Txt "Please enter a username and password for the new user:"]
```

Next, we deploy this task to allow the chair to add users to the CM system:

```
addUser :: Task Void
addUser =
  addUserForm =>> λuser →
  addUserDB user #>>
  endMsg ?>> ok
where endMsg = [Txt "A new user has been added"]
```

Together, cancel, void, and ok form a group of tiny but useful combinators:

```
ok      :: Task Void
ok      = buttonTask "Ok" void

cancel :: Task Void
cancel = buttonTask "Cancel" void

void    :: Task Void
void    = return_V Void
```

The task buttonTask label t is a library function that performs task t when the button with the label is pressed:

```
buttonTask :: String (Task a) → Task a | iCreateAndPrint a
```

The type Void is similar to Haskell's () value, and is defined as:

```
:: Void = Void
```

Exercises

4. *Hello!*
Create a task that asks the name of a user, and then replies with "Hello" and the name of the user.

5. *To !>> or to ?>>, that's the question*
Open the CM system project file, and find the function addUser (in the main module CM.icl). Alter the ?>> combinator into !>>. Compile and re-run the application. What is the effect of this change?

6. *Enter a prime number*
Create a workflow that uses the <| combinator (see module StdiTasks.dcl) to force the user to enter a prime number.

7. *Tearing User apart*
In Section 2.2, a User editor task was created with which complete User values can be edited. Create a new workflow in which the user has to enter values for the fields one by one, i.e., starting with the login name, and subsequently asking the password, email and role. Finally, the task should return the corresponding User value.

8. *Adding users*
Create a workflow that first asks the user a positive (but not too large) integer number n, and subsequently have him enter n values of type User (use the seqTasks combinator for this purpose (see module StdiTasks.dcl). When finished, the names of these users should be displayed.

2.7   Choice: Breakable Tasks

The monadic combinators presented in the previous section are useful for sequential composition. Obviously, realistic workflows also require *choice*, and this is provided by the iTask system using the following basic combinator:

(-||-) **infixr** 3 :: (Task a) (Task a) → Task a | iData a

The left-biased task t -||- u is finished as soon as either t or u has finished, or both. The combination of monadic composition and choice leads to a number of useful derived combinators. We continue by discussing some examples of such combinators.

Tasks constructed with the monadic combinators rigidly force the user to perform the given tasks in the prescribed order, and finish only when the very last task has been performed. For real world cases, this is sometimes to restrictive: we want to model the fact that a user can choose to *abort* her work. The break combinator models this behavior by lifting the result to a Maybe value:

```
break :: (Task a) → Task (Maybe a) | iData a
break t =
    (t       =>> return_V o Just)
    -||-
    (cancel #>> return_V Nothing)
```

The task break t performs t and wraps the result in the Just constructor from the Maybe type. However, at any time before finishing t, the user also has the option to perform the cancel task, consequently returning Nothing instead.

The use of Maybe values, as in the definition of break, is a common functional programming idiom. Because many tasks yield such values, it is useful to define an alternative =>> combinator:

```
try :: (Task (Maybe a)) (a → Task b) (Task b) → Task b | iData b
try t succeed fail =
    t =>> λx →
    case x of
      Nothing → fail
      Just x' → succeed x'
```

The task try t succeed fail performs task t first. If this yields a Just value, then it proceeds with succeed, providing it the result of the first task. If the first task returns Nothing, it proceeds with the task fail.

Another useful alternative =>> combinator is breakable which combines the use of break and try:

```
breakable :: (Task a) (a → Task Void) → Task Void | iData a
breakable t succeed = try (break t) succeed void
```

The task breakable t succeed allows t to be cancelled. If this task yields a result, it is provided to succeed. Otherwise, the value Void is returned. As an example of this combinator, we turn the addUser task for the program chair (defined at the end of Section 2.6) into a task that can be aborted:

```
addUser :: Task Void
addUser =
    breakable addUserForm
            (λuser → addUserDB user #>>
                      endMsg ?>> ok)
where endMsg = [Txt "A new user has been added"]
```

2.8   Recursive Tasks

So far we have introduced monadic sequential composition and choice. The next key ingredient is to allow *recursive* workflow specifications. Recursion is

fundamental to define computations that may run arbitrarily long. First we start
with a useful combinator that can be found in the iTask API, namely, `foreverTask`:

```
foreverTask :: (Task a) → Task a | iData a
```

The task `foreverTask t` repeats task `t` infinitely many times. In the CM system,
this combinator is used to define the main task. Because we do not know how
long the user will be logged in, she is offered the same choice whenever a chosen
task is finished:

```
main :: User → Task Void
main user =: {User | login = {loginName}, role} =
  welcomeMsg ?>> foreverTask (chooseTask homeMsg userTasks)
where
    welcomeMsg = [ H1 [] ("Welcome " +++ loginName), Br ]
    homeMsg    = [ Txt "Choose one of the tasks below or select a task that "
               , Txt "has been assigned to you from the list on the left"
               , Br, Br
               ]
    userTasks  = case role of
                    Chair → [ ("Show users",       showUsers)
                            , ("Add user",         addUser)
                            , ("Show papers",      showPapers)
                            , ("Assign reviewers", assignReviewers)
                            , ("Judge papers",     judgePapers)
                            ]
                    PC    → [ ("Show papers",      showPapers)
                            , ("Mark papers",      markPapers user)
                            ]
```

Besides the column containing the main tasks of the current user, as described
in Section 2.2, the user is provided a choice, using the function `chooseTask`:

```
chooseTask :: HtmlCode [(String, Task a)] → Task a | iData a
```

The task `chooseTask msg ts` displays the message `msg` and allows the user to choose
one of the tasks from the list `ts`, which contains several tasks accompanied by a
description.

The choices available for the CM system are defined in `userTasks`, depending
on the role of the current user. Note that we only described a selection of the
choices in these lecture notes.

2.9 Multi-user Workflow

So far, the examples that we showed are single-user applications only. However,
workflow systems usually involve arbitrarily many users. The iTask system supports multi-user applications by providing the function `multiUserTask`, which has
exactly the same type as the function `singleUserTask`. The former allows you to
switch identity easily, while the latter assumes a fixed identity. In a multi-user
application, tasks need to be assigned to specific users. The iTask system provides
two combinators which assign a task to a specific user:

```
(@:)    infix 3 :: UserId (String, Task a) → Task a | iData a
(@::)   infix 3 :: UserId (Task a)         → Task a | iData a
```

The task uid @: (msg, t) assigns a task t to a user identified by uid accompanied by a message msg. No message is required when we use the @:: combinator.

Unfortunately, these combinators do not provide full control over an assigned task: we also want to suspend, delete, or reassign such an assigned task. The iTask toolkit provides several functions to manage spawned tasks. First, we spawn a task using the following function:

```
spawnWorkflow :: UserId Bool (String, Task a) → Task (Wid a) | iData a
```

The task spawnWorkflow uid active (label, t) spawns a new workflow process t to the user identified by uid and activates the task immediately if the active flag is set to True. Otherwise, the spawned task is suspended for the moment. The function returns a handle of type Wid a which identifies the spawned workflow. The task getWorkflowStatus wid provides the status of the spawned task identified by this handle wid:

```
:: WorkflowStatus = WflActive    UserId
                  | WflSuspended UserId
                  | WflFinished
                  | WflDeleted
```

```
getWorkflowStatus :: (Wid a) → Task WorkflowStatus
```

The iTask library provides several functions which allow us to alter the status of a spawned task:

```
waitForWorkflow    ::            (Wid a) → Task (Maybe a) | iData a
activateWorkflow   ::            (Wid a) → Task Bool
suspendWorkflow    ::            (Wid a) → Task Bool
deleteWorkflow     ::            (Wid a) → Task Bool
changeWorkflowUser :: UserId (Wid a) → Task Bool
```

The task waitForWorkflow wid waits until the workflow process identified by wid is finished. Since the process might be deleted already, the result is a Maybe value. Furthermore, the functions activateWorkflow, suspendWorkflow, and deleteWorkflow allow us to activate, suspend, or delete a spawned workflow process, respectively. We can also decide to reassign a spawned process to a different user using the function changeWorkflowUser.

These functions give full control over assigned tasks to different users, which is required for many workflow scenarios. In the CM system, the program chair assigns reviewers to submitted papers. Ideally, the program chair makes a decision on all submissions when all reviews have been completed. Unfortunately, real life is usually less structured: some papers require additional reviewing and some reviewers may fail to deliver before the deadline. Hence, we structure this process as a set of spawned tasks.

Multi-user applications often require some kind of login ritual, which is facilitated by the following function:

```
workFlowTask :: [StartUpOptions] (Task ((Bool, UserId), a))
                (UserId a → (String, Task b)) *World → *World | iData b
```

The task `workFlowTask opts t f world` takes a task `t` which provides us with some kind of identification of the current user. Then, this identification is provided, together with an additional result from the task `t`, to the task `f`. This is the task that the user performs when she is logged in successfully, such as the the function `main` as defined for the CM system in Section 2.8. Additionally, the function `workFlowTask` takes some options and a unique world.

Exercises

9. *Number guessing*
Create a workflow specification in which a user identified by 1 enters an integer value $1 \leq x \leq 100$, after which a user identified by 2 has to guess this number. At every guess, the application should give feedback to user 2 whether the number guessed is too low, too high, or just right. In the latter case, the workflow returns the guessed number in a `Just` value. User 2 can also choose to give up, consequently, returning `Nothing` as the result.

Optional: The result of user 2 is provided to user 1, who has the chance to respond to the guess with a personal message.

10. *Number guessing in a group*
Extend the previous exercise to a fixed set of persons 0..x in which user 0 determines who is the next person to try to guess the number.

11. *Tic-tac-toe*
Create a workflow specification for playing the classic 'tic-tac-toe' game. The tic-tac-toe game consists of a 3 × 3 matrix. User 1 places × marks in this matrix, and user 2 places ○ marks. The first user to create a (horizontal, vertical, or diagonal) line of three identical marks wins. The specification has to ensure that users only enter marks when it is their turn.

3   Semantics

In this section we present a small semantic model of the iTask system. Its main purpose is to explain the rewriting behavior of an iTask program.

During evaluation, the state of an iTask program is represented by a *task tree*, i.e., a tree structure in which the nodes are formed by task combinators, such as `=>>` and `-||-`, and the leaves are formed by basic editors, such as `editTask` and buttonTask, but also return_V. We represent this task tree by means of the following algebraic data type:

```
:: TaskTree = Return    Val
            | Bind       ID              TaskTree (Val → TaskTree)
            | EditTask   ID String    Val
            | .||. infixr 3 TaskTree TaskTree
            | .&&. infixr 4 TaskTree TaskTree
```

The constructors Return and Bind correspond with return_V and =>>, EditTask with editTask, and .||. with -||-. We introduce the iTask combinator t -&&- u, and represent it by t .&&. u. In the case study in Section 2 we did not use this combinator, but it belongs to the basic repertoire of the iTask system, therefore we include it here. In the task t -&&- u, both subtasks t and u are available to the user. The composite task is finished as soon as both subtasks are finished. Hence, it differs from -||- in which termination is controlled by the first subtask that finishes. Also, its type is more general, because the types of the return values of the subtasks are allowed to be different, the type of this operator in the iTask system is (Task a) (Task b) → Task (a,b) | iData a & iData b. The function parameter of the constructor Bind can be any function, and hence can use choice and recursion in the usual way. With this approach, we obtain a simple algebraic data type representation of iTask programs.

In contrast with the iTask combinator functions, the Bind and EditTask constructors are also parameterized with an ID value. These identification values are required to relate events to task editors, which is the reason why they occur at every EditTask combinator. Since the function value of the Bind constructor can only be numbered once its argument is provided, numbering is deferred until this result is known. The ID value keeps track of the number to continue with, once numbering is resumed in the resulting task tree of the function.

Tasks are numbered by a list of integers, in a way that is similar to the numbering of sections in a book, but in which the least significant number is in the front of the list rather than in the back. On top level, tasks are assigned integer numbers starting at 0. These task identifiers, ID, are straightforwardly represented as a list of integers:

```
:: ID :== [Int]
```

Whenever a task is replaced by its successor, the id is incremented by the function nextID:

```
nextID :: ID → ID
nextID [x:xs] = [x+1:xs]
```

For every ID value id it holds that nextID id ≠ id. This allows us to distinguish inputs for a task from inputs to its successor.

The function splitID generates a list of task identifiers for subtasks of a task with the given id:

```
splitID :: ID → [ID]
splitID xs = [[0, x : xs] \\ x ← [0..]]
```

This function adds two numbers to the identifier, one number for the subtask and one number for the version of this subtask. If we would use the same number for both purposes, one application of the function nextID would incorrectly transform the identification of the current subtask to that of the next subtask.

In the iTask system, these identification values are generated automatically to guarantee a systematic way of identifying all (sub)tasks of a task tree. This systematic numbering is captured in the following definition:

```
nmbr :: ID TaskTree → TaskTree
nmbr _ (Return v)      = Return v
nmbr i (Bind _ t f)    = Bind k (nmbr j t) f    where [j,k:_] = splitID i
nmbr i (EditTask _ s v) = EditTask i s v
nmbr i (t .||. u)      = nmbr j t .||. nmbr k u where [j,k:_] = splitID i
nmbr i (t .&&. u)      = nmbr j t .&&. nmbr k u where [j,k:_] = splitID i
```

In the rewriting function that we discuss below, we assume that the argument TaskTree has been numbered using nmbr. By convention we assign [0] as identification to the root of the task tree.

The focus of the semantic model is on the rewriting behavior of task trees, and less on the actual values that are passed around. Therefore, we use a simplified representation of values: it is a basic value of type String or Int, or even just a VOID value, or a pair of values:

```
:: Val = String String | Int Int | VOID | Pair Val Val
```

Whenever a user manipulates one of the available task editors or commits herself to a final value, she generates an *event* that must be handled by the current task tree. In the simplified semantic framework, an event is intended for an editor with some identification value id. The user either *edits* the current value to new for that editor (Event id (Edit new)), or *commits* the current value that is hosted by that editor by pressing the commit button (Event id Commit). Another special event, NoEvent, is required for *normalizing* a task, which is explained below. This event is usually not generated by a user executing a task, but corresponds roughly to a refresh event in the iTask system.

```
:: Event     = Event ID EventKind | NoEvent
:: EventKind = Edit Val | Commit
```

Now we have all the ingredients for the semantic model. An iTask program is modeled with a TaskTree and the user actions are modeled as a list of Event values. These events are subsequently *applied* to the current task tree, and result in a new task tree. We denote the application of an event e to a task tree t with t @ e, where @ is an overloaded operator defined by the following type class:

```
class (@) infixl 9 a b :: a b → a
```

In the case of an event sequence (a list of events) es we apply this sequence to the given task tree t and obtain a resulting task tree by t @ es:

```
instance @ t [e] | @ t e where (@) t es = foldl (@) t es
```

Analogously, in the case of a list of task trees l and an event e, then we apply this event to all elements by l @ e:

instance @ [t] e | @ t e **where** (@) l e = map (flip @ e) l

The instance of @ to a task tree and event defines the single rewrite step:

instance @ TaskTree Event **where**
  (@) (Bind i t f)   e =
    case t @ e **of**
      Return v → normalize i (f v)
      u   → Bind i u f
    where normalize i t = nmbr i (t @ NoEvent)
  (@) (EditTask i n cur) (Event j eKind) | i == j =
    case eKind **of**
      Edit new → EditTask (nextID i) n new
      Commit   → Return cur
  (@) (t .||. u)   e =
    case t @ e **of**
      Return x → Return x
      t   → **case** u @ e **of**
                Return x → Return x
                u   → t .||. u
  (@) (t .&&. u)   e =
    case [t,u] @ e **of**
      [Return v, Return w] → Return (Pair v w)
      [t, u]   → t .&&. u
  (@) t   _ = t

The semantic model shows that the ID values play a dominant role in the rewriting of task trees. As mentioned earlier, the Bind constructor provides its ID value to its function argument, once its argument value is known. The EditTask constructor reacts only to edit and commit events that are targeted to that task. The .||. and .&&. constructors pass events to their subtasks and check if the root of the task tree can be rewritten after the reduction of the subtasks. Although the iTask combinator -&&- has not been discussed in Section 2, its semantic counterpart .&&. tells the story: only if both subtasks t and u terminate and yield a value v and w respectively, then t .&&. u also terminates and yields Pair v w. Finally, all other tasks, such as return tasks, ignore all events. It is assumed that all task expressions considered here corresponds to task expressions in the real iTask system. This implies that the subtype of cur and new in an expression (EditTask i n cur) @ (Event j (Edit new)) are equal, i.e. it is impossible to change an editor for integers dynamically to an editor for pairs of integers.

    A properly numbered task tree remains correctly numbered after reduction. Editors that receive a new value get a new number by applying the function nextID to the task identification number. The numbering scheme guarantees that a certain number cannot occur in any other subtask. If the left-hand task of the Bind operator is rewritten to a normal form, the new task tree is the result of f v. The application of normalize (nextID i) to this new task tree guarantees that it is well formed and properly numbered within the surrounding task tree.

    In conclusion, the handling of events for a task tree is somewhat similar to reduction of combinator systems or in λ-calculus. An essential difference of such a reduction system with the task trees considered here, is that all required information is available inside a reduction system and the evaluation of inputs for task trees needs a (sequence of) event(s) as additional information.

4 Related Work

In the realm of functional programming, many solutions that have been inspiring for our work in the iTask system have been proposed to program web applications. We mention just a few of them in a number of languages: the HaskellCGI library [18]; the Curry approach [14]; writing XML applications [10] in *SMLserver* [11]. A sophisticated system is WASH/CGI by [24], based on Haskell in which HTML is produced as an effect of the CGI monad whereas we consider HTML as a first-class citizen, using data types. Instead of storing state, WASH/CGI logs all user responses and I/O operations. These are replayed when it is required to bring the application to its desired, most recent state. In the iTask system, we replay the program instead of the session, and restore the state of the program on-the-fly using the storage capabilities of the underlying iData. Forms are programmed explicitly in HTML, and their elements may, or may not, contain values. In the iTask toolkit, forms and tasks are generated from arbitrary data types, and always have a value. Interconnecting forms in WASH/CGI are achieved by adding callback actions to submit fields, whereas the iData toolkit uses a functional dependency relation.

Two more recent approaches that are also based on functional languages are Links [7] and Hop [23]. Both languages aim to deal with web programming within a single framework, similar to the iData and iTask approach. Links compiles to JavaScript for rendering HTML pages, and SQL communicates with a back-end database. A Links program stores its session state at the client side. Notable differences between Links and iTask (and iData) are that the latter has a more refined control over the location of state storage, and even the presence of state, which needs to be mimicked in Links with recursive functions. Compiling to JavaScript gives Links programs more expressive and computational power at the client side: in particular Links offers thread-creation and message-passing communication, and finally, the client side code can call server side logic and vice versa. The particular focus of Hop is on rendering graphically attractive applications, like desktop GUI applications can. Hop implements a strict separation between programming the user interface and the logic of an application. The main computation runs on the server, and the GUI runs on the client(s). Annotations decide where a computation is performed. Computations can communicate with each other, which gives it similar expressiveness as Links. The main difference between these systems and iTask (and iData) is that the latter is restricted to thin-client web applications, and provides a high degree of automation using the generic foundation.

iData components that reside in iTask are abstractions of forms. A pioneer project to experiment with form-based services is Mawl [4]. It has been improved upon by means of Powerforms [5], used in the <bigwig> project [6]. These projects provide *templates* which, roughly speaking, are HTML pages with *holes* in which scalar data as well as lists can be plugged in (Mawl), but also other *templates* (<bigwig>). They advocate compile-time systems, because this allows one to use type systems and other static analysis. Powerforms resides on the client-side of a web application. The type system is used to filter out illegal user input. Their and our approach make good use of the type system. Because iData are encoded by ADTs, we get higher-order forms for free. Moreover, we provide higher-order tasks that can be suspended and migrated.

Web applications can be structured with *continuations*. This has been done by Hughes, in his arrow framework [16]. Queinnec states that "A browser is a device that can invoke continuations multiply/simultaneously" [22]. Graunke et al. [12] have explored continuations as one of three functional compilation techniques to transform sequential interactive programs to CGI programs. The Seaside [8] system offers an API for programming web pages using a Smalltalk interpreter. When waiting for new information from the browser, a Seaside application is suspended and continues evaluation as soon as input is available. To make this possible, the whole state of the interpreter's run-time system is stored after a page has been produced. This state is recovered when the next user event is posted such that the application can resume execution. In contrast to iTask, Seaside can only be a single-user system. Our approach is simpler yet more powerful: every page has a complete (set of) model value(s) that can be stored and recovered generically. An application is resurrected by restarting the very same program, which recovers its previous state on-the-fly.

Workflow systems are distributed software systems, and as such can also be implemented using a programming language with support for distributed computing such as D-Clean [25], GdH [21], Erlang, and Java. On the other hand, iTask makes effective use of the distributed nature of the web: web browsers act as distributed rendering resources, and the server controls what is displayed where and when. Furthermore, the interactive components are created in a type-directed way, which makes the code concise. There is no need to program the data flow between the participating users, again reducing the code size.

Our combinator library has been inspired by the comprehensive analysis of workflow patterns of over more than 30 contemporary commercial workflow systems [1]. These patterns are typically based on a Petri-net style, which implies that patterns for *distributing* work (also called *splitting*) and *merging* (*joining*) work are distinct and can be combined more or less arbitrarily. In the setting of a strongly typed combinatorial approach such as the iTask system, it is more natural to define combinator functions that pair splitting and merging patterns. For instance, the combinator -||- that was introduced in Section 2.7 pairs the *or split* and *synchronizing merge* patterns. Conceptually, the Petri-net based approach is more fine-grained, and should allow the workflow designer greater flexibility. However, we believe that we have captured the essential combinators of these systems. We plan to study the relationship between the typical functional approach and the classic Petri-net based approach in the near future.

Contemporary commercial workflow tools use a graphical formalism to specify workflow cases. We believe that a textual specification, based on a state-of-the-art functional language, provides more expressive power. The system is strongly typed, and guarantees all user input to be type safe as well. In commercial systems, the connection between the specification of the workflow and the (type of the) concrete information being processed, is not always well typed. Our system is fully dynamic, depending on the values of the concrete information. For instance, recursive workflow can easily be defined. In a graphical system, workflow is much more static. Our system is higher order: tasks can communicate tasks, work can be interrupted and conditionally moved to other users for further completion. Last but not least: we generate a complete working multi-user directly from the specification. Database storage and retrieval of the information, version management control, type driven generation of web forms, handling of web forms, it is all done automatically and the programmer only needs to focus on the workflow specification itself.

5 Conclusions

In these lecture notes we have presented the iTask system, which is a domain specific language for the specification of workflows, embedded in Clean. The iTask system uses the specification to generate a multi-user interactive web-based workflow application. We think the notation that is offered by the iTask system is concise as well as intuitive and support this claim by showing (parts of) the implementation of a CM system prototype as a case study, as well as a small semantic model of the rewriting behavior of iTask applications.

The iTask toolkit uses many features that are known in the functional programming community, and puts them to good use: a compositional, combinator based approach to construct workflows, strongly typed system in combination with generic programming, dynamic run-time behavior, higher-order tasks that can be suspended, passed to other users, and resumed.

At the time of writing, the work on iTasks has made further progress. We are working on a new option for the evaluation of tasks on the client side using Ajax technology in combination with an efficient interpreter for functional languages [17]. We are refactoring the internal structure of the iTask toolkit to make it better suited for future experiments and enhanced creation of its GUI.

Besides demonstrating the iTask toolkit, we hope to have also shown how functional programming can provide solutions to challenging problems.

Acknowledgements

The authors would like to thank Erik Zuurbier for the many discussions on the state-of-art of contemporary workflow systems and as a source of many examples, and Wil van der Aalst for commenting on the difference between the combinator approach and contemporary workflow specification languages. We also want to thank Doaitse Swierstra for his valuable input on this paper.

References

1. van der Aalst, W., ter Hofstede, A., Kiepuszewski, B., Barros, A.: Workflow patterns. QUT technical report, FIT-TR-2002-02, Queensland University of Technology, Brisbane, Australia (2002)
2. Achten, P.: Clean for Haskell98 programmers - A quick reference guide (July 13-21, 2007),
   `http://www.st.cs.ru.nl/papers/2007/achp2007-CleanHaskellQuick-Guide.pdf`
3. Alimarine, A.: Generic functional programming - Conceptual design, implementation and applications. PhD thesis, Institute for Computing and Information Sciences. Radboud University Nijmegen, The Netherlands (2005); ISBN 3-540-67658-9
4. Atkins, D., Ball, T., Benedikt, M., Bruns, G., Cox, K., Mataga, P., Rehor, K.: Experience with a domain specific language for form-based services. In: Usenix Conference on Domain Specific Languages (October 1997)
5. Brabrand, C., Møller, A., Ricky, M., Schwartzbach, M.: Powerforms: declarative client-side form field validation. World Wide Web Journal 3(4), 205–314 (2000)
6. Brabrand, C., Møller, A., Schwartzbach, M.: The <bigwig> project. In: ACM Transactions on Internet Technology, TOIT 2002 (2002)
7. Cooper, E., Lindley, S., Wadler, P., Yallop, J.: Links: web programming without tiers. In: de Boer, F.S., Bonsangue, M.M., Graf, S., de Roever, W.-P. (eds.) FMCO 2006. LNCS, vol. 4709, pp. 266–296. Springer, Heidelberg (2007)
8. Ducasse, S., Lienhard, A., Renggli, L.: Seaside - A multiple control flow web application framework. In: Ducasse, S. (ed.) Proceedings of the 12th International Smalltalk Joint Conference, ESUG 2004, Technical Report IAM-04-008, Koethen, Germany, November 7, pp. 231–254. Institut für Informatik und Angewandte Mathematik, University of Bern, Switzerland (2004)
9. Elliot, C.: Tangible functional programming. In: Proceedings of the 12th International Conference on Functional Programming, ICFP 2007, Freiburg, Germany, October 1-3, pp. 59–70. ACM Press, New York (2007)
10. Elsman, M., Larsen, K.F.: Typing XHTML web applications in ML. In: Jayaraman, B. (ed.) PADL 2004. LNCS, vol. 3057, pp. 224–238. Springer, Heidelberg (2004)
11. Elsman, M., Hallenberg, N.: Web programming with SMLserver. In: Dahl, V., Wadler, P. (eds.) PADL 2003. LNCS, vol. 2562, pp. 74–91. Springer, Heidelberg (2003)
12. Graunke, P., Krishnamurthi, S., Findler, R., Felleisen, M.: Automatically restructuring programs for the web. In: Feather, M., Goedicke, M. (eds.) Proceedings of the 16th International Conference on Automated Software Engineering, ASE 2001. IEEE CS Press, Los Alamitos (2001)
13. Hanna, K.: A document-centered environment for Haskell. In: Butterfield, A., Grelck, C., Huch, F. (eds.) IFL 2005. LNCS, vol. 4015, pp. 196–211. Springer, Heidelberg (2006)
14. Hanus, M.: High-level server side web scripting in Curry. In: Ramakrishnan, I.V. (ed.) PADL 2001. LNCS, vol. 1990, pp. 76–92. Springer, Heidelberg (2001)
15. Hinze, R.: A new approach to generic functional programming. In: Proceedings of the 27th International Symposium on Principles of Programming Languages, POPL 2000, Boston, Massachusetts, USA, January 2000, pp. 119–132 (2000)
16. Hughes, J.: Generalising monads to arrows. Science of Computer Programming 37, 67–111 (2000)

17. Jansen, J., Koopman, P., Plasmeijer, R.: Efficient interpretation by transforming data types and patterns to functions. In: Nilsson, H. (ed.) Proceedings of the 7th Symposium on Trends in Functional Programming, TFP 2006, Nottingham, UK, April 19-21, pp. 157–172 (2006), ISBN 978-1-84150-188-8

18. Meijer, E.: Server side web scripting in Haskell. Journal of Functional Programming 10(1), 1–18 (2000)

19. Plasmeijer, R., Achten, P.: The implementation of iData - A case study in generic programming. In: Butterfield, A., Grelck, C., Huch, F. (eds.) IFL 2005. LNCS, vol. 4015, pp. 106–123. Springer, Heidelberg (2006)

20. Plasmeijer, R., Achten, P., Koopman, P.: An introduction to iTasks: defining interactive work flows for the web. In: Horváth, Z., Plasmeijer, R., Soós, A., Zsók, V. (eds.) Central European Functional Programming School. LNCS, vol. 5161, pp. 1–40. Springer, Heidelberg (2008)

21. Pointon, R., Trinder, P., Loidl, H.: The design and implementation of Glasgow distributed Haskell. In: Mohnen, M., Koopman, P. (eds.) IFL 2000. LNCS, vol. 2011, pp. 53–70. Springer, Heidelberg (2001)

22. Queinnec, C.: The influence of browsers on evaluators or, continuations to program web servers. In: Proceedings of the 5th International Conference on Functional Programming, ICFP 2000 (September 2000)

23. Serrano, M., Gallesio, E., Loitsch, F.: Hop, a language for programming the web 2.0. In: Proceedings of the 11th International Conference on Object-Oriented Programming, Systems, Languages, and Applications, OOPSLA 2006, Portland, Oregon, USA, October 22-26, pp. 975–985 (2006)

24. Thiemann, P.: WASH/CGI: server-side web scripting with sessions and typed, compositional forms. In: Krishnamurthi, S., Ramakrishnan, C.R. (eds.) PADL 2002. LNCS, vol. 2257, pp. 192–208. Springer, Heidelberg (2002)

25. Zsók, V., Hernyák, Z., Horváth, Z.: Distributed pattern design in D-Clean. In: Proceedings of the 1st Central European Functional Programming School, CEFP 2005, Budapest, Hungary, vol. 33 (2005)

Author Index